Also by Walter J. Boyne

WALTER J. BOYNE

SIMON & SCHUSTER

NEW YORK • LONDON • TORONTO

SYDNEY • TOKYO • SINGAPORE

CLASH OF TITANS

TITANS

WORLD

WAR II

AT SEA

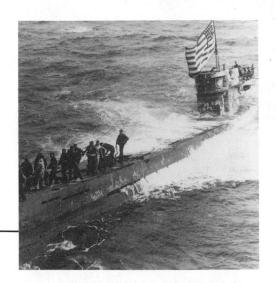

SIMON & SCHUSTER
Rockefeller Center
1230 Avenue of the Americas
New York, NY 10020

SIMON & SCHUSTER and colophon are registered trademarks
of Simon & Schuster Inc.

DESIGNED BY BARBARA M. BACHMAN

Manufactured in the United States of America

10 9 8 7 6 5 4 3 2 1

Library of Congress Cataloging-in-Publication Data
Boyne, Walter J., date.
    Clash of Titans: World War II at sea / Walter J. Boyne.
        p.   cm.
    Includes bibliographical references and index.
    1. World War, 1939–1945—Naval operations. I. Title.
    D770.B675   1995
    940.54'59—dc20   95-5432   CIP
ISBN 0-684-80196-5

PHOTO CREDITS

Robert Lawson: 20–21, 25, 39–42, 51, 52, 55, 58, 68–72
U.S. Naval Institute: 1–19, 22–24, 26–38, 43–50, 53, 54, 56, 57, 59–67

ACKNOWLEDGMENTS

A book on naval surface warfare was quite a departure from my past efforts; I had, of course, always been interested in the subject, and read fairly widely, but never to the extent that I pursued aviation subjects. Once absorbed in the task, however, I found it fascinating, particularly since I was able to call upon the talents of some experts who could tell me the difference between beam and width, wall and bulkhead, floor and deck, and most difficult of all, ship, boat and vessel.

The research proved to be wonderfully exciting, because of the vast literature that exists and the many surviving veterans who experienced the great adventure of World War II at sea. The bibliography reflects only a part of my reading, but it does offer a rich and varied menu for anyone who wishes to learn more about *the* most fascinating period in the history of naval warfare.

I want to thank the Department of the Navy for its cooperation and, most especially, the Naval Institute, where Dottie Sappington and her excellent researchers and staff personnel made the gathering of many of the photographs such a pleasure. My thanks to Robert Lawson, an excellent photographer and naval researcher in his own right.

My heartfelt gratitude goes also to Norman Polmar, the internationally renowned expert on naval matters, who patiently guided me through the task, and who put up with my comparative ignorance in naval matters. Norman has the faculty for spotting not only errors of fact, but also errors in context, chronology, spelling, usage, format and everything else, and doing so with wit and humor—sometimes caustic. Professor Paolo Coletta, a naval scholar, also vetted my work and gave me many pointers, as well as insight into many of the great personalities of the navy and naval aviation. Steve Llansos, who often works with Norman Polmar, was of great help, providing not only corrections, but many informative bits of anecdotal information. Captain James Hay, a distinguished submariner, was helpful both with advice and with suggestions for source material. Henry Snelling performed his usual masterful job of editing the manuscript as it was written, and then helped in cutting it down to size.

I wish to thank also my friends at Simon & Schuster, especially my helpful and encouraging editor, Bob Bender, who has such an intuitive feel for content and direction. He is ably assisted by Johanna Li, who keeps us both on track. Working with Gypsy da Silva, copy supervisor, is a joy and a revelation—no one else could point out so many mistakes in so charming a manner. Thanks, too, to the vigilant Fred Chase, my copy editor. Finally, I want to thank my agent, Jacques de Spoelberch, for his usual support and assistance.

WALTER J. BOYNE
Ashburn, Virginia,   July 17, 1994

5

THE INVASION
OF NORWAY
April 9–10, 1940

Tromsø

Narvik

SWEDEN

FINLAND

IRELAND

GREAT
BRITAIN

North Sea

NETHERLANDS

Königsberg
April 10

Trondheim

NORWAY

Bergen

Kristiansand

Oslo
Blücher
April 9

ESTONIA

LATVIA

LITHUANIA

EAST
PRUSSIA

POLAND

DENMARK

GERMANY

London

Eastbourne
Portsmouth
Margate
Dover

Dunkirk
Calais
Boulogne
BELGIUM

June 6, 1944

Dieppe

NORMANDY

English
Channel

Brest

Lorient

St. Nazaire

Paris

FRANCE

SWITZ.

Atlantic
Ocean

SOUTH
AMERICA

Bay of
Biscay

Montevideo

Graf Spee
Dec. 17, 1939

Pacific
Ocean

PORTUGAL

SPAIN

Marseilles

Toulon
Aug. 15, 194

Mediterranean
Sea

Warships sunk
Invasions
Evacuations

Tangier

Gibraltar

SP. MOROCCO

Nov. 8, 1942

Mers
el Kebir

Oran

Nov. 8, 1942

Algiers

Nov. 8, 1942

Fedala

Port Lyautey
Rabat
Casablanca

ALGERIA

Atlantic
Ocean

MOROCCO

Kms.
0   200

0   200
Miles

©A·Karl/J·Kemp 1995

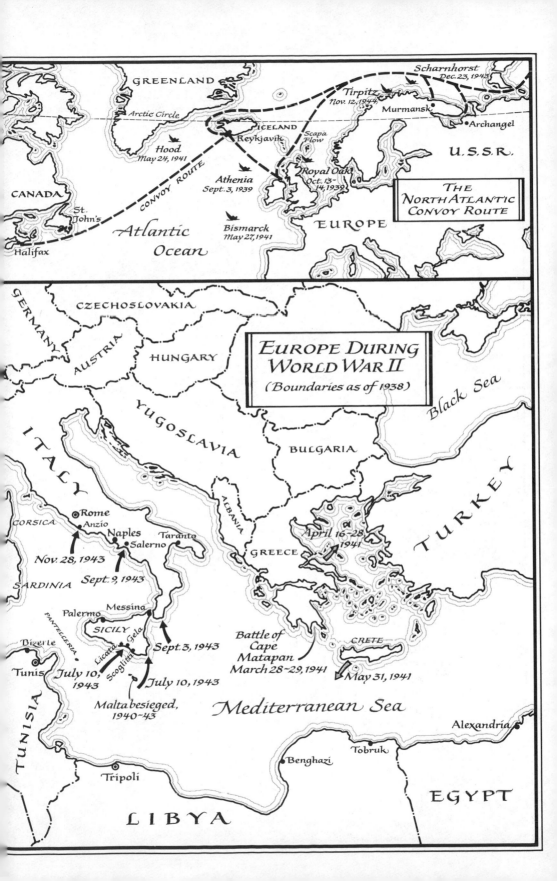

THE NORTH ATLANTIC CONVOY ROUTE

GREENLAND

Arctic Circle

Scharnhorst
Dec. 23, 1943

Tirpitz
Nov. 12, 1944

Murmansk

Archangel

U.S.S.R.

ICELAND
Reykjavik

Scapa Flow

Hood
May 24, 1941

CONVOY ROUTE

Athenia
Sept. 3, 1939

Royal Oak
Oct. 13–14, 1939

CANADA

St. John's

Atlantic Ocean

Bismarck
May 27, 1941

EUROPE

Halifax

EUROPE DURING WORLD WAR II
(Boundaries as of 1938)

GERMANY

CZECHOSLOVAKIA

AUSTRIA

HUNGARY

YUGOSLAVIA

BULGARIA

Black Sea

ITALY

CORSICA

Rome
Anzio

Nov. 28, 1943

Naples
Salerno

Taranto

ALBANIA

GREECE

April 16–28, 1941

TURKEY

SARDINIA

Sept. 9, 1943

Palermo

Messina

Bizerte

PANTELLERIA

SICILY

Licata
Gela

Sept. 3, 1943

Battle of Cape Matapan
March 28–29, 1941

CRETE

May 31, 1941

Tunis

July 10, 1943

Scoglitti

July 10, 1943

Malta besieged, 1940–43

Mediterranean Sea

Alexandria

TUNISIA

Tripoli

Benghazi

Tobruk

EGYPT

LIBYA

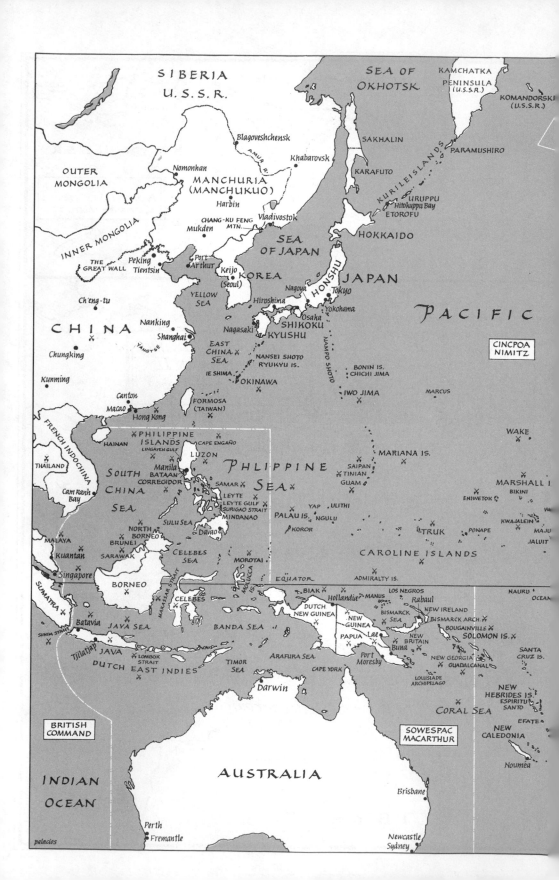

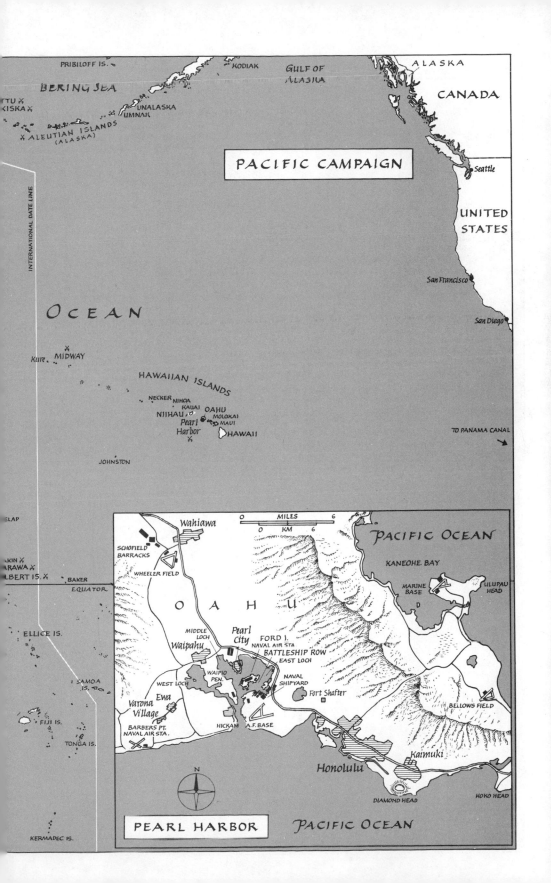

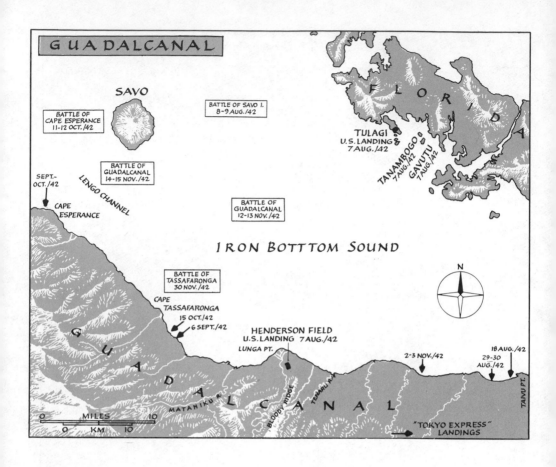

Contents

This book is dedicated to the men and women of all nations who served in the navy or merchant marine during World War II. Their vital duties were difficult and demanding, and rarely gained attention except when stark tragedy was involved. They served in all seasons, in all weathers, often under the most difficult conditions of combat, and they served well.

PREFACE

Some historians view World War I and World War II as a single war extending from 1914 to 1945, separated only by an armistice in which the combatants gathered strength to renew the contest. With the passage of time came changes in alliances; in the first great war, Italy and Japan were on the Allied side, while in the second, they were part of the Axis powers.

The first segment of this long conflict, from 1914 to 1918, was for the most part a war of continental powers. However, sea power was vital in sustaining the Allies with food and weapons, while for the Central Powers, the submarine campaign was of critical importance. From this experience, it can be seen that sailors are at least as subject as others to Santayana's admonition that those who cannot remember the past are condemned to repeat it. The lessons that should have been writ large from experience in the First World War had to be relearned in the Second. This derived in part from the ordinary human experience, but to a greater degree from the fact that many of the most critical strategic and even tactical decisions were made on the basis of political rather than military criteria.

In World War II the war at sea was the most far-reaching conflict in history, ranging across all the oceans of the world, involving all seafaring nations, some as combatants, most as victims.

Ironically for a continental power like Germany, the best chance the Axis nations had to win the war in either the European or Pacific theaters was by the effective use of sea power. However, Germany was too short-sighted to invest the necessary resources in submarines in time to win, while Japan was so arrogant and contemptuous of her enemies' will to fight that she was unable to assess the dangerous gamble she had taken.

The European sea campaigns were distinctly different from those of the Pacific theater. In Europe, especially in the Battle of the Atlantic, the Germans waged war with their submarines almost exclusively; after the first year of the war, their few capital ships were assigned a primarily passive role. With the exception of the invasion of Norway, the active campaigns they did undertake were for the most part ineffective.

In the Pacific, Japan entered the war with an emphasis on land- and sea-based air power, submarines and, to a large degree, upon its battleships. The United States was still wedded to the concept of the battleship as the decisive instrument; the enormous losses at Pearl Harbor led the United States to adopt the carrier as the principal weapon.

When war began, the navies of the major combatants, with the exceptions of Germany and Russia, were in a better state of preparedness than were their respective armies or air forces. During the budget-constrained Great Depression, the little money available had been lavished on ships and on officers and men who were smartly trained, if not always for war. Yet despite their years of training, in the final analysis, each navy learned to fight only after it had been in battle, the voluminous plans and precise training exercises of the prewar years proving for the most part as futile as the endless polishing of brass.

The critically important naval campaigns were inextricably intertwined with both land and air campaigns in each theater operation. In Europe, the sea campaign almost determined the outcomes of the land campaigns; a more substantial (and easily affordable) investment by Germany in its submarine force could well have defeated England, shut off a critical flow of supplies to the Soviet Union and prevented the invasions of both North Africa and Europe. In the Pacific, after the initial Japanese onslaught, the United States and its Allies conducted parallel land and sea campaigns, as General Douglas MacArthur strove to return to the Philippines while Admiral Chester Nimitz fought to secure a chain of island bases. It was a policy that only a country with the enormous resources of the United States could have successfully undertaken. Both strategies became increasingly dependent upon air power for their success, and, as in Europe, both benefited from Allied code-breaking activities.

The full import of the major naval campaigns is better understood if some of the lesser known, but vastly interesting, elements of the war are examined. This includes the participation of the smaller navies; the difficulties in mustering and mastering the amphibious forces required for invasions; the mining wars that silently sank so many ships; and the technological war, where the advantage lay first with one side and then the other, until the Allies accumulated so great a scientific edge that victory was assured. Seemingly disparate subjects, they are united by a common thread: incongruity. The French and Italian navies both fought bravely under desperate circumstances; the countries that endured the most humiliating evacuations also participated in the most successful invasions, and technological progress, while seemingly rapid, actually moved in fits and starts.

Strangely enough, the men doing the fighting, the enemies engaged in a war in which quarter was rarely asked and even more rarely given, had almost everything in common except their ideologies. If one looks dispassionately at the war at sea, forgetting that World War II was a war waged by the Allies against two truly evil empires, one cannot fail to be impressed by the bravery, ingenuity, persistence and warrior-nobility of combatants on both sides.

The proud bearing of the sailors is all the more striking in view of the universal hardships. Sailors of all nations fought on uncomfortable ships, were often poorly fed, worked long hours in absurd shifts, submitted to unrelenting discipline and were subject not only to the terror of the enemy's guns, bombs, torpedoes or depth charges, but also to the horrifying power of the sea, which could rise up suddenly to destroy vessels as large as destroyers. All men in all navies suffered from loneliness and feared anonymous death at sea. Yet almost all served honorably, believing in their respective causes and fighting hard until the very end.

Like the intensity of the conflict, the degree of their sacrifice was masked by the immensity of the oceans upon which it was conducted, and by an implacable invisibility. When the battle was over, both sides disappeared, the loser sliding beneath the sea that claimed so many, the victor to a different battle, and perhaps a different fate.

The war at sea was long, hard-fought and for a time in each theater, uncertain as to outcome. The following pages will chart the causes, courses, climaxes and costs of that war.

1.

A Swift Beginning
to a Long War

World War II at sea opened with a sudden fury in September 1939 as German surface ships and submarines began a systematic attack that almost brought Great Britain to her knees. The range and intensity of the battle increased steadily for the next six years as the war spread to almost every major body of water in the world, embroiling all of the great and many of the smaller naval powers in bitter battles of unimaginable size and variety.

In the North Atlantic, the U-boats savaged convoys carrying desperately needed supplies to Great Britain and the Soviet Union. In the Mediterranean, British and Italian surface forces engaged in sharp battles as the Royal Navy sought to prevent the reinforcement of Axis forces in Africa. In the Pacific, Japan's chosen new weapon, the carrier task force, was soon engaged by its American counterparts in ferocious combat, each nation's aircraft carriers exchanging attacks like two boxers in mid-ring while surface forces became for the most part mere cornermen, never close enough to see the enemy, much less attack it.

There was fighting on the water anywhere the interests of the Axis and the Allies conflicted—in the South Atlantic, the Baltic, the Aegean, the Indian Ocean, on rivers, especially in the Soviet Union and in Burma, on many other inland seas and on numberless lakes. Warships matched the geography in variety; aircraft carriers became the primary instrument, but the greatest battleships in history still slugged it out in classic ship-of-the-line encounters; destroyers and cruisers slashed at each other and at the transports they escorted, while fast motor torpedo boats dueled with larger targets. There were a myriad of fascinating improvisations—repair-ships-turned-gunboat by means of bolted-on armor plate, or battleships turned into aircraft carriers by deleting a turret and adding a launch platform. As the war grew more desperate, suicide weapons evolved—human torpedoes, midget submarines and kamikaze aircraft.

As always there were two underlying common denominators for success or failure in battle: the valor of the sailors and the wisdom of their leaders. In the navies of all nations, the officers and men, from ship captain down to the lowest-ranking sailor, fought well and bravely with what they had, often against hopeless odds.

The wisdom of the leaders was not so equitably divided. The Allies had far better leadership from their heads of state all the way through the chain of command to the admirals commanding the fleets. Although there were exceptions, the leadership of the Axis navies suffered by comparison at every level of command.

Yet the Axis nations—Germany, Italy and Japan—scored initial triumphs at sea of such magnitude that it seemed to them, and to many on the Allied side, that they had won the war. Yet the Allied nations persevered, and as time wore on, their enormous preponderance in resources, coupled to superb intelligence systems and far better leadership, ensured the hard-earned victory.

The Cost of Disarmament

The victory would not have been so hard-earned if the Allies had been better prepared for war. There is no little irony in the fact that a major cause for World War I was the naval armament race between Germany and England, while a major cause for World War II was the almost mindless quest for naval disarmament.

The pressure to disarm was primarily economic rather than altruistic; Great Britain, its economy ravaged by the Great War, could no longer afford to rule the waves by a building race; it attempted instead to retain its primacy by arms limitation agreements. In the mixture of euphoria of peace and the tribulations of declining economies, none of the democratic nations could foresee that future aggressor nations, defeated Germany and ascendant Japan, would take advantage of the disarmament conferences to precipitate another world war.

Equally important, few understood (as Hitler did) that a nation peacefully disarming itself was stifling its industry, while a renegade nation busily arming itself was invigorating its economy.

It thus first became policy, and then fashion, to preach naval limitations and disarmament. In a world already economically drained, the prospect of reducing arms expenditures was wildly popular, and a series of treaties and agreements followed that halted naval building in its tracks. At no time in the long process did the United States and Great Britain realize the extent to which each treaty worked to the advantage of future belligerent nations, and to their own immense disadvantage.

THE WASHINGTON CONFERENCE

At the suggestion of Great Britain, a naval arms limitation conference began in Washington on November 12, 1921. This was the equivalent of the more contemporary SALT talks, and had the same goals. The treaty that resulted was signed on February 6, 1922. It provided that a ratio of capital ships be established for Great Britain, United States, Japan, France and Italy, in the respective proportion of 5:5:3:1¾:1¾. A ten-year holiday from building capital ships was declared, and a limit of a displacement of 35,000 tons was placed on battleships. (The future was foreshadowed in that the United States was reading the Japanese diplomatic codes during the conference, giving it a great advantage.)

Japan accepted the agreement with the proviso that the United States could not strengthen its Pacific fortifications west of Hawaii, and that Britain would not strengthen Singapore. The conference was a brilliant diplomatic victory for Japan, for the United States had two oceans to defend, and England, three. The result was for Japan to be left in a position with far better base facilities and an *effective* strength ratio in the only ocean it had to defend, the Pacific, of 5:3 over the United States and 5:2 over Britain.

Japan was not content however; the apparent subordinate position in the parity ratio, despite the net advantage it provided in the Pacific, became grist for the mill of ultranationalists, who interpreted it as an insult. It was not; the ratios had been selected on the basis of the current naval thinking that an attacking force had to have a two-to-one superiority over a defending force to be successful. The 5:3 ratio was thought to be a safeguard. (But American and English admirals also protested the ratio, believing that it gave too much to Japan.)

Nonetheless, the term "5-5-3" became the equivalent of a "54-40 or Fight" slogan for the militant Japanese nationalists. Comprised primarily of junior officers and the growing Japanese middle class, they were united in a hatred of the white race and a desire for military supremacy. The popular image for their movement became the *Kodo-Ha*, the "Way of the Emperor"; they called for the military to redeem the government from corrupt politicians.

The United States chose to regard the treaty limits as an upper limit rather than a goal, and American shipbuilding came to a virtual halt, with only two additional ships commissioned by 1934. President Herbert Hoover's administration was the first since the eighteenth century in which not a single keel for a major naval vessel was laid down.

The Washington Conference was followed by a series of further treaties, each of which eroded the power of the democratic nations because the aggressor nations did not abide by the agreements. Japan broke each agreement as soon as it became convenient to do so, responding to the heightened fervor of its national politics. The country was in the clutch of a right-wing revolution that between 1930 and 1932 had carried out assassinations of four major political figures and two attempted coups, all designed to strengthen Japan's expansionist policies. In each of the assassinations, the young officers responsible were not punished, being regarded as "pure youths" acting for the good of the country. A situation grew up in which there were in effect two governments, one civil and one military, with the latter exercising the decisive power.

In 1931, the extremists put forward as national policy the ancient Japanese idea of *Hakko Ichiui*, the bringing of the eight corners of the world under one roof: Japanese world hegemony. The first step toward this goal was the invasion of Manchuria in 1931. A vast territory was brought under Japanese control, with the "Empire of Manchukuo" being made a puppet state in 1932. In 1933, Japan withdrew from the League of Nations in response to criticism of its militant activity. By 1934, the extremists were able to demand that Japan have naval parity with the United States and Great Britain. Not content with numerical equality, the Japanese plans called for the creation of a technically superior navy, composed of submarines of the latest design, advanced torpedoes superior to those of any other country, and indigenous-designed super-battleships of greater displacement than any others in the world, and carrying the largest guns.

Although the policy of naval disarmament had by now failed utterly, neither the United States nor Great Britain was aware of it. The American economic Depression continued to inhibit shipbuilding, while England still struggled under the infamous Ten Year Rule, which forestalled rearming if a war were not perceived as imminent within the next ten years. The Royal Navy personnel strength fell below that of the year 1894, the army was reduced to cadre status, and the tiny Royal Air Force remained equipped with fabric-covered biplanes not much advanced over those used in 1918.

The principal proponent of this virtual unilateral disarmament, Neville Chamberlain, was then Chancellor of the Exchequer. Immortalized—or stigmatized—as Prime Minister for his "peace in our time" comments upon his return from the 1938 Munich sellout of Czechoslovakia, his earlier attempts at appeasement, directed to Japan, are less well known. Chamberlain, a former mayor of Birmingham and unswervingly dedicated to a balanced budget, was so opposed to rearmament that he advocated a reconsideration of Great Britain's ties with the United States. He advised reestablishing cordial terms with Japan and moving away from what he and his peers termed the Yankee "braggadocio of Yahoodom." Chamberlain formally recommended to the Cabinet that Japan be informed that England was not linked to America, and suggested that a ten-year nonaggression pact be proposed. Great Britain and Japan were to decide mutually on spheres of influence in Asia, and ignore American interests.

Yet even as Chamberlain proposed, Japan disposed, abrogating the Washington Treaty on December 30, 1934. The result, which had no effect whatever upon Chamberlain's popularity or credibility, was that Britain offered to abandon America, only to be rebuffed by Japan. Japan was soon joined by Germany in seeking approval for rearmament, and the British government was only too happy to renege on the Treaty of Versailles and on Britain's supposedly immutable friendship with France. Hitler had stunned Europe with his renunciation of the Versailles treaty by resuming conscription for an army of thirty-six divisions and announcing the existence of the Luftwaffe. He now sent a personal representative, Joachim von Ribbentrop, to England (together with forty planeloads of personnel and equipment) to negotiate a naval treaty.

Ribbentrop, exercising the lack of diplomatic charm that would win him world fame, brusquely demanded that England immediately agree to a treaty that would allow the Third Reich a surface fleet 35 percent the size of the Royal Navy, and, if Germany so desired, *parity* in submarines. Despite being appalled by Ribbentrop's breach of traditional diplomacy, the British government agreed. Germany had demanded a duck dinner, and England eagerly provided the duck.

Disarmament in a World Racing to War

Disarmament and the political climate in which it flourished encouraged the exercise of aggression by Italy, Germany and Japan. It resulted in the nominally powerful navies of the United States and Great Britain becoming hollow, unbalanced forces, lacking the numbers and variety of ships their global responsibilities demanded. Both were severely undermanned in both officer and enlisted ranks, and their reserve components were overage and undertrained. Realistic training was almost nonexistent.

This might not have been as catastrophic if the national leaders had adopted policies reflecting the status. Henry Stimson, then Secretary of State for Herbert Hoover, and later to be Secretary of War for Franklin D. Roosevelt, had protested the Japanese actions in Manchuria strongly. For three consecutive years, 1932, 1933 and 1934, the Navy General Board informed the government of Japan's quest for dominance and its goal of naval supremacy. The board advised the Roosevelt administration to decide whether it intended to defend the Philippines long enough for a U.S. relief force to arrive. If it did, then Manila would have to be extensively fortified at great expense, and naval construction would have to be accelerated. If it did not, then the United States should renounce its Asian policy and leave the field to the Japanese.

Roosevelt chose to follow a middle path, refusing to fortify Manila, enter a naval race with Japan or forsake U.S. commitments in Asia. Instead he chose to remind Japan of its treaty obligations, while trying to avoid a crisis. It was an ostrich policy, but one calculated to get him reelected.

The British government received the same advice on Singapore from within its own military. All through the 1930s, England conducted its activities as if it were still a great power in Asia. But thanks to its policy of disarmament and attitude of appeasement, when Japan attacked, Britain lacked the resources and the will to resist.

In the United States, the navy was in a relatively favored position, thanks to the affectionate regard in which it was held by President Roosevelt, who had been Assistant Secretary of the Navy during World War I, and was the de facto Secretary of the Navy for his first two administrations. As a result, although the battleship was still considered the decisive instrument, a great deal of experimentation was conducted with operating dive-bombers and torpedo planes off carriers. The United States was fortunate to have Admiral William Moffett, who, though infatuated with airships, also backed Admiral H. T. Mayo and Rear Admiral Hugh Rodman in their belief in carrier aviation. And, in 1934, Representative Carl Vinson of Georgia, a member of the Naval Affairs Committee, pushed legislation to begin building to treaty limitations. (Today, the USS *Carl Vinson* is one of the navy's most powerful nuclear aircraft carriers.)

The Japanese also believed that the biggest guns would decide the next contest, but like the United States, developed lighter, faster carriers carrying many aircraft. The man who had done the most to build up Japanese carrier capability was Admiral Yamamoto Isoruku, who would lead the Combined Fleet, and who, coincidentally, had been the primary Japanese naval adviser at the disarmament conferences.

The German naval leadership fell in 1928 to Vice Admiral Erich Raeder, who earlier had been assigned to write the official German naval history of World War I, *Der Krieg Zur See (The Sea War)*. In his research, Raeder was influenced by the relative success of German merchant raiders like the *Emden,* and determined that was the correct path for the German navy to follow in the future. Raeder kept his navy completely apolitical, while he prostituted himself to Adolf Hitler, telling him first that a surface navy was necessary to maintain connections between Germany and East Prussia, then separated by Polish territory. (Ironically, the last great effort of the German navy in World War II would be in the doleful winter and spring of 1945, conducting the tragic evacuation of refugees from East Prussia to Germany as the Russian armies surged forward.)

As his confidence grew, Raeder next used France as the nominal enemy, suggesting Germany have a fleet at least equal to that of its old foe. In January 1939, he presented his Z Plan, which called for a fleet capable of challenging Britain by 1948 with the raider tactics he had come to prefer: he envisioned sending out strong raiding parties of battleships, battle cruisers and aircraft carriers to decimate English shipping.

Hitler knew his man, and promised Raeder all he wished, even allowing him to dream of an ultimate world fleet, an enormous armada of eighty battleships and dozens of carriers, which, after finishing off England and the United States, would have a final climactic duel for world domination with Japan. More importantly, Hitler assured Raeder that there would be no war before 1944.

Raeder ignored the lessons of submarine warfare, and began, with severely limited means, to build up a surface fleet. The ships he built were excellent, but their numbers were so few that when war began in 1939, he felt betrayed by Hitler. Raeder was obsessed with the idea that the modern German navy would never surrender as the Kaiser's navy had, and would instead go down with flag waving and guns firing. Yet he did not resign, and instead regularly put his ships at risk in support of Hitler's plans, confident until the end of his career that he alone knew what was good for Germany's navy. As the events of the war demonstrated, his advocacy for the navy was over time transformed into an identification of the German navy's goals with his own goals. He consistently failed to develop a wartime strategy, just as he failed to anticipate what might happen if war came earlier than promised.

If there is any justice in war, it perhaps may be found in the fact that of all the combatant nations, the naval leaders of Germany and Japan, Erich Raeder and Yamamoto Isoruku, were the greatest failures. Their countries developed fine ships and trained brave crew members for them; but the two leaders established and executed policies that, when war came, would condemn their navies to total defeat.

THE DIE IS CAST

"Winston is back."

This proud if apprehensive message was sent out by the Board of Admiralty to all Royal Navy ships when Winston Spencer Churchill became the First Lord of the Admiralty for the second time, on the day England declared war upon Germany, September 3, 1939.

Churchill, three months shy of sixty-five, not a member of the Cabinet since 1929 and vilified in the press for years over his role in the Gallipoli campaign and his party switching, began his new duties with his usual vigor. The Admiralty, unlike the War Ministry and the Air Ministry, had direct operational control of its forces. Churchill relished the exercise of power, and his ability to do so in 1939 appeared to be even greater than it had been in 1914.

In 1939, his First Sea Lord was Admiral of the Fleet Sir Dudley Pound, a grim, unsmiling man whose four-year tenure would be marked by both notable successes and resounding failures. Pound was strongly criticized because he so often deferred to Churchill, but he was far from being the only senior British officer to do so.

To all external appearances, Churchill should have been reasonably content with the apparent relative positions of the Royal Navy and its opponent. There was no German High Seas Fleet, and Italy had not come into the war. The Royal Navy was ready to fight the Battle of Jutland, that classic battleship engagement of World War I, again, but the Germans lacked the wherewithal to be the opponent. Instead, Raeder could only pursue a vastly shrunken version of his grandiose raiding plans.

Appearances were deceiving, for despite its superiority in numbers, the various naval treaties of the 1920s and 1930s had left the Royal Navy saddled with older vessels. It was especially deficient in the capability of its aircraft carriers and in the quality of the planes of the Fleet Air Arm. Compared to their American counterparts, the British carriers were too short-ranged.

The Fleet Air Arm, which had not received its own funding base until 1938, went to war with obsolete, obsolescent or ill-conceived aircraft. Only the obsolete Fairey Swordfish, a cumbersome biplane referred to affectionately as the "Stringbag," proved to be an effective weapon, remaining operational until May 1945. It would be months before modern aircraft like the Hawker Sea Hurricane or the U.S. Grumman Martlet (Wildcat in the United States) appeared on British carriers.

One of the hidden dangers of the long period of naval disarmament revealed itself as soon as war broke out and the submarine threat became an actuality. There was a critical shortage of cruisers, destroyers and, most especially, the smaller ships that were vitally needed for escort work with the convoys.

More important than any of these, however, was a leadership malaise that kept the Royal Navy technically backward and lacking proficiency in the skills required for war. In the previous twenty-one years, the Royal Navy had reverted to a nineteenth-century way of life, where polished brass, gleaming paint and a full social life were the dominant factors.

RELATIVE STRENGTHS

The Home Fleet felt secure at Scapa Flow in the Orkneys, the great ships entering and leaving port not far from where the Imperial German Navy had scuttled itself on June 21, 1919. The Home Fleet consisted of five battleships, two battle cruisers (including what had for twenty years been considered the most powerful ship in the world, HMS *Hood*) two aircraft carriers, sixteen cruisers, seven destroyers and twenty-one submarines.

At ports along the English coast to Liverpool, there were distributed an additional two battleships, two carriers, five cruisers and fifty-four destroyers. Other warships were stationed around the globe, and there were also the fleets of the dominions to draw upon. And by formal agreement between Britain and France, the French fleet was concentrated in the Mediterranean.

Facing this formidable array, Grand Admiral Raeder had at his disposal only seven heavy warships, the most important of these being the two fast but undergunned battleships, the *Gneisenau* and the *Scharnhorst*. The press had made much of three so-called pocket battleships, the *Admiral Graf Spee*, *Admiral Scheer* and *Deutchsland*. These, officially called *Panzerschiffen* (armored ships), were supposed to be fast enough to escape any ship they could not outgun. This was not the case; the French battleships *Strasbourg* and *Dunkerque* were specific counters to the pocket battleships, and the British battle cruisers *Hood, Renown* and *Repulse* were faster and had greater fire power. Armed with six 11-inch guns, and capable of 26 knots, the three German Admiral-class ships had been built under the 10,000-ton limitation on cruisers, but actually displaced 12,100 tons. Like some Japanese vessels, the pocket battleships used welded steel hulls, a radical departure from the standard riveted naval construction at the time.

Raeder's other large warships were pre–World War I battleships, the coal-burning naval training ships *Schleswig-Holstein* and the *Schlesien*, useful only as floating artillery. The mighty *Bismarck*, which was to have a short, event-filled history, and the *Tirpitz*, which would become the apotheosis of the "fleet-in-being" concept, were not yet complete.

The remainder of the German navy was inexplicably weak, given the magnitude of the rest of the Nazi rearmament program, with only three heavy cruisers—*Hipper, Prinz Eugen* and *Blücher*—six light cruisers, seventeen destroyers, and fifty-seven U-boats. Of the submarines, ten were "Baltic ducks," too small for service in the Atlantic, and eight were not ready for service. There were in addition a number of armed merchant ships, some of which would be unleashed to follow in the famous footsteps of Count von Luckner's raider in World War I.

If the British were weak in naval air power, the Germans were virtually powerless, thanks in great part to Field Marshal Hermann Goering's jealous insistence on controlling all aviation matters. Keels for two aircraft carriers, the *Graf Zeppelin* and the *Peter Strasser* (named for a distinguished World War I zeppelin commander), had been laid down, but work soon ceased on the latter, and it was in fact offered to the Soviet Union in fulfillment of part of the weapons promised in the infamous prewar pact. The *Graf Zeppelin* was never completed, riding out its war at anchor as a warehouse for exotic Asian wood. Seized as war booty, it capsized under tow en route to the Soviet Union, in part because its decks were so heavily laden with freight cars of loot.

Goering did not permit the Luftwaffe to act sufficiently on the navy's behalf later in the war, when land victories had provided air fields from Norway to the Spanish border. The Germans had developed some excellent specialized aircraft, including the Focke Wulf FW 200 long-range reconnaissance plane, and the Heinkel He 115 torpedo plane. In addition, standard Luftwaffe aircraft like the Junkers Ju 88 and Heinkel He 111 did excellent work when assigned maritime missions. Unfortunately for the German navy, Goering would neither allow a separate naval air arm nor commit an adequate amount of Luftwaffe support, even early in the war when it was available.

Raeder, no matter how surprised at Hitler's decision for an early war, nonetheless sent as many warships as he could into the Atlantic prior to the invasion of Poland. All eighteen U-boats capable of Atlantic duty were on station, and twenty-one more were deployed in the North Sea, while the *Deutschland* and the *Graf Spee* had already been sent to their respective North and South Atlantic stations.

Despite the seeming heavy odds, some factors favored the German navy. The Royal Navy had to stretch itself thin to defend against threats at every possible point. The appearance of a pocket battleship was sufficient to cause panic in the Admiralty. The German captains recognized this, and tried to promote as much confusion as possible, moving from point to point over wide ocean ranges. Even more than in World War I, the very concept of a German fleet-in-being was inhibiting to England, which proceeded to take the next six years to overcome the limited number of German capital ships.

SURFACE ACTION

The surrender of the Imperial German Navy and its subsequent scuttling at Scapa Flow in 1919 had a profound pathologic effect upon Grand Admiral

Erich Raeder and many of the captains who commanded warships in the new German navy. In a memorandum written on September 3, 1939, Raeder spelled out his disappointment with Hitler's breaking his promise, indicating how much stronger the German fleet could have been if war had been delayed. And he included the significant statement that "The surface forces, moreover, are so inferior in number and strength to those of the British Fleet, that even at full strength, they can do nothing more than show that they know how to die gallantly and thus are willing to create the foundations for reconstruction."

Raeder's recidivist philosophy echoed the cries after the scuttling at Scapa Flow. During World War II, it would have a terminal effect upon the lives of thousands of younger officers and seamen who were killed when their captains refused to surrender even when the fight was obviously lost.

"Raeder's dictum" was at sharp tactical variance with Hitler's nervous insistence that German surface units not engage enemy forces of greater power. A German ship captain was thus torn by two directives, one to fight at any cost, and the second not to fight unless victory was assured.

A "doomed to fail" mentality surfaced early, with the ineffective and ultimately disastrous cruises of the *Graf Spee* and the *Deutschland*.

2.

GERMANY SAILS
FORTH

The *Graf Spee* and the *Deutschland* had been sent to sea before the outbreak of war, the *Spee* on August 21, the *Deutschland* three days later. The latter ship's initial foray was far less dramatic than that of the *Spee*.

The *Deutschland* was the first of the new German battleships launched, the first to enter combat and the last to stop fighting. The gloomy, shell-freighted future was not foreseen when she was commissioned in March 1931. Proudly christened the *Deutschland*, the ship was ostensibly a 10,000-ton cruiser permitted by the terms of the Treaty of Versailles. In fact she was the first of the *Panzerschiffen*, displacing 15,500 tons fully loaded, and carrying six 11-inch guns in two triple turrets. These guns could throw a 670-pound high explosive shell for fifteen nautical miles, and both German shells and explosives were of the finest quality. The use of an electrically welded hull and diesel engines had resulted in a weight saving of 550 tons. Powered by eight M.A.N. diesels of 6,750 horsepower each, the total 54,000 shaft-horsepower could propel the *Deutschland* at 26 knots. She had cost the equivalent of $19 million, very expensive for the time, disproportionately so given the competition for armament funds in the Weimar Republic, which had financed her. She was bombed by Spanish Republican planes in the harbor at Ibiza, Spain, on May 29, 1937, with 109 casualties.

FIRST WAR CRUISE

The *Deutschland*, under the command of Captain Paul Wenneker, moved out from her hiding place in the south of Greenland, to sink the British SS *Stonegate*, 5,044 tons, on October 5, 1939, and the Norwegian SS *Lorentz W. Hansen*, 1,918 tons on October 9. Wenneker then committed one of the classic errors of the war, the capture of the U.S. merchantman *City of Flint*, a gaffe that must have streaked Hitler's hair with gray. The *City of Flint* had made headlines on September 3 when she rescued more than 200 survivors of the *Athenia* and then safely transported them to New York, along with twenty-nine American refugees fleeing the outbreak of war in Europe. Joseph Aloysius Gainard, captain of the *City of Flint*, had been torpedoed in 1918 when serving as an ensign aboard the naval transport *President Lincoln*. After loading a general cargo, he sailed again from New York on October 3, 1939, headed for Liverpool and Glasgow. The *City of Flint* was halted five days later, 1,260 miles from New York, by the *Deutschland;* a German prize crew was put aboard, Gainard and his crew made prisoners, and the swastika flag run up. The German crew evaded the British navy (not too difficult a task at this early stage of the war) and made it to Tromsö, Norway, on October 21. The Norwegians, anxious to protect their neutrality, refused admission to the Germans, who next went to Murmansk, where the prize crew claimed "havarie," the traditional privilege of sanctuary for damage incurred at sea. The Soviet authorities forced the vessel back to sea, insisting that if havarie were invoked, the Americans on board could not be considered prisoners.

Meanwhile the United States had initiated a tidal wave of diplomatic protest and the German Foreign Office was scurrying about, trying to find a face-saving way of making amends. The *City of Flint*, her Nazi crew now officially kidnappers, had the British Home Fleet hot on her trail. By keeping close to the Norwegian coast, she reached Haugesund, Norway, where she was again refused entry. The Germans realized they'd never make it through the gathering British forces, and anchored anyway. The Norwegians promptly arrested and interned the Germans, while setting Gainard and his crew free to return to New York. Gainard was awarded the Navy Cross—the first to be given in World War II—and subsequently called back to duty. He was serving in the rank of captain when he died on board his ship on December 23, 1943. On November 23, 1944, the *Sumner*-class destroyer *Gainard* (DD 706) was named for him; the ship earned the Navy Unit Commendation at Okinawa.

Unable to endure the *Deutschland*'s bumbling, Hitler ordered her home; she slunk into Gotenhafen on October 17; a month later Hitler, without consulting Raeder, peremptorily changed her name to *Lützow*.

In the 1940 invasion of Norway, the *Lützow* was badly damaged by shore-based guns. As she returned home for repair she was struck by torpedoes from the British submarine *Spearfish,* blowing off both propellers and the rudder; tugs lugged her home ignominiously to save her from sinking. Repaired, she was torpedoed by a Bristol Beaufort on June 12, 1941, and sent back to dry dock in Kiel. *Lützow* next missed the mass attack on convoy PQ-17 in July 1942 by running aground in northern Norway. By 1944 she was providing artillery support for Nazi troops retreating along the Baltic coast; she had almost come into her own, for the shells of her 11-inch guns were credited with delaying the Red Army's capture of Memel by several weeks. In 1945 she was finally sunk in the Kaiserfahrt canal by a 12,000-pound Tallboy bomb dropped from a British Avro Lancaster. Defiant, if ill-served by luck, the *Lützow* was brought back to an even keel, serving as a fort in the last days of the war, firing her 11-inch guns at advancing Soviet tanks. When the Russian troops finally arrived within small-arms range, the *Lützow* was deliberately blown up on May 4, 1945. The *Deutschland/Lützow* may have been a late bloomer, but she outlived Hitler by four days.

THE GENTLEMAN RAIDER

Yet as ineffective, not to say counterproductive, as the *Deutschland*'s voyage had been, it had strained British strength to the limit in attempting to find her. That episode plus the more fruitful efforts of the *Graf Spee* validated Raeder's concept that numerous hard-hitting German raiders could seize the initiative from the Royal Navy and disrupt English shipping.

The Royal Navy regarded the threat so seriously that no fewer than eight battle groups searched for the *Graf Spee* as it raided shipping in the South Atlantic. Ironically, this massive force, disrupting the Royal Navy's ability to operate in exactly the way Raeder wished, would never engage with the *Graf Spee*. That honor would instead go to Force G, the cruisers *Ajax, Achilles* and *Exeter,* summoned from their operating areas in the South Atlantic by a man with the true Nelson touch, Commodore Henry Harwood, on board the *Ajax*.

The *Graf Spee* slipped through the British fleet and established itself in the South Atlantic, with her supply ship *Altmark* (soon to figure in another intrusion in Norwegian waters). There she began a classic raiding foray. Forty-five-year-old Captain Hans Langsdorff was a veteran of Jutland, well liked by his men, and ultimately, by his captives, perhaps the highest honor that could be accorded him.

Langsdorff executed Raeder's raiding policy with precision and élan, mystifying the Royal Navy with widely spread appearances in the South Atlantic and the Indian Ocean. Between September 30 and December 7, 1939, the *Graf Spee* sank nine cargo ships, totaling 50,089 tons. In that process Langsdorff did not kill a single sailor or passenger on any of these ships. He treated his captives with a sympathetic courtesy, and embarked them either upon European-bound neutral shipping, or on the *Altmark*.

His cruise might have been longer if he had been more ruthless, for two of his last victims, the *Doric Star* and the *Tairoa*, had sent out their RRR (attacked by surface raider) signal, along with their positions, and the Royal Navy at last had a recent fix on the area in which the *Graf Spee* was operating, near the eastern coast of South Africa. Other raiders usually sent a barrage of shells into the victim's radio shack at the first sign of a transmission. Langsdorff, ever the gentleman, was lenient in this regard, not firing until necessary, and even congratulating the brave radioman on the *Tairoa* who had kept up a continuous stream of traffic until a 4.1-inch shell blew up his equipment. It was good theater, but poor warfare.

But the *Graf Spee*'s captain recognized that he had to find a new base of operations. From his final victim, the 3,895-ton *Streonshalh*, he had captured documents that indicated the optimum position to intercept merchant ships coming out of the River Plate, near Montevideo, Uruguay. By radio from Berlin he learned that four British cargo vessels were due to leave Montevideo on December 10, and that decided him. He would steam to the South American coastal area to score successes against the Britain-bound grain and refrigerated meat ships, and then return to Germany. His engines needed a complete shipyard overhaul and were given to smoking badly at inopportune times.

Commodore Harwood's ships were widely separated as Langsdorff had envisioned, the *Exeter* off the Falklands, the *Achilles* off Rio de Janiero, while the *Ajax*, fortuitously, was off the River Plate. Harwood wrestled with the puzzle of the *Graf Spee*, trying to determine where he would go if he were in Langsdorff's place. He plotted the *Graf Spee*'s sinkings, assessed the various merchant routes, and guessed that Langsdorff would head for Montevideo. He called for his squadron to join *Ajax* there.

Harwood and Langsdorff exemplify in many ways the difference between the British and German commanders. The British warship captains were typically pugnacious and determined to engage in battle no matter what the odds. The German commanders were reluctant to begin battle unless the odds were heavily in their favor. It was not a question of fearing death; Langsdorff took care later to prove that wasn't so. It was instead an unreasonable caution about losing a ship.

Harwood was well aware that by any standards the *Admiral Graf Spee* constituted what was known in naval parlance as a "superior force." The German ship had a greater weight of fire than the three cruisers, being able to throw 4,708 pounds of shell in a single salvo, compared to the cruisers' combined salvo weight of 3,136 pounds. The *Graf Spee* was also more heavily armored than any of the British ships, able to withstand the 6-inch shells of the *Achilles* and *Ajax*, and vulnerable only to the 8-inch shells of the *Exeter*. It also had a marginal advantage in being the first German ship to be equipped with radar, a rather primitive 80cm Seetakt with a useful range of nine miles. *Exeter* displaced 8,390 tons; *Ajax* and *Achilles* each displaced about 7,000. The *Graf Spee* displaced 12,000 tons.

Harwood's orders were succinct: "My policy with three cruisers versus one pocket battleship. Attack at once. By day act as two units. First Division (*Ajax* and *Achilles*) and *Exeter* diverged to permit flank marking. First Division will concentrate gunfire." (Flank marking meant registering the fall of fire from the side, i.e., calling where the shells fell.) In other words, superior force be damned.

At 0552 on the morning of December 12, 1939, the *Graf Spee* sighted the masts of the *Exeter* at a distance of twenty miles. Eight minutes later the English squadron sighted a trail of diesel smoke from the *Spee*'s ailing engines, and sped to the attack.

Langsdorff, having already made up his mind to engage an escorted convoy, believed that his heavy guns could so damage any cruiser or destroyer that it would be unable to shadow him. But at 0616 hours he learned that he faced not one but three cruisers, which he correctly identified as the *Exeter*, *Ajax* and *Achilles*, all three of them capable of speeds as much as 6 knots greater than his own. Knowing he had to fight and destroy them, he increased his speed and climbed into what would become his Achilles heel, the unarmored control tower. There he had great visibility, but no protection from the storm of steel about to be unleashed upon him. Nonetheless, at 0617, when he had closed to just under twelve miles, he opened fire on the *Exeter*. The British cruiser responded three minutes later, followed in sixty seconds by the *Achilles* and *Ajax*.

German gunnery was excellent, straddling *Exeter* with the third salvo, destroying the two Supermarine Walrus spotter aircraft and killing the crew of the starboard torpedo tubes. The next salvo hit cleanly, putting the ship's B turret out of action and killing most of the people on the bridge. Two more direct hits followed, and smoke and flames billowed upward from the *Exeter*, now being steered by its captain, F. S. Bell, from a secondary position. Wounded in the face, Bell had his orders relayed verbally to the manual steering station aft, with the usual delay and confusion attendant to the loss of normal communications.

Langsdorff was worried about a torpedo attack from the two light cruisers and shifted fire from the *Exeter* to the *Ajax* and *Achilles*, his second error since electing to engage. The battered *Exeter*, listing and presumed conquered, attacked with torpedoes; Langsdorff avoided them, but, disconcerted, turned sharply to the left and laid down a smoke screen. He thus gave up the initiative, and effectively the battle, only twenty minutes after it had begun.

The contest now played out like terriers harassing a wounded German shepherd. Langsdorff, doubtless dismayed by the aggressive tactics, again concentrated on *Exeter*, which hit the *Spee* with another salvo from its 8-inch guns. The *Exeter*'s A turret was displaced and not functioning, its fire-control equipment was inoperative and the ship's list had worsened, but its engines were running, and Captain Bell was preparing to ram the *Graf Spee* if all else failed.

The *Graf Spee*'s salvos now hammered *Ajax*, knocking out her two after turrets at 0725, and there followed an exchange of torpedoes from the two ships, loosed at 9,000 yards' range. Both ships avoided the missiles, but *Graf Spee* was steaming at 24 knots toward Montevideo, and despite her damage still firing accurately enough to carry away *Ajax*'s topmast.

The *Graf Spee* had been hit by three 8-inch and seventeen 6-inch shells. A huge hole had been opened in her bow and critical portions of the superstructure were knocked out, including a plant for purifying the fuel and lubricating oil used by her engines. The 6-inch guns of the two British cruisers, while unable to penetrate the *Spee*'s armor, wreaked havoc on the upper decks, killing and wounding the men manning the secondary armament. There were thirty-six killed and fifty-nine wounded among the *Graf Spee*'s crew, and considerable damage done to the water-distilling machinery, the bakery and the galley. None of the sixty-two British prisoners on board was injured, maintaining Langsdorff's perfect record. Langsdorff, exposed in the relatively unprotected control tower, was not spared, being twice wounded in the head, and rendered briefly unconscious. He may have suffered a mild concussion.

Langsdorff sought sanctuary at Montevideo, getting approval for his decision from Admiral Raeder and a furious Hitler. A mendacious diplomatic game ensued, each side dissimulating. The British were the clear winners. Langsdorff asked to remain for fifteen days to repair the ship fully. The British pretended to demand that he leave within twenty-four hours, as international law seemed to require, but in truth wanted him to stay for at least three or four days until the ships they said were already on station, the *Ark Royal* and *Renown*, actually arrived.

Persuaded that the British were waiting in overwhelming force, Langsdorff's options dwindled to three: a fighting passage to Buenos Aires, in the hope that he could get better treatment from the Argentine government; accepting internment in Montevideo; or scuttling the *Graf Spee* in the estuary of the River Plate.

Langsdorff sent these three options by radiogram to Raeder on December 16, requesting a decision. Raeder and Hitler discussed the problem, Hitler this time arguing for a fight to the death, but deferring to Raeder for a final judgment, as he did so often in naval matters. The latter then advised Langsdorff to try to extend his time in neutral waters, and approved his decision to fight his way to Buenos Aires, if possible. He ordered: "*No* internment in Uruguay." Then, somewhat ambiguously, Raeder added, "Attempt effective destruction if ship is scuttled."

The British force waiting off the River Plate still consisted of the battered *Ajax* and *Achilles*, reinforced now by the *Cumberland,* a 10,000-ton cruiser with eight 8-inch guns, built to the Washington Naval Treaty specifications. Harwood, the force commander, disposed his forces to cut off the *Graf Spee,* but estimated that Langsdorff had at least a 70 percent chance of escaping. Once free, he might well have gotten home, as the *Altmark* was almost to do.

Langsdorff elected to scuttle, transferring most of his crew to the German merchant ship *Tacoma* to go to Buenos Aires to seek sanctuary as "shipwrecked sailors."

With his senior officers and a minimum crew of eight petty officers, Langsdorff took the *Graf Spee* out of Montevideo harbor in front of thousands of onlookers who hoped to see a last gallant battle. Instead, the battleship, her classified equipment stripped or destroyed, was anchored just outside Uruguay's three-mile limit. The German flags were hauled down, the time fuses set, and the skeleton crew embarked in a motorboat that set course for Buenos Aires.

At 2000, twenty minutes after Langsdorff departed, the charges went off and the *Graf Spee* blew up, settling to the bottom with her distorted upper works still visible.

The Argentinians were less receptive than the Germans had hoped, and the crew was interned, probably saving their lives; for had they been repatriated, most of them would have returned to combat as submariners, and few would have survived. More than 500 elected to remain in Argentina after the war.

Langsdorff, having attended to the many details, borrowed a pistol from the German embassy, and sat down to write three letters. Two were to his family. The third was to the German ambassador in Buenos Aires, stating that he wished to prove by his death that the "fighting services of the Reich were ready to die for the honor of the flag." A possibly apocryphal story says that he wrapped himself in the German naval ensign. Then, with the morbid Prussian military outlook that any situation can be improved by another death, he shot himself.

LIFELINE TO THE NORTH

After the *Graf Spee* had been sunk, Admiral Raeder fought back by becoming even more militant, advocating the attack in the west that the generals wished to postpone, and continually stressing the need to occupy Norway. In time Hitler became enamored of the idea as well, in part because he viewed the Norwegians to be Aryans of the best type for his new racial order. From this point on, Hitler retained a curious belief that Norway would be the pivotal theater of war, and he tied up thousands of men in occupation duty until the very end.

After secret preparation by a small bank of skilled staff officers, led by General Nikolaus von Falkenhorst with Captain Theodor Krancke representing Raeder, the plan for the occupation of Norway was signed by Hitler on March 1, 1940. It called for the utmost effort from the German navy to effect simultaneous landings at seven Norwegian ports over 1,200 miles of coastline. It was incredibly risky given the British command of the seas, and had only one thing to recommend it: total surprise. It was one of the most daring of Hitler's military moves, a much more radical departure on his part than many of his later decisions in the war, and thoroughly atypical. Despite the *Graf Spee* disaster, Raeder had done what few men could do: cause Hitler to trust him in the coming campaign in Scandinavia.

Germany depended upon Sweden for more than 40 percent of its iron ore, importing 15 million tons annually. In the summer, the ore went to the port of Luleå, and then down the Gulf of Bothnia to Germany. From October to April, however, this route was iced in, and the ore went from the iron fields at Gällivare by rail to Narvik, Norway, and then down the Innereled (inner leads or the Leads), the waterway threading between Norway's coast and the myriad offshore islands, to Germany.

The English were equally determined to seize Norway, and if Raeder was an advocate on the German side, Winston Churchill was his rabid opposite number.

There began a curious seesaw effect in which each English or German step in preparing to invade Norway would cause the other side to take an additional countermeasure, a converging process that would culminate in early April 1940. The Allies, unlike Hitler, had difficulty in finding a pretext for launching an aggressive invasion of a friendly neutral country. The answer seemed to come with the Soviet invasion of Finland on November 30, 1939. The Soviet armies suffered grievously. What was expected to be a walkover turned into a grisly bloodletting for the hapless Soviet army, with the gallant Finns exciting the world's imagination and leading to the possibility of joint Anglo-French intervention on their side.

Out of touch with reality, England and France seriously discussed adding the Soviet Union to their list of enemies, despite being so ineffective to date in their war with Germany. Plans were crafted to bomb the Russian oil fields in Baku (at a time when only leaflets were being dropped on Germany by British bombers) in addition to placing an army in the field in Finland.

The tension was heightened on February 16, when on the explicit instructions of Churchill, the British destroyer *Cossack* violated Norwegian neutrality and boarded the *Altmark*, the *Graf Spee*'s supply ship, now returning with 299 British sailors on board as prisoners. The rescue was done with élan, the cry "The navy's here!" going up with the boarding, the successful execution of which imparted pride to England and an excuse to Hitler.

Prime Minister Neville Chamberlain, who had been so inexorably wrong about the peace, persisted in his equally bad decisions about the prosecution of the war. He too now championed the plan to invade Norway, secure Narvik, then move across the Gällivare ore fields, adding to it the confident assurance that both Norway and Sweden would acquiesce in this "protection." It was an impossible dream; both nations rejected the idea of armed intervention by any power on any pretext.

It was still early in the war, and the years of peace and low budgets had eradicated British expertise with amphibious operations and invasions. The general run of the Allies' preparations was hopelessly muddled, with protracted delays, divided command structure and only inadequately equipped second-line troops available. By March 12, however, a decision had been made to land troops at Narvik, Trondheim and Bergen. Then the Finns succumbed to a renewed Soviet attack on March 13, 1940, removing the one excuse for intervention.

In the meantime, General von Falkenhorst was continuing his planning, counting on six army divisions, 1,000 aircraft and the entire German navy to execute the campaign. The Germans hoped to have the support of a militant pro-German minority of the Norwegian population, under the leadership of Vidkun Quisling, whose name soon would became a synonym for "traitor." Quisling had been a military attaché to Finland and was for a period of time Minister of War, before leaving government to found the National Unity Party, a quasi-fascist organization. He made a good impression on Hitler, but did not receive the full backing of General von Falkenhorst, who reacted as most patriots do to traitors, even those of enemy nations. Quisling was immediately repudiated by his people, and after a two-week "reign" effectively replaced by the Germans with Josef Terboven. At war's end, the ruthless Terboven committed suicide somewhat untidily with a stick of dynamite; Quisling, his name forever infamous, was shot by a Norwegian firing squad.

THE CAMPAIGN IN NORWAY

With the troops previously designated for the invasion of Norway now disembarked because of Finland's surrender, England nonetheless persisted with Operation Wilfred, the mining of the Leads beginning on April 6. The start was postponed by two days, in part to prepare for the expected German reaction. Word of the intended mining had leaked to Germany, and on Admiral Raeder's advice, Hitler agreed to the invasion, code-named Fall Weseruebung (Weser Exercise), to begin on the morning of April 9, 1940. The initial element of the offensive, the invasion of Denmark, went off almost without incident, with German troops occupying the country by the early morning of the 9th.

German planning for the invasion of Norway was vastly complicated by the long distances to be covered and the differences in speeds of the ships involved. Because all landings were to be simultaneous, the ships intended for Narvik, some 1,000 miles away, had to begin departing on April 3. The main forces, embarked on faster warships, left on April 7 and 8.

Hitler, mindful of world opinion about powerful Germany striking at smaller neighbors, had determined to keep the initial forces as small as possible, and to attempt to maintain the appearance of a peaceful takeover. British command deficiencies facilitated the execution of the German plan to an amazing degree.

At this stage of the war, Britain's political ineptitude was matched by that of her military leaders. The Commander-in-Chief of the Home Fleet, Admiral Sir Charles Forbes, had already made so many miscalculations of German intent that he was known within the fleet as "Wrong-Way Charlie" and he added to his errors in the Norwegian campaign. The British soldiers ultimately disembarked in Norway were under the command of Major General P. J. Macksey, who refused even to speak with his co-equal, Admiral of the Fleet Lord Cork and Orrey. The two men operated completely independently (even though they were equal commanders) with no definition of their individual or joint responsibilities. All three men, Forbes, Macksey and Lord Cork, were continually supervised and overruled by Churchill and Pound in the Admiralty, who intervened at the individual ship level.

Raeder had no way of knowing of the British leadership crisis when he advised Hitler that the prospective invasion was in fact impossible in the face of British sea power *unless* complete surprise was maintained. If it were so maintained, then the invasion could succeed, but the navy would immediately have to return to bases in Germany and leave support of the army to the Luftwaffe. Raeder knew that once the enemy was alerted, few German ships would get home. Even with surprise, Raeder expected to lose half of his ships, but as soon as the key ports and airfields were seized, the army could be supplied directly from Germany. Ships could go through the Kattegat to Oslo, all under the protection of German air power.

Raeder and Hitler agreed that the game was worth the candle, and the invasion was launched with a surge of initial successes—and some losses. Falkenhorst's plan functioned perfectly, with Group One (ten destroyers) carrying 2,000 troops to Narvik without incident.

Group Two had some problems. The heavy cruiser *Admiral Hipper* (completed in 1939; 10,000 tons; eight 8-inch guns) and four destroyers were taking 1,700 troops to Trondheim when two of the destroyers had a chance encounter with the British destroyer *Glowworm*, under the dauntless Lieutenant Commander G. B. Roope. The *Glowworm* had parted company with the sizable British fleet engaged in Operation Wilfred in order to search for a sailor swept overboard.

The German destroyers called for help from the *Hipper,* which charged in with a barrage of 8-inch shells, then tried to ram the *Glowworm.* Roope managed to turn swiftly enough to ram the enemy instead, tearing a great 130-foot hole in the *Hipper*'s starboard side. *Glowworm* then drifted away, to blow up and sink. Roope was posthumously awarded the Victoria Cross, the first to be won by a member of the Royal Navy in World War II and the first of three to be won in Norway. *Hipper* was able to continue on to Trondheim, which was secured.

While Churchill, Pound and Forbes continued to bicker over which wrong tactic to pursue, the Germans swiftly executed the rest of the invasion. The Norwegians were beginning to wake up to the danger, and their ships and coastal batteries were given authorization to fire on unknown vessels that seemed hostile.

Group Five, comprising the pocket battleship *Lützow* (née *Deutschland*); the *Hipper*'s sistership, the cruiser *Blücher,* with division commander Rear Admiral Otto Jummetz on board; and the 5,400-ton cruiser *Emden,* headed for Oslo with 2,000 troops. The decision to send these valuable ships through the fifty-mile-long Oslo Fjord is a measure of the risks Raeder was willing to take. At the Drobak Narrows, the fjord is less than 500 yards wide. There were sited the 11-inch and 8-inch coastal guns the Norwegians had obtained almost a half century before from the great German Krupp arms firm. They had never been fired in anger.

The *Blücher* had to slow to 12 knots to navigate through the Drobak Narrows; the Norwegians waited until the ship was in white-of-eye range, then unleashed a torrent of shells. Shattered, the *Blücher* was finished off by torpedoes fired from shore-based tubes; she rolled over and sank in the icy waters at 0630, taking with her more than 1,000 officers and men.

The hapless *Lützow* also took three 11-inch shells, but got away; the remaining troops were disembarked south of the fortresses, which they took by storm. Alerted, King Haakon VII, his family and the Norwegian government escaped to the countryside, and afterward, to England. Oslo fell later in the day to German airborne troops.

Despite the loss of ships, the rest of the invasion was equally successful. Kristiansand was taken by Group Two; the light cruiser *Karlsruhe* was torpedoed on its return voyage on April 9 by the British submarine *Truant,* and had to be finished off by the German torpedo boat *Greif.*

Group Three's light cruiser *Koenigsberg* was hit by shore batteries at Bergen; she limped to shelter at the Skoltegrund Mole in Bergen harbor. She entered history the next morning as the first major warship to be sunk by aircraft, after an attack by Fleet Air Arm Skuas.

By nightfall of April 9, General von Falkenhorst was able to radio Hitler that Norway and Denmark were secured. It was an incredible feat, which matched German discipline and daring against a self-indulgent British command setup and bad luck. The British never recognized the importance of air power in the theater, while the Germans flew in more than 1,000 aircraft to take control of the skies. It was the decisive difference.

The German navy's losses had not been as severe as Admiral Raeder had expected, but the British were—at last—alerted, and descended in a fury upon the German ships that did not immediately race for home.

In Narvik harbor, the loss of a German tanker had delayed the departure of the ten large German destroyers that had landed General Eduard Dietl's elite 3rd Mountain Division to take the city. In Horatio Hornblower style, Captain B. A. Warburton-Lee in *Hardy* led four other destroyers—*Hotspur, Havock, Hostile* and *Hunter*—in a snow-shrouded dawn assault on Narvik harbor on April 10.

There they quickly sank the German flagship, the *Wilhelm Heidkamp*, and the *Anton Schmidt*, and severely damaged the *Hans Luedemann, Diether von Roeder* and *Hermann Kuenne*. As the British destroyers withdrew they were ambushed by the *Georg Thiele* and *Bernd von Arnim*, whose accurate gunfire drove the disabled *Hardy* onto the shore and set the *Hunter* on fire. In the melee, *Hotspur* collided with *Hunter*, inflicting a fatal wound. *Havock* and *Hostile* broke clear without major damage, sinking the German ammunition ship *Rauenfels*, effectively depriving the surviving destroyers of shells.

Warburton-Lee was awarded a posthumous Victoria Cross for inflicting decisive damage against a superior force, which was left for the coup de grâce by the aging 31,520-ton battleship *Warspite* and nine destroyers. These burst into Narvik harbor on April 13, and sank all of the eight remaining German destroyers.

The land campaign in Norway, while beyond the scope of this book, began with an Allied assault on Narvik on April 24 that finally took the city on May 28, forcing General Dietl's troops into the countryside after a hard fight. Events in the south had already undone this success. On May 10—the same day that Winston Churchill succeeded Neville Chamberlain as Prime Minister—the German army started its offensive against Holland, Belgium and France. By May 28, Belgium had surrendered, the British Expeditionary Force was backing into Dunkirk and the French leaders were beginning their precipitate rush to surrender. The evacuation of Narvik was begun on June 7, the culmination of a doleful series of military fiascoes.

One more British naval tragedy was to come. The aircraft carriers *Ark Royal* and *Glorious* had arrived from the Mediterranean on June 2 to cover the evacuation of Norway. The *Glorious* was assigned the task of recovering the precious RAF Gloster Gladiators and Hawker Hurricanes that had finally been put ashore at Bardufoss, and which had claimed thirty-seven victories over the otherwise invincible Luftwaffe. None of the pilots had ever landed on a carrier before, and the Hurricane was considered too "hot" to even try. But eight Hurricanes and ten Gladiators made it, each one breaking hard to a halt, then being manhandled forward so that the next could land.

Human error bordering on criminal negligence intervened to void this gallant effort. The captain of the *Glorious*, G. D'Oyly Hughes, a winner of the Victoria Cross in World War I, steamed at a moderate 17 knots, did not keep any patrol aircraft flying and failed to have anyone on lookout in the crow's nest; more importantly, he neglected to have any torpedo planes spotted on the deck, ready to attack. He was encumbered by the Hurricanes and Gladiators, but given the situation, these could have been trundled over the side if necessary to save the ship.

Guided by Luftwaffe reports, the *Scharnhorst* and *Gneisenau* tracked the *Glorious* down at 1600 hours on June 8. If in the next half hour Hughes had been able to send off three or four Swordfish, the battle might have ended differently. The German battleships opened fire at 1630, at a range of sixteen miles, hitting the *Glorious* with the second salvo. The two escorting destroyers, *Acasta* and *Ardent*, laid down a smoke screen but further hits sank the *Glorious* at 1740. Only forty-three crewmen were saved; the RAF fighters and all but two of their pilots were lost.

The destroyers made gallant torpedo attacks before being blown to bits themselves, with only three survivors between the two ships. One torpedo from the *Acasta* did strike the *Scharnhorst*, disabling a turret, and flooding two engine rooms. The difference in British and German naval tradition manifested itself; where a Harwood or a Warburton-Lee would have thrown the wounded *Scharnhorst* had they been its commander on the rest of the British evacuation fleet, the German Vice Admiral Wilhelm Marschall pulled his ships out of the battle and headed for Trondheim, letting the *Ark Royal* and the other ships escape a certain slaughter. The *Gneisenau* was torpedoed on June 29 on the way home to Germany by the British submarine *Clyde;* both German battleships were to spend the next few months as they spent most of the war: under repair.

For the Allies, the debacle of Norway was masked by the catastrophe of the surrender in France, but some lessons were learned. The British became more sensitive to the need for planning amphibious operations well in advance, a determination that would later lead to the costly but valuable experience at Dieppe. They also became more aware of the need for a clearly defined command channel to be observed by the Cabinet and the Admiralty.

The Germans learned a great deal as well. Admiral Raeder and Hitler had experienced the power of the Royal Navy as it reacted, and realized that it could not be surprised by an invasion of the homeland. It was obvious that it would be impossible for the severely weakened German navy to attempt an invasion of England unless absolute air supremacy was established and maintained by the Luftwaffe, so that the Royal Navy could be suppressed. This would lead to the Battle of Britain between the Luftwaffe and the RAF.

Overall, Raeder and Hitler had correctly assessed the risks and won an impressive victory that would yield positive results for years to come. Germany now outflanked the British Isles, and had at comparatively low cost solved the problem of iron ore deliveries. The importance of Norwegian ports was somewhat diminished by the fact that the entire French coast was now available, but that was a serendipitous happening that no one could have anticipated.

Just as no one could have anticipated the British fighting the French.

3.

THE LION GROWLS

Hitler and Churchill were equally sensitive to the importance of the French fleet, although the Fuehrer was understandably intoxicated by the scope of his three major victories in the first ten months of the war. France, the bitter enemy of 1871 and 1918, was prostrate, at a cost of fewer than 50,000 German casualties; the comparison with the millions of German dead in World War I made the achievement all the greater. Germany ruled Europe from Scandinavia to Spain, and from the Atlantic coast to the Soviet Union. (The latter had occupied Estonia, Latvia and Lithuania during June 15 and 16, 1940, and seized Bukovina and Bessarabia two weeks later. For the moment, Hitler could do nothing about it.)

But most of the French fleet was outside Hitler's power. Wishing to avoid it being scuttled, Hitler ostentatiously renounced all claim to the fleet in the armistice terms, except for a few conditions that gave him plenty of room to maneuver later.

Churchill was not prepared to accept Hitler's word on the matter, for the addition of the French fleet to the strength of Germany and Italy could be overwhelming. Eager to lash out at a target that would prove Britain's power and resolve, his War Cabinet forbade all French ships in British ports to put to sea, planning to seize them in Operation Grasp. Simultaneously, there would be an assault upon the powerful French squadron at Mers-el-Kebir, near Oran in Algeria: Operation Catapult. The French had two battle cruisers, *Dunkerque* and *Strasbourg;* two older battleships, the *Provence* and *Bretagne;* a seaplane carrier, the *Commandant Teste;* six of the large *Tigre*-class destroyers; and miscellaneous other smaller ships. The *Dunkerque* was the first of the new generation of capital ships, being laid down in 1932; along with the *Strasbourg,* she was looked upon as a counter to the German pocket battleships.

On July 3, 1940, the British commander, Vice Admiral Sir James Somerville, a Francophile, gave the commander of the French squadron, Admiral Marcel Gensoul, a list of four options:

1. Put to sea and continue the war on the British side;

2. Sail his ships to a French West Indian port, and demobilize them;

3. Sail with a minimum crew to a British port; or

4. Scuttle his ships in the harbor.

Gensoul was given six hours to reply; if he failed to agree to one of the choices, Somerville was ordered to use all the considerable force at his command to destroy the French ships.

Somerville's fleet consisted of the battleship *Hood,* long considered to be the most powerful warship in the world, and soon to be engaged in a fiercer struggle; the battleships *Resolution* and *Valiant,* both from World War I, but each carrying eight 15-inch guns; the ubiquitous carrier *Ark Royal,* which, like the *Hood,* had a pending rendezvous; plus two light cruisers and twelve destroyers.

When the ultimatum expired, first the *Hood* and then the others began the firing. The *Bretagne* was blown up almost immediately, the smoke and steam from her explosion masking the other ships. In the confusion, the *Strasbourg* and some destroyers managed to escape to Toulon. The *Dunkerque* was heavily damaged, set on fire and beached; two days later, Swordfish from the *Ark Royal* struck her with torpedoes.

The Vichy government of unoccupied France broke off diplomatic relations with England on July 4, but the British were not finished. On July 8, the tiny aircraft carrier *Hermes,* the first carrier to be built from the keel up, launched six Swordfish against the pride of the French fleet, the *Richelieu,* stationed at Dakar and considered by many to be the equal of any battleship in the world. One torpedo damaged the *Richelieu*'s propeller and rudder, putting her out of action for a year.

The attacks completely soured relations with French commanders in North Africa, so much so that when the Allies invaded in 1942, there was some fierce French resistance. On balance, the raid gave England satisfaction, but it probably accelerated French collaboration with Germany.

The Anglo-French antagonism was solidified by the complete fiasco of Operation Menace, a joint British–Free French expedition on September 23, 1940, to seize Dakar and the battleship *Richelieu*. The French fought back so brilliantly that Churchill called the operation off.

VICTORIES IN THE MEDITERRANEAN

Circumstances had deprived the French fleet of any active role in the war; as the muddied water settled at Mers-el-Kebir, the Italian fleet was valiantly preparing for a war it did not want.

An unfair image has grown up concerning the Italian navy's lack of combativeness, much of it stemming from British accounts that almost inevitably are colored with malicious, if understated, humor about the enemy's conduct in battle.

Notwithstanding this, the Italian navy served its country and its allies well in World War II, executing almost 35,000 sorties between June 10, 1940, and September 8, 1943. In that time the Italian navy transported hundreds of thousands of men and millions of tons of matériel across the Mediterranean to Libya, Tunisia and Greece. In many hard engagements, it lost 393 vessels, including eleven cruisers, forty-four destroyers and eighty-six submarines. During the same period, the Royal Navy lost 238 ships of 412,000 tons to German and Italian action in the Mediterranean. It was not a totally one-sided war.

The Italian armed services had been sold short by Benito Mussolini's vainglorious aspirations. As France was being humiliated in the spring of 1940, Il Duce became convinced that Germany would settle with Britain within three months. Unable to bear the possibility of not sharing in the spoils, Mussolini preemptorily forced Italy into the war two years before the navy was scheduled to be ready, just as Hitler had done with the German navy. The navy itself was essentially royalist and had a pervasive contempt for Fascism, and was appalled to be allied with Germany, the traditional enemy, against Britain, the traditional ally.

Between the wars, Italian naval contractors had done remarkable work in modernizing older vessels while at the same creating the sleekly lined *Littorio* class of 30-knot, 42,000-ton battleships, armed with nine 15-inch guns. The design team for these was led by the inspector general of the Italian Navy Construction Corps, Umberto Pugliese, who also devised the unusual "Pugliese cylinders" used for underwater protection. These very effective devices consisted of hydropneumatic cylinders placed between the ship's side and the bulkheads, to serve as shock absorbers to torpedo explosions.

The *Littorio* (the Italian name for the fasces of the Roman lictors, the symbol of the Fascist party), *Vittorio Veneto* (celebrating a World War I victory) and *Roma* were rushed to completion, the first two available three months after Italy's entrance into the war. The *Roma* was completed in June 1942.

Yet despite modern ships, capable officers and eager (if harshly disciplined) sailors, the Italian fleet had grave handicaps. Mussolini, an ardent advocate of air power, had insisted that all of Italy was itself an aircraft carrier, and denied both carriers and an independent naval air force to the Italian navy. Limits on vision and on budgets also deprived the Italian navy of the research and development required for such indispensable equipment as radar. Even by the end of the war, when radar was standard issue on the ships of every other major navy, the Italians had only a few primitive sets on the largest ships. The *Littorio* received an EC.3/bis Gufo (Owl) set in September 1941, but a fully operational set was not available until a year later. Phonetically for English speakers, the Gufo was aptly named, for it had a poor performance and was highly unreliable to boot.

There were also logistic and training problems. Fuel oil was in short supply; the navy began the war with 1.8 million tons, sufficient for only nine months' steaming. For some inexplicable reason, the Italian navy did not plan on having night engagements, and was neither trained nor equipped for them. At night, the main turrets of Italian warships were not manned, even when on a combat sortie. The Regia Aeronautica (Italian air force) did not regard support of the navy as a primary mission, and consequently communication and coordination was never conducted on a professional basis. (The Regia Aeronautica did, however, conduct expert reconnaissance and determined bombing attacks on its own initiative, even attacking Gibraltar.)

With the French fleet removed by the armistice, the Royal Navy's Mediterranean Fleet did not, ship for ship, match the strength of the Italian navy. But it far surpassed the Italian navy technologically, and had an ever-improving air support. Although the Italian navy's intelligence gathering was good, it did not compare to the British insight into Axis communications. And finally, and probably most important, the Royal Navy had an overwhelming psychological advantage: its imposing fleets had made "courtesy calls" on Italian ports for the past eighty years and it was no coincidence that the Italian Naval Chief of Staff, Admiral Arturo Riccardi, kept *The Life of Nelson* on a table by his bed.

It was Italy's misfortune that a modern Nelson, Admiral Sir Andrew Browne Cunningham (nicknamed, of course, "ABC"), had become Commander-in-Chief, Mediterranean, on May 14, 1940. Fifty-six years old and the very image of a sea dog with wind-reddened skin and a rugged face, he was a master of his craft, able to con his own ship or direct the work of a fleet with equal ease.

Admiral Cunningham had a difficult task in the Mediterranean, for his forces would be within range of Italian air attack for much of the distance between Sardinia and Alexandria in Egypt. Although the Regia Aeronautica did not cooperate effectively with the Italian navy, it was capable of strikes that Cunningham assessed as more effective than those of the Luftwaffe.

The initial forces at Cunningham's disposal were not great—the World War I battleships *Warspite, Malaya* and *Royal Sovereign;* the small aircraft carrier *Eagle* (converted in 1924 from a Chilean battleship under construction, the *Almirante Cochrane*) and carrying only three Sea Gladiator fighters and eighteen Fairey Swordfish torpedo planes; five cruisers and seventeen destroyers.

Yet Cunningham plunged into the heart of the Mediterranean, Mussolini's *Mare Nostrum*, shaking off determined air attacks to engage Vice Admiral Inigio Campioni's two modernized battleships, the *Conte di Cavour* and *Giulio Cesare*, which were escorting a convoy. In this first encounter, on July 9, 1940, off the Calabrian toe of Italy, Cunningham set the tone for future battles: when the *Warspite*'s 15-inch shells struck aft of the funnel on the battleship *Cesare*, Campioni elected to withdraw immediately.

THE DUCE STRIKES—OUT

Mussolini ordered the invasion of Greece to begin on October 29, 1940, expecting a victory in two weeks. Nine days later, the Greeks went over to the offensive, and drove the Italians back into Albania, beginning a debacle from which Hitler had to extract his Italian ally.

Great Britain, taking heavy civilian casualties from the German bombing of its cities (about 6,400 dead and 8,700 injured in October), nonetheless pledged assistance to Greece, reducing the momentum of the victorious British offensive in Cyrenaica, North Africa. In this case, Winston Churchill once again put political considerations above the advice of his military counselors, even though most predicted that it would be impossible to contain the German forces when they arrived to bail out the Italians.

TARANTO

The idea for an attack on the Italian fleet in the harbor at Taranto, located inside the heel of the Italian boot, originated with Rear Admiral A. Lumley St. G. Lyster, who commanded the carriers *Illustrious* and *Eagle* under Cunningham. Lyster had picked up the idea from maneuvers during the 1935 Ethiopian crisis, and had been its advocate ever since. Operation Judgement, as it was called, was an extraordinarily bold concept, involving the first-ever strike of carrier-based aircraft on a fleet within a naval base. It, of course, presaged Pearl Harbor.

Launched in 1939, the *Illustrious* was as modern as the *Eagle* was antiquated; its heavily armored deck contributed considerably to its 23,000-ton displacement, but its aircraft capacity of thirty-six was small compared to its U.S. and Japanese contemporaries. Although both ships carried the ubiquitous Swordfish, of which 2,391 were built, the *Eagle* also had a squadron of twelve new two-seat Fairey Fulmar eight-gun fighters. Not up to the standards of the Battle of Britain, the Fulmar was adequate for the Italian aircraft it would encounter.

Reconnaissance flights by fast, American-built Martin Maryland aircraft operating out of Malta had shown that the Italian fleet was at anchor in Taranto, with at least six battleships, five cruisers and numerous smaller ships. The warships were defended by an extensive barrage balloon network (which had some gaps because of a recent wind storm), and both shore-based and shipboard antiaircraft batteries.

Mechanical defects on the *Eagle* prevented her from participating, but the *Illustrious* sailed from Alexandria on November 6. At 2040 hours on November 11, the first twelve Swordfish, led by Lieutenant Commander Kenneth Williamson, of No. 815 Squadron, took off for a 170-mile strike at Taranto; another nine, led by Lieutenant Commander J. W. Hale of No. 819 Squadron, followed twenty minutes later.

The attack was of classic simplicity. The Swordfish cruised in at 90 knots and 6,000 feet altitude, eight in one group, four in another that had moved out of position in the clouds. In each wave a single "Stringbag" was sent over land to drop a line of twelve flares behind the ships at anchor, silhouetting them for the torpedo planes. The flare ship then went on to bomb oil tanks and other targets.

Williamson's group dove in from out of the west, wind whistling in the myriad struts and wires of the gangly Stringbags, leveling out just above the water to send their Mark XII torpedoes into the line of battleships. Williamson was shot down just as he released his torpedo; he and his observer were rescued and made prisoners.

Twenty minutes later, Hale's group repeated these tactics, along with one straggler who came in thirty minutes after the first wave.

By 0250 on the twelfth, all but two Swordfish made it back to the *Illustrious;* the next day, photo reconnaissance showed the *Conte di Cavour* sunk and the *Littorio* and *Caio Duilio* so badly damaged that they would be out of the war for months. The Italians immediately removed the rest of their fleet to the better-defended harbor at Naples, which greatly reduced the danger of Italian attacks on Allied convoys.

CAPE MATAPAN

The British merchant ships supplying Greece were a natural target for the Italians, who put a powerful force to sea on March 27, 1941. The battleship *Vittorio Veneto* carried the commander, Vice Admiral Angelo Iachino; she was supported by eight cruisers in the 10,000-ton class, six with eight 8-inch guns and two with ten 6-inch guns.

Iachino's force was the prize Admiral Cunningham was seeking, and he mustered all his ships to engage. His battleships—*Warspite, Valiant,* and *Barham*—were modernized veterans of World War I, and not fast enough to catch the Italians, but Cunningham had the advantage of superior intelligence reports. Iachino would compound his own problems by making a series of mistakes, including twice ignoring aerial reconnaissance reports that gave accurate information on the strength and position of the British fleet.

Cunningham's forces included the newly arrived carrier *Formidable* (of the *Illustrious* class), four cruisers and thirteen destroyers. On March 28, the cruisers, under Rear Admiral Henry D. Pridham-Wippell, engaged one Italian division of cruisers for almost forty minutes before withdrawing. Iachino had studied Jutland and was rightly suspicious of any English captain who did not throw himself headlong into battle. Instead, he ordered his own cruisers to reverse course, to lure Pridham-Wippell into range. *Vittorio Veneto* unleashed a total of twenty-nine salvoes at Pridham-Wippell's cruisers, which turned and fled. As this action was taking place, Iachino, totally misinterpreting his reconnaissance reports, was steaming blithely toward Cunningham's main force.

Two torpedo attacks, one by British land-based aircraft, and one by Swordfish from the *Formidable*, at last alerted Iachino to his danger. The *Vittorio Veneto* began to withdraw at a speed of 28 knots. Cunningham realized that his only chance was another torpedo attack. He sent five Swordfish, led by Lieutenant Commander J. Dalyell-Stead. Three of the Swordfish made a head-on attack, while two attacked from the port side. The *Vittorio Veneto* had already avoided nine torpedoes that day; she would elude four out of five more. The fifth torpedo struck on the port side, above the outer port propeller, stopping the engines. Italian damage-control parties swarmed through the ship, trying to stop the leaks, correct the list and get the engines started again. The *Vittorio Veneto* got under way and was soon reported making 20 knots, only 4 knots slower than Cunningham's undamaged battleships, now more than fifty miles away. Unless stopped again, the *Vittorio Veneto* would reach the protection of German shore-based aircraft before the British battleships could arrive to dispatch her.

Another torpedo attack was launched even as Cunningham's forces steamed at maximum speed toward the *Vittorio Veneto*, which was now covered on both sides by a line of cruisers. The Swordfish put one torpedo into the cruiser *Pola*, while the *Vittorio Veneto* limped on.

Iachino, so ill-served by the reconnaissance efforts of both the Luftwaffe and Regia Aeronautica that he didn't believe the reports he now received, was still blissfully unaware of the position of Cunningham's forces. He assigned two cruisers, *Zara* and *Fiume*, along with four destroyers, to assist the *Pola* back to harbor. It was this unlucky collection, steaming at night with gun crews asleep, turrets trained fore and aft, that Cunningham fell upon. With guns sighted at the point-blank range of 3,800 yards, the order was given to fire. British searchlights fastened on to the Italian ships, and the *Warspite*, *Barham* and *Valiant* sent rapid-fire broadsides of 15-inch shells into their hulls.

Within three minutes the Italians lost the cruisers *Zara* and *Fiume* and the destroyer *Alfieri*. Moments later, the destroyer *Carducci* was sunk, but the most bizarre moment of the night was yet to come.

The original mission of the newly sunk Italian ships was the protection of the damaged *Pola*, now drifting, guns trained in the evening fore-and-aft position. Captain Philip J. Mack, whose handling of his destroyer force had earlier displeased Cunningham immensely, now entered history by sending a boarding party from HMS *Jervis,* complete with cutlasses and bloodcurdling yells, to capture *Pola.* Instead of a ship-of-the-line sword fight, they found instead only 256 members of the original crew of 800, many of them drunk. They were taken prisoner and the *Pola* torpedoed.

Thus, in Cunningham's words, "Matapan might be assumed to have knocked the heart out of the Italian fleet," with three cruisers and two destroyers sunk and a battleship damaged. Twenty-four hundred Italian officers and men were killed, most by shell fire, the rest by drowning; perhaps most galling to the Italians was the rescue of more than 100 of their sailors by their Greek enemy. The British lost one plane and its two-man crew.

The Battle of Matapan, the Royal Navy's greatest victory since Trafalgar, came at a crucial time, for the British were about to conduct their third and fourth major evacuations of the war—from Greece and then from Crete—and the shattered Italian fleet did not intervene. If it had, as it could have done even despite its losses, the course of the war in North Africa might have been changed drastically. Even with the Italian navy quiescent, however, the Royal Navy would be mauled savagely for the next few months by the Luftwaffe and by U-boats.

For the moment, however, Britain rejoiced at the good news of the Battle of Matapan, which was soon followed by another Cunningham triumph, his conduct of Operation Tiger. Churchill knew that the Germans had a newly arrived armored division that posed a dangerous threat to Great Britain's armies in North Africa. The Prime Minister, ignoring the still formidable threat of a German invasion, ruthlessly took tanks from Britain-based units, and ordered that they be sent through the Mediterranean at top speed. For most of the long stretch, Cunningham's ships were vulnerable to Luftwaffe bombers, torpedo boats and submarines, as well as to surface units of the Italian fleet if they should appear. Cunningham accepted his responsibility, using the opportunity to be reinforced with badly needed warships and to include a convoy of tankers in the operation. He sailed his force the length of the Mediterranean in the face of German and Italian opposition, delivering the cargo to Wavell on May 12. It comprised, in part, 238 tanks and forty-three Hurricane fighters, both needed to meet Rommel's offensive.

The Admiralty breathed a little easier, as Matapan and Operation Tiger should have assuaged Churchill's lust for combat temporarily. It would flare again in May 1941, as events transpired in the North Atlantic.

DEATH RIDE OR DEATH WISH? THE *BISMARCK*'S FIRST AND LAST SORTIE

The *Bismarck*'s death ride was, from start to finish, a concatenation of egregious mistakes, some seeming almost to be a wish for failure. The long battle at sea, which electrified the world as it was played out, might be compared to a game of giveaway checkers, in which each opponent plays to lose. The loss of the *Bismarck* can be attributed directly to a series of bad decisions made by its Fleet Commander, Admiral Guenther Luetjens, who truly wrested defeat from the jaws of victory.

It must be admitted, however, that Luetjens had plenty of help. Grand Admiral Erich Raeder made the first and gravest of the long series of errors by remaining dedicated to his concept of surface raiders even at a time when his submarines were coming close to being a war-winning weapon. Despite the fact that he had few ships at his disposal, he persisted with his dream of attacking Great Britain's shipping in all the corners of the globe, developing what came to be called the "double-pole" strategy. He planned to have German surface ships make distant raids upon British shipping and at the same time confront the Royal Navy in the Baltic Sea. Raeder was still convinced that the hit-and-run tactics of the *Graf Spee* were profitable, and went so far as to issue a study indicating that battleships were the key to the future in naval warfare, superseding submarines. In essence, Raeder wanted his ships, including his precious super-battleship the *Bismarck*, to attack unprotected convoys, a naval oxymoron.

By the spring of 1941, Raeder should have been able to draw a different conclusion from the wealth of evidence available to him. The *Graf Spee* was scuttled after sinking about 50,000 tons of shipping. The *Admiral Scheer,* rebuilt as a cruiser in 1940, had sunk seventeen ships with a total of 113,233 tons on a prowl in the Indian Ocean before sneaking back into Germany in March 1941. Other than their sinking of the *Glorious,* the *Gneisenau* and the *Scharnhorst* had but one brief season of raiding success. During the first eight weeks of 1941, they sank a total of 122,000 tons of shipping before returning to base. To this must be added the 370,000 tons sunk over a longer period of time by the six much smaller armed merchant raiders, which included the famed *Atlantis, Komet, Orion, Pinguin, Thor* and *Widder.* The combined totals were insufficient to have a decisive effect on the war.

The ambiguity of the Seekriegleitung (Naval War Staff) orders to sink ships, but not to engage enemy warships, vitiated the commanders on the scene. The *Gneisenau,* the *Scharnhorst* and the *Admiral Scheer* had all been turned back by hopelessly outclassed British armed merchant cruisers. On November 23, 1939, the 16,700-ton *Rawalpindi*, under Captain E. C. Kennedy, fought the two German battleships savagely, her guns blazing even as she sank beneath the shattering 11-inch broadsides. Afraid that they had been reported, the two German ships returned home. A year later, on November 5, 1940, the 14,000-ton *Jervis Bay*, commanded by Captain E. S. F. Fegen, fearlessly engaged the *Admiral Scheer;* the merchant cruiser was sunk within twenty minutes, but she saved the convoy she was escorting. Fegen received the Victoria Cross posthumously, as too many of its winners did.

It was true that widespread raiders caused the British fleet a tremendous problem, but Grand Admiral Raeder was unwilling to recognize the improvement in British tactics, and most importantly, the growing impact of intelligence, radar and aircraft on sea warfare—not only on the outcome of battle but also on logistics. No matter how many ships Raeder put to sea, each had to have tankers and cargo ships stationed at remote destinations for refueling and resupply. The Royal Navy searched for these systematically, using decrypted radio messages and radio homing techniques to place the hunters, aircraft and radar-equipped ships in the right place to intercept them. The ocean was vast, but the Royal Navy located and sank the support vessels, effectively diminishing the utility of the raiders.

Yet so beguiled was Grand Admiral Raeder with his concept that on April 2, 1941, he issued an operational directive for the *Bismarck*, stating that the decisive object in the struggle with Britain was the destruction of her trade. He commented that gaining control of the sea was the best means of achieving this objective, but admitted that it was not possible with the forces available to him, "given the constraint that we must preserve our numerically inferior forces." Then he went on to say, "Nevertheless, we must strive for local and temporary command of the sea in this area [the North Atlantic] and then gradually, methodically and systematically extend it."

This was sheer pie in the sky, based on his hopeful—wistful might be a better term—premise that "the enemy will assume that *one* battleship will be enough to defend a convoy."

To implement his philosophy, Raeder envisioned sending out the large battleships *Bismarck* and *Tirpitz* and the heavy cruiser *Prinz Eugen* on their maiden missions, in company with the *Gneisenau* and the *Scharnhorst*, stipulating that "the objective of the *Bismarck* is not to defeat enemies of equal strength, but to tie them down in a delaying action, while preserving her own combat capability as much as possible, so as to allow the other ships to get at the merchant vessels in the convoy. The primary target in this operation is the enemy's merchant shipping; enemy warships will be engaged only when that objective makes it necessary and it can be done without excessive risk."

These fantasy orders completely discounted the Royal Navy's visceral determination to destroy the German surface fleet. The degree of Raeder's error is illustrated by the measure of the Royal Navy's effort. To make sure that the *Bismarck* was sunk, the Royal Navy ruthlessly stripped other theaters, including precious convoys of their escort, ultimately deploying no fewer than six battleships, four battle cruisers, two aircraft carriers, thirteen cruisers, thirty-three destroyers, eight submarines, plus patrol aircraft—the largest naval force so far assigned to a single mission in the war.

Raeder persisted with his planning even when it was obvious that the *Tirpitz* was not ready for sea and neither the *Scharnhorst* (undergoing engine overhaul) nor the *Gneisenau* (torpedoed in the inner harbor at Brest) would be available.

The *Bismarck* was an enlarged, more heavily armed version of the *Gneisenau* and *Scharnhorst,* with her dimensions, displacement and configuration determined by a number of external factors, including the size of berthing facilities at Wilhelmshaven, the size of the Kiel Canal connecting the Baltic to the North Sea, and the space available for the power plant necessary to meet the specified speeds. Yet the long, graceful lines, flowing from her "Atlantic" clipper bow to streamlined cruiser stern, blessed the *Bismarck* with a beauty characteristic of German designs of the period. The ships of the *King George V* class, the nearest British counterpart, had square-jawed bows and simple sterns, not aesthetically so pleasing, and less able to handle rough weather.

According to construction specifications, the fully loaded *Bismarck* displaced 53,546 tons; it was 823¼ feet long, and had a beam of 118 feet. The dimensions are difficult to comprehend in the abstract, but the *Bismarck* was so huge that in the coming battle even the impact of 14-inch shells was localized and could not be felt throughout the ship.

Captain Ernst Lindemann insisted that the *Bismarck* be referred to as "he," in deference both to its namesake, the great Prussian Chancellor, and to the masculine warrior tasks awaiting it. On one speed run in the Baltic, "he" reached a top speed of 30.8 knots, more than the design had called for. At full speed, with the three sets of Brown Boveri Curtiss-type steam-driven turbines generating 150,000 horsepower, the *Bismarck* carved through the water with a minimum bow wave; there was little vibration. The design speed was 30 knots.

The four turrets each had two 15-inch guns mounted; these were directed by a sophisticated fire control system that used Zeiss stereoscopic range finders. Radar was used only for sea surveillance and range finding at night or during foul weather, but it had both less range and less accuracy than the optical equipment. The radar was also sensitive to the shock of the 15-inch guns firing. Neither Fleet Commander Luetjens nor Lindemann really understood radar; they were aware of the principles involved, but lacked extensive experience in its use, and this would contribute to later difficulties.

The superior German armor, called *Wotan weich* and *Wotan hart*, had significantly greater tensile strength than previous armor. The traditional German emphasis on armor over either speed or firepower is evident in the ratios between the weight allocated to armor, armament and power. In the case of the *Bismarck*, this relationship was 40:17:9. For the British battle cruiser *Hood*, the relationship was 30:12:12. The *Bismarck*'s armor was distributed to protect the most vital areas, varying in thickness at different points, to make up 40 percent of the ship's weight. At the thickest points in belts along the side, the armor was 12.6 inches. The upper deck also varied, reaching 4.5 inches. A shield of armor 1.97 inches thick provided protection to the upper deck; it could not deflect incoming heavy shells, but instead would detonate them before they struck the armored deck below, a concept similar to the reactive armor technology currently used on tanks.

The four 15-inch gun turrets (designated from fore to aft as Anton, Bruno, Caesar and Dora) received the maximum protection, with armor ranging in thickness from 5.12 to 14.17 inches; to compensate for this weight, the secondary armament was lightly protected with armor from 1.57 to 3.94 inches, and the gun crews would suffer in the coming battle. The 15-inch guns could reach out almost twenty-three miles, and as events would prove, the accuracy of *Bismarck*'s gunners was superb.

But not everything was perfect. To achieve a tight turning radius, two rudders, each of 260 square feet, were operated in parallel by an electrically driven steering mechanism. During the intensive Baltic Sea trials the rudders were locked in a neutral position and an attempt was made to steer with differential power on the propellers. Their effect was minimal, because the port and starboard propeller shafts were aligned along converging lines with the center propeller shaft, reducing their capacity to turn the ship by asymmetric thrust. No thought was given to seeing what would happen if the rudders were locked hard over—a grave error. (Recent investigation of the sunken hull also suggests that faulty welds near the stern weakened the ship, making it more susceptible to torpedo damage.)

The *Bismarck*'s nominal range of 9,280 miles at 16 knots was 1,000 miles less than that of the *Scharnhorst* or *Gneisenau*, giving further rise to questions about some of Luetjens's later decisions.

Perhaps the strangest element in the *Bismarck*'s sortie is the naive faith that Raeder and Luetjens professed in the secrecy of the operation, and of the ship's ability to break into the North Atlantic undetected by the British.

In his memorable book on his service on the *Bismarck*, Baron von Muellenheim-Rechberg recounts how, as the great ship was preparing for sea, the local people speculated on the mission. Then, the day before *Bismarck*'s scheduled secret exit from Gotenhafen (formerly the Polish city of Gdynia) the fleet band serenaded the crew with "Muss Ich Denn" (Must I Leave?), the traditional departure song—a dead giveaway, if any were necessary.

None was. British cryptologists were aware that the sailing was imminent, and in the usual fashion laid on reconnaissance flights in just the right places to mask the fact that the German radio signals were compromised. Further, the native populations of Denmark, Sweden and Norway were hostile to the Nazis, and routinely reported German ship movements. Less routinely, a friendship had developed among Colonel Roscher Lund, the Norwegian military attaché in Stockholm; Major Toernberg, the chief of staff to the head of Swedish Intelligence; and Captain Henry W. Denham, the British naval attaché in Stockholm. The Lund-to-Toernberg-to-Denham pipeline provided exact information that, confirmed by reports from coast watchers and warships, including the Swedish cruiser *Gotland* and merchant vessels, would enable British reconnaissance planes to track the *Rheinuebung* force. Ironically, the British Admiralty knew of *Bismarck*'s departure before Adolf Hitler learned of it.

On May 19, 1940, at 0200, preceded by minesweepers and destroyers, the *Bismarck* sortied, followed by the equally untried *Prinz Eugen*, nominally 10,000 tons but actually a 19,000-ton displacement cruiser with eight 8-inch guns. The two ships were very similar in appearance, and could easily be confused, especially given the German camouflage of the period, in which the bow was painted darker and a "bow wave" placed farther aft. *Prinz Eugen*, commanded by a classmate of Lindemann, Captain Helmuth Brinkmann, survived the war, only to initiate a new age of conflict by being sunk in the atomic tests at Bikini.

Already at sea in support were fourteen U-boats, the Italian submarine *Barbarigo*, nine tankers, and nine supply, weather or observation vessels, each one a plum for the Royal Navy to pick.

Vice Admiral Luetjens had previously tried to postpone the sailing until the *Scharnhorst*, or even better, the *Bismarck*'s brother-ship, *Tirpitz*, could participate. Grand Admiral Raeder had refused, citing the coming invasion of Crete as a reason for disrupting British supply lines, and diverting strength from the Mediterranean. A sailor for thirty-four years and by nature a melancholic man, Luetjens accepted the decision stoically; he was prepared to die for his fatherland in a heroic way. Unfortunately, his death would also mean the death of most of the 2,221-man complement of his battleship, who had no choice in the matter. Most of them would endure the battle locked in the sterile gray bowels of the ship, uncertain of what their fate would be until the cold dark waters came crashing in.

Luetjens's fatalism may be discerned in a series of subsequent decisions that frittered away his main advantages: speed and the vastness of the ocean. Already 200 tons short of fuel oil because of a refueling accident at Gotenhafen, he first elected not to refuel at Grimstad fjord (apparently because it was not in the operations order), south of Bergen and the first stop in Norway, and subsequently declined later to refuel from either the tanker *Wollin* or the *Weissenburg*. At Gotenhafen, the fuel tanks could have been topped with approximately 1,200 tons of fuel, almost 14 percent of *Bismarck*'s 8,700-ton capacity, an amount that would have made a crucial difference in the outcome of the battle.

At midnight on May 22, Vice Admiral Lancelot Ernest Holland departed Scapa Flow in HMS *Hood,* with the *Prince of Wales* and six destroyers. Only fifteen minutes later, Luetjens left his own destroyers behind, and the *Bismarck,* leading the *Prinz Eugen,* took advantage of foggy weather to steam out at 24 knots to the Denmark Strait, which runs between Greenland and Iceland.

The English reacted violently to the German sortie. The Commander-in-Chief of the Home Fleet, Admiral Sir John Cronyn Tovey, began marshaling the forces that would grow to enormous strength and would—in spite of errors and interference—find and sink the *Bismarck* by only the barest possible margins. As would happen so often during the war, the individual acts of common sense that compensated for the ill-laid plans of the commanders would largely be unacknowledged and unrewarded.

Tovey, energetic, fiery, a devout Christian with a good appetite for life, always "sane and optimistic" in the view of his former boss, Admiral Cunningham, knew that his every action would be scrutinized by that master naval strategist Winston Churchill. The latter was determined to put paid to the *Bismarck,* to the point that he would later commit an unforgivable breach of naval etiquette.

Luetjens, lulled by incorrect Luftwaffe reconnaissance reports that the British fleet did not seem to be alerted, decided to head south toward his target, an Atlantic convoy, confident that he would have no difficulty with the single British battleship he expected to find escorting it.

The last days of the *Bismarck*'s saga are so complex that it is helpful to be specific about dates and times, the latter given in British double summer time.

May 23, 1941, 1922 Hours

The patrolling British cruiser *Suffolk* spotted the *Bismarck* in the Denmark Strait at seven miles' range. The 10,000-ton *Suffolk* immediately sought cover in the fog, knowing that broadcasting a report of her find was more important than trying to take on the *Bismarck* with eight 8-inch guns. The *Norfolk*, commissioned in 1928, two years after the *Suffolk*, encountered the *Bismarck* at six miles' range at 2032. The *Bismarck* was ready this time, and fired, but *Norfolk* got away to begin the game of shadowing her prey, now heading southwest at a maximum continuous speed of 28 knots. Luetjens and Lindemann were startled when deciphered British radio traffic revealed that they were being tracked by radar. The sense of being visible to an enemy they could not see loomed large in the Germans' minds, especially since the first salvo at the *Norfolk* had knocked out the *Bismarck*'s forward radar. Luetjens signaled for *Prinz Eugen* to take the lead; its forward radar was still working.

Luetjens could have now made a reasonable, defensible decision to return to Norway; his location was known and he must have realized that the Royal Navy was moving in for the kill. Nevertheless, he plunged on to the southwest, ignoring both the power of radar to track his course and the potential strength of the Royal Navy.

With the *Bismarck*'s position fixed, Tovey was able to direct all of his resources toward a climactic battle. The first ships able to engage the German fleet would be the legendary battle cruiser *Hood*, long the flagship of the Royal Navy, and the *King George V*-class battleship *Prince of Wales*, new and not really ready for combat.

The *Hood* was named for Admiral Sir Samuel Hood, who had fought brilliantly against the French in the time of Napoleon. For twenty years she been regarded as the most powerful warship in the world. It is difficult to assess how potent a symbol of British naval power the *Hood* became between the wars. Often painted white, as spruce as a ship could be, and possessing a particularly powerful, graceful profile, she visited most of the British empire and was venerated by the thousands who saw her pass by. Yet her reputation had inadvertently served her ill, for she was repeatedly passed over for modernization until 1939, when she was scheduled to receive additional vertical and horizontal armor. The outbreak of war canceled the modification, and the *Hood* went to war in essentially the same configuration as in 1918, the last battle cruiser to be launched during World War I. Her armored deck could not withstand plunging fire, and there was insufficient fire protection between turrets and between magazines.

Vice Admiral Holland gave chase, knowing that the *Norfolk* and *Suffolk*, trailing the German warships by a dozen miles, would be able to lead him to the battle. The *Hood*'s captain, Captain Ralph Kerr, had the same invidious position that Captain Lindemann held on the *Bismarck*—second in command on his own vessel.

Conscious of the *Hood*'s vulnerability, Holland determined to engage at the closest possible range, avoiding plunging fire by keeping the trajectory of the German shells flat. Holland was also well aware that the *Prince of Wales* still had deficiencies in her armament. Both the *"Princes,"* German and English, had put to sea unprepared. Civilian contractors from Vickers and Armstrong worked on the *Prince of Wales* even as their counterparts from Siemens labored on the *Prinz Eugen*.

May 24, 1941, 0535 Hours

At 0535 hours, British lookouts on the *Prince of Wales* picked up the German ships at seventeen miles' distance; the Germans, already alerted by their sophisticated hydrophone equipment, which tracked the water-borne sounds of the British ships, picked up the smoke and masts of the British ships visually ten minutes later. Gunnery officers on both ships trained their guns and waited for the order to fire.

Holland at this point had the option of joining the *Suffolk* in shadowing the *Bismarck*, and waiting until Tovey was able to bring the *King George V* and other ships to attack. Instead, he elected to attack head-on, closing at a combined speed of 56 knots. The attack had the benefit of reducing his profile to the German gunners, but it meant that only his forward batteries could engage; instead of having all eighteen of his big guns (nine on the *Hood*, nine on the *Prince of Wales*) firing, he had only ten. Concerned about the *Prince of Wales*'s lack of experience, Holland, unlike Harwood and his cruisers with the *Graf Spee*, decided to fight his two ships as a unit. Inexplicably, he did not maneuver so that the *Suffolk* and *Norfolk* could harass the Germans from the rear with their 8-inch shells and torpedoes.

When the range fell to just under fourteen miles, Holland opened fire with his forward turrets, sending four 15-inch shells screaming toward what he thought was the *Bismarck,* but was in fact the *Prinz Eugen* in the lead.

Luetjens delayed response for a long moment; his orders were not to engage capital ships. As he waited, his gunnery officers tensed with excitement, eager for battle; finally, Luetjens called over the intercom, "Permission to fire."

The *Bismarck*'s first salvo was short, then the traditional "ladder" of three salvos bracketed the *Hood.* First gunnery officer Lieutenant Commander Albert Schneider, much beloved by his crew, had found his target immediately, and ordered full salvos from all four main turrets in rapid fire.

The *Prince of Wales* joined the battle at 0553, handicapped by the heavy rolling seas breaking over her low bow and spraying water over the primary range finders. Captain John Catterall Leach had the courage and wisdom to fire not at *Prinz Eugen* in the lead, as Holland had ordered, but instead at the correct primary target, the *Bismarck.* Leach's first salvos fell 1,000 yards short.

The *Prinz Eugen* began firing with her 8-inch guns. At 0557, shells from the *Prinz Eugen* ignited unprotected ammunition standing ready to be fired—a sign of lax discipline developed in the easy campaigns in the Mediterranean—causing a fire on the deck of the *Hood* that facilitated the *Bismarck*'s optical equipment providing the exact range.

The *Hood* and the *Prince of Wales* turned on a course almost parallel to the enemy to bring their aft turrets to bear, with the latter ship registering three fateful hits on the *Bismarck. Prinz Eugen* shifted fire to the *Prince of Wales* as seven of the eight shells of the fifth salvo from the *Bismarck* churned the sea around the *Hood.* The eighth shell, 798 pounds of the finest German artillery engineering, smashed through the *Hood*'s thin deck armor—as little as one inch amidships and only three inches over the magazines—plunging into the 4-inch-gun antiaircraft magazine near the aft main turrets. Then, in an exact backdraft replication of the "bloody ships" blown up at Jutland, the fire spread to a 15-inch gun magazine, exploding hundreds of tons of ammunition and breaking the *Hood* in two. Multicolored columns of smoke and flame soared hundreds of feet into the sky, bits of flaming aluminum tumbling along with entire turrets, as a concussive wall of sound swept across the sea and the *Prince of Wales* was bathed in an orange glow.

No one on either side could believe it; one moment Britain's mightiest warship was about to release her first full salvo; the next moment she was snapped in half like a matchstick. When the smoke cleared slightly, the bow of the *Hood* was seen projecting almost straight up; as it hung there, her forward guns fired, probably by accident, possibly as one last defiant gesture by men who knew they were going to die. More than 1,400 men, including Admiral Holland and Captain Kerr, went down with the ship; only three were saved. Six minutes had passed since the *Hood*'s first salvo was fired, signaling the start of the battle.

Scarcely daring to credit what he had just seen, Admiral Luetjens ordered the *Bismarck* to join the *Prinz Eugen* in firing on the *Prince of Wales*, now turning to avoid the *Hood*'s wreckage, but still plunging toward the enemy. Holland had kept his two ships close together, and the firing data for the *Hood* easily served for the *Prince of Wales*, a slight shift of the *Bismarck*'s guns putting them immediately on target. A 15-inch shell from the *Bismarck* demolished the *Prince of Wales*'s bridge, killing everyone but Captain Leach and a signal officer. Four 15-inch shells from the *Bismarck* and three 8-inch shells from the *Prinz Eugen* battered the British ship. Navigating from an auxiliary control station, with his ship badly damaged and only four guns operational, Captain Leach swung the *Prince of Wales* about, made smoke and disengaged at 0614.

No blood lust had risen in Luetjens. Where almost any British commander would have immediately fallen on the *Prince of Wales* and destroyed her, he elected to break off combat. Technically, he was adhering to Raeder's instructions; in fact he was sealing his own doom. Luetjens already had preliminary damage reports and knew the *Bismarck* was taking on water and leaking fuel. Nonetheless, if he had pursued and sunk the *Prince of Wales*, he could have continued on course, back the way he came, 1,000 miles to Norway and safety.

The intensely private Luetjens never explained his orders; he didn't do so now as he headed south toward the convoy despite the damage from three 14-inch shell hits from the *Prince of Wales*. The crucial damage came from one that struck the port side and exited through a five-foot-wide hole on the starboard side. Although above the waterline, it was below the bow wave, and the *Bismarck* took on 2,000 tons of seawater, some of which contaminated the fuel supply. Both bilge pumps and fuel-oil pumps were inaccessible, preventing the water from being pumped out and isolating 1,000 tons of fuel.

Engineering personnel recommended that the *Bismarck* be slowed and flooded aft, raising the bow so that the damage could be repaired. Luetjens refused. By 0700, however, a report indicated that there was only 3,300 tons of available fuel remaining. A reasonable course to Brest, one that would evade the places where Luetjens expected the strongest concentrations of

British ships, would involve a curving, 2,000-mile route—100 hours at the most economical speed of 20 knots. At 20 knots, the *Bismarck* burned approximately 19.8 tons of fuel per hour; it would require 1,980 tons of fuel to reach Brest, leaving a margin of 1,320 tons, little enough if there was further combat along the oily trail now marking *Bismarck*'s passage.

Ironically, 330 miles to the southeast, Admiral Tovey's force of *King George V, Repulse,* Victorious, and five cruisers was facing an equally pressing fuel supply problem; British ships were notoriously short-ranged, and did not yet refuel at sea. Tovey was driving northwest to intercept the *Bismarck* while the redoubtable Force H, champions of the Mediterranean, was summoned to steam north to intercept the *Bismarck* if it should outrun its pursuers.

The *Bismarck* took advantage of the weather to detach the *Prinz Eugen* at 1814, sending her on ahead on the same course as the *Bismarck* wheeled through a 270-degree turn to cross her own track and steer to the southeast, trying to reach the protection of Luftwaffe planes and a line of U-boats some 690 miles off the coast of France. Tovey's problem was to bring the *Bismarck* to battle before she reached that line, and to do so before the British ships ran out of fuel.

Stopping the *Bismarck* meant first of all maintaining contact, and the *Norfolk, Suffolk* and *Prince of Wales* trailed her in formation on her port side, zigzagging just out of range of the 15-inch guns. Radar contact was maintained only intermittently; it was lost on the outbound (port) leg of the zigzag, and recovered on the inbound (starboard) leg. The three-ship unit was commanded by Rear Admiral William F. Wake-Walker in the *Norfolk,* who had elected to track the German battleship and make sure she was intercepted by superior forces, rather than attempting to sink her himself. In principle, his decision was the correct one, but it raised the ire of both Admiral Pound and Winston Churchill. The latter, immediately thinking in terms of a court-martial, sent insulting inquiries about Wake-Walker's intentions for "reengaging" the *Bismarck*. It was the wrong criticism; Wake-Walker was quite right not to try to engage the *Bismarck* with his inferior force. The British navy would have been better served if the Admiralty had spotted the flaw in maintaining station only to port, instead of shadowing the *Bismarck* on the starboard side as well.

Meanwhile, Tovey had concluded that the only solution was a torpedo attack by Swordfish off the *Victorious*. At 2200 the *Bismarck* was 120 miles away when the *Victorious* launched nine Swordfish and six Fulmar fighters. The mission had the trappings of a suicide attack: 90-knot biplanes took off from the pitching deck of a carrier into terrible weather to attack the most powerful antiaircraft defense afloat. But attack they did, hitting the *Bismarck* with one torpedo, and, *mirabile dictu,* all but two Fulmars making it back. On board the *Bismarck,* the antiaircraft fire was so noisy that Captain Lindemann's orders could not be heard. Seaman Hans Hansen, the *Bismarck*'s helmsman, took responsibility for the steering and skillfully avoided all the torpedoes but one.

Unfortunately for the British, the one 18-inch torpedo that hit home had been a surface runner and struck the strongest section of the *Bismarck*'s armor, inflicting negligible damage. One man, Warrant Officer Kurt Kirchberg, was killed by the concussion effect inside, the *Bismarck*'s first death of an ultimate 2,007.

Admiral Tovey was disappointed with the results of the torpedo attack, and knew that his chance to catch the *Bismarck* were dwindling as fast as his fuel supplies.

May 25, 1941 (Luetjens's Birthday), 0230 Hours

The Germans were experts with hydrophones, and soon determined there were no ships to their starboard. When they detected the British ships on an outbound leg of their zigzag, the *Bismarck* turned smartly to starboard and executed a 270-degree turn to cross her track thirty miles behind the British ships. The *Bismarck* then accelerated to the maximum speed her damaged bow would permit, driving east toward the Luftwaffe and safety.

The British radar operators, exhausted like everyone else in the battle, at first assumed that the disappearance of the enemy battleship from the radar screen would be corrected on the next turn in or on the one following. A natural desire to believe contact would be regained resulted in a delay until 0500 hours before the loss of contact with the *Bismarck* was reported to Tovey—and to a furious Admiralty. The British fell into a desperate panic, with Admiral Tovey's force steaming determinedly in the wrong direction to the southwest, while Churchill was convinced that Luetjens had doubled back and was heading for the Denmark Strait.

Even though German headquarters had advised Luetjens that British radio traffic indicated that they had lost radar contact, Luetjens apparently could not believe that he had at last broken free, after thirty-one hours of continuous radar surveillance. His radar operators continued to receive British radar signals, but they did not comprehend that the British were too distant to receive the reflected radar waves. This misapprehension does not excuse Luetjens for sending two radio messages to Berlin. The simple logic of the situation meant that he should have maintained radio silence, especially since the messages he sent were hardly urgent. Alternatively, he could have used the *Kurzsignalverfahren* technique, a short-signal procedure that was still immune to radio direction finding.

Instead, he sent a short signal at 0700 and then a longer one at 0900, which reported that he was still being followed, persistent radar coverage made disengagement impossible and he was short of fuel. To the British, desperately seeking to make contact by surface vessels, aircraft and submarines, his communications were a godsend, but in the style of this battle, they promptly bobbled the information.

The HF/DF (Huff-Duff) high-frequency/direction-finding radio fixes, while not as precise as they might have been, were correctly interpreted at the Admiralty, and fixed the *Bismarck*'s position well to the southeast of where she had last been reported. But, acting on Tovey's previous instructions, the Admiralty furnished not the *Bismarck*'s position but the raw data to Tovey. The specialists whom he depended upon to plot it were on destroyers released to be refueled; the people who received the data were not well qualified and misplotted it, placing the *Bismarck* far to the north of its real position. Tovey, who had been steaming in the wrong direction to the southwest, now reversed course in the wrong direction to the northeast. He would ultimately spend eight hours flailing about, and wind up 150 miles from the *Bismarck*. It was an impossible distance unless the *Bismarck* was stopped by another air strike by the Swordfish.

Berlin responded to Luetjens's messages with heartiest congratulations on his birthday from Raeder, and a frosty message from Adolf Hitler, who undoubtedly sensed that matters were deteriorating. And they were, in part through utter indulgence by the Chief of Staff of the Luftwaffe, whose son served on the *Bismarck*. General Hans Jeschonnek, whose mismanagement of the Luftwaffe would lead him to suicide on August 18, 1943, inquired about the ship's destination. He was told Brest, and the message was intercepted by British intelligence.

May 25 should have been a day of buoyant hope for the *Bismarck;* every hour was bringing it closer to safety, and as yet there was no further contact with the pursuing British forces. Yet Luetjens made a lugubrious speech to his crew, telling them they would fight until the last shell had left the barrels and "For us seamen, the question now is victory or death!" The effect upon morale was disastrous; officers violated regulations by wearing their life jackets and discipline began to wane.

May 26, 1941, 0300 Hours

Forced by the fuel shortage to steam at only 20 knots, the *Bismarck* nevertheless edged toward safety, hour by hour. If Luetjens had originally refueled when he could have, he might have steamed at 28 knots and slipped out from under the British like a baserunner stealing home. But it was not to be. An RAF Consolidated Catalina flying boat of No. 209 Squadron, Coastal Command, based at Lough Erne, Ireland, was detailed to fly south of the *Bismarck*'s projected direct route. The aircraft was a potential international incident, for it was piloted by Flying Officer Dennis Briggs, RAF, with twenty-six-year-old Ensign Leonard B. "Tuck" Smith, USN, as copilot. Smith was one of a group of sixteen American pilots who volunteered to familiarize the British with their new Catalinas, and then were integrated into the squadrons, in technical violation of the U.S. Neutrality Law.

Almost seven hours into their patrol an unbelieving Smith looked straight out of his cockpit window to see the *Bismarck* slinking along. The Catalina dropped down out of the clouds to within 500 yards of the *Bismarck*, to be met with a withering fusillade of antiaircraft fire. Smith jettisoned the four depth bombs they were carrying and the *Bismarck* veered. As the Catalina climbed away, Briggs got off a sighting message, giving what he thought was *Bismarck*'s position.

He was more than twenty miles off, but it was close enough. The *Bismarck* was now about 700 miles due west of Brest. Tovey's battleships were 135 miles to the northeast, too far away to catch up unless the *Bismarck* was somehow stopped or slowed. Now everything rested on the shoulders of Force H, commanded by the dashing, aggressive and good-natured Admiral James Somerville, a man of colorful language who was willing to take risks. (One story about Somerville, often told but too good not to repeat, conveys his salty character and his relationship with his boss, Admiral Cunningham. When Cunningham learned that Somerville, already a Knight of the British Empire, had been made a Knight Commander of the Bath, he radioed the following: "Congratulations, but isn't twice a knight at your age rather overdoing it?")

Force H was just 100 miles away, standing between the *Bismarck* and safety. Somerville dispatched the cruiser *Sheffield* forward to make contact with the beleaguered battleship. Unfortunately, he did not pass this information along to the *Ark Royal*, now being readied to strike as soon as she was within range. The 22,000-ton *Ark Royal*'s streamlining of the deck and island superstructure, combined with good hull design, resulted in a top speed of 31.75 knots and good sea-keeping qualities.

There was a considerable difference between operating in the calm Mediterranean and the pitching seas of the North Atlantic, where the deck might rise and fall fifty feet in the time it took for a takeoff, and where wind speed across the deck approached 50 miles per hour, almost the Swordfish's takeoff speed. The Swordfish crews of the *Victorious* had little experience but successfully operated in similar filthy weather. The seasoned veterans of the *Ark Royal* knew they could do as well. Long-range versions of the Swordfish, with extra fuel tanks and no torpedo, relieved Briggs's Catalina of spotting duties and began to maintain continuous coverage.

Fifteen torpedo-armed Swordfish were launched from the *Ark Royal* at 1540; despite their expertise, the pilots were deficient in ship identification and launched eleven torpedoes at the *Sheffield*, much to their embarrassment. Brilliant shiphandling saved the *Sheffield*, which had the forbearance not to fire on the Swordfish.

Yet the attack was somewhat fortunate, for it revealed that the Duplex magnetic-pistol firing mechanisms fitted to the torpedoes were malfunctioning. When the red-faced Swordfish pilots landed back on the *Ark Royal*, they demanded that standard contact pistols be installed.

The second strike was launched at 1915; fifteen aircraft bored through the thick clouds that reached down to within 700 feet of the water. They were directed by radar to the *Sheffield*, which then gave them the heading of 110 degrees to the *Bismarck*, twelve miles away.

The *Bismarck* was at battle stations, supplementing its usual wall of antiaircraft fire with large-caliber shells fired into the sea to create waterspouts. The Swordfish split up, attacking from all sides. Of the thirteen torpedoes dropped, two struck the battleship. One hit amidships on the port side, where its explosion was contained by the underwater protection system. The second torpedo crashed into the stern area, striking near the steering gear room and jamming the rudders in a 12-degree right turn. All of the Swordfish returned safely.

The *Bismarck* began two complete 360-degree turns, firing at *Sheffield* as she went. Damage-control parties fighting to regain steering control uncoupled and centered the starboard rudder, but were unable to free the port rudder.

With violent applications of asymmetric power, the *Bismarck* labored on in the heavy seas at about 8 knots, weaving 60 degrees between northeast and northwest, her snaking course converging with that of the ships coming to kill her.

The comedy of errors was almost over. Luetjens had a final mistake to make, the gravest of all. Unable to steer, the *Bismarck* could not avoid the overwhelming British forces converging upon it. Luetjens could have scuttled his ship and surrendered, enabling his 2,220 surviving crew members to live. Instead, with Wagnerian bombast, he signaled: "Ship unable to maneuver. We will fight to the last shell. Long live the Fuehrer." Then, apparently unable to resist an open microphone, at two minutes before midnight he announced: "We will fight to the last in trust in you, our Fuehrer, and a rockhard trust in Germany's victory."

May 27, 1941, 0847 Hours

The odds were terribly uneven, but the *Bismarck* was still dangerous, and Tovey wished to take no chances. His command ship was the *Rodney*, 38,000 tons with nine 16-inch guns. (She and her sister, the *Nelson*, were reduced versions of a class of ships canceled after the Washington Naval Treaty. They were known as the "Cherry Tree" class, because they had "been cut down by Washington.") In addition, Tovey had the battleship *King George V*, with ten 14-inch guns, with the cruisers *Dorsetshire* and *Norfolk;* it was enough to begin a bloody pummeling.

The *Rodney* opened fire first, followed at 0848 by the *King George V*. The *Bismarck* replied at 0850, the wallowing sea ruining its normally accurate fire. The ship that had sunk the *Hood* in six minutes did not register a single hit in this engagement. A storm of British shells tore out the *Bismarck*'s fire control, blasted the superstructure and displaced the guns. By 0931, the last main turret of the *Bismarck* was silenced, and the British ships shortened their range, firing point-blank into the battered hull.

At 1020 scuttling charges were set off within the *Bismarck*. All watertight doors were opened and the surviving crew members were told to save themselves.

The British battleships, short on fuel and running low on ammunition, ceased fire at 1022. The *Rodney* had fired 380 16-inch shells and the *King George V* had fired 339 14-inch rounds. With the other ships, 2,157 additional shells of smaller caliber had smothered the *Bismarck*, plus twelve torpedoes from the *Rodney*. Of these more than 400 shells had hit, and the enemy ship now lay a broken mass, no gun able to fire, burning from stem to stern—but floating still.

The cruiser *Dorsetshire* delivered two torpedoes at close range into the starboard side, then circled to place another in the port side. The combination of shells, scuttling charges and torpedoes finally caused the *Bismarck* to roll over and sink at 1046, a victim of Raeder's dream and Luetjens's mismanagement.

The *Dorsetshire* and the destroyer *Maori* picked up 110 men before a submarine scare forced them to leave the area. Between 500 and 600 sailors were left to drown. A further five were rescued, three by a U-boat and two by a German weather ship.

The *Bismarck*, the largest and most modern capital ship ever built in Europe, arrived on the scene just a little too late; it was as if the world's greatest horse-drawn carriage had appeared just after the introduction of the Ford Model T. Radar and aircraft combined to spell the doom of battleships in general, and the battleship-raider in particular.

BITTER LOSSES IN THE MEDITERRANEAN

The Royal Navy's moment of triumph over the *Bismarck* was soon diminished with a series of catastrophies in the Mediterranean. These began with losses to German air power in Greece and Crete (to be covered later), followed by a litany of disasters that almost destroyed the Royal Navy in the Mediterranean. On November 13, 1941, Lieutenant Friedrich Guggenberger, first commander of the *U-81*, fired four torpedoes at the aircraft carrier *Ark Royal* when she was just fifty miles east of Gibraltar. One torpedo struck the starboard boiler room, bringing the ship to a halt; many personnel were removed, including the key electricians. Water in the center boiler room put the main electrical switchboard out of action, and power to the pumps was lost. The next day, after fourteen hours under tow and only twenty miles from Gibraltar, the *Ark Royal*, survivor of many trips to Malta and victor over the *Bismarck*, capsized and sank. Guggenberger was later awarded the Oak Leaves to his Knight's Cross. (He went on to command another submarine, the *U-513*. She was sunk in July 1943, but he survived to become a prisoner of war.)

Twelve days later, patrolling between Crete and Cyrenaica, Admiral Cunningham was having tea in his bridge cabin on the battleship *Queen Elizabeth* when he heard three noises that he first took to be antiaircraft guns opening up. He ran to the bridge and saw the battleship *Barham* stopped, and already listing heavily to port.

As he watched, the 31,000-ton dreadnought, laid down in 1913, rolled on her side, men scrambling across the dripping black hull. A minute passed and there was an ear-splitting explosion as a main magazine went up in a cloud of yellow-black smoke that hid the stricken ship from sight. When the smoke cleared, the *Barham* was gone, the only English battleship to be sunk at sea by a U-boat. (The loss was captured on motion picture film, and is stunning to watch.)

Cunningham later called the attack "a most daring and brilliant performance on the part of the U-boat, which fired from a position about 200 yards ahead of the *Valiant*." The *U-81*, commanded by Lieutenant Hans-Dietrich Freiherr von Tiesenhausen, had slipped through the escorting ships and fired a spread of four torpedoes. Three hit home, and the *U-81* broached in the resulting explosion and was seen sliding along the side of the battleship *Valiant* before escaping.

The twin loss of the *Ark Royal* and *Barham* had not yet been digested when news was received of the defeat inflicted upon the U.S. fleet at Pearl Harbor, followed by the December 10 sinking of the *Prince of Wales* and the *Repulse* by Japanese land-based bombers from Saigon. The toll increased on December 15, when the *U-557*, captained by Lieutenant Commander Heinz Paulshen, sank the cruiser *Galatea* off Alexandria; the *U-557* was lost in a collision on its return trip.

Admiral Cunningham was trying to see how he could spread his ships even thinner to cover the Mediterranean, when on the night of December 18, 1941, the Italian submarine *Scire* made her way under the direction of her captain, Commander Prince Junio Valerio Borghese, to within one mile of the port of Alexandria. He released three Maiales (pigs), special two-man torpedoes designed by Teseo Tesei, using a standard 21-inch torpedo as a basis. Two crewmen, wearing what today would be called scuba gear, straddled the pig, which was twenty-two feet long and carried a warhead of 661 pounds of explosives. The pig had a speed of about 2.5 knots, and an endurance of five to six hours.

The three Italian pigs followed destroyers in through the entrance gate and made their way into the harbor at Alexandria. Lieutenant Durand de la Penne and Sergeant Major Emilio Bianchi made their way to the battleship *Valiant*; the torpedo stopped running and the two men literally dragged it across the sea floor to rest fifteen feet beneath the *Valiant*'s hull. Captured and brought on board after they surfaced and swam to a buoy, they refused to talk and, on Admiral Cunningham's orders, were thrown in the brig—directly over their torpedo. Ten minutes before the torpedo was timed to explode, they asked to see the *Valiant*'s captain, Captain R. D. Morgan, and warned him that the ship was about to be sunk. Morgan mustered all hands on deck, sent the Italians back to the brig and waited for the explosion. It came, and the *Valiant* settled to the bottom, the two daring frogmen somehow managing to escape.

Meanwhile, Captain Antonio Marceglia with Lance Corporal Spartaco

Schergat passed under the torpedo nets around the battleship *Queen Elizabeth* and fastened their charge to her bilge keel. The explosion sent the ship to the bottom of the harbor, upright, and like the *Valiant,* out of the war for a long time. The crew members were also captured.

The third crew, Captain Vincenzo Martellotta and Sergeant Major Mario Marino, sank the large Norwegian tanker *Sagona,* in the process damaging the British destroyer *Jervis.* The two men swam ashore and, with considerable sangfroid, walked into town, exchanged a five-pound note, caught a train for Rosetta, where they were captured the following day while en route to dinner with a policeman. They had hoped to get a boat and be picked up the following day by the submarine *Zaffiro.*

It was not the end of the British losses; on the same night that the manned torpedoes struck, the cruiser *Neptune* and the destroyer *Kandahar* wandered into an Italian minefield twenty miles east of Tripoli and were sunk. Cunningham's fleet had been bled down to three cruisers and some destroyers, a shadow of its former self, and there were untold months of bitter fighting still to come. Any commander other than Cunningham would probably have been undone by the serial tragedies, which reflected upon the standards of training and vigilance of his fleet. He was shielded by his past accomplishments and by his aggressive nature, which promised future triumphs.

4.

Submarine
Warfare
in the West

First Blood

At 1400 hours on September 3, 1939, the signal "Commence hostilities against England immediately" was sent to all U-boats. This was followed an hour later by an admonition to adhere to standing operational orders, which defined five categories of shipping that could, like warships, be attacked without warning. These included ships known to be carrying war goods, ships engaged in military activity (e.g., fueling a warship), cargo ships sailing with a warship escort or in convoy, armed merchant ships and troopships.

At 1945 that night, Lieutenant Fritz-Julius Lemp of *U-30*, one of the first ten boats of the Type VIIA class, raised his periscope and saw a huge merchant vessel steering westward on a rolling sea, 250 miles northwest of Ireland.

Lemp was close enough to be able to tell that the ship was a passenger liner, yet it is inconceivable that he would simply have disobeyed his orders not to sink such ships. Almost certainly, his desire to succeed persuaded him that this was a legitimate target.

His torpedo, the first of more than 40,000 fired during the war, was accurate, ripping open the port side of the SS *Athenia*, a 13,581-ton passenger liner of the Donaldson Atlantic Line. The explosion eliminated the bulk-head separating the engine and boiler rooms and the flood of seawater caused the *Athenia* to take on a sharp list almost immediately.

Lemps suffered a sinking feeling himself when he surfaced and became aware that it was the passenger ship *Athenia* sending out SOS signals. Help came swiftly enough for more than 1,300 people to be rescued; the ship did not sink until 1040 the next day. One hundred twelve lives were lost, including twenty-eight Americans; most of the dead were trapped in the third-class and tourist dining rooms when the stairs to the upper decks were blown away by the explosion.

The world press resounded with indignation, with inevitable comparisons with the *Lusitania* freely made. The Germans immediately (and sincerely) denied responsibility. Propaganda Minister Dr. Joseph Goebbels first insisted that it had to be a British torpedo or mine, as there was no German ship within 200 miles of *Athenia*'s position; he next accused Churchill of blowing the ship up for propaganda purposes.

It was not until late in September, when Lemp arrived back in port to report personally that he had sunk the *Athenia* to commander-in-chief, U-boats, Captain Karl Doenitz, that the stunning truth became known to the German high command.

Scale is always important in military foul-ups, and it was Lemp's good fortune to have made a mistake of such colossal proportions that he could not be punished for it. Even his sinking of the *Athenia* in honest error could not be admitted because of the strident Nazi official denials. The matter was covered up, the *U-30*'s war diary was altered (supposedly one of only two such alterations in the entire war) and the crew members were cautioned not to reveal what had happened. (Lemp went back to a successful career until losing his life on May 9, 1941, when he was captain of *U-110* and British depth charges forced it to the surface. Aware that the precious Enigma machine on board would be compromised, he attempted to reboard his vessel to scuttle it and was shot in the process. Ironically, his old boat, *U-30*, had a relatively charmed life. After a combat career in which it sank seventeen ships, it became a training boat and survived until April 5, 1945, when it was sunk in a bombing raid.)

The *Athenia* incident had important results for both sides. The British immediately assumed that the Germans were going to undertake unrestricted submarine warfare, and took every step they could to combat it, including the immediate institution of the convoy system. Hitler went to the opposite extreme, ordering that no attacks be made on any passenger ship, no matter what the circumstances.

The whole affair was but a hint of what was to come in the months ahead: the Battle of the Atlantic. The U-boats were very effective, sinking 221 ships of more than 750,000 tons in the first four months of the war. Of these, 47 ships of almost 250,000 tons had been sunk in the North Atlantic, a serious but not grievous loss. But Doenitz had too few boats to be decisive, and the initial "surge" of thirty-nine fully operational submarines in the Atlantic and the North Sea soon dwindled as they returned to port to resupply. In December 1939 only four ships were sunk, just under 16,000 tons.

Always wishing to be on the offensive, Churchill established "Units of Search," a combination of an aircraft carrier and cruiser to hunt down the pocket battleships. He also decreed that groups of destroyers and smaller vessels would seek out and attack submarines with what would today be called hunter-killer teams. The Units idea seemed to meet with some success on September 14, when four destroyers sank the U-39, a large Type IXA boat (1,178 tons' submerged displacement), as she attacked the carrier Ark Royal. The flurry of self-congratulation on the first sinking of a German submarine in World War II ended when it was realized that the torpedoes fired by the U-39 had exploded prematurely—and if they had not, the carrier would probably have been sunk instead.

These fleeting suspicions were confirmed a few days later when Lieutenant Commander Otto Schuart in U-29 became the hero that Lemp had hoped to be. Schuart positioned himself in the Bristol Channel, between Wales and the southwest of England, where German naval intelligence told him a British aircraft carrier might be found. (From early in the war until 1943, the German naval intelligence B-Dienst capability to read British codes gave their submarines a tremendous advantage. The ciphers had been cracked during the Italian invasion of Ethiopia, when the Royal Navy had mustered considerable strength in the Mediterranean, and was generating an enormous amount of radio traffic without the rigors of wartime communications discipline.)

On the evening of September 17, Schuart detected the 22,400-ton carrier Courageous turning into the wind to recover some of her normal complement of forty-eight aircraft. Three torpedoes were fired at a distance of just under two miles; two struck the Courageous, causing so violent an explosion that Schuart thought that U-29 was being depth-charged by some unseen assailant. The Courageous, sister ship of the Glorious, and like her a hybrid built on the thin hull of a 1916 vintage light battle cruiser, broke up and sank within fifteen minutes, carrying the captain and 518 of his men with her. The concept of hunting units was quietly dropped.

THE BULL OF SCAPA FLOW

Scapa Flow, a land-locked anchorage in the Orkney Isles, 15 miles in length and 8 miles wide, had long served as a base for the British fleet. It was an ideal target for the German navy, representing as it did the height of British power and the degrading nadir of the scuttled World War I High Seas Fleet. Unknown to the Germans, it was also a victim of the interwar disarmament program, and as a result lacked adequate antiaircraft and sea defenses.

Aerial reconnaissance revealed that on the northern side of Kirk Sound, the eastern entrance to the fleet base, the blockships used to bar the entrance were separated by a fifty-foot-wide passage. A good submarine captain could slip through the gap on the surface at night, submerge and attack a battleship or an aircraft carrier. Getting out might be a problem, but that was a sacrifice Doenitz—and the commander he chose—were prepared to make.

Doenitz, a classic micromanager who knew all of his commanders personally, and who met almost every submarine returning from patrol for a personal debriefing, had picked Lieutenant Guenther Prien for the task. Prien had been the first U-boat captain to sink a cargo ship, and scarcely two months into the war was widely recognized as a submarine "ace," as much to be admired as von Richthofen had been for his aerial victories in World War I.

Prien was not ordered to undertake the task, but Doenitz knew his man, and Prien volunteered himself and his ship. The crew members, who naturally had no say in the matter, were somewhat perplexed when Prien ordered fuel and supplies to be off-loaded prior to sailing, indicating a very short voyage. He told them nothing until they arrived off the entrance to Scapa Flow on October 13, 1939. They settled to the bottom, 300 feet below the surface, as comfortably as forty-eight men jammed into a submarine can be. Prien told them of the mission—and to get some rest.

At 1915 on October 13, Prien surfaced the *U-47* and began conning the submarine like a whitewater canoe, the swift-running slate gray tidal waters propelling him through the angled blockships, whose unseen anchor chains represented hazards to his rudders and propellers. Prien commanded a good U-boat; the *U-47* would see fifteen months of active wartime service and sink thirty-four ships, all under his command. Commissioned in 1938, she was one of twenty-four Type VIIB boats. The Type VIIB had originated directly from a list of requirements by Captain Doenitz to improve the range, torpedo load and the maneuverability of the Type VII class. Twin rudders were fitted to improve turning capability, range was increased from 4,300 to 6,500 miles, and fourteen rather than eleven torpedoes were carried.

At twenty-seven minutes after midnight, the *U-47* was inside Scapa Flow. To Prien's dismay, most of the British fleet was not there. Alerted by the presence of German aerial reconnaissance flights to expect a bombing raid, the Royal Navy had gone to sea, leaving few targets behind. Of these, only one was of consequence, the battleship *Royal Oak*, riding peacefully at anchor below the town of Scapa, most of her crew of 1,264 officers and men asleep. The *Royal Oak* was completed in 1916 at a cost of £2.5 million; she displaced 33,500 tons when fully loaded and carried eight 15-inch guns. Too slow for operations now, with a top speed of only 22 knots, she was still a powerful vessel—and the only game in town.

Identifying ships in a strange harbor, with only a fading aurora borealis for light, is difficult; Prien recognized the *Royal Oak*, but thought the *Pegasus*, a 6,900-ton seaplane carrier, was the 32,000-ton battle cruiser *Repulse*.

It is worth noting here that, films and books notwithstanding, in most combat situations, the U-boat captain did *not* do the actual aiming and firing of the torpedoes. He ordinarily served as ship commander, selecting the target and directing the attack, while the first watch officer actually placed the U-boat into position, aimed and fired.

At 0058 hours, the first watch officer, Lieutenant Englebert Endrass (later an ace U-boat commander himself), fired a salvo of four torpedoes at the *Royal Oak* at a range of 9,000 feet. One jammed in its tube, and two missed. The third caught its target in the bow. As the English crew raced to inspect the damage, Prien ordered the stern tube fired; this torpedo missed or malfunctioned. Despite a gaping hole, most of the *Royal Oak*'s damage was above the waterline, leading its captain, William Benn, to decide that there had been an internal explosion—it was simply unthinkable that an enemy submarine could be loose in Scapa Flow. The damage was relatively slight and no alarm was given.

Prien had turned south to make his escape, the crew swiftly reloading the torpedo tubes. But a last look at the *Royal Oak* showed her apparently undamaged, so he reversed course and went in to attack again, closing to within 4,800 feet before Endrass fired three torpedoes. This time the *Royal Oak* exploded with a blast that shook the harbor; she sank within fifteen minutes, 833 men losing their lives.

Now the harbor defenses burst into activity, searchlights sweeping the water and destroyers coursing back and forth dropping depth charges. The *U-47* fought the current and slipped out of Scapa Flow a little after 0200 on October 14.

Before the *U-47* reached Wilhelmshaven, the crew painted a crude bull on the conning tower, and Prien was already being referred to as "The Bull of Scapa Flow."

Admiral Raeder and the newly promoted Rear Admiral Doenitz were ecstatic, knowing that Hitler would respond well to a feat of daring executed with such skill that even Churchill spoke with admiration of it to Parliament. Prien received the Iron Cross, First Class immediately upon docking; every man on the crew received the Second Class of the order.

More was to come. The Nazi equivalent of a ticker-tape parade was held in Berlin, and Hitler personally invested Prien with the Knight's Cross of the Iron Cross, a very high honor at the time, and the first to be awarded a submariner.

Prien soon returned to his work as a submarine ace, eventually destroying a total of almost 200,000 tons of shipping in addition to the *Royal Oak*. Ironically, the first of the U-boat aces was also among the first to be killed. Early on the morning of March 8, 1941, the *U-47* was caught by destroyers and heavily depth-charged. Prien's submarine broke the surface of the water, then dove again, to be followed by more depth charges. These provoked a massive internal explosion within *U-47* that caused an enormous ball of orange fire to be observed deep within the water (possibly onboard torpedoes exploding), and another first for a man of many firsts—underwater immolation.

THE TRUTH BEHIND THE TRIUMPHS

Given the magnitude of these initial victories, it appeared that Germany had entered the war well prepared to conduct a vigorous submarine campaign. In fact, however, Admiral Raeder had overruled then Captain Doenitz's suggestions for a large submarine building program, and allocated the submarine forces a subsidiary role in his balanced Z Plan fleet. The result was that Germany had not even built to its treaty limits, which would have allowed seventy-two submarines. When war came Raeder acknowledged that the U-boat fleet was the best means of harming Britain, and sought Hitler's approval for an accelerated building program. This was denied on the basis of priorities—the army and its tanks had to come first. With the Mobilization Program of 1939, a large submarine-building program was approved, calling for 118 boats in 1940 and 368 in 1941. From 1942, U-boats were to be built at the rate of twenty-three per month. With an estimated 10 percent loss rate figured in, Doenitz would have 320 U-boats on hand by October 1943. As things worked out, he actually had 426 U-boats in March 1943, but of these, only 255 were operational because of his strictly enforced training and overhaul requirements.

The lack of German preparedness, reflected in the small number of submarines it was able to maintain at sea for the first eighteen months of combat, was offset by British diffidence to antisubmarine warfare. When the budget cuts came, the Admiralty clung to its capital ships, and eliminated its Antisubmarine, Minesweeping and Trade Divisions. Cutting the Antisubmarine Division was an obvious folly, especially in view of the light in which Asdic was held as the answer to submarines. (The name "Asdic" purportedly derives from Anti-Submarine Detection Investigation Committee, but this long accepted explanation has recently been challenged as a wartime subterfuge.) In any event, Asdic grew out of pioneering work by the French scientists Chilowski and Langevin, and developed by Dr. R. W. Boyle. The first Asdic set—essentially an oscillator hung over the ship's side, a transmitter to send out the characteristic "ping" and a receiver—was first used at sea in 1920 on the armored cruiser *Antrim*. By 1939, five Asdic types had been developed that could detect submarines at up to 1,500 yards' range under good conditions. Unfortunately, the possible range error could be as much as twenty-five yards—at a time when depth charges had a killing radius of only seven yards. The sonar equipment developed by the United States derived from information on Asdic, but lagged behind British efforts until World War II. The major flaw of Asdic/sonar equipment was that it could not detect a submarine on the surface, nor amidst the multiple engine sounds of a convoy.

Once again the economics of disarmament won out in the face of an arming enemy. Tight military budgets also forced decisions in which the small ships that would be used to escort convoys and combat submarines were not built, in the blithe hope that they could be quickly built when war started.

Britain was also hampered because its myopic view of the role of naval aviation was almost as bad as that of the Germans. The Fleet Air Arm had been reestablished as a separate air service in 1937, but the long years of domination by the Royal Air Force had left it with a fleet of obsolete aircraft that were completely outclassed by any land-based air force and by the U.S. and Japanese naval air forces. Fortunately, good relations had been established with the orphan of the Royal Air Force, Coastal Command, which had received lower priority in the RAF because its mission was to support the Royal Navy. Over time the two services were able to work together to establish an effective antisubmarine capability.

GERMAN SUBMARINE STRENGTH

Germany entered the war with thirty small, 250-ton coastal submarines, referred to as "Baltic ducks," eighteen Type VII 500-ton Atlantic boats, and eight Type I and Type IX 700-ton large Atlantic boats: a total of fifty-six, of which forty-six were available for operations. In the first year of the war, by straining every element of his command, Doenitz managed to average thirty-three operational U-boats with fourteen operating in the North Atlantic. At the high point, twenty-one U-boats operated there in November; the low point was at Christmas 1939, when no German submarines were in the North Atlantic. During the year, twenty-eight submarines were lost, a number exactly offset by twenty-eight new boats.

It is important to understand that the U-boat was much more a torpedo boat than a submarine. It spent the vast majority of its time surfaced, its low profile difficult to see at night, or at a distance. The Type VIIC submarine, the most numerous of the German U-boats, with 567 built during the war, had a 17-knot sustained surface speed on its diesel engines and could travel submerged at 7.6 knots for one hour on its electric motors. For longer duration, dependent on currents, it could move submerged for 130 miles—at 2 knots, that is, sixty-five hours of dull, cold cruising. Absolute maximum range, surfaced, was 8,850 miles at the most efficient speed. When the batteries that powered its electric motor were discharged, it took as long as seven hours' running on the surface to charge them. A maximum of fourteen torpedoes or up to thirty-nine mines were carried. Maximum allowable diving depth was 309 feet—a depth often successfully exceeded. *Red October*s they were not—but a simple, hard-hitting, lethal weapon they were.

THE FIRST TEN MONTHS: OPERATION FROM HOME BASES

The weakness of the U-boat fleet was obscured by the rich number of targets, and by the Royal Navy's lack of experience in antisubmarine warfare. The Admiralty, its faith based on prewar exercises in which Asdic was highly successful, had repeatedly assured the Parliament that it did not intend to reinstitute convoys in the event of war. Despite the navy's strong faith in it, Asdic was in fact installed in only about 180 warships when war broke out; of these, more than 150 were destroyers, which had many duties other than sub hunting. As a result, the first convoy had been established immediately before the outbreak of the war.

After the September 3 sinking of the *Athenia*, the British Admiralty required convoys on principal routes for ships able to steam at a speed of 9 to 14.9 knots. Ships capable of speeds faster than 15 knots were believed more or less immune to submarine attack—a false assumption, given the German ability to read British shipping instructions and position their submarines accordingly. Ships traveling at less than 9 knots were simply on their own. These requirements were later changed to permit "fast" and "slow" convoys, the former capable of speeds of 9 to 14.8 knots, the latter capable of speeds from 7.5 to 8.9 knots. In reality, speeds were lower for both types of convoys.

These criteria meant there was an enormous amount of shipping sailing independently, and it was from these easy targets that most U-boat kills would be made. In September 1939, fifty-three Allied and neutral ships totaling 195,000 tons were sunk, none in convoy.

The disposition of convoys and the extent of their coverage changed over the years, and depended in great part upon the number and types of escorts. Initially, convoys originated only at the Thames and at Liverpool (coded OA and OB respectively), and were given close escort only to a point 12.5 degrees west—as little as 200 miles from the west coast of Ireland. The outward-bound convoy would then maintain its formation for another twenty-four hours, before scattering to sail independently to their respective ports of call. Next to the unescorted inbound ships, they became the U-boats' favorite victims. The escort vessels would wait at the 12.5-degree point for a homeward-bound convoy from Halifax (HX) or Freetown (SL) to arrive for escort to the port.

The convoy was of course tied to the speed of its slowest ship, and would, by the middle of the war, typically be an array of forty to forty-five ships in four columns, separated 1,800 feet laterally and 1,200 feet longitudinally, and covering a five-square-mile area of the sea. It was difficult to maneuver such a mass of ships, particularly with captains inexperienced in convoy operations, and there was a tendency on the part of individual masters either to surge ahead or lag behind (they were called "rompers")—and in doing so, to become prime U-boat targets.

If there were only a few escorts, as was usually the case in the beginning, they would be placed around the convoy to cover front and sides, assuming that even a 9-knot convoy would be faster than a submerged submarine, which thus could not approach from the rear. If there were more escorts, they would cover the rear and the flanks as well.

When war began, the Royal Navy had just over 180 destroyers and sloops on hand, and these had many other duties. Consequently some convoys had only a single warship for protection. As the war progressed, Operations Research specialists discovered that it was advantageous to increase the number of ships in the convoys. As more sloops, corvettes, frigates, destroyer escorts and destroyers became available, the density of the escorts increased and they adopted more aggressive formations.

Despite their numerical successes, initial operations of the U-boats were handicapped by faulty torpedoes, which resulted in a scandal that rocked the German navy. Time after time, U-boat commanders would correctly position their submarines, take careful aim and fire torpedoes that failed more often than not. The torpedo malfunctions were many and varied. Some, like premature explosions or circling, were hazardous to the U-boat. Others, which included broaching the surface and drifting off the aimed course line, were wasteful, and left a track to the submarine. The most frustrating faults, however, were an inability to maintain a correct depth and a failure to detonate, either on contact or by magnetic pistol. This was agony; to be reproached subsequently by naval headquarters for poor performance was an insult.

Very early in the war German U-boats suffered two great missed opportunities because of defective torpedoes. The first was the attack by *U-39* on the *Ark Royal* on September 14, 1939. Guided by Lieutenant Gerhard Glattes to within the point-blank range of 2,400 feet, the *U-39* sent two Type G7a compressed-air-driven torpedoes against the carrier, only to have both explode prematurely. The *Ark Royal*'s escorts, including the *Foxhound*, followed the trail of bubbles back, saw the submarine clearly, and depth-charged *U-39* to the surface, where its crew was captured. *U-39* sank, to become the first and perhaps the most important U-boat loss. If her torpedoes had worked and sunk the *Ark Royal*, the *U-39* might have changed the course of later events, including the loss of the *Bismarck*.

A little more than a month later, the *U-56*, under the command of Lieutenant Wilhelm Zahn, sent three torpedoes against the battleship *Nelson*, which had on board Winston Churchill, Admiral Sir Charles Forbes, Commander-in-Chief of the Home Fleet, and the First Sea Lord, Admiral Sir Dudley Pound. Zahn's torpedoes did not explode prematurely. Two did not explode at all, merely striking the side of the *Nelson* with a metallic thunk that registered on the *U-56*'s listening devices; the third exploded harmlessly at the end of its run.

The greatest failure of the German torpedoes, however, came during the Norwegian campaign, rendering the U-boat arm virtually impotent in fruitless attacks on many British warships. With fully effective torpedoes, hits would have been scored on a battleship, seven cruisers, seven destroyers and five transports—the resulting carnage would have done much to save the German navy from being mauled.

Eventually, the U-boat commanders' fury forced an investigation, in which it was found that the German Torpedo Inspectorate, which was responsible for testing torpedoes, had conducted only *two* tests on the engineering change designed to correct the depth-regulating mechanism and that neither of these tests had been totally satisfactory—German torpedoes had in fact never been officially cleared for military service!

Development of the magnetically operated detonating device (magnetic pistol) had started in 1915. It was designed to be detonated by a ship's magnetic field as the torpedo passed a few yards beneath the keel of the target; the resultant explosion directed upward caused much more damage than a conventional strike on the side of a ship. (Later German analysis of a six-month period in 1942 showed that it took 806 torpedo hits to sink 404 ships, whereas with a properly operating magnetic pistol, one hit per target would have sufficed.) Further research revealed that both magnetic and contact pistols were failure prone. Anything but a head-on impact caused the contact pistol to fail; a glancing blow rendered it useless. The Torpedo Inspectorate had ignored complaints from the field that began in Spain in 1937; it responded to continuing complaints from destroyer and torpedo boat crews through 1939 and 1940 by blithely contending that there must be something wrong with the crews using them—the torpedoes could not be to blame.

The result of the investigation was an immediate shake-up with the responsible people being court-martialed. Ultimately, only two high-ranking officers were sentenced to six months in jail, comparatively light punishment in the draconian Third Reich, and an indication to some observers that the trial was a cover-up. (The U.S. Navy had almost identical problems for almost identical reasons; the corrective actions taken were similar, but no one went on trial.)

Had it not been for the faulty torpedoes, the U-boats, despite their pitifully small numbers, would have wrought even greater damage during the first ten months of the war, especially in view of the totally unexpected opportunity provided by the blitzkrieg's successes in Europe in the spring of 1940. Raeder had pressed for bases in Norway from which to operate submarines; by June 1940, he had Norway and the entire western coastline of

Europe down to a friendly Spain, 3,000 miles of access to the Atlantic, compared to the 300 miles that the Kaiser's navy enjoyed in World War I.

The first German navy contingents traveled from Wilhelmshaven through Paris to the French Atlantic coast in June 1940, the first submarine, Lemp's *U-30*, arriving on July 5. French bases were an unbelievable windfall that effectively doubled the number of submarines Doenitz had on hand because it reduced by half their time spent going to and from operational areas. (And, in contrast, added 30 to 40 percent to the distance British convoys had to travel to reach a safe port.)

Good Hunting From French Ports

Even though the opéra bouffe preparations for Operation Sea Lion (the invasion of England) diluted Doenitz's strength, he immediately addressed his new opportunities with a prudent enthusiasm. To maximize the effect of the limited numbers of submarines he had, Doenitz decided to husband his forces periodically by keeping just a few boats at sea, then fielding as many as possible to score a big victory over a convoy. He was convinced that his *Rudeltaktik* (wolf pack tactics), extensively developed in 1918 and practiced in training exercises to a limited degree in the years between the wars, would be successful. The key to his operations was the vastly improved radio communications system, which permitted him personally to direct the operations of each individual submarine from his headquarters.

In addition, Doenitz had finally succeeded in persuading Admiral Raeder and Hitler to increase the U-boat building program substantially. He also kept many of his boats in the Baltic training crews rather than on patrol. Despite his slender resources, Doenitz enjoyed a success out of all proportion to the assets at his disposal.

In the German view, submarine warfare was a matter of addition and subtraction, with the emphasis on subtraction. Britain had begun the war with approximately 2,000 merchant ships (not counting about 1,000 coastal vessels) with a combined capacity of about 21 million tons; to this could be added the three million tons of shipping seized from countries occupied by Germany and by a projected 1.2 million tons in new construction annually.

Britain normally required 55 million tons of imports each year to feed her people and keep her factories running; of this, 15 million tons was food: fresh meat, grain, produce. With true British pluck, these needs were sharply reduced. (An odd side effect was that the health of many British citizens improved over the war because shortages forced them to eat a better balanced diet than had been their custom.)

Admiral Doenitz knew how close Germany's U-boat fleet had come to defeating England in World War I. He determined on a "tonnage war" in which the goal was to sink the maximum number of tons of shipping, wherever and whenever they could be found. He wished to sink ships faster than Britain could build them, and thus strangle British imports.

The tonnage policy permitted Admiral Doenitz to move his ships to the areas where the hunting was rich and the defenses light. Just as he had set a goal of 300 operational submarines as the necessary size of his force, he now set a goal of 800,000 tons of shipping per month as the key to victory. He believed, and preached, that if German U-boats could sink shipping at that average rate, 9.6 million tons annually, Britain would be brought to her knees.

Up to June 1940 Germany had sunk 701 ships, for 2,335,847 tons, an average of 233,548 tons per month, or about 29 percent of the magic 800,000-ton goal. June had been the biggest month, for the flurry of activity involved in first supplying embattled France, and then evacuating the troops from Dunkirk had drawn off escort vessels and provided both submarines and airplanes with a plethora of targets. One hundred forty ships were sunk, for 585,496 tons, a figure that would not be surpassed until April 1941.

As 1940 passed, the sinkings from all causes rose to a new level: 719 ships sunk for a total of 2.4 million tons. The U-boat commanders continued to concentrate on ships sailing individually—convoys were too risky—and preferred working in the mid-Atlantic, beyond the range of land-based aircraft.

Hermann Goering, intoxicated by the Luftwaffe's successes in Poland, Norway, the Low Countries and France, was pleased with its performance against English shipping as well. During May 1940, attacking small ships averaging only 3,200 tons, his planes sank more than 158,000 tons—forty-eight ships. During the same period, Doenitz's U-boats were able to sink only thirteen ships, totaling about 56,000 tons. From his position of strength, Goering bitterly opposed cooperation with Doenitz, and only grudgingly allocated aircraft to Battle Group (really a bomber group) 40 to do reconnaissance for the U-boat arm.

KG 40 was sparingly equipped with the Focke-Wulf FW 200 Condor, a four-engine civilian airliner converted to military service as a reconnaissance bomber. (It would be more than six months until Hitler himself ordered the transfer of these aircraft to naval control, doing so while Goering was absent on a hunting trip.) The few that were available proved deadly in the extreme, performing so well that Churchill referred to the Condor as the "Scourge of the Atlantic."

There were occasional moments of cooperation between the Luftwaffe and the U-waffe. On October 26, 1940, a Condor caught the luxury liner *Empress of Britain* (42,348 tons) northwest of Donegal Bay, Ireland, hitting her with two bombs and causing a fire that soon swept from bow to stern. Excellent damage-control work put out the fire, and the ship was taken under tow. The FW 200 had reported the position of the vessel to Doenitz, who sent First Lieutenant Hans Jenisch in *U-32*. Jenisch sank the *Empress of Britain* on October 28 with two torpedoes. (Two days later, *U-32*, a type VII A boat, was sunk in turn by the British destroyers *Harvester* and *Highlander;* Jenisch was taken prisoner.)

Over both the short and the long run, however, Doenitz never received the degree of aerial support he required, and that could have been provided him. In a grievously poor application of resources, Goering's bombers were instead employed in the indiscriminate bombing of British cities, a task that brought few rewards and much revenge.

The submarine sinkings were considerably augmented by mines laid in shipping lanes by German submarines, destroyers, surface raiders and aircraft. By December 1940, 1,280 ships totaling 4,746,878 tons had been sunk worldwide. In the North Atlantic, 398 ships totaling 2,054,689 tons had been sunk. Thirty-two U-boats were lost in the same period.

The worldwide average was 296,670 tons, only 37 percent of the total Doenitz deemed necessary to win the war. Yet Admiral Doenitz was not displeased, and would have disagreed strongly with Winston Churchill's later assertion that "Nothing of major importance occurred in the first year of the U-boat warfare." Doenitz was aware that his average number of ships on station had been pathetically small, and that this would change for the better. He knew that the torpedo problem had been substantially corrected. And he knew that his wolf pack tactics would succeed.

THE FIRST HAPPY TIME: JULY TO OCTOBER 1940

Every nation at war is hungry for heroes, and the U-boat arm was able to supply many—some, sadly for them, only for a brief period. Guenther Prien, having seized headlines at Scapa Flow, maintained them with a series of sinkings that were trumpeted by Goebbels's propaganda agency. Others who surged to the fore included Lieutenant Commander Otto Kretschmer, who commanded the *U-23* and then *U-99*, and was the top-scoring U-boat ace of the war, with 266,629 tons and forty-four ships sunk in only eighteen months; Lieutenant Commander Englebert Endrass, Prien's first watch officer and then commander of *U-46;* and Lieutenant Commander Joachim Schepke (*U-3*, *U-19*, and *U-100*), who had earned the Oak Leaves to the Knight's Cross when he was killed on March 17, 1941.

In a period when there was only a monthly average of twelve U-boats at sea (compared to an average of forty-five during a peak period in 1917), these captains and their colleagues attacked both convoys and merchant vessels sailing independently, to sink 217 ships, totaling more than one million tons. Only six U-boats were lost, providing a basis for a new statistic used by Doenitz: the exchange rate, which began at an encouraging 217 to 6, or 36 to 1.

The peak period of the first "Happy Time" came with the introduction of wolf pack tactics on two convoys. The first of these, SC-7, sailing from Sydney to Liverpool in October 1940, consisted of thirty ships traveling at 7 knots—four stragglers had already been attacked, and three sunk. For the first eleven days, the convoy was escorted only by the 1,000-ton sloop *Scarborough;* bad weather and U-boats had already cost three more ships. Later, four additional warships, the sloops *Fowey* and *Leith* and the corvettes *Heartease* and *Bluebell,* joined as escorts. These were scarcely enough as U-boats, capable when surfaced of twice the convoy's speed, began to gather. The *U-48* (Lieutenant Commander Guenther Kuhnke) picked off two ships but was driven off by a Short Sunderland flying boat, the famous "flying porcupine," so called for its formidable defensive armament.

U-48 reported the convoy's position, and, following the *Rudeltaktik*, a patrol line consisting of the *U-46*, *U-99*, *U-100*, *U-101* and *U-123* positioned across the oncoming convoy's path. On the night of October 18, 1940, the wolves worked on the surface, close to the convoy, rendering the vaunted Asdic useless. With a calm sea and targets soon well illuminated by flames, the U-boats attacked in turn, some coming back for a second shot. In the midst of the convoy they found targets all around them, and fired bow and stern tubes in rapid succession at the hapless ships, whose thin skins and volatile cargoes rendered them so vulnerable. Before morning, sixteen ships were sunk, and the rest scattered to be picked off by single hunters. In the *U-99* Kretschmer, firing torpedoes with the assurance of a pool hall hustler,

sank six ships of 28,066 tons and damaged another. In the *U-101*, Lieutenant Commander Fritz Frauenheim sank three ships of 10,650 tons and
torpedoed two more. The *U-99*, *U-100* and *U-123*, with all torpedoes gone,
departed for home, while the remaining boats, supported by *U-28* and *U-38*,
took up station nearby, 250 miles northwest of Ireland. Convoy SC-7 had
lost twenty-one ships of 79,592 tons.

The U-boats did not have long to wait. The *U-47* had located HX-79,
consisting of forty-nine ships moving at better than 9 knots—a fast convoy.
HX-79 was heavily escorted, with the destroyers *Whitehall* and *Sturdy*, four
"Flower"-class corvettes—*Hibiscus*, *Heliotrope*, *Coreopsis* and *Arabis*—a
minesweeper, three antisubmarine trawlers and the Dutch submarine *O-21*.

With Kretschmer absent, Guenther Prien, the Bull of Scapa Flow, now
commanded the wolf pack, subject always to the flood of directions stream-
ing directly from Admiral Doenitz's headquarters in Lorient, France. The
U-boats attacked in the evening on October 19, repeating the previous
night's success, and finding more targets when the seven-ship convoy H-
79A came into range.

Short on fuel, and exhausted by the stalking, the submarines fired all
of their torpedoes and sank twelve ships for another 75,069 tons.

At his battle headquarters, Doenitz followed the course of the battle,
delighted as he saw his *Rudeltaktik* validated in combat. Thirty-three ships
sunk in two nights, 155,000 tons of shipping gone—and no submarines lost.
It was indeed a happy time for the submariners. Doenitz knew the British
viewed such a convoy loss as even worse than a defeat in a major land battle, for it was a defeat in their own element, the sea.

For the men of the merchant marine, it was a sustained horror; defenseless on tiny ships that were barely able to contend with the wild North
Atlantic, they were exposed to predatory attacks that their escorts were too
inexperienced to repel. The explosions were so violent that many sailors
went down with their ships, unable to scuttle through the gangways and up
the ladders to the pitching deck. Those that made it over the side were little better off, risking a dive into oil-slicked and often burning waters, trying
to avoid the thrashing propellers and the undertow, only to find themselves
swiftly going numb in the freezing waters. Immersion for more than fifteen
minutes meant unconsciousness, for thirty minutes, death. If there had
been time to get some boats and rafts away, or if the drowning ship spat
back wreckage that could be climbed upon, they then had to wait for the attack to finish. Their fellow ships were not allowed to stop to pick up survivors, and only the bravest or most experienced escorts would do so while

the attack was going on. When a fortunate few were saved, they were brought to port to be crewed up for another voyage—and often, another sinking. Ironically, it took decades before the U.S. and British governments recognized the merchant marine sailors as veterans, entitled to the benefits given military members for their war service (even though the merchant marine sailors had received higher pay at the time).

The Happy Time surge meant that more boats had to come back for replenishment, and the average number at sea declined, reaching a low point of eight in January 1941. Then the numbers began to rise as new production and newly trained crews began to flow together. By March, the average number of boats on station had risen to thirteen, shooting up steadily to thirty-two in June. It fell off to twenty-seven in July, then rose to a new high of thirty-eight in November before dropping back to twenty-five in the rotten weather of December 1941. The total strength of the U-boat arm had stayed just about the same, as losses in 1941 (thirty-one) equaled new construction.

In 1941, the shipping losses correlated with the increase in the number of submarines only through June, by which time 480 ships totaling 2,884,307 tons had been sunk. The numbers fell off drastically in July, with forty-three ships and 120,975 tons sunk worldwide. In the North Atlantic, only twenty-three ships were sunk for 98,000 tons. It was the first sign that British countermeasures were becoming more effective.

The sea change had earlier been signaled with ferocity by the Royal Navy, which was improving both in numbers and expertise. Four U-boats (*U-37*, *U-49*, *U-70* and *U-99*) had been assigned to attack convoy OB-293. On the night of March 7, Commander Prien in *U-47* was surprised by the destroyer *Wolverine* and sunk with depth charges. The Germans made no mention of Prien's death for weeks. Hitler was afraid of the adverse affect upon morale, and decided not to reveal the U-boat hero's death until it could be paired with some exceptionally good news from the U-boat war.

More bad news followed a week later when five U-boats (*U-37*, *U-74*, *U-99*, *U-100* and *U-110*) and six Italian submarines (*Velella*, *Brin*, *Argo*, *Mocenigo*, *Emo* and *Veniero*) ambushed the homeward-bound forty-one-ship convoy HX-112. (The German and Italian submarine forces did not work well together, and the latter were subsequently assigned their own, less crucial operational areas; eighty-six Italian submarines were sunk during the war, twenty-one of them in the Atlantic.)

It was bad luck for the wolf pack that the convoy's escort group was commanded by the redoubtable Commander (later Captain) Donald Macintyre, who earned three Distinguished Service Orders and one Distinguished Service Cross in becoming one of the finest escort commanders in the Atlantic. A versatile man, Macintyre was also a naval pilot and after the war became a distinguished historian. His newly formed 5th Escort Group had five destroyers and two corvettes, and his excellent use of the group was a portent for the future.

The submarines made contact with convoy HX-112 on March 15, but the escorts kept the submarines at bay until the following night, when the ace Kretschmer slipped within the convoy and in rapid succession sank three tankers and two cargo ships totaling 34,505 tons. As Kretschmer departed the area, Lieutenant Commander Joachim Schepke glided in with the *U-100*. The radar operator on the destroyer *Vanoc* suddenly saw a contact on her starboard side, only a half mile away—the *U-100* surfacing, the first successful location by the new Type 286 radar. Without a moment's hesitation, *Vanoc* rammed the *U-100*, crushing Schepke against his conning tower; only six of his men survived.

(The Type 286 was considered to be "better than no radar at all," but it was not until the ten-centimeter Type 281 came into general use that surface ships had a decisive advantage against a surfaced U-boat at night or in bad weather.)

Even as the *Vanoc* picked up *U-100* survivors, Kretschmer's *U-99* was next located by the Asdic of Macintyre's ship, the destroyer *Walker,* which attacked with six depth charges. (Coincidentally, the leading British antisubmarine ace was Captain F. J. Walker, whose 2nd Escort Group sank twenty submarines.) Badly damaged, the *U-99* was forced to surface. Before it sank, its crew members leaped overboard, swimming to reach the nets the *Walker* had dropped alongside. Among them was the catch of the year, Captain Otto Kretschmer, the U-waffe's leading ace. It meant four years in a prisoner-of-war camp for him, but it also probably meant life, for he would have continued as a U-boat commander until he was killed. (Kretschmer's brother, Hans, had been killed on a reconnaissance flight over Scapa Flow to check on the results of Prien's mission there.) After the war, Kretschmer rose to the rank of admiral in the West German navy. He had much for which to thank the *Walker*'s crew. In postwar reminiscences, some of the *Walker*'s crew members saw symbolism in the fact that the *U-99* had as its *Abzeichen*, or good-luck charm, a horseshoe with its ends pointed down. The *Walker*'s insignia was a horseshoe with the ends pointed up—so its luck would not run out.

In addition to the improved British defenses, Admiral Doenitz found political events conspiring against him as the United States became ever more overt in its support of Britain.

ALL AID SHORT OF WAR

President Roosevelt's first step in preparing the United States for war had been in 1937, when he saw to yet another "neutrality law" being passed, this time permitting the sale of munitions on a "cash and carry" basis. Inasmuch as only Britain and France had the cash or the ships in which to carry, it was a clear rebuff to Germany—one that Hitler noted but ignored.

Roosevelt was more forthcoming in his January 4, 1939, State of the Union Address, in which he expressed concern about the encouragement the current neutrality legislation provided "aggressor" nations, and for the first time used the phrase "short of war" to describe methods to help the democracies. After war broke out on September 1, 1939, he issued a proclamation of a Neutrality Zone as an extension of the Monroe Doctrine, warning belligerent ships to stay at least 300 miles away from countries in the Western Hemisphere, with the exception of Canada and European colonies. The effect of this was to channel German warships into areas where the hard-pressed British and Canadian forces could more easily cope with them.

Britain and France were already short of hard currency, even as their respective purchasing commissions sought to buy up aircraft and munitions of every kind. Although there was opposition in Congress from isolationists like Senators Burton K. Wheeler, William Borah and Gerald Nye, the U.S. military forces welcomed the Allied purchases, for they expanded the American industrial base. As war became more probable, this attitude soon changed, however, for the U.S. armed services were desperately short of matériel of every kind.

Roosevelt's personal political predilections were reinforced even before the German invasion of France on May 10, 1940, by the assiduous courtship of that master of emotion, Winston Churchill. Nonetheless, Roosevelt clearly saw where the United States's interests lay, and when Great Britain was at its nadir after the defeat of France, he openly questioned its ability to continue. Churchill rallied to overcome his doubts, showing his determination at Mers-el-Kebir, and using his charm and diplomatic genius to bring Roosevelt to his side, step by step.

Roosevelt demonstrated just how serious the world political situation was in June 1940 by signing a $4 billion "Two-Ocean Navy" bill, authorizing the U.S. Navy to double its tonnage to 2,500,000. It was perhaps the most important prewar legislation, for it laid the foundations for victory in both the Atlantic and the Pacific. Then, on June 19, 1940, Roosevelt lent credence to his policies by creating a "War Cabinet" that included two Republicans. "Colonel" Frank Knox became Secretary of the Navy, and former President Hoover's Secretary of State, Colonel Henry L. Stimson, became Secretary of War, a post he had earlier filled for the Taft administration. Neither man dissembled: both believed war with Germany was coming and that the United States had better prepare for it.

His new Republican appointees and the massive ship-building program gave Roosevelt the leverage to turn necessity into opportunity by forging an agreement with Churchill under which fifty "overage" destroyers and ten Coast Guard cutters were transferred to the Royal Navy—clearly an act of war from the point of view of the Axis. In exchange, Great Britain ceded ninety-nine-year leases on sites for military, air, and naval bases in the West Indies, and gave the United States bases in Newfoundland and Bermuda as gifts. It was such an obviously good horsetrade for the United States that even isolationist legislators could not cavil.

Obtaining the destroyers was both a diplomatic and a military triumph for Churchill, for the savage fighting in Norway, at Dunkirk, and around the rest of the world had depleted Britain's destroyer strength; she had fewer than eighty available for service in the spring of 1940 and her situation had worsened with the fall of France.

Any residual American opposition to this deal was swamped on September 27, 1940, when Japan joined the Axis by signing the Tripartite Pact. Japan was America's "natural enemy," and her alignment with the Axis diminished the little sympathy remaining for Germany.

The pot for war was boiling, as was Hitler, who had to endure these increasingly bellicose acts because, by any measure, the United States "short of war" was preferable to the United States at war. It was a matter of timing; he did not wish to fight the United States until he had settled with the Soviet Union and Britain.

The next step was far more important and ultimately decided Hitler's fate: the Lend-Lease agreement of March 11, 1941, which Winston Churchill described to Parliament as "the most unsordid act in the history of any nation." The Lend-Lease Act committed the United States to total economic support for England in her war against Germany, an about-face from the isolationist policies of the preceding twenty years, and one that convinced Republican opponents that Roosevelt was hell-bent for war. The agreement would have profound effects upon World War II and in the decades following it, for while it was originally intended solely to sustain Great Britain, it was extended to the Soviet Union after the German invasion of June 22, 1941. The die-hard anticommunists in the U.S. Congress suddenly found themselves supporting the Bolshevik cause. Thus are the ways of politics.

5.

THE TIDE BEGINS
TO TURN

1941: DISAPPOINTMENT FOR DOENITZ

The Lend-Lease Act was signed only four days after Prien's *U-47* had been sunk and five days before Schepke was killed and Kretschmer captured. Admiral Doenitz, preoccupied with a sudden rise in the U-boat loss rate, which approached 20 percent, probably did not recognize Lend-Lease's full import at the time. He was instead concentrating on maximizing the "yield" of his U-boats by assigning them 200 miles farther to the west, away from the increasingly vigorous British antisubmarine efforts.

From Doenitz's point of view, attacking where he could gain the most sinkings at the least cost in U-boats made obvious sense. It served him ill, however, by masking the rising tide of Allied defenses. Although his original tactics seemed to pay off (and they did handsomely, for another two years), they were not adequate to meet the combined onslaught of four new elements that were gradually introduced by the Allies as their technology improved. These included:

1. An increasing number of superior ship and aircraft radars.

2. An increase in the numbers of very long range aircraft.

3. A growing proficiency of the escort groups.

4. The increased efficiency of HF/DF (Huff-Duff) radio detection, which plotted the transmissions required by Doenitz's method of central control, and turned them against him.

These were the primary elements; each was augmented by an amazing proliferation of devices, weapons and techniques that, in concert with the intelligence-gathering breakthroughs, eventually overwhelmed the U-waffe. In effect, Doenitz's successes, which reached crisis proportions in 1942 and 1943, were done on the cheap by moving from soft spot to soft spot. German effort was concentrated on increasing the number of its submarines, and less emphasis was placed on technology. In contrast, the Allied emphasis on technology meant that in a matter of time superior enemy weaponry would be available everywhere, and there would be no more soft spots.

Germany's blindness to the importance of the technological war was an anomaly for a country noted for its scientific and engineering achievement. The basic capability was there, but the autocratic state was the wrong environment for the widespread experiments that had to be conducted to arrive at a fruitful course of action. In both the United States and Great Britain, the best scientific minds were recruited and given not only autonomy for the development of their seemingly arcane projects, but were also subsequently sometimes given *authority* over their military counterparts! The authority derived through military channels, but nonetheless it was both unmistakable and well exercised.

The German difficulties were compounded by an inability to discipline themselves to select from an array of opportunities and ruthlessly pursue the most promising. Admiral Doenitz was certainly not alone in this; Reich Marshal Goering was both too lazy and intellectually incapable of appreciating advanced technology, and Hitler, in his one-man-band role as Head of State, Commander-in-Chief of the Armed Services and Commander-in-Chief of the Army (and occasionally, of individual units down to battalions), was distrustful of the claims made by his technocrats. As a result, German technology lagged throughout the war until it was apparent in mid-1943 that the odds against Germany had grown so great that only miraculous technological breakthroughs could save her. Some remarkable advances were indeed made, but they came too little and too late.

A significant event passed unnoticed on May 27, 1941, when convoy HC-129 became the first to be escorted all the way across the Atlantic. Doenitz's own figures told him that since the beginning of the war only 10 percent of U-boat successes had been achieved against convoys, while 60 percent of U-boat losses had occurred attacking them. He failed to make the necessary inference that if *all* shipping were to be convoyed, and *all* convoys escorted for their entire route, the U-Waffe would be rendered virtually impotent.

The tonnage sunk through June 1941 had been marginally satisfactory: 1.8 million tons in the North Atlantic, of 2.9 million tons worldwide. A straight-line projection would indicate 3.6 million tons for the year in the North Atlantic and 5.6 million tons worldwide. The latter represented 58 percent of the desired goal of 800,000 tons per month, and was not bad given the number of U-boats available. Had the trend continued, the additional submarines joining the fleet could reasonably have expected to exceed the 800,000-tons-per-month goal by a decisive margin.

But German U-boat sinkings would drop drastically in the following six months. Only 151 ships, totaling 621,510 tons, were sunk in the North Atlantic, at a cost of twenty-three U-boats. This represented a yield of only 6.5 to 1, compared to 26.5 in the first six months. Suffering a defeat, Doenitz suspected that it was due to Allied intelligence, and demanded assurance that the German naval Enigma machine was not in fact compromised. He was assured that it was not, and could not be, just as Hitler had been assured so many times. Neither man ever learned how well and fully Enigma had been compromised. Information gained by Enigma decryption was code-named Ultra by the Allies, and was jealously guarded and prudently used.

THE INTELLIGENCE WARS

Nowhere were there less likely warriors than the coterie of Cambridge mathematicians and scientists at the Government Code and Cipher School at Bletchley Park, fifty miles north of London. Their opposite numbers in Doenitz's Naval Intelligence sections were far more military. Nonetheless, the two teams waged an unending war against each other, with the Germans doing much better than they are generally given credit for. The British were seriously overmanned; Bletchley Park employed as many as 10,000 people at one point, and was the major British organization devoted to solving the German ciphers. The Germans had at least seven units working in cryptanalysis, with far fewer total personnel. With the Fuehrer's rigid instructions on the need-to-know basis of security, cooperation was difficult.

Two of the men most responsible for the attack on Pearl Harbor laying a wreath at the Tomb of the Unknown Soldier at the Arlington National Cemetery in 1927. Vice Admiral Nagano Osami is presenting the wreath; at his extreme left is young Captain Yamamoto Isoruku. Nagano's insistence on a preemptive attack on the United States at Pearl Harbor, and Yamamoto's masterly planning, plunged Japan into an unwinnable war, creating many more fallen unknown soldiers and sailors.

In late May of 1938, the battle cruiser HMS *Hood* exemplified the Royal Navy at its finest; painted in a light gray, immaculately maintained, the *Hood* was widely regarded as the most powerful ship in existence. Ironically, its very reputation denied it the necessary modifications that might have saved it in battle.

San Pedro, California, 1938. It was scenes of great ships like the *Arizona* in the foreground and the *Mississippi* and *New Mexico* in the background that inspired many a young lad from a Kansas farm or a Pennsylvania mine to run away and join the navy to see the world. Some still serve, forever locked within the hulk of the *Arizona*, now a monument in Pearl Harbor.

Life was good aboard spit-and-polish cruisers like the *Astoria* and the *Indianapolis* before the war. The *Astoria* (center) was lost in the 1942 Battle of Savo Island debacle; the gorgeous Curtiss Seagull biplanes—unused in the battle—turned out to be a liability when Japanese shells turned them into torches. In 1945, the *Indianapolis* (left), after delivering the essential components of the atomic bomb to Tinian, was sunk by the Japanese sub *I-58*, with a tragic loss of life.

The USS *Ward*, many rivets yet undriven, just days before its launch on June 1, 1918; as the sign indicates, the keel had been laid only 14 days earlier. The destroyer *Ward* sank no German U-boats in World War I, but did fire the opening shot of U.S. involvement in World War II, when it shelled, depth-charged and sank a Japanese midget submarine one hour before the Japanese attack on Pearl Harbor on December 7, 1941.

5

6

The last of the so-called pocket battleships, the *Admiral Graf Spee*, had a mildly successful commerce raiding career before being scuttled by her crew off Montevideo on December 17, 1939, in the first great defeat suffered by the German navy in World War II.

The *Graf Spee* was harried to its doom by a British team of cruisers, *Exeter*, *Ajax* and *Achilles*. This, the *Achilles*, had the longest career, transferring to the Royal New Zealand Navy in 1936, returned to the Royal Navy in 1943 and transferred to India in 1948 and renamed the *Delhi*.

Italian battleships, like Italian planes and cars, were notable for their sleek beauty. This is the *Vittorio Veneto* at anchor in 1940; she was to have a very busy war, undertaking fifty-six missions, and being heavily damaged in several engagements. The *Vittorio Veneto* was surrendered with the bulk of the Italian fleet on September 11, 1943; after the war she was returned to Italy and broken up for scrap.

Not yet complete in December 1940, the mighty *Bismarck* points its handsome flared clipper bow up the Elbe to complete work at the Blohm and Voss shipyards. The *Bismarck*'s naval career would be short and tempestuous.

Called "The Rube," the *Reuben James*'s name can be traced back to the battles with the Barbary pirates. The proud old four-stacker became instantly world-famous on October 31, 1941, when, guarding a British convoy, she was torpedoed by a German U-boat and became the first U.S. warship lost in World War II.

The cruiser *Indianapolis*, sailing with President Franklin D. Roosevelt on board. Roosevelt was a navy man through and through, and was never happier than when on shipboard; his perseverance in establishing the funding for a "Two-Ocean Navy" in 1940 was a fundamental factor in the victories that ensued after 1943.

A post-strike photo of one of the most important naval air attacks of World War II, the British Fleet Air Arm raid by Fairey Swordfish torpedo planes on the Italian fleet in the harbor at Taranto on the night of November 11–12, 1940. Two damaged cruisers of the *Trento* class are shown here amidst the oil slicks and debris from other ships. The success of the raid had an impact on Japanese thinking and was emulated in the attack on Pearl Harbor.

A Japanese Type A midget submarine, one of five released from *I*-class submarines in the Pearl Harbor attack, and similar to the one sunk by the *Ward*. Technically not suicide weapons, they were nonetheless murderous to their crews; of the ten Japanese crewmen involved in the attack, only one survived.

A Japanese aircrewman took this shot of Ford Island during the Pearl Harbor attack at about 0800 on December 7, 1941. A torpedo is shown striking the USS *West Virginia* (center), and smoke is rising from the USS *Curtiss* in the lower left. In the background are the crucial fuel storage tanks that the Japanese fortunately ignored.

A famous photo showing the enormous destruction caused by Japanese bombing and strafing at Pearl Harbor.

One of the great unsung heroes of the war, Captain Joseph J. Rochefort, in a photo taken in 1943. Rochefort was a genius whose intuitive understanding of cryptanalysis gave the United States an inestimable advantage in deciphering Japanese codes.

Grand Admiral Karl Doenitz ran the German U-boat fleet with an iron hand. Despite an inadequate number of vessels and faulty torpedoes, his submarines came close to winning the Battle of the Atlantic. Despite his dour appearance, Doenitz had charisma, and he imparted the force of his personality to all of his subordinates, officers and men. He tried to meet every returning U-boat personally.

Admiral Doenitz might have had the number of submarines he required if Germany had not persisted in building large capital ships like the *Gneisenau*, shown here during its famous run up the English Channel on February 11, 1942. Her end was ignominious; disarmed by Hitler's orders in February 1943, she remained a useless hulk until March 23, 1945, when she was sunk as a block ship.

18

19

The first of a new class of ships, the Royal Navy's *King George V* might not have been the handsomest ship afloat, but it was rugged and capable; during the war it would gain more and more antiaircraft firepower, as the battleship's role changed from ship-of-the-line conflict to support of aircraft carriers. Here it sails as the flagship of the British task force in the Western Pacific, on March 30, 1945.

The French built beautiful ships, and it was agony for the French navy to lose them to the Germans. There was worse to come, for the remnants of the French navy would be savaged first by the Royal Navy and then by the U.S. Navy as the war was brought to Africa. This is the battleship *Jean Bart*, showing damage received from the November 8, 1942, Allied attack during Operation Torch.

An impossible scene before the war, but simple expedience during Operation Torch. Army Air Force Curtiss P-40s launched from a navy escort carrier on November 8, 1942. They did not return to land aboard, but went on to bases already seized in the Allied invasion.

22

The *Prinz Eugen* was to bear a charmed life, surviving all the rigors of World War II without loss of its crew and ending its days as a target for atomic tests at Bikini. The dark camouflage paint on the bow is intended to foreshorten the ship; note the false bow wave aft. This deception may have worked in the engagement with the *Hood*, which took the *Prinz Eugen* under fire first, rather than the more dangerous *Bismarck*.

23

The utter misery of winter sea duty is evident, as sailors hammer away at the ice that covers the destroyer, now safe in port. Life on board the smaller ships was especially hard, with ice forming not only outside but inside the living spaces.

24

A little more than a year old, the valiant *Hornet*, which carried James Doolittle's B-25s on their raid on Japan, lists after an attack by Japanese planes in the Battle of Santa Cruz, October 26, 1942. Her death agony was prolonged; it took four bomb hits and sixteen torpedoes, from both Japanese and U.S. vessels, before she finally sank.

25

The famous USS *Wasp* burns fiercely after the Japanese attack off San Cristobal Island in the Solomons on September 15, 1942. The *Wasp* had inadequate antitorpedo protection, and her thousands of gallons of aviation fuel stored on board made her (like all carriers) virtually a floating bomb. Three torpedoes fired by the Japanese submarine *I-15* ignited uncontrollable fires that caused her to be abandoned. She did not sink immediately, however, and the U.S. destroyer *Lansdowne* had to finish her off with torpedoes.

26

The gallant cruiser *San Francisco*, as beautiful as her namesake city, survived massive damage meted out on the night of November 12–13, 1942. Hit first by a torpedo-bomber that crashed into her after control stations, she took forty-five hits, two of them from the 14-inch guns of a Japanese battle cruiser. Fortunately, all airplanes and other flammables had been removed, and no massive fire ensued.

27

The British-built Japanese battleship *Kongo*, which decimated Guadalcanal's Henderson Field with its firepower, succumbed to an attack by the U.S. submarine *Sealion II*, sinking off Formosa on November 21, 1944. Japanese ships were built with scant consideration for crew comfort or safety.

28

The *Essex*, first of a new class of carriers that, in early 1943, began to turn the Pacific war in favor of the United States. Shown here at sea on May 20, 1945, during the Okinawa campaign, she carries both Grumman F6F Hellcats and Vought F4U Corsairs.

29

The "Big E," the mighty *Enterprise*, distinguished herself at Midway. Although her Douglas Devastator torpedo bombers suffered disaster at the hands of Japanese fighters and flak, her Douglas Dauntless dive-bombers attacked the enemy carriers and reversed the trend of the war.

The U.S. submarine fleet was hugely successful, sinking the Japanese merchant marine and cutting off the home islands from food and water and matériel. This is the USS *Barb*, winner of many Presidential and Navy Unit Citations, as well as victor over seventeen Japanese ships of 96,628 tons in its fifteen-month wartime career.

Vice Admiral Charles A. Lockwood, just presented the Legion of Merit on February 25, 1944, was the Commander Submarine Force, Pacific Fleet. He was beloved by the crewmen, for he battled the bureaucracy as hard as he did the enemy. He was a true submariner, and his wise, aggressive handling of U.S. submarines made him one of the war's great commanders.

32

HMS *Warspite*—a true fighting ship. The *Warspite* took hits at Jutland in World War I, but survived to smash German destroyers at Narvik; damage the *Giulio Cesare* off the toe of Italy; slug it out in the Battle of Cape Matapan; participate in the surrender of the Italian fleet at Malta, just as it had participated in the surrender of the German fleet at Scapa Flow in 1918; take a guided missile hit off Salerno; bombard Normandy on D-Day; and fight the Japanese in the Pacific. Her reward for thirty years of glorious service was to be broken up by a scrap dealer in 1947.

33

The all-time champion sub-killer, the destroyer escort USS *England*. Captained by Lieutenant Commander Walton B. Pendleton, the *England* killed five Japanese submarines and finished off a sixth between May 19 and May 30, 1944; more importantly, the six submarines were the Japanese scouting line intended to alert Admiral Toyoda about American intentions in the Battle of the Philippine Sea.

As previously noted, the Germans had gained an initial advantage from the decryptions made during the 1935–1936 crisis Italy had precipitated with Ethiopia. By September 1941, the German Horchdienst (Listening Service), was working with the Naval Intelligence Division Beobachtungs-dienst (Observation Service, often called B-Dienst), to gather British signals. The decryption section, xB-Dienst, was reading British signals with some ease; by February 1942, employing 700 people, it was able to interpret as much as 80 percent of radio intelligence on convoy movements. This was an inestimable advantage for Doenitz, one that was maintained through June 1943—a pivotal time in the Battle of the Atlantic, as will be shown.

This spectacular intelligence success—quite unusual in Germany, where the intelligence services were as much at war with each other as with the enemy—made 1942 such a banner year for the submariners that it led to the oft-quoted comment from that most quotable of statesmen, Winston Churchill: "The only thing that ever really frightened me during the war was the U-boat peril."

The Germans staked the security of their radio transmissions on the Enigma machine, which David Kahn describes so expertly in his *Seizing the Enigma*. The standard Engima machine consisted of a keyboard by which the enciphered message was input to the machine, which used a series of electrically connected revolving drums and cable plugs to randomly "scramble" the letters for transmission. The recipient on the other end had a similar machine that permitted him to decipher the letters he received. The Nazis, with their usual hubris, were convinced that the Enigma machines were impossible to compromise even if one were captured.

But few things are impossible when brains and money are applied as lavishly as they were at Bletchley Park, where counter-Engima machines, nicknamed "bombes," were created to unscramble the signals. It became a sheer mechanical wrestling match, the bombes (which ultimately numbered more than sixty) being fed the Enigma signals and mindlessly grinding out the permutations (augmented by captured material and German operator errors) until meaningful messages in German were generated.

(There is a small but growing opinion that in the precomputer mainframe age, the bombes could not have worked as they have been reported to do. If this is true, it follows then that the most important information supposedly gathered by the Bletchley Park system was in fact as Hitler suspected, a leak from within, and that Ultra, then and now, was a cover-up for the espionage.)

The first Luftwaffe Enigma signals were broken in the spring of 1940. Similar success with the German navy's codes eluded Bletchley, and their decryption became even more difficult after November 1941, when the U-waffe began enciphering messages even before they were placed in the Enigma enciphering machine—a double encoding.

The German navy imposed further problems in February 1942, when a fourth rotor was added, multiplying the number of permutations so that decoding seemed, to the Germans, to be a mathematical impossibility, for with only three rotors the number of permutations approached 160 trillion. The additional rotor effectively blacked out Enigma intelligence until December of that year.

Still, on at least two occasions Doenitz suspected that the Enigma ciphering capability was compromised and ordered special investigations. The Communications Service, under Rear Admiral Eberhard Maertens, investigated itself both times, and on the second occasion came back with this answer: "There is no real basis for acute anxiety as regards any compromise of operational security. . . . The more important ciphers do not seem to have been compromised, despite their constant heavy use and occasional loss." In other words: *die Tuenche*, a whitewash.

This nonanswer led Doenitz to presume that the uncanny precision with which British antisubmarine warfare forces were appearing at U-boat rendezvous points resulted from poor security, what Hitler always complained about as "the leak," or high-frequency detection, or simple accident. No one allowed himself to suspect that the enemy was deciphering Enigma, even though the company that had developed the machine had offered it commercially long before the war—and even though the Royal Air Force's encoding machine was derived from the same basic patents!

On the opposite side, the British analysis of German signal traffic regarding the rerouting of convoys revealed in mid-1943 that the Germans were reading English signals, as indeed they were on an almost real-time basis. The codes were changed, and xB-Dienst was unable to penetrate them again.

The intelligence war was hard fought, and although the Allies ultimately held the upper hand, the German cryptanalysts distinguished themselves. It is sometimes held that Ultra was the deciding factor in winning the Battle of the Atlantic; it was not. Rather, it was an extraordinarily important component that orchestrated a vast symphony of technological achievements that would defeat the U-boat. But before this technical symphony was rendered, Doenitz used simpler percussion instruments to play a tune that almost achieved his goal.

PEARL HARBOR AND *PAUKENSCHLAG:*
THE SECOND HAPPY TIME

If the Japanese attack on Pearl Harbor was a surprise, Hitler's incredible decision to declare war on the United States on December 11, 1941, was stupefaction squared. Given the furious American indignation against Japan, it is entirely possible that Roosevelt would have been unable to follow the "Germany first" strategy agreed upon with the British at the March 1941 ABC-1 (American British Conference) meetings had Hitler not indulged himself.

Hitler's action was probably as much relief as pique; the Americans had made life difficult for German submarines by continually extending the areas in which they would cover convoys. The U.S. destroyer *Greer* and *U-652* exchanged the first shots on September 4, 1941, and first blood was drawn when the U.S. destroyer *Kearny* was damaged later that month. American anger flared when the destroyer *Reuben James* was sunk on October 31, 1941, by the redoubtable Lieutenant Commander Erich Topp in *U-552*. (He ultimately sank thirty-four ships totaling 193,684 tons—and survived the war.)

Incredible as it may seem, the United States was even less prepared for antisubmarine warfare in January 1942 than Great Britain had been in September 1939. Part of the problem stemmed from the general lack of American military preparedness, but a major portion must be attributed to one of the seminal figures of the war, Admiral Ernest J. King, who soon became both Commander-in-Chief, U.S. Fleet (COMINCH), and also Chief of Naval Operations (CNO). This was an unprecedented concentration of power, one that enabled King to resist instruction from everyone but President Roosevelt and the Secretary of the Navy.

Admiral King was an extraordinary figure, with a varied background in cruisers, battleships and submarines. He learned to fly at the age of forty-seven, and became captain of the aircraft carrier *Lexington* in June 1930. Later, as Chief of the Bureau of Aeronautics, he was central to the selection of the aircraft with which the navy began World War II. His wide experience made him one of the first to develop the concept of separating the battleships from cruisers and aircraft carriers, knitting the latter two into hard-hitting task forces.

He was a man of powerful and generally unpleasant personality; he disliked and distrusted almost everyone, with the British at the top of his list. His attitude was universally reciprocated by all but the most extreme loyalists on his staff; over time he battled all comers, confident that he alone knew not only what was right but also what was morally correct.

Nonetheless, while full credit must be given King for the masterful way in which he put heart and punch back into the Pacific fleet after Pearl Harbor (the battles of the Coral Sea and Midway were going on at the time of the German U-boat thrust on the East Coast), he nonetheless must bear the responsibility for the total failure to anticipate the German submarine incursion, and for the six long months it took to combat it. Because he had not provided sufficient smaller ships for escort duties, King refused to institute convoys, insisting that a weak convoy was worse than none at all, despite clear evidence from the British that this was not so.

The result was slaughter on a scale that no one could have imagined, least of all the incredulous German submariners, who found the richest, safest hunting of their careers.

OPERATION *PAUKENSCHLAG* — A ROLL OF DRUMS

Doenitz immediately requested that the naval staff allow him to send twelve of his large 1,153-ton Type IX U-boats to strike off the U.S. East Coast. The naval staff refused, allowing only six to go, the rest being required to remain off the Azores. In fact, only five were ready. Doenitz ordered these to positions between the Gulf of the St. Lawrence River and Cape Hatteras, with haughty instructions to sink only vessels over 10,000 tons.

The shipping traffic was so dense in the area that the U-boats were unable to take advantage of all their targets, and seven smaller Type VII boats were called in to supplement them. To stretch the Type VII's limited range, extra fuel was stored in every available spot, including drinking water tanks, trimming tanks and even the compensation tanks, an extraordinarily risky business that doubled the danger of every dive until the fuel was burned off. Various "cruise control" techniques were adapted to extend the range. All of the efforts were worthwhile even though it extended to five weeks the time required to prepare the boats.

The yield was fantastic as the boats moved gradually south along the East Coast, browsing among the shipping like a hungry guest at a banquet buffet. The concept of a blackout was resisted by the American tourist trade, and the tankers sailed down the coastline outlined perfectly by the glimmering lights of cities and the flickering neon of roadhouses. The submarines were guided through the shallow waters by lighthouses and buoys still lit to mark the channels; targets obligingly steered straight courses between the buoys, simplifying the shooting.

The slaughter began with the sinking of the British freighter *Cyclops* on January 12; it was the first of seven to be sunk within a week by Lieutenant Commander Richard Hardegen in *U-123*, a Type IXB boat that would sink a total of thirty-seven ships in her forty-nine months of service.

American antisubmarine warfare lurched into operation, with private yachts, small aircraft and the Civil Air Patrol being employed. By April 1, twenty-three large and forty-two small coast guard cutters, three submarine-chasers, twelve ancient wooden-hulled Eagle boats (built by Ford in 1918) and an assortment of armed trawlers were pressed into the search. Britain lent the United States ten corvettes and twenty-four creaking coal-burning trawlers, while the U.S. Army and Navy Air Forces contributed 170 planes and the first of the blimps. It was hardly sufficient for a danger area that extended from Canada to the Caribbean and beyond.

The first U-boat kill was scored on the night of April 13–14, 1942, when *U-85*, a Type VIIB boat, was sunk by the USS *Roper*, captained by Lieutenant Commander H. W. Howe. The *Roper* was a four-stacker, built in World War I—but one of the first American destroyers to have radar. The *Roper* was steaming south from Norfolk at 18 knots when her radar picked up an object 2,700 yards away. Not wishing to fire on a friendly vessel, Howe closed to 700 yards, then caught the wake of a torpedo passing his port side; offended but undaunted, he closed to 300 yards, bathed the *U-85* in the beam of his 24-inch searchlight and opened fire with 3-inch guns while machine guns cut down the German crewmen on deck. The submarine dove and the *Roper* put down eleven depth charges. In the shallow water off the coast it was a certain kill, and twenty-nine bodies were recovered the following morning. Howe got the Navy Cross and the navy got a boost in morale: the U-boats could be found and sunk.

As resistance stiffened along the eastern coast of the United States, the U-boats increased in number and moved their operations farther south to new fields in the Gulf of Mexico, the West Indies and the Caribbean, which yielded rich tanker targets coming from Curaçao and Aruba. Subsequently U-boats operated all the way to the Panama Canal and then Brazil. The easy pickings bred contempt; Lieutenant Commander Werner Hartenstein in the *U-156* shelled a shore refinery at Aruba while his colleagues were sinking a further seven tankers offshore. Another entered the harbor at Saint Lucia and torpedoed the British passenger liner *Lady Nelson* and a cargo ship. In May submarines began laying minefields off seaports, but it was soon recognized that this was less profitable than using torpedoes against the sitting ducks.

The nation grew appalled at the navy's apparent inability to cope; Secretary of War Stimson, Army Chief of Staff General George C. Marshall and their sympathetic British counterparts put pressure on Admiral King to reorganize. Marshall, normally the quiet diplomat, sent a stiff message on June 19, 1942, telling King that failure to effectively protect shipping was endangering the entire war effort. The enemy had sunk seventeen out of seventy-four ships allocated to transport army materials; and 22 percent of the bauxite fleet, carrying aluminum ore for the aircraft industry, had been sunk, along with a similar portion of the Puerto Rican fleet.

Admiral King took umbrage at what he regarded as a conspiracy of like-minded Anglophile scoundrels, but managed to reply in measured tones, still insisting that his theory of close escort and air support was correct. As his staff grew in expertise and began to better understand the information being provided them by the hard contest and from their British allies, King began to receive internal pressure to undertake some of the actions that he opposed. But it was not until May 20, 1943, that he established the Tenth Fleet as the antisubmarine warfare organization for the navy—and even then he kept it under his personal supervision. He did have the good sense, however, to appoint Rear Admiral Francis S. Low (a man, typically, King did not like) as his Assistant Chief of Staff, and let him run the operation, which Low did very effectively.

In mid-1942, though, the carnage went on, moving southward with the ease of the pickings, in conformance with Admiral Doenitz's idea that a ship sunk anywhere detracted from the total tonnage available to the Allies. Anyone examining British import statistics in late 1942 would have agreed with him; British imports fell 33 percent below 1939 levels, to 34 million tons. More frightening, with monthly consumption of bunker fuel running at 130,000 tons, Britain had only 300,000 tons in storage. If the tankers were stopped, catastrophe loomed in two and one half months.

Imperceptibly, an extensive combination of U.S. and British measures began to take effect, especially when an "Interlocking Convoy" system was instituted, an intricate organization that eventually provided cover for shipping throughout the Atlantic Ocean by using an early form of linear programming. As it took effect, Doenitz brought his boats back from the East Coast of the United States to the mid-Atlantic.

DOENITZ MOVES UP

The second Happy Time for U-boat men had been ecstasy for Doenitz. Allied shipping losses for the year 1942 were 1,662 ships, totaling 7.8 million tons; in the Atlantic, 1,006 ships were sunk for 5.5 million tons. Only eighty-six submarines were lost, 7.2 per month, while twenty per month were being commissioned. Doenitz believed that his tonnage warfare concept was working, especially since most of the lost ships were loaded with war matériel—there were so many targets his captains could elect not to attack empty ships riding high in the water.

There were unexpected further rewards. Admiral Raeder had sent a German task force composed of the cruiser *Hipper* and pocket battleship *Lützow* and six destroyers on Operation Regenbogen (Rainbow) to attack JW-51B, a Russia-bound convoy of fourteen freighters, closely escorted by seven destroyers, with heavier ships in more distant support, including the light cruisers *Jamaica* and *Sheffield* (the latter had been an accidental Swordfish target during the *Bismarck* chase).

In the ensuing engagement, the *Hipper* took three hits, and on the basis of a message from naval headquarters "to exercise restraint if you contact enemy of comparable strength," broke off the engagement. It was the typical no-win situation for the German commander on the spot, who was instructed to engage at whatever cost—as long as he did not lose any of his own ships.

Not a single ship in the convoy was sunk, and Hitler learned of the incident from the BBC! In a protracted rage that time did not allay, he demanded that the big ships be scrapped, their guns used in fixed fortifications, and their crews transferred to submarines, industry or the infantry. Raeder, realizing at last that his Z Plan had been a chimera, resigned effective January 30, 1943. He recommended two officers to succeed him, one of them Doenitz, who was appointed in his place and promoted to Grand Admiral. Raeder's last message to Hitler was a plea to protect his navy and his successor from Hermann Goering. (There were at least two other farewell notes that echoed similar warnings about Goering, from Luftwaffe generals Ernst Udet and Hans Jeschonnek.)

The events went to Grand Admiral Doenitz's head, and, imprudently, he openly claimed that his U-boats were in an unassailable position to win the war in the Atlantic. The first three months of 1943 were in fact encouraging, even though U-boat losses soared to forty; still, 476,349 tons had been sunk, but the 155 merchant vessels yielded only a 3.8 to 1 ratio.

Then disaster struck. In May, only thirty-four ships (163,507 tons) were sunk with the loss of forty-one submarines—the ratio had been inverted to 3 to 4. In June, only four ships were sunk, at a cost of seventeen subs, a 1 to 4 ratio. In the first six months of the year, 113 submarines had been sunk, and with them the irreplaceable experience of their crews.

On May 31 Doenitz came to the Berghof, Hitler's famous mountain residence, for a conference with the Fuehrer, to report that he had withdrawn his submarines from the North Atlantic to positions west of the Azores, an admission that the Battle of the Atlantic was "temporarily lost"—and implicitly a recognition that the war was lost, for in 1943, Germany was on the defensive in every theater, including the skies over Germany.

Allied technology and production had triumphed at last, though there were still twenty-four hard months to be fought. From June to December 1943, the German victories in the North Atlantic declined to fifty-seven merchant ships of 304,572 tons; 167 U-boats were lost.

Eighty-nine of the U-boat losses stemmed from the Bay of Biscay "blitz," in which the British saturated the area with new weapons. Doenitz reacted by requiring the U-boats to travel in company on the surface, arming them with additional antiaircraft guns, and railing at their commanders. Yet he understood better than anyone that with the improved Allied antisubmarine weapons, the U-boat as it had existed since World War I was obsolete. What was needed was a submarine with a high submerged speed, one that could travel faster underwater than a convoy moved, and could attack without surfacing with new homing torpedoes. Doenitz's heart must have ached to realize that an experimental streamlined, fish-shaped boat had achieved a submerged speed of 23 knots in early 1940. But bureaucratic indifference and the press to manufacture standard submarines had blocked production of any of the new type.

It was a German tragedy, for his U-boat men had exhibited unparalleled courage and skill in the first four years of the war and achieved great results. They would continue to do so for the last two, even in the face of soaring losses, declining sinkings and Doenitz's inability to provide them with the weapons they required.

TECHNOLOGICAL TRIUMPHS

The Allied forces grew in size, sophistication and cooperation on a scale beyond the ability of their German opponents to comprehend. This is illustrated by one of the most fundamental issues of the war: ship construction. Doenitz was convinced that the combined British-U.S. ship construction capability would be limited to 1.2 million tons per year by their antiquated shipyards and the general shortage of labor. The United States, however, built eighteen new shipyards in 1941, and in 1942, American merchant ship production rose to 6.1 million tons. To this must be added 1.8 million tons of British construction, to total 7.9 million tons—just exceeding the worldwide loss figure of 7.8 million. In 1943, the combined U.S. and British construction equaled 14.6 million tons, while losses had declined to 3.2 million. Doenitz's estimate was off by 1,000 percent. Liberty ships slid off the ways at the rate of three a day, and in a burst of showmanship, one was rushed from keel laying to launching in *four days*. There is no evidence that these figures were reported to Hitler, but if they had been, the Fuehrer would not have believed them any more readily than he believed the reports of massive Soviet tank production, for the same reasons, and with the same results.

The Battle of the Atlantic was officially noted as the premier Allied problem at the Casablanca Conference in January 1943, when it was agreed that the defeat of the U-boat "must remain a first charge upon the resources of the United Nations." One result of this charter was the astounding Allied growth in antisubmarine capability, which had grown slowly at first but was now increasing at a geometric rate, in marked contrast to Doenitz's arithmetic approach to the problem. Much of the progress was interrelated—developments in radar could be used in both ships and aircraft, as could improvements in depth charges. A brief summary of individual elements of the total response follows, but it is useful to comment that as so often happened during the war, the ability and initiative of those at the operational level often overcame the blunders and delays imposed by their headquarters.

Operational Intelligence

The British set up an Operational Intelligence Center (OIC) in 1937 under the leadership of Lieutenant Commander Norman Denning. Over time, the OIC was able to route merchant ships away from known U-boat concentrations, although German Naval Intelligence countered this with their own decryption activity. The OIC's knowledge of the individual U-boats from construction, through training, combat sorties and so forth became so intimate that they could estimate what a U-boat captain might do under most circumstances, and be able to take action to frustrate it.

The OIC concept was only reluctantly adopted by the Americans as the Atlantic Section, Operational Intelligence after a special briefing to Admiral King; however, once adopted, it worked closely with its British counterpart and gained the same degree of almost uncanny proficiency in anticipating German moves. Also, in both the British and American intelligence centers, officers whose careers would have otherwise been terminated because of physical disabilities were able to distinguish themselves.

Similar organizations were operating in Germany, but they were spread among a number of agencies, and did not have the "playing fields of Eton" spirit of enthusiasm and cooperation. They were inhibited by security concerns, which were focused more on possible retribution by the Gestapo than on loss of information to the enemy. Consequently, they did not function as well.

Aviation Versus Submarines

The Coastal Command, formed by the Royal Air Force in 1936 along with Bomber Command and Fighter Command, was the RAF's poor relation, forced to operate with limited numbers of inadequate equipment. In September 1939, Coastal Command's primary strength was ten squadrons of "Faithful Annies," the Avro Anson, the militarized version of the civil 652. This was a twin-engine aircraft of mixed construction, similar in size to, but not so modern as, the American Beech Model 18. The Anson had a "not to exceed speed" of 170 knots (presumably attainable only in a vertical dive), an offensive load of four 100-pound bombs and a range that confined it to coastal patrol.

Some of the Anson's shortcomings were overcome in the Lockheed Hudson, a military development of the Model 14 airliner; 1,338 were purchased by the RAF and another 1,302 were provided under Lend-Lease. The Mark I Hudson had a speed of 246 miles per hour and a range of 1,960 miles; it carried four machine guns and 1,400 pounds of bombs or depth charges. Later models of the Hudson had greater performance, but all were a handful to the pilot to take off and land after the docile Anson. The Hudson was rugged and performed invaluable service in a number of theaters. In an unusual version of reciprocal Lend-Lease, RAF Hudsons of No. 53 Squadron operated out of Rhode Island and helped drive Doenitz's U-boats farther south during the Happy Time.

In 1939, the Coastal Command had two squadrons of the very effective Short Sunderland, which became known to the Germans as the *Fliegende Stachelschwein* (Flying Porcupine) because of its heavy ten-gun armament.

The Sunderland had a flight duration of thirteen and a half hours and a maximum range, with overload fuel, of 2,880 miles at 144 knots. It was a good tough airplane, liked by its crews and beloved by downed airmen it rescued, but it was complex to build and production was slow—there were only thirty-four in service by June 1940.

With the same sort of effort that it took to drink American-brewed tea, the Royal Air Force swallowed its pride to buy an American flying boat, the Consolidated Model 28 Catalina. This extraordinary workhorse, as useful at sea as the Douglas DC-3 was on land, was designed by the famous Isaac M. Laddon, and first flown on March 21, 1935. With its single high wing mounted on a pylon and sporting retractable wing-tip floats, the Catalina was a winner from the beginning. The first of the 129 ordered by the RAF went to No. 240 Squadron, followed by No. 209 Squadron, which used it to find the *Bismarck*.

The Catalinas had a quoted top speed of 179 miles per hour, but the word among the crews was that it "took off at 120, cruised at 120 and landed at 120." Its maximum patrol range of 2,545 miles reduced the area in which a submarine could cruise undetected, but there remained gaps in air coverage around Greenland and the Azores where Doenitz concentrated his U-boats, out of range of Allied aircraft.

The aircraft that could have closed these gaps already existed, the Consolidated B-24 Liberator. No. 120 Squadron, the first RAF unit to be equipped with the B-24, became operational in September, flying out of Iceland and North Ireland. Accidents and transfers bled its strength down, so that by August 1942, there were only five remaining, despite its proven effectiveness. Thus the Royal Air Force made exactly the same mistake that Goering had made with the Luftwaffe. Instead of allocating aircraft to the vital battle against the submarine, all bombers were sent to Bomber Command to engage in what proved to be the less than decisive area bombing of Germany.

Acquiring the Liberator was doubly difficult for Coastal Command. Admiral King scorned the idea that long-range patrol bombers could reduce the submarine threat. In addition, he was partial to the Pacific theater and diverted Liberators to the Pacific that could have been used far more profitably in the Atlantic.

Delays in delivery and fitting new equipment and armament prevented the buildup of B-24s for antisubmarine warfare until mid-1943. From that point on, however, they provided constant surveillance, often under terrible weather conditions. Some historians have said that failure to provide the very long range B-24s would have permitted the U-boats to win the Battle of the Atlantic. B-24s were, however, just part of the air power being brought to bear.

Escort Carriers

In December 1940, to combat the Focke-Wulf Condor menace, the Royal Navy mounted catapults on HMS *Pegasus*, a 1918 vintage seaplane carrier that had been loitering behind the *Royal Oak* during Prien's U-boat attack. Three Fairey Fulmar fighters were carried, and three more "Fighter Catapult Ships" followed, some equipped with Hawker Hurricanes.

In April 1940, some cargo vessels were designated Catapult Aircraft Merchantmen—CAM ships—and modified to carry a single Hawker Hurricane to be fired off in a one-way trip to engage. The first of these, a symbol of desperation, the SS *Michael E*, set sail on May 27, 1941; it was torpedoed and sunk before it could launch its first Sea Hurricane, but thirty-four more CAM ships followed. The first success was scored by Lieutenant R. W. H. Everette, who shot down a Condor, the first of five that would fall to "Hurricat" guns in 1941.

The CAM ships were supplemented by the Merchant Aircraft Carrier (MAC ship). Six 8,000-ton grain carriers and six 11,000-ton tankers were fitted with a simple flight deck and had three or four Swordfish or Sea Hurricanes stationed on board. There was no hangar deck, so the planes were always kept on the flight deck. The ships continued to carry their main cargo, and were phased out as more escort carriers became available.

The most effective solution, the escort carrier, had actually been introduced earlier, the first of these being the *Audacity* in September 1940, converted by the British from the captured German cargo ship *Hannover*. The six Grumman Martlet II fighters (the Wildcat) could not only take off but land on the escort carrier, a very useful attribute in the minds of the pilots, who enjoyed the unexpected luxury of private cabins and baths. They enjoyed it only briefly, however, for the *Audacity* was sunk by three torpedoes from the *U-751* (Lieutenant Commander Gerhard Bigalk) on December 21, 1941. Nonetheless, the principle was sound and the *Audacity* became the forerunner of the hordes of escort carriers that would follow.

The escort carrier had the specific backing of both President Roosevelt and Admiral King, who believed that merchant ships could be fitted with a flight deck and be used to escort convoys. The conversion of the diesel-powered C-3 merchant ship *Mormacmail* began on March 18, 1941. With a displacement of 13,500 tons, she was commissioned as the *Long Island* on June 2, 1941. Her 362-foot-long, 70-foot-wide flight deck was equipped with a single catapult and an elevator by which aircraft could be moved to the hangar deck below for storage and repair. The British received four modified versions of the *Long Island* in the spring of 1942: the *Archer, Avenger, Biter* and *Dasher.*

The escort carriers helped the B-24s bridge the gaps in the Atlantic coverage, arriving just in time to frustrate a huge U-boat offensive Admiral Doenitz launched to halt the convoys.

The continuous presence of an aircraft was sufficient to keep a U-boat submerged; killing the U-boat, however, required more sophisticated equipment than existed when the war began.

The Electronic War

The German effort was hoisted on its own petard in part because the Doenitz system of centralized control required an astonishing number of radio transmissions. The Allies were able to continually improve their Huff-Duff equipment (high-frequency direction-finding), which was placed first on a ring of land stations spread around the Atlantic, whereby a U-boat's position could be established by fixes plotted from her radio transmissions. At least three HF/DF sets were necessary to get a precise location, and more helped. By 1942 shipborne HF/DF sets were available. Initially, only one ship in a convoy would have the equipment, which was useful in establishing the direction of the U boat. Later, when two or three HF/DF ships were in the same convoy, they could get accurate position information. The HF/DF equipment was often the convoy's best warning that it was being shadowed by a submarine. Aircraft were dispatched to investigate, their radar sets giving special attention to the indicated direction. The first HF/DF-directed kill was the *U-587* on March 27, 1942, in an attack on convoy WS-17.

Radar became available on more and more ships and aircraft as 1943 progressed. The first Air-to-Surface Vessel (ASV) Mark I model radar was heavy and unreliable, but by 1943, more than sixty different radar types had been created, tested and either adopted or abandoned. The great leap forward came in the 1940 British development of centimetric radar, which the Germans had investigated but discarded as impossible to perfect. The first ship model was known as 271M, while the first airborne was called ASV III. The American equivalent of the latter, installed in the Liberator, was the SCR-517. With this equipment, a submarine could be detected at a distance of twelve miles or more—no matter what the weather.

Detecting a submarine was only the first step; next, it had to be visually identified and bombed. One deficiency of even the later radars was that the image on the screen improved until the aircraft got within three quarters of a mile, and was then lost in the clutter from the sea surface. (The effect was similar to that encountered with Asdic, which lost its target when it passed over it.)

To offset this failing, the Leigh Light was developed. This was a 24-inch naval searchlight first mounted in the belly of a Vickers Wellington so that it was automatically controlled by the 1.5-meter ASV II radar, with 20 degrees of movement in the horizontal and vertical planes. Its brilliant white light would reach out 5,000 yards. The aircraft radar picked up the surfaced submarine, and guided the aircraft to its unsuspecting target. The U-boat, hoping that the night and weather cloaked it, would suddenly be bathed in a brilliant white light and then depth-charged before it had time to submerge. From June 4, 1942, the Leigh Light was used with success in the Bay of Biscay, augmenting the RAF's intensive daylight offensive against the U-boats entering and leaving French ports. After the debut of the Leigh Light, German submarines were told to cross the Bay of Biscay submerged, by day or by night, unless they were forced to recharge their batteries. The much slower submerged transit speed had the effect of reducing the number of submarines on patrol.

The U-boats gained a temporary respite in July 1942 by introducing long-range Junkers Ju 88C fighters to hit British antisubmarine aircraft in the bay, but by November, British Bristol Beaufighters had suppressed them. A more difficult problem arose when the season for French tuna fishing arrived in late July. There were so many small fishing boats out, each of which gave the same reflection as a submarine conning tower, that the British could not find their targets.

The offensive in the Bay of Biscay finally broke down because of German countermeasures. They had discovered the ASV Mark II radar in a Hudson that had crashed in Tunisia, and created the Metox—the name was taken from the French firm that produced it—a simple receiver that picked up radar transmissions in the ASV II frequency band of 113–500 megacycles. Metox used the FuMB aerial 2, a crude wire-strung wooden cross called the *Biscayakreuz* (Biscay Cross), which had to be manually installed and removed each time the boat submerged. Soon most U-boats were fitted. Any not so equipped were supposed to accompany one that was during the journey across the Bay of Biscay. The number of U-boat detections quickly declined.

This situation revealed a clear difference in the relative ingenuity of the two enemies. The British were ready with the next generation ASV III 10-centimeter (actually, 9.7) radar, which the Metox could not detect. Once again the U-boats reported being attacked without warning, and German Naval Intelligence became convinced that the British were homing in on radiations from the Metox and exerted extreme effort to reduce these to a minimum. The Germans were stunned when an H2S radar set (the equivalent of the ASV III) recovered from a crashed bomber near Rotterdam revealed that 10-centimeter radar was not only possible, but operational. A forced draft effort resulted in the creation of the FuMB 76 Naxos-U, designed to detect 10-centimeter radiations, but these did not reach U-boats until October 1943, and then proved ineffective. The FuMB 26 Tunis, an effective radar warning system for U-boats, did not arrive until late May 1944.

Allied inventiveness continued to reach new heights. The Americans introduced high-definition 3-centimeter radar, which made picking up a submarine's conning tower or even its periscope possible. To this was added Magnetic Airborne Detection (MAD), which was useful in detecting the steel hulls of U-boats in shallow water, and localizing them for attack after they had been detected by other means.

Escort and Support Groups

The Royal Navy had longed to kill U-boats, not merely keep them away from the convoys. And just as in 1944, when it was finally recognized that the way to defeat the Luftwaffe was to use the bomber formation as bait for Allied fighters, now the convoys were to defeat the U-boats by being bait for the Escort and Support Groups.

The Commander-in-Chief of the Western Approaches, Admiral Sir Max Horton, has been described by his biographer as "poacher turned gamekeeper," for he had been a submariner first, sinking many enemy ships, including the cruiser *Hela* in World War I. In World War II, he led the antisubmarine effort that mastered the U-boat threat.

Admiral Horton was able to conceive not only the scale of the escort and support groups required to safeguard the convoys, but also the intense training required to do their job. He approved an increase in the size of convoys, based on the Operations Research findings that the number of ships sunk was independent of the number of ships in a convoy. Increasing the size of convoys reduced their number, which allowed a greater ratio of escort ships. At about the same time the general shortage of escort vessels began to ease as American and British production got under way, and a mixture of new destroyer escorts, corvettes, frigates and escort carriers began operating together. These small ships built in the hundreds and almost as uncomfortable as a submarine and nearly as dangerous to the crews, permitted the formation of the two-tier defense system.

The first tier was the standard convoy escort, which grew in size and complexity as the war progressed, and whose purpose was to fend off U-boat attacks. The second tier was to be the independent support group, composed of a mix of small ships and, where possible, an escort carrier. These were vectored in on the U-boats, and stayed with them until they were sunk. This was the kind of action that the Royal Navy had longed for, as did its allies in the Royal Canadian and U.S. navies.

One of the most frustrating aspects of convoy protection was being unable to pick up survivors of torpedoed cargo or warships. In the midst of a convoy battle, stopping was obviously impossible, for the cargo ships' mission was to get through, and the warships' mission was to sink submarines. So in 1943 rescue trawlers were added to the convoy, their task to rescue victims of sunken ships. They themselves were designated a desirable target by Admiral Doenitz, who considered killing merchant crews as important as sinking merchant ships.

As the escort groups gained experience, the two-tier system worked in concert with HF/DF, radar and very long range patrol planes to doom the U-boat force. A frustrated and embittered Admiral Doenitz in 1944 ordered his U-boat captains to "Remain surfaced. Shoot your way through to the convoy with Flak [antiaircraft guns]." The desperate order was a recipe for defeat and the continued heavy losses soon required it to be rescinded.

Improvement in Weapons

Coastal Command and the Fleet Air Arm had started the war carrying bombs that were ineffective against submarines; in 1940, they converted to depth charges, which were far more effective, especially when it was possible to set the detonation depth at twenty-five feet. Shipboard depth-charge settings could be varied, and the depth charges were modified ultimately to reach great depths before exploding.

The depth charge became the standard antisubmarine weapon, as guns and conventional torpedoes were of little use. The depth charge (familiarly called the "ash can" in the U.S. Navy) was a hollow drum filled in the earlier years with Amatol explosive and fired by a hydrostatic pistol, preset to explode at a specific depth. By April 1942, Torpex explosive, 30 percent more powerful than Amatol, was brought into use. The lethal radius of the 300 pounds of Amatol used was about twenty-five feet, but damage could be caused at a much greater distance. A small variety of depth charges was created, the largest being the Mark X, which had 2,000 pounds of the improved Minol explosive and could be set to detonate at a depth of 1,500 feet, far below the U-boat's operating depth.

The air-dropped depth charge became much more effective with the introduction of radar altimeters, which not only measured height precisely, but gave pilots the confidence to descend in foul weather to a minimum altitude. The MK VIII depth charge, which entered service during the winter of 1942, was designed with nose and tail fairings that added to the accuracy of aim, and that broke off on impact, reducing its velocity so that its detonating pistol would have time to explode at the desired twenty-five-foot depth. With the improved depth charges, air warfare took on a new and lethal meaning for the U-boats; ultimately 47 percent of their losses could be attributed to aircraft, which sank 388 submarines and assisted in forty-five other kills.

Along with improved depth charges came improved tactics in their use. The finest escort commander of the war, Commander "Johnnie" Walker of the 2nd Escort Group, perfected what he termed the "creeping attack." The U-boats used hydrophones to listen to the propellers of an attacking ship, and would turn away at an opportune moment. With the creeping attack, one vessel would maintain contact at about 1,000 yards astern and direct another up the U-boat's path, where the latter ship's propeller noise would be masked by that of the U-boat itself. When the second ship was in position, the shadowing escort would give the signal, and a shower of depth charges would be delivered, either by rolling them off chutes or firing them from the depth-charge thrower, essentially a reinforced mortar that could fire out to about seventy-five yards to explode in a pattern around the submarine. The U-boat command never received word of Walker's tactics, for no survivors reached home to tell the tale.

Walker devised his methods to conform to the way depth charges were launched—over the side or rear as the escort vessel pulled away. A device was needed to launch depth charges ahead of the ship, so that sonar contact could be maintained. One had been demonstrated in 1917; it was called a howitzer, and like its land namesake, threw its projectile forward in a high arc. This reappeared in modified form in 1942 as the "Hedgehog," a battery of twenty-four 65-pound bombs mounted on spikes (whence the nickname) that were ripple-fired 600 feet ahead of the ship. They landed in an oval pattern, 120 by 140 feet, landing roughly twelve feet apart to provide a descending shower of steel for the submarine to travel through. Each Hedgehog bomb contained thirty pounds of Torpex and would explode on contact—a hit was fatal. (Smaller ships were equipped with the "Mousetrap," which had four or eight rounds.) Those that did not hit did not explode and disrupt the sonar surveillance as depth charges did. A later development, the "Squid," combined the area advantages of the Hedgehog with the insured detonation quality of the depth charge.

Life on a Sub-chaser

Living conditions aboard a submarine were miserable, but they were scarcely better on the escort vessels attacking them. Some, like the numerous "Flower" class, were so small that "they would roll on wet grass" and sometimes for days and weeks at a time had to plow their way through waves that threatened to swamp them. Most voyages commenced with all on board being deathly seasick for a few days. All of the escorts were cold, wet on deck and below decks. The great escort commander Captain Donald Macintyre writes of the rough weather opening rivets in the hulls, so that there was a constant slosh of water on the deck, and of steel bulkheads below decks coated with rime ice. Wearing wet clothes twenty-four hours a day and subsisting on a diet of corned beef, bread, cocoa and coffee did nothing to relieve the situation.

GERMAN COUNTERMEASURES

Admiral Doenitz never wavered (even after the war, in his memoirs) from his adherence to his tonnage theory of warfare; during the war he moaned about the genuine opportunity lost by not having a 300 U-boat fleet when the war began. Then, given the pathetic state of British equipment and training, he almost certainly would have won the Battle of the Atlantic by mid-1941.

Despite its limitations, however, the U-boat fleet came close to winning even with its reduced numbers, and the greatest credit for this must go to the U-boat captains and crews, who endured terrible living conditions and the horror of combat on mission after mission, even though the odds of their survival declined steadily after 1943. In the course of the war, 28,000 of the total of 40,000 German submariners died at their posts. (The British lost 30,132 merchant seamen to all causes.)

Doenitz himself lost two sons to the war. Peter was drowned when *U-954* was sunk attacking a convoy on May 19, 1943. Klaus, by Doenitz's personal intervention, had been transferred from U-boat duty subsequent to

Peter's death, and was in medical school at Tuebingen. While on a holiday, Klaus took a ride on a reconnaissance sortie by torpedo boat *S-141* in the English Channel. Allied destroyers were encountered, and *S-141* was sunk. Klaus was not among the survivors.

The principal German response to the growing Allied antisubmarine measures was increased production. By October 1942 there were 365 U-boats in Doenitz's inventory, of which the creditable number of operational craft was 196. At the same time, U-boat designs had been considerably improved. Hulls had been strengthened to permit dives to greater depths and to increase resistance to depth charges. In an attempt to combat the increasingly effective Allied air attacks, a wide variety of heavy antiaircraft armament was added for protection. It took extreme courage to man these guns and return the fire of an attacking bomber, but the submariners had courage in abundance. The addition of the antiaircraft weaponry, though, had adverse effects upon the U-boats' performance. They increased drag, and made the vertical center of gravity so high that there was an increased tendency to roll. Some submarines were converted into "Flak" U-boats, being armed with two 20mm quadruple mounts and one 37mm gun, and carrying fewer torpedoes to compensate.

Germany delayed fitting radar on board U-boats because of space limitations, but by June 1942, the need was so obvious that work was begun. Initial installations were unsatisfactory, and it was not until Luftwaffe ship-detection radar was incorporated as the FuMO 61 Hohentwiel U in 1944 that really satisfactory results were obtained.

The Snorkel

It was obviously necessary to reduce the time a submarine spent on the surface, vulnerable to detection and attack; some means of providing air to the submerged submarine had to be found so that the diesel engines could be used for propulsion and for charging the batteries. A patent for an extensible air mast had been taken out in 1933 by Lieutenant Commander J. H. Wichers of the Royal Netherlands Navy, and the air mast was used on four Dutch submarines by 1938. The concept was revived in 1943 by Dr. Hellmuth Walter, who would develop the next generation of U-boats, which have had a profound influence on today's navies.

Admiral Doenitz backed Walter's idea. The snorkel was basically an air tube that could be extended and retracted like a periscope, with a valve on the top that prevented water washing over it from entering. When the valve closed in rough seas, the galloping diesel engines repeatedly drew their air from the submarine itself, changing the pressure rapidly and causing terrible pains in the sinuses and ears of the crew.

Tests were relatively satisfactory, although the crews protested the snorkel's use, and Type VIIC U-boats began to be equipped with the device in September 1943. The first boat to use the snorkel operationally, the *U-264*, was lost on her first mission, which further increased apprehension about the device. Commanded by Lieutenant Hartwig Looks, *U-264* had the misfortune to run into the formidable 2nd Escort Group, five sloops commanded by Johnnie Walker. Walker's group was on a roll, having scored five sinkings in ten days when it forced the *U-264* to surface; its crew was captured and relentlessly interrogated about the snorkel.

By the summer of 1944, however, Allied air and sea power was so great that the snorkel was gratefully accepted as a means of avoidance, keeping in the relative safety of the depths. As experience with the device grew, so did success, to the point that the U-boats were able to intrude again in areas previously regarded as safe by the British.

Snorkels could only be used at speeds up to 6 or 7 knots, which increased the time needed to get to and from operational areas. Improved models were strengthened and streamlined and could be used at speeds of 10 to 11 knots, but none of these was brought into service before the war ended.

Torpedoes

Marked improvements had been made in German torpedoes, but the first really revolutionary change came in early 1943 with the "Fat" torpedo (Federapparat—Spring-Loaded), which, after a specified distance, began to run in a circle, increasing its chances of hitting a ship in a convoy. The Fat torpedo was improved to the LuT (Langen unabhangiger Torpedo—Independent Torpedo) type, which could be released at great distances from a convoy, and was programmed to follow it on selected courses and preset depths. It, too, would run in great wide circles, constantly curving back in on the target area. LuT became operational in February 1944.

The next step was the Dackel (Slow-Worm), which ran in a pattern and was used for attacks against ships in a harbor. Based on the standard G7e electric torpedo, it traveled at only 9 knots so that its larger battery gave it a thirty-five mile range, zigzagging or circling for as long as four hours. The Dackel was too long for use in a U-boat, but the fast attack E-boats fired it against Allied channel shipping.

The first German acoustic torpedo, the T4 Falke (Falcon), was introduced in mid-1943, and then was superseded by the T5 Zaunkoenig (jenny wren) beginning on August 1, 1943. Allied intelligence called it the GNAT (German Naval Acoustic Torpedo). The Germans fired 640 of the Zaunkoenigs in action and obtained about thirty-eight hits. Part of their problem was that the Allies had been made aware of the existence of the Zaunkoenig and developed the Foxer, a device towed astern of a ship to make noise and attract the torpedoes, much as aircraft now deploy flares to decoy heat-seeking missiles. The Royal Canadian Navy developed the Cat, which had a higher-pitched noise than Foxer, serving the same purpose.

Further developments in torpedo guidance systems were made by the Germans, including wire-steered, magnetic, ultrasonic and passive-acoustic, but there was insufficient time remaining for Germany to bring them to operational status.

The U-boat command placed emphasis on defensive measures as well, including the Pillenwerfer, a discharge of an effervescent substance intended to simulate the body of the submarine and to reflect the sonar waves. It did not fool the experienced Asdic operator for long. Stealth warfare was introduced when snorkels and periscopes were coated with a buna (synthetic rubber) compound to reduce radar reflectivity.

New U-boat Types

The first of ten Type XIV tankers was commissioned on November 15, 1941. Called Doenitz's "milk cows," they were used to refuel and resupply U-boats at sea, thereby extending their time on station. Refueling was extremely hard on the crew members, who had to don bathing suits to wrestle with hoses and hawsers in the frigid ocean waters, but it eventually became almost routine. It was actually possible to refuel while submerged, as the *U-977* (famous for its postwar snorkel trip to Argentina) demonstrated. On the first tanker sortie by the *U-459*, no fewer than thirteen submarines were refueled and reprovisioned, the first being the *U-108* on April 22, 1942. Warm rye bread, fresh from the milk cow's bakery, received a rousing welcome from crews accustomed to eating the insides of "white rabbits," the mold-encrusted loaves they had brought with them on departure.

The tankers, with their 432 tons of transferable fuel, were a principal factor in the success of the Type VII boats off the American coast, but they lasted for but a brief period. Allied intelligence had rapidly ferreted out their locations, often waiting to strike until a U-boat was alongside reprovisioning. Of the ten Type XIV tankers, one was lost in 1942, seven in 1943 and the rest in 1944.

German U-boats were also used in the minelaying role, eight of the large XB type being built especially for the task. The XB boats had thirty vertical tubes through which mines could be released, and twelve on each side; seventy-two mines were carried, thirty in containers on the deck. Six of the XBs were lost at sea. The surviving boats were *U-219*, which the Japanese took possession of after the German surrender and redesignated *I-505*, and *U-234*, which was handed over to the Allies after the surrender.

A group of three large and seven medium-size Italian submarines were also used to transport technical material and raw materials to and from Japan. These were given the cover names of *Aquila I* through *Aquila X*. Of the first five attempts, three made it to Singapore, where they were interned by the Japanese, Mussolini having fallen in the interim. No boats made it back to Europe, and no others succeeded in reaching Japanese waters. (The Japanese managed to get two of their four own large cargo submarines, laden with vital raw materials, through to German bases in France.)

Better success was obtained from the Type IXD boats, which could carry 245 tons of supplies, including 120 tons of tin, fifteen tons of molybdenum, eighty tons of rubber and a ton of miscellaneous high-value items. Six submarines made it back from Japan with such loads, but only shortly before the end of the war.

Doenitz, shaken by his acknowledged loss of the Battle of the Atlantic, was now forced to place his hopes on some remarkable new submarine designs, the undersea equivalent of the advanced jet and rocket aircraft.

Once again Doenitz must have cursed the loss of time. In 1933, Admiral Raeder had refused to back development of the fish-shaped single-propulsion U-boats advocated by Dr. Walter, based on his hydrogen peroxide closed-cycle engine system, which did not require oxygen from the atmosphere to operate. These boats were to be true submersibles and faster underwater (27 knots) than when surfaced, the vital characteristics that could combat the Allied dominance in the air and at sea. Now, in June 1942, Doenitz had the Walter engine rushed into development. The first experimental Walter boat, the *V-80*, was built in 1940; it could make just over 26 knots submerged, for short periods. The first production boats were the *U-792*, launched on September 28, 1943, and the *U-794*, launched on October 7. These experimental submarines were designated Type XVIIA.

However, the Walter engine system was simply too advanced and complex and there was insufficient development time to iron out all the bugs. The new hull and steering designs gave problems as well, and none of the Walter boats entered operational service. One inhibiting factor was that their hydrogen peroxide fuel, called Aurol, was also needed in the V-2 rockets. After the war, the promise of the closed-cycle engine was superseded by nuclear power.

Admiral Doenitz had another wonder submarine, the Type XXI, known as the "Electro" boat, like the Walter boat intended to be a true submersible. The design was suggested to Doenitz and Dr. Walter by ministerial counselors Dr. Frierich Schuerer and Hermann Broecking at a conference in Paris in November 1942. Schuerer and Broecking carried great weight, having been in submarine design since World War I, and being responsible for the design of the ubiquitous Type VII.

Equally radical except for its power source, the Type XXI used an extremely advanced hull design combined with the reliable MAN diesel engines for surface running and charging the batteries for electric power. For the first time, however, the electric motors had more horsepower than the diesels—4,200 compared to 4,000, and there was a separate 225-horsepower electric motor for silent running. The Type XXI boats had a submerged speed of 16 knots for one hour, or could run at 4 knots for seventy-two hours without recharging batteries. For the crew members, the greatest change was in comfort. The 251-foot boat had a beam of 21 feet, 9 inches and displaced 1,819 tons submerged. Consequently, there was room for the crew members to stretch out, and officers even had private quarters. A deep freeze for food was provided, and torpedoes were loaded hydraulically rather than by hand.

The attack method proposed for the Type XXI was also different from previous submarines. Once a target had been picked up by radar or hydrophone, the submerged submarine was to have proceeded at full speed toward it and, without using its periscope, attack using sonar bearings.

A huge construction program plan was headed by a former manufacturer of fire-fighting equipment, Otto Merker, a friend and fellow Swabian of Minister of Armaments Albert Speer. The submarines were to be built in nine sections by thirteen factories situated well inland. The sections, some weighing as much as 165 tons, were equipped with their machinery and electrical gear, and transported by canal barge to the dockyards for assembly. The 1944 program called for 1,300 Type XXI U-boats to be produced at the rate of forty per month. It would replace the Type VII and Type IX in construction. Because the Type XXI was too large for use in coastal waters, a smaller version, the Type XXIII, was designed for that purpose. If fate had allowed the two new designs to be sent to sea in quantity, Admiral Doenitz would undoubtedly have won another round in the Battle of the Atlantic.

Although the massive production scheme was fraught with problems (not least of which was the Allied bombing of canal walls, leaving the U-boat sections high and dry), 118 Type XXI boats were completed before the war was over. The first operationally ready Type XXI boat, the *U-2511*, captained by Lieutenant Adalbert Schnee, reached Norway on March 18, 1945, and began her first operational patrol on April 30. By mid-May, a further thirty to fifty Type XXI boats would have been ready for sea.

On May 4, Doenitz, now the new Fuehrer, ordered all U-boats to cease hostilities and return to base. The returning *U-2511* made a mock attack on a British cruiser and a destroyer, and Schnee returned home confident that he would have sunk them if he had fired, for the Type XXI could fire off eighteen torpedoes in twenty minutes from its six bow tubes.

The Type XXIII 250-ton coastal boat had a high-speed hull design similar to the Type XXI. The first Type XXIII boat, *U-2321*, entered service on June 12, 1944; by the end of the war, sixty-two more would follow. The Type XXIII was ideal for its purpose—fast, highly maneuverable and difficult for surface ships to locate. It had a successful career, gaining the distinction of making the last sinkings of the war on May 7, 1945, at 2300, when the *U-2336* sank the British merchantmen *Avondale Park* and *Sneland*, each with a single torpedo. (Earlier in the day, a Coastal Command Catalina sank the *U-320*, the last U-boat to be lost in the war.)

Additionally, nine different types of midget submarines and human torpedoes were created. These, like so much of the advanced German research and development effort, proved to be irrelevant to the war effort, worthy of the cliché "too little too late."

FINAL ASSESSMENT

After Grand Admiral Doenitz admitted losing the Battle of the Atlantic on May 24, 1943, the fight was far from over, but the conditions of battle were reversed. The submarine was now stalked instead of being the stalker, and the kill ratio increasingly favored the Allies.

In the last six months of 1943 the Germans lost 141 submarines, and there were few experienced submariners to replace the crews. In 1944, the tonnage sunk shrank to 175,031 and the ratio worsened to thirty-one merchant ships to 242 U-boats. In the first five months of 1945, relaxed Allied convoy discipline and improved submarines made a slightly better showing, with nineteen ships sunk for 122,729 tons; 151 submarines were lost in achieving this.

Admiral Doenitz had staked his strategy on the wolf pack tactics that might have won World War I. The same tactics might possibly have won World War II if they could have been employed with good torpedoes by 300 U-boats in the long months before the Allies developed the right mix of antisubmarine weapons and tactics. But the Allied powers evolved a fateful, multi-pronged combination. The intelligence from Enigma was used to reroute the ever larger convoys, which were provided with continuous air and surface escorts. Both air and surface escorts were provided with continually improved electronics and weapons in lavish quantities. Taken together, the submarines were denied their stealth advantage and forced to attack convoys on Allied terms, which resulted in their destruction.

Leadership

The Allies surpassed the Germans technically and in production, and completely outclassed them in terms of leadership. Admiral Doenitz had Hitler's moral support and little else; he had to win his production allocations by fighting Goering and lobbying Speer, who, being the Fuehrer's man, attended first to Hitler's primary interest, the army. In contrast, Roosevelt and Churchill were both passionately fond of their navies, and supported them well. In the fall of 1942, Churchill had established an Anti-U-boat Warfare Committee with himself (naturally) as chairman, along with his chief scientific adviser, Lord Cherwell, the chiefs of staff of the services and pertinent members of government. In the United States, Roosevelt's Office of Scientific Research and Development (OSRD) performed roughly the same function. OSRD was headed by Dr. Vannevar Bush, who had direct and comfortable access to Secretary of War Stimson and Secretary of the Navy Knox, as well as to the President's informal chief of cabinet, Harry Hopkins. Nowhere in Germany could be found a similar group marshaling the same great weight of talent and able to act independently without fear of retribution.

The Allies also had far better commanding officers and a superior assignment system. While Doenitz had some advantage in running his operation with an iron hand and surprisingly small numbers, there was no way he could compete with the depth and breadth of the leadership provided by the British and American naval officer corps. Not always—in fact, rarely— were they beloved figures, but Admirals King, Cunningham, Somerville, Horton and others were superb leaders in their own right, and had no counterpart in Germany. And regardless of their personal faults, these admirals followed the general Allied practice of tolerance for unusual personalities—as long as they delivered. Among these might be numbered the great escort captain Johnnie Walker, who literally worked himself to death by heart attack in scoring his twenty kills; Donald Macintyre, invalided out of flying duties because of shingles, and sent to surface ships; Rodger Winn, crippled from youth by polio, but *the* irreplaceable figure in the British Operational Intelligence Center, who was able by force of personality to make Admiral King come to terms. Winn also collapsed from overwork, but he survived to see victory in the Atlantic. There were many others among the Allies, and there were few similar to them on Doenitz's staff.

At the submarine captain level, it was different; superb German submarine commanders emerged, men who understood their weapons and their tactics, and who often prevailed against impossible circumstances. They were in every way the equal of their opponents, and gained their lasting respect.

Envoi

The Battle of the Atlantic was truly titanic, tying up billions in resources and hundreds of thousands of men in a desperate struggle. Although the German U-boats had a chance to win the war while the Allies were getting ready to fight, it soon became a colossal mismatch. It is a measure of Germany's toughness and determination that it was able to fight on for six long years against such heavy odds. The Allies had an overwhelming advantage in technology, ships, planes, men, money and matériel; it took until mid-1943 to assemble the combination that would stifle the submarines. Once assembled, the U-boats never had another chance.

Even though the Allied shipping losses were staggering, they do not convey the scale of the Allied success. Approximately 2,850 merchant ships were sunk, totaling almost 14.7 million tons, but in the process, the Germans lost 821 submarines, an unacceptable ratio. Against these monumental figures, each one replete with individual human suffering, must be cast another, even more gigantic number.

In the same period, there were more than *300,000* individual voyages of merchant ships across the Atlantic, and hundreds of thousands more undertaken in the coastal waters of the United States and Great Britain. As we will discuss later, gigantic invasions were launched, one directly into North Africa, others into Sicily and Italy, and the greatest of all into Normandy via the British Isles. The German submariners were not even aware of the North African invasion and did not inhibit the invasion of France in the least, gaining only a handful of sinkings from the largest target of the war.

Statistically, the 2,233 merchant ships sunk in the North Atlantic represent .007 percent of the number of transatlantic passages, and an even smaller percentage of the total targets available. This figure in no way minimizes the seriousness of the German threat to shipping, to the people of the British Isles who depended upon the imports or to the armed forces of the United States, Britain and the Soviet Union. But it does indicate that Germany once again underestimated the true proportions that a world war would assume, as it also did with aircraft, armor and personnel. Hitler had wanted to run a smash-and-grab operation that, in his own words "poached other people's countries." The Battle of the Atlantic was another demonstration of how naive he was.

6.

HEADY VICTORIES, DISMAL DEFEATS

In Japan since the turn of the century, the supreme command of the military services was independent of and superior to the government. Military leaders could report their intentions to the Emperor, who, powerless to overrule them, always acquiesced; the same military leaders could then proclaim imperial approval of their actions. As a result, politicians tended to concentrate on civilian (business) interests. Military matters, including those involving national policy, were left in the hands of the army and navy, which were themselves at odds. It was inevitable that no unified national policy could be enunciated, nor any grand national strategy created.

The military hold on the government was strengthened when it was stipulated in 1936 that the service ministers of the army and the navy had to be on the active duty list. This gave the military control of the government, for it could topple a cabinet by withdrawing its minister, or prevent a new cabinet from taking power by refusing to nominate a minister.

There was no supreme command. A very rough counterpart to the American Joint Chiefs of Staff was the *Dai-hon'ei*, the Imperial General Headquarters, which functioned only in time of war. It was composed of the chiefs of staff of the army and navy and their associates, and the ministers of the army and navy, active, serving members of their respective services. To establish some feedback, if not control, the government established the *Dai-hon'ei seifu renraku kaigi*—the Imperial Headquarters–Government Liaison Conference, a "bolt-on" committee to align the government with the conduct of the war. It was attended by the Prime Minister—for most of the war, until the fall of Saipan in mid-1944, General Tojo Hideki—the Foreign Minister, and the members of the Imperial General Headquarters.

The Japanese military hierarchy, which appeared as monolithic to the Allies as that of the Nazis, was split and split again. The primary dichotomy was the army and the navy. Within the army, however, there were many factions, the most vociferous of which demanded aggressive action to expand the empire. Other elements railed against the bureaucrats and the wealthy *zaibatsu* class, which they felt defiled the ancient Japanese ways. These dissident groups used assassination as an ordinary business practice; the result was to create terror within the government and destroy discipline within the army, for the senior officers were afraid to punish the younger men on fear of death. A concept of *gekokujo* emerged, in which insubordination to achieve a higher—usually more radical—cause was regarded as proper and healthy. Junior officers are regarded as important assets by all countries, but only in Japan were they able, quite literally, to call the shots, conducting what one author has called "government by assassination."

The army and the navy competed for funds on the basis of their ability to accomplish the mission of expanding Japan's influence. Until it was badly bloodied by the Soviet Union in 1937 and 1938 in the mini-wars conducted in Manchukuo (Manchuria), the army always advocated expansion to the north, and more than 3,000 exchanges of gunfire had taken place with Soviet troops. After two major battles—minor wars—in 1937 and 1938–1939, in which the Japanese were thoroughly trounced by Lieutenant General Georgi Zhukov, the Japanese army began to come around to the navy's point of view that the empire should be expanded to the south.

Yet the army remained predominant in Japan, its prestige deriving from the samurai warrior tradition. The navy's grand strategy derived from simple logistics; having, like all the navies in the world, converted to oil-burning ships, it had to have an assured oil supply. Being totally dependent upon imported oil, it was natural that the navy's strategy should lean toward securing the oil-rich Dutch East Indies as a national resource.

LESSONS LEARNED AND UNLEARNED

Japan determined that it would achieve autarchy by edging toward the east, in an early domino-effect conquest that took it into Korea and Manchuria, and then south into China. The next step was the expulsion of European and American influence from Asia—America from the Philippines and its other Pacific island possessions; England from Hong Kong, Singapore and Burma; and the Dutch from the Dutch East Indies. It was a wildly ambitious program, but consistent with the Japanese view of the world—and with current events, for as Germany became more powerful, the Pacific colonies of France, Great Britain and the Netherlands became easier prey.

At the same time that Japan evolved this policy of conquest, it overlooked the most critical lesson of World War I, the absolute importance of an island empire's maintaining its sea communications at all costs. Nearly succumbing to German U-boat warfare, England had survived because it managed to preserve its maritime communications. Japan completely ignored this need, and did not plan for the necessary merchant or anti-submarine-warfare ships to do the same thing, nor did it provide the requisite technological development. When the U.S. submarine fleet was at last perceived as a genuine menace, the Japanese navy could deploy fewer than fifty anti-submarine-warfare ships over an ocean battlefield that ranged from the Aleutians to India. Instead, the Japanese navy concentrated on replicating Tsushima, the major battle by which it defeated the Russian navy in 1904. It planned to lure the U.S. fleet (the principal enemy in its war plan since 1909) across the Pacific. En route, the superior U.S. fleet would be whittled down by submarines and air attack, until finally there would be a fleet engagement, which the Japanese would win. In this, as all through the Pacific war, the Japanese looked to what would now be called the best-case scenario, eschewing the possibility of a worst case.

Although both nations were proud, a total lack of understanding prevented the United States from realizing that *any* failure on its part to agree to Japanese demands was regarded by the Japanese as a loss of face. They in turn were unable to see that the United States expected concessions in negotiations from both sides. Thus protracted arms-limitation conferences, even though apparently satisfactorily resolved, caused tremendous resentment and fueled the passionate fires of the younger Japanese officers, who demanded superiority in naval strength.

AN ECONOMIC COFFIN CORNER

The situation in the mid-1930s saw the United States determined to halt Japanese incursions in Asia, but unwilling to spend the funds necessary to do so. Japan saw expansion by conquering other countries as a right that was of no concern to anyone else. When this "right" became a necessity, Japan had maneuvered itself into an economic corner: to achieve its goal of autarchy, it had to expand, yet to expand it became more dependent upon the outside world for its resources. It was particularly dependent upon its most hated potential enemy, the United States, which supplied 66 percent of Japan's machine tools, 50 percent of its copper, 75 percent of its scrap steel, 80 percent of its fuel oil and 90 percent of its aviation fuel. Until 1941, every mile of Japan's naked aggression was paved with "made in the USA" war matériel.

Japan's initial expansion in China in 1931 was reinvigorated by the "China Incident," which began at the Marco Polo Bridge near Peking, on July 1, 1937, a date that could well be used as the start of World War II. There followed a series of incidents that led inevitably to war with the United States:

December 13, 1937: the sinking of the USS *Panay;*
December 14, 1937: the "Rape of Nanking": 250,000 Chinese massacred;
July 18, 1940: Roosevelt calls for a "Two-Ocean Navy";
July 25, 1940: Japan occupies northern Indochina;
July 26, 1940: America embargoes fuel, lubricating oil and steel scrap to Japan and freezes Japanese assets;
September 17, 1940: Germany, Italy and Japan sign the Tripartite Agreement;
July 26, 1941: Roosevelt nationalizes the armed forces of the Philippine Commonwealth and appoints Field Marshal Douglas MacArthur to be Commanding General of the United States Army Forces, Far East;
August 9, 1941: Roosevelt and Churchill's Atlantic Conference warns Japan that further expansion could lead to war;
October 18, 1941: General Tojo Hideki becomes Prime Minister, retaining the War Ministry, and confirming Japan's thrust to war;
November, 1941: the United States and Japan continue fruitless negotiations;
November 26, 1941: the Japanese naval strike force sails for Hawaii;
December 7, 1941: Japanese attack Pearl Harbor.

Who Were the Goats?

The United States was ill-prepared for the Japanese attack. Those in command did not exert themselves and their forces to the same hard degree that the Japanese did. The result was disaster at Pearl Harbor, the Philippines and, for 100 blazing days, the rest of the Southwest Pacific. Admiral Husband Kimmel and Lieutenant General Walter Short, the army commander, were immediately sacked and subjected to years of congressional investigaton. Both men had been excellent officers, who would undoubtedly have served well. But they had not taken all the steps that were necessary, they had not forced their subordinates to work as hard as they should have, they ignored compelling intelligence and they had made a variety of errors, both of omission and commission. Kimmel's most egregious error was a failure to do the necessary reconnaissance, preferring to continue training with his Catalinas rather than use them to patrol. His second worst mistake was to decide *not* to install antitorpedo nets for the battleships at anchor, which might have cut his losses by 70 percent. Short also failed in reconnaissance, both short- and long-range, and did not have his forces at the proper state of alert. Neither man deserved the congressional and press opprobrium heaped upon them, but the attack happened on their watch and they had to take the blame.

The Japanese Fleet

The Imperial Japanese Navy came into the war uncertain about its prosecution, performed brilliantly for a brief period of time, and then was hammered into submission, its ships sunk, its sailors drowned, its aircraft destroyed. As was the case in their aircraft industry, the Japanese had created their shipbuilding expertise by closely following foreign practice until they acquired sufficient skills to embark upon indigenous designs. Ships built after 1930 were primarily the product of their own system, built to their own specifications. The rapid rush to independence was not without its hazards, however. Lacking the centuries of warship-building experience of their opponents, inevitably there were gaps in their grasp of basic design data. Manufacturing difficulties also arose from the practice, continued until World War II, of using both British and metric measurements.

The Japanese introduced some structural innovations, including integration of armor into the basic structure of the ship. Deficiencies manifested themselves in unusual ways, however; for example, a shortage of welding rods and trained welders limited the amount and the quality of welding done in Japanese shipyards. Some ships using part welded construction suffered a complete failure of welds, the most famous being the highly touted light cruiser *Mogami*.

Japanese designers, particularly Vice Admiral Hiraga Yazura, liked to cram extremely heavy armament into their ships; the result was a series of disasters that caused the entire *Fubaki* class of destroyers to be rebuilt as well as the cruiser *Mogami*. It was a case of reach extending beyond grasp.

Japanese crews received the same severe treatment as their infantry brothers; sections slept and messed in their work areas, and personal hygiene was accomplished with cold salt water at troughs at the deck edge. Rations on board ship were adequate during the first part of the war, but grew steadily worse as time went on. Submarines received the best rations, averaging about 3,300 calories per day per man, far above other Japanese civil and military allotments except for senior military and government officials.

By sacrificing all creature comforts and even things considered essential in Western navies—adequate fire suppression, medical facilities, damage-control materials—Japanese warship performance nonetheless compared favorably to that of their potential enemies.

The performance envelope was pushed by exceedingly realistic training exercises, ignoring the safety considerations that stifled the practice operations of other navies. It was not unusual for collisions to occur in large-scale fleet maneuvers or for as many as 100 seamen to be killed in accidents in a single fleet maneuver. What would have resulted in a congressional investigation in the United States was simply hushed up. The Japanese were prepared to pay the price to be ready for war. Because of the close control of the civilian populace by the military, no notice was given of the extent of the losses, and there were no protests.

The Japanese trained extensively for night engagements, and developed superior searchlights and pyrotechnics; this would pay off during destroyer and cruiser engagements in the early part of the war before the widespread use of radar. The Japanese relied heavily on the use of their excellent 24-inch Long Lance torpedoes in both their cruisers and destroyers; U.S. cruisers, having deleted their torpedo tubes, were at a disadvantage in the opening battles.

Also, the Japanese destroyers and cruisers were captained by the toughest, most aggressive breed of commander, willing to risk ships by closing fast and not breaking off the engagement until it was settled. The same combativeness was sadly lacking at fleet commander levels.

YAMAMOTO TAKES COMMAND

The Combined Fleet, commanded by Admiral Yamamoto Isoruku, was a formidable force, consisting of ten battleships, ten carriers (six fleet and four light), eighteen heavy cruisers, twenty-four light cruisers, 111 destroyers and sixty-four submarines. It was a relatively modern force, short-ranged by American standards, but crafted to fight the war that had been planned for so long. It would soon be reinforced by two new super-battleships, the *Yamato* and the *Musashi*, the largest battleships ever built, each perfect examples of the Japanese theory that their ships must be superior to their American counterparts.

Only five feet three inches tall and weighing 130 pounds, Yamamoto nonetheless was never described as small, for he had a powerful personality that engaged the friendship of Japanese and foreigners alike even though he could be extremely rude and outspoken. He liked scotch, cigars and geishas; one, Umeryu, would be the love of his life. He traveled extensively, and knew from firsthand observation that Japan could not compete with the industrial might of the United States in a war of long duration. Despite his cosmopolitan outlook, Yamamoto believed, as his countrymen did, that Japan was a great power that deserved hegemony in Asia.

In many ways, Yamamoto's early career was similar to Admiral King's. An advocate of air power, though not a pilot as King was, Yamamoto was captain of the carrier *Akagi* and pressed for the buildup of carriers at the expense of battleships. He headed the Naval Aviation Department, the equivalent of the U.S. Bureau of Aeronautics, and spearheaded the development of many of the aircraft with which Japan began World War II. There was bitter opposition to carriers in the Japanese "battleship navy," but the Diet thought so much of Yamamoto that it sanctioned the creation of a separate fleet of aircraft carriers in addition to the traditional battle fleet of battleships, cruisers and destroyers.

Admiral Yamamoto opposed war with the United States quite openly, and his most quoted statement is from a letter in which he wrote that if ordered to fight "I shall run wild for the first six months or a year, but I have utterly no confidence for the second or third year." Yet his subsequent actions are in stark contrast to this belief, for he prepared the concept of an aerial strike on Pearl Harbor. His plan was rejected by the Naval General Staff, which did not feel that an attack on Pearl Harbor was absolutely necessary for the success of the drive to the south, and that such an attack would have only a 40 percent chance of succeeding.

They also were concerned that too much depended upon surprise and that the risks involved in refueling in the North Pacific in the winter were too great.

Using a tactic he would repeat, Admiral Yamamoto threatened to resign if his plan was not adopted. He would have served his nation better if instead he had threatened to resign if Japan planned war upon the United States.

Yamamoto relied on the assistance of his best people to do the actual detailed planning: Rear Admiral Onishi Takijiro, Japan's foremost aviation authority, and an air ace in the war with China; Rear Admiral Fukudome Shigeru, who had advocated withdrawing from the Tripartite Pact to avoid war with Britain and the United States and, oddly enough, was not a great advocate of air power; and Commander Genda Minoru. Genda had been an air attaché in London during the time of the British attack on Taranto in November 1940, and used it as a model for the attack on Pearl Harbor. He brought in Commander Maeda Kosei, an expert on torpedo bombing, and Commander Fuchida Mitsuo, who would be the airborne commander. These three men developed new methods for dropping torpedoes and drastically intensified bombing training. Without ever being told of their ultimate missions, crews were trained in Kagoshima Bay in Kyushu, which resembled Pearl Harbor in some essential respects. Just as the Japanese had honed their night-fighting skills for cruiser and destroyer engagements, so now did they train their already skilled aircrews.

Responsibility for operational command of this vast array of ships and aircraft was given to a man who had no aviation experience and was opposed to the attack, because he was senior. Vice Admiral Nagumo Chuichi was directly responsible for the swiftest, most comprehensive series of naval victories in history but is now virtually unknown to the American public, nor is he greatly celebrated by the Japanese, even though his uniform and medals are displayed at the Yasukuni Shrine near Tokyo. It was Vice Admiral Nagumo who led Japan's naval forces on a 100-day rampage, beginning with the brilliantly executed attack on Pearl Harbor. He went on to command the Darwin Strike Force, which bombed Australia and whipped the British at Ceylon; life was less kind to him subsequently, for his on-the-spot decisions cost the Japanese victory at Midway. Twice removed from key positions, he ended his life on July 7, 1944, by *seppuku*, ritual suicide, in a dank cave at Jingoku-dani, the "Valley of Hell" on Saipan.

The reluctant Vice Admiral Nagumo believed that there were too many unknowns, and that it would be impossible to maintain secrecy. Grouchy and forbidding to all but his innermost circle of officers, curiously similar in physical appearance to Yamamoto, Nagumo knew that, since 1909, Japan had planned to lure the American fleet toward Asia, whittle it down and defeat it on the open ocean. Now, almost overnight, all the years of planning and training were being discarded for Yamamoto's sneak attack.

To the South and to Pearl Harbor

In what would become a familiar style, Japan's war plan was extraordinarily complex, ranging over a far-greater area than the Allies had considered possible. Allied intelligence had expected a thrust to the south, but not of the dimensions of the Southern Operation, which encompassed Hong Kong, Malaya, the Dutch East Indies, Guam, Wake Island and the Philippine Islands. The possibility of a simultaneous attack on Hawaii was considered beyond Japanese capabilities.

Vice Admiral Nagumo's powerful force sortied from Hitokappu Bay at 1800 hours on November 26, 1941. The heart of the strike force consisted of six carriers: the just commissioned *Shokaku* and *Zuikaku* (seventy-four aircraft, 34-knot speed); Yamamoto's old ship, the *Akagi*, and the *Kaga* (seventy aircraft, 26 knots); and the sister ships *Hiryu* and *Soryu* (fifty-three aircraft, 25 knots).

The carriers were supported by two pre–World War I battle cruisers converted to high-speed battleships with eight 14-inch guns, the 29,330-ton *Hiei* and *Kirishima;* two heavy cruisers, *Chikuma* and *Tone;* the light cruiser *Abukuma;* eleven destroyers; and three submarines. Eight tankers and supply ships provided en route support.

In addition to Nagumo's task force, Yamamoto had sent forward a submarine force consisting of twenty-seven submarines. Staged out of Kwajalein in the Marshall Islands, they proceeded to Hawaii by a southern route. Five large submarines, *I-16*, *I-18*, *I-20*, *I-22* and *I-24*, each carried midget submarines stored on the deck.

The midget submarines were the brainstorm of a hero of the Russo-Japanese war of 1904–1905, Captain Yokoo Noriyoshi, and work began on them in 1933. Code-named "Target A," all five, with their crews, would be lost; the one survivor, Ensign Sakamaki Kazuo, became the first Japanese prisoner of war of World War II.

The weather was perfect for Nagumo's purposes, enough clouds to hide the fleet's passage, but calm enough to permit refueling operations. Only one vessel was sighted, a Japanese cargo ship.

Weekend Torpor in Paradise

A grave problem in the U.S. command structure in Hawaii was masked by an apparent cordiality and an abundance of meetings. Years of peacetime routine, in which roles and missions were sharply defined and competed for, resulted in a failure of communication at the top that had disastrous results.

Perhaps more importantly, as much as the U.S. Army and Navy played at war games, concerns over safety and leisure time vitiated the results. In short, the American commanders were not serious, despite the warnings and despite having conducted war games featuring a carrier-borne attack from the north.

The Commander of the Hawaiian air force was Major General Frederick L. Martin, a big man, but not entirely well. As commander of the 1924 Round-the-World flight of Douglas World Cruisers, he had flown into a mountain in the Aleutians, survived the crash and walked out—typical of his innate toughness. Yet Martin was a diplomat, aware of the interservice arguments and particularly sensitive to the fact that the navy regarded the Army Air Corps Brigadier General Billy Mitchell's crusade against battleships with particular anger. Martin did much to rectify the situation, working closely with his opposite number in the navy, Rear Admiral Patrick N. L. Bellinger (later Deputy Chief of Staff to Admiral King), who had arrived in Hawaii on October 30, 1940, two days before Martin. Bellinger had initiated U.S. naval air warfare by taking rifle-fire hits while reconnoitering Mexican defenses in Vera Cruz in his Curtiss AB-3 flying boat in April 1914. The two men cooperated to prepare the remarkable March 31, 1941, Martin-Bellinger report, which stated that in the near future the Japanese might make a surprise early morning air attack that would destroy the fleet. They proposed the establishment of a 360-degree system of aerial reconnaissance patrols extending out to the limit of their aircrafts' range. Recognizing the shortage of patrol aircraft, they indicated that such patrols should be initiated upon receipt of intelligence that a raid was imminent. It was a remarkable forecast, but its recommendations were ignored.

Magic

The one area in which the United States had outstripped the Japanese was in deciphering and analyzing radio traffic. Even though Vice Admiral

Nagumo was extremely security conscious, removing the crystals from the radios to make sure no accidental transmission broke radio silence while the rest of the Japanese navy maintained an extensive radio hoax to conceal his departure, U.S. Naval Intelligence in Hawaii was hauntingly aware of a lapse in contact with two carrier groups. In retrospect, this was the most severe war warning of all, but was not interpreted as such.

As with the Japanese services, cooperation at lower levels was always better than at the top, and a brilliant army cryptanalyst, the Signal Corps Reserve Lieutenant Colonel William F. Friedman, working with Lieutenant Commander Alwyn D. Kramer of Naval Intelligence, cracked the Japanese Purple *diplomatic* code in August 1940. Friedman's group had built a duplicate of the Japanese machine, which, like the Enigma, used a keyboard, but instead of rotors had a selective device that encoded each letter separately. The feat was given the cover name Operation Magic.

Not unnaturally, security about the breakthrough was a problem; Magic's importance was so great that distribution of the information was extremely limited. As difficult as it was to decipher the code, it sometimes took longer to make a meaningful translation, for the Japanese used many obscure references and allusions difficult to render into English.

At the time, no Japanese military code had yet been broken, but a relatively small group of intensely motivated officers and men in both the army and the navy would attack the problem with an animal ferocity. The results were, without exaggeration, war-winning.

But even if there had been no intelligence other than the November 27, 1941, war warning from Admiral Harold Stark, the chief of naval operations, the U.S. reconnaissance efforts were seriously flawed. General Short was not conducting sufficient short-range reconnaissance. Admiral Kimmel elected to restrict the long-range reconnaissance of his Consolidated PBYs, concentrating on training missions instead, so that they would be ready for an encounter between the two navies. The great compensating factor was that Nagumo, too, was remiss in his reconnaissance efforts before, during and after the attack; of this, more later.

The United States was blessed by the fact that its Pacific aircraft carriers were not in Pearl Harbor on December 7. The USS *Enterprise* was en route back to Pearl after delivering a squadron of marine fighters to Wake Island (where they would do remarkable work in the next month). The USS *Lexington* had sailed for Midway Island on December 5. The two ships embodied the bulk of the navy's carrier air power, for the USS *Saratoga* was still on the West Coast. (The *Yorktown* and the brand-new *Hornet* were in the Atlantic.)

The most important of the navy's and marines' 250 aircraft in Hawaii were newly arrived Consolidated PBY-3 and PBY-5 flying boats. New aircraft entering squadron service typically require maintenance to bring them to combat standards, and there was a severe shortage of spare parts. If truly rigorous methods had been taken—as they would be in almost every instance later, even when the war was obviously won—more of the planes could have been actively patrolling.

*N*IITAKA *Y*AMA *N*I *N*ABORE

The order *Niitaka Yama Ni Nabore* (Climb Mount Niitaka) given to Nagumo's force on December 2 was a metaphor for the difficulty of the attack, for Mount Niitaka, in Formosa, was the tallest mountain in the Japanese empire. Nagumo, having avoided his greatest fear, premature detection, had brought his task force to a position 200 miles north of Oahu, in a spot that U.S. war games had predicted, and well within the range not only of Kimmel's PBYs but also Short's few B-17 and obsolete B-18 bombers.

The fact that agents in Hawaii had confirmed that the U.S. carriers were not in port worried Nagumo. Had security been compromised? Were U.S. dive-bombers about to attack his carriers? He knew when the *Enterprise* and the *Lexington* had left, but where were the *Yorktown* and the *Hornet*, which he believed to be in the area? Incredibly, he made no great effort at reconnaissance to find them. He concentrated instead on the eight battleships and nine cruisers lying at anchor, the majority of their crews ashore enjoying themselves. To Nagumo, this was his mission; the battleships represented the main threat to the flank of the Southern Operation, and had to be destroyed.

At 0530, Nagumo ordered that both the cruisers *Tone* and *Chikuma*, both hardy warriors that would make their influence felt through most of the war, each catapult an Aichi E13A1 float plane (later to be called "Jake" by the Allies) to reconnoiter Pearl Harbor. It was adequate for the attack, but totally inadequate to determine where U.S. carriers might be located.

With the same ensign Togo had flown at Tsushima flying from the *Akagi*, the Japanese first attack force of 183 aircraft began taking off at 0600, a green lamp waved in a circle signaling each takeoff, recorded for history by Japanese cameramen who caught the stern-faced pilots with their white *hachimaki* headbands staring straight ahead. It was an emotional moment; in the finest Japanese naval tradition of aping the English, Yamamoto sent a message derived from Nelson at Trafalgar: "The rise or fall of the empire depends upon this battle: everyone will do his duty with utmost efforts."

The launch was not easy, for the carriers were pitching and rolling, and the takeoffs had to be coordinated with the change in pitch. Led by Commander Fuchida, the attack formations assembled with practiced efficiency in thirty minutes. Nagumo prudently kept thirty-nine of the Zeros over the carriers as a defense, their pilots miserable with the assignment.

It was a powerful force for the time, one that the Japanese could well be proud of. The forty-two Zeros assigned the air superiority role over Hawaii were the best carrier aircraft in the world, flown by the best carrier pilots. The eighty-nine Nakajima B5N Kate bombers were similarly advanced, making both the British Fairey Swordfish and the awkward American Douglas TBD Devastator seem primitive by comparison. Acompanying them were fifty-two Aichi D3A Val dive-bombers, not quite so advanced over their counterparts, the Douglas SBD Dauntless or the German Junkers Ju 87 Stuka, but adequate for their role.

Forty-nine of the eighty-nine Kates carried 1,800-pound armor-piercing bombs that the Japanese had modified from 16-inch battleship shells. The remaining Nakajima B5Ns were armed with specially modified torpedoes, suitable for use in Pearl Harbor's shallow waters.

In his effort to tighten the air defense of Hawaii, General Martin had requested operational control of the newly arrived—and more than a little mysterious—radar sets from General Short. Short denied the request, insisting that the radars be maintained under the control of the Signal Corps until training on them was completed.

The young soldiers being introduced to the truck-mounted SCR-270B radar sets were eager to learn. The Fort Shafter and Koko Head units made the first sighting at 0613, followed by Kaawa, Kawailoa and Opana at 0645, picking up *Tone* and *Chikuma* reconnaissance planes.

In a temporary operations room at Fort Shafter, a young pursuit pilot, doubtless fretting about performing a ground-pounder's duty, manned the central Information Center. Lieutenant Kermit Tyler's only experience with radar had been a similar four-hour shift a few days before; he had had no formal training, and could not be expected to appreciate what the sightings meant. Despite the plots, schedules were schedules, and by 0700 the radar stations began shutting down, a lengthy procedure in itself. At the Opana station, Privates George Elliot and Joseph Lockard kept their radar on line to get some extra practice. At 0702, they plotted a large formation only 127 miles away.

Elliot and Lockard, excited, called the Information Center. Lieutenant

Tyler analyzed the information, recalled that a flight of B-17s was due in from the West Coast, and called them back, telling them not to worry. Tyler would not be aware of the attack until he got a call from Wheeler Field at 0800.

FIRST BLOOD

While the phosphorescent blobs of light were moving inexorably across the Opana radar tube, there were other more violent signs of war. Lieutenant William Woodward Outerbridge was on his second patrol in command of the USS *Ward*, an overage destroyer whose keel had been laid down on May 15, 1918, and was launched fifteen days later on June 1 to set a building record. Similar to the four-stackers given to Great Britain, the 30-knot ship was named for Commander James Harmon Ward, the first naval officer killed in the Civil War. Old or not, Outerbridge was proud of her, and pleased to be pulling duty off Pearl Harbor instead of the North Atlantic.

At 0357, Outerbridge received word that the minesweeper *Condor* had sighted what it thought was the periscope of a submarine in a restricted area one and three-quarter miles from the entrance to Pearl Harbor. He ordered general quarters and searched the area, in vain. (It was learned later that a midget submarine had entered Pearl Harbor at 0430, circled Ford Island and left again—this was probably the sub the *Ward* was seeking.)

Outerbridge was awakened at 0637; the repair ship *Antares*, towing a target, was in sight, with a small submarine following it, evidently intending to enter Pearl Harbor.

As the *Ward* hurtled toward the submarine, the two boilers it had on line pushing the Parson turbines as fast as they would go, Outerbridge closed to 100 yards before giving the order to fire the opening American shot of World War II. The first shot missed, but the second hit the conning tower at the point-blank range of seventy-five yards; as the *Ward* passed over the diving submarine, Outerbridge called for the depth charges to be rolled off the stern. At 0645 the submarine was boxed by the charges and it sank in 1,200 feet of water, the kill confirmed by oil and debris.

Outerbridge immediately sent a message to Pearl Harbor: "We have attacked, fired upon, and dropped depth charges upon submarine operating in defensive sea area." The message, with its stark import, was never delivered to the commanders at Pearl Harbor. There had been too many reports of submarines in the past and this was considered another false alarm.

The morning's excitement was just beginning for Outerbridge and his crew as the *Ward* captured a motor-driven sampan and its Japanese crew, inexplicably in the same forbidden area as the submarine. Shortly thereafter, they saw smoke in the sky over Pearl Harbor.

(Outerbridge would go on to a distinguished career, fighting in both the Atlantic and the Pacific and rising to command Destroyer Division 136. After the *Ward*, he became captain of the modern destroyer *O'Brien*, which was struck twice by kamikaze aircraft off Okinawa. The *Ward* had been relegated to a role of fast transport, and was badly hit by kamikazes off Leyte on December 7, 1944, exactly three years to the day after she sank the midget submarine. Abandoned and burning, but still afloat, the tough old veteran had to be destroyed by U.S. forces. In what sounds like a Hollywood script, the task fell to Commander Outerbridge of the *O'Brien*, who with sadness in his heart sank his old ship, his first command, with gunfire.)

FUCHIDA EN ROUTE

The approach to Oahu had been obscured by clouds, but Commander Fuchida used his radio direction finder to home in on local radio stations, which obligingly informed him that the target area was covered only by broken clouds and that visibility was good. At 0645, just as the first midget submarine was sinking, the second attack force of 168 planes was taking off, consisting of seventy-eight Val dive-bombers, fifty-four Kate level bombers and thirty-six Zeros.

Over Kahuka Point, the northernmost tip of Oahu, at 0740, correctly believing that the first wave had achieved complete surprise, Fuchida gave the predetermined signal, a "Black Dragon" pyrotechnic flare. This ordered the torpedo-bombers to attack the fleet first, followed by the high-level bombers and then the dive-bombers. Some of the level and dive-bombers were assigned to attack airfields, including the army's Hickam, Wheeler and Bellows Fields, and the navy installations at Ford Island, Kaneohe and Ewa.

The Zeros did not see the first Black Dragon, and Fuchida fired a second flare, a mistake, for it was interpreted by Lieutenant Commander Takahashi Kakuichi to mean that his dive-bombers were to attack first. The resulting confusion was probably fortunate for the Japanese, for it compressed the time of the attack into the period when the American response was least effective.

At 0749, Fuchida sent his attack signal and Japan launched itself at the

United States with a fury that would not abate until August 1945. In his own writing, Fuchida records that his radioman tapped out in Morse code the signal to the attacking pilots, "To, to, to, to . . ." short for *totsugeki* (charge). Moments later, he sent "Tora, Tora, Tora," the signal that the surprise had been complete, to Nagumo.

Initially the attack was easier than the practice exercises. Fearing sabotage, the army had its planes lined up in neat rows, perfect for strafing runs by Lieutenant Commander Itaya Shigeru's fighters. Led by Lieutenant Sakamoto Akira, twenty-five Vals, obsolete-looking with their fixed gear, plummeted earthward and dropped their 550-pound bombs on Wheeler Field. Moments later, another fifty-two Vals, from *Zuikaku* and *Shokaku*, struck Hickam Field and Ford Island; others hit Kaneohe, where the bulk of the patrol planes were sitting. Twenty-six of the thirty-six precious PBYs were destroyed and six were heavily damaged. Three Catalinas out on patrol survived.

BELLINGER'S MESSAGE

The stark message "AIR RAID, PEARL HARBOR—THIS IS NO DRILL" was sent out at 0758 by Admiral Bellinger, who from his hillside position could see, as the Japanese pilots did, the disposition of ships in Pearl Harbor, as tidy as the aircraft at Wheeler Field. Just over a thousand feet from the navy yard lay Ford Island, and along its southeast shore was Battleship Row. There, a few yards off shore, the battleships were moored to sturdy quays. The *California* was in the berth farthest to the south; north of her were the *Maryland* and the *Oklahoma*, moored as a pair; then came the *Tennessee* and the *West Virginia*, also paired, followed by the *Arizona*, which had a small repair ship, the *Vestal*, alongside; at the northeastern point lay the battleship *Nevada*. The *Pennsylvania* was across the harbor, in dry dock at the navy yard with two destroyers, the *Cassin* and *Downes*. Around the harbor were five cruisers, twenty-six destroyers and minecraft and various other auxiliary ships. The Japanese had found a textbook target, lacking only the carriers to be perfect.

The hard training of the missions in Kagoshima Bay bore fruit as the Kates struck Battleship Row from the east, with, thanks to Kimmel's concern about getting under way rapidly, no nets to impede their torpedoes. The *West Virginia* took the first of a half-dozen bomb and torpedo hits at 0756. Showing grace under pressure, an inexperienced ensign, Roland S.

Brooks, directed the damage-control parties while Lieutenant Claude V. Ricketts ordered prompt counterflooding measures, which succeeded in preventing the "Wee Vee" from capsizing; the *West Virginia* settled to the bottom upright, her antiaircraft guns still blazing. Ricketts's action saved many lives; only 105 were killed out of the 1,541 on board. (He would make further history by being the first man to rise from the enlisted ranks to four-star admiral.) Just astern of the *West Virginia*, the *Arizona* absorbed several hits. The *Oklahoma*, south of the *West Virginia*, capsized from five of the excellent 1,764-pound Japanese torpedoes that tore great gaping holes in her side—no depth control or exploder problems. Out of 1,354 officers and men on board, 415 were lost.

The *Nevada*, old but agile, got under way without any assistance, but took a torpedo nonetheless and was then hit by five bombs. Despite the damage, *Nevada* kept up an intense antiaircraft fire that still did not prevent the diving Vals from making three more hits; she was beached at Waipio Point to prevent her sinking in the main entrance channel.

It was the *Arizona* for which the greatest punishment was reserved. At 0756, an 1,800-pound bomb smashed through the number two gun turret to explode the forward ammunition magazines; as with the *Hood*, a gigantic tower of flame rose up as the ship broke in half. Moments later, the first in a string of bombs exploded deep inside, while six more marched aft to the stern. Mortally wounded, the *Arizona* sank, killing 1,103 of her 1,411 officers and men, and becoming the instant, permanent symbol of Pearl Harbor, just as Pearl Harbor would become the symbol of the war. At 0804 the *California* was struck by two torpedoes; she settled slowly to the bottom. The battleships *Tennessee* and *Maryland*, screened by their sister ships, were damaged by bombs but did not sink.

On the northwest side of Ford Island, the decommissioned target ship *Utah*, berthed where the carrier *Saratoga* usually tied up, was hit by two torpedoes and capsized. Near her, the scout cruiser *Raleigh* kept up a protective fire for the defenseless *Utah* while being torpedoed and dive-bombed herself. Expert damage control, directed largely by junior officers, kept her afloat. The destroyer *Monaghan*, on her way to support the *Ward*, found her own midget submarine and rammed it, then rolled out a pattern of depth charges to sink it.

The Japanese air attack was thoroughly professional and well executed; the Japanese aircraft were methodical; after dropping their bombs or torpedoes, they swept back to machine-gun soldiers and sailors. Sporadic opposition began as ship and shore antiaircraft started firing wildly, then settled down to greater effect. All over the harbor, the stark trauma of exploding bombs, wounded comrades and utter pandemonium called forth individual acts of heroism, some noticed and rewarded, many more passing undetected in the heat of battle. Young ensigns, normally relegated to minor duties, found themselves the senior officers on board and fought their ships gallantly. Shipfitters waded their way through fire, oil and water to control damage; shipmates were hoisted on backs and carried up the tilted ladders to safety; wounded men stayed at their guns and fought.

Vice Admiral Nagumo had achieved his mission's objective in the hard-hitting first attack. American battleships were no longer a threat to the flank of the Southern Operation.

American resistance began to stiffen as the Japanese continued their attack on parked aircraft and other targets of opportunity. Five young army air force pilots managed to get their Curtiss fighters off from a small auxiliary field at Haleiwa, and conducted a series of sorties until 1000. Although there was no briefing, and certainly no air control from the ground, the pilots had no problem finding the enemy. In the course of two sorties, Second Lieutenant George S. Welch scored four victories and Second Lieutenant Kenneth M. Taylor scored two before returning to Wheeler to rearm.

The ground and ship defenses were fully alerted by the time the second attack force struck at 0850. It had flown down the eastern side of Oahu, and curved in from the south to attack the same targets.

It was war on the Japanese scale, one that had proved effective in China. Eighteen Kates struck the patrol planes already burning at Kaneohe Naval Air Station again, while twenty-seven more attacked Hickam Field; nine others picked out targets on Ford Island. To the Japanese, this was the preferred way to fight a war: a small number of excellent aircraft flown by highly trained pilots in a sneak attack on a virtually undefended target. Three years later, when the B-29s began their assault, the Japanese complained bitterly that the Americans were not fighting fair by using advanced equipment in such tremendous quantities.

The battleship *Pennsylvania,* in dry dock but still capable of putting up a limited antiaircraft barrage, was struck by a single 551-pound bomb that killed eighteen men. Forward in the same dry dock, the destroyers *Downes* and *Cassin* were incinerated by intense fires set off by bombs intended for the *Pennsylvania,* with their own fuel, torpedoes and depth charges contributing to the conflagration. (Later, new hulls were built to their old design, and given their old hull numbers.)

Because the second wave of the Japanese attack appeared to come from the south, all of the initial American search efforts to find the Japanese carriers were made in that direction, 180 degrees out of phase—none of the visual or radar reports of Japanese aircraft coming in from the north were considered.

By 1000 the only Japanese aircraft over Hawaii was the Kate from which Commander Fuchida assessed the damage; he concluded that a second attack was necessary and flew back to persuade Admiral Nagumo to make it.

The Americans were making a damage assessment as well. Initially, it seemed to be utterly disastrous. Casualties included 2,403 killed and 1,178 wounded. Five battleships were sunk and three were damaged, one seriously. Three light cruisers (*Raleigh*, *Helena* and *Honolulu*) suffered moderate damage. Three destroyers received devastating damage; one, the *Shaw*, had her bow blown off. The minelayer *Oglala* capsized, the repair ship *Vestal* was beached and the seaplane tender *Curtiss* was badly damaged by a crashing plane. On the Oahu airfields, at least 188 aircraft were destroyed, with another 100 badly damaged.

The Japanese had missed some prime targets whose destruction would have provided a far longer breathing space for them, although it would be months before U.S. commanders realized this. No attack was made on the 4.5 million barrels of fuel and oil in the tank farms, nor did the vital machine shops in the dock area receive much damage. The submarine base went unscathed, and the nine submarines at anchor during the raid would go out to wreak havoc on Japanese merchant shipping.

Had the machine shops and the fuel dumps been destroyed, it would have taken eighteen months or more to get Pearl Harbor back in operation. Fleet operations would have had to have been conducted from West Coast ports, adding 5,000 miles to each sortie. The repair of a single ship, the *Yorktown*, so crucial to the battle of Midway, would have been impossible.

It was considerations such as these that led Commander Fuchida to press the case to Admiral Nagumo for a second attack. His was the last plane to return to the *Akagi*, and he found most of his aircraft already refueled and rearmed, ready to go for another strike. Commander Genda, flushed with success, wanted to find the enemy carriers and attack them.

Nagumo considered the matter carefully. He had lost only twenty-nine planes in the course of the attack although several others were damaged upon returning to the ship. The loss of the five midget submarines was not yet known to him. After evaluating everything, and listening to the usual negative counsel of his Chief of Staff, Rear Admiral Kusaka Ryunosuke, Nagumo ruled against a second attack, and steamed away northward at high speed. He had accomplished his assigned mission; he did not know where the enemy aircraft carriers were, and he felt that there were at least fifty land-based bombers operational on Oahu that could attack him.

The attack on Pearl Harbor was over, but the stunned American defenders did not know it, remaining on alert and reacting to false alarms.

RESULTS

Admiral Yamamoto's attack on Pearl Harbor has been decried by U.S. historians such as Samuel Eliot Morison, who described it as "strategic folly," a politically "irredeemable blunder" and in short, "imbecilic" because it involved Japan in a fatal war. It has been defended by surviving members of the Japanese Naval Staff, such as Admiral Fukudome Shigeru, who maintained that Japan had no choice but to go to war, and Pearl Harbor provided a gain of two years' time in which anything might have happened.

Vice Admiral Fukudome's postwar reasoning illustrates the utter blindness of Japanese thinking, for it excludes the possibility that Japan could have chosen not to be an aggressor nation. For Fukudome, the China Incident, the incursion into Indochina and the oil of the East Indies were truly only Japan's business, and the adverse U.S. reaction meant war. It simply did not register that Japan could have maintained a strong defensive posture, eliminated the drain of the China Incident and reestablished good relations with the United States and England by concentrating on its own industrial development and forswearing aggression. The remarkable progress seen from 1955 to the present might have begun in 1941; Japan could have become a major supplier of arms and ships to the Allies, and peacefully and by economic means established a true Co-prosperity Sphere by 1945.

In the entire process, however, the greatest Japanese mistake was their failure to gauge how the American and British public would respond. The Japanese leaders had no idea of the lengths to which England and the United States would go to win a war on their own terms. Just as they had always planned on the best-case scenarios in their war games, so did the Japanese imagine the best-case diplomatic scenario, in which the wounded and war-weary Anglo-Saxon powers, led by Chamberlain-style weak reeds, would surrender their interests in the Far East, and with them interest in Australia, India and Hawaii. Instead they had run into a buzz saw; it turned out that the Allies *liked* to fight, particularly when they began to win.

The sad truth is that the Japanese forces that executed the attack with such brilliance deserved better leadership, and should not have been ordered to begin the process by which they and their country would be utterly destroyed.

The war would continue from December 7, 1941, to August 15, 1945. Japan would ride high for less than 10 percent of that time; there would be 100 days of cheaply won glory, creating an enormous Pacific empire. From the 101st day, however, Japan was on an irreversible slide to defeat.

7.

THE RELUCTANT
NAGUMO
RAMPAGES

THE WILD RUN BEGINS

The great naval historian Samuel Eliot Morison aptly likened the Japanese multi-pronged southern advance to the tentacles of an octopus, dangling down into the fabled Indies and seizing everything en route. It was a very greedy octopus indeed, one that ultimately embraced more than it could consume. But even more amazing than the speed and efficiency with which Japan seized the resources and the defensive perimeter was the very austere means employed. The Japanese army and navy parceled out their forces as meticulously as a pharmacist compounding a prescription, and the unwilling Dutch, British and American patients had to swallow their medicine. Only ten Japanese divisions and three brigades were allocated to the Southern Army under General Count Terauchi Hisaichi, which had as its task seizure of all American, British and Dutch possessions over the immense area of the South Pacific.

In this operation, all of the interservice rivalry that plagued Japanese General Headquarters was forgotten in the intricately linked movements that joined the army, navy and their respective air forces together in a blitzkrieg that outsped and outfought anything Hitler had done or would do.

The basic tactics were superb. The navy would escort troops to an invasion area; air cover would be provided by land-based aircraft if within range, or by carriers if not; when the invasion took place, the first objective was to seize or build an airfield. Units of the army or navy air forces would fly in to help overwhelm local defense forces and to provide cover for the next operation. (It should be noted that the navy operated both carrier-based and land-based aviation, and did not hesitate to shift carrier units to operate from land bases as required.)

There was almost a balletlike quality to the tactics the Japanese imposed upon their enemies, who far outnumbered them in the aggregate. But by concentrating overwhelming forces under the cover of air power at each location, the Japanese defeated the Allies, and as they did so they built up an aura of invincibility that they soon believed themselves.

The aggressive moves Japan had made in Indochina prior to Pearl Harbor would prove to be the key to much of the operation, because in the early weeks of the campaign air superiority was provided from bases in southern Indochina where prepositioned troops were available for the multiple invasion routes. The navy assembled its ships into task forces, with warships to cover the transports as they conducted the first ship-to-shore invasions of the war, one of the most spread out in history. Japanese planning was evident in their pioneering deployment of large landing ships that launched landing craft, foreshadowing the extensive American use of similar craft a few years later. The Japanese Type A landing craft were simple adaptations of civilian craft; 49 feet long, with a 12-foot beam, they were fitted with a bow ramp, carried up to 100 men at 8 to 10 knots, and were armed with one or two light machine guns. Unopposed, they functioned well; in heavy seas or against determined opposition, the lightly built craft were highly vulnerable.

OVERALL PLAN

While the Allies stolidly believed that Japan was capable of undertaking only one major movement at a time, the planners in the land of the Rising Sun had allocated the resources to undertake multiple strikes over a vast area. The Pearl Harbor Special Attack Force was under Nagumo's command, and later supported operations in the south and in the Indian Ocean. The Southern Force, under the command of Vice Admiral Kondo Nobutake, was to convey the invasion forces to conquer the Philippines, Malaya and the Dutch East Indies. Vice Admiral Inouye Shigeyoshi was tasked to capture Guam and Wake Island.

The Japanese navy displayed extreme flexibility in its operations, shifting task forces from one area to another as needed, and achieving both concentration and surprise. The maneuvers were often intricate and depended upon good communication, excellent timing and a measure of good fortune. All three elements attended Japanese operations as they moved to inhale an empire at a gasp.

Phase one of the assault was to conquer the Philippines, Wake Island, Guam, Hong Kong and Malaya. Phase two saw the tentacles merging to enfold the Dutch East Indies, from the westernmost tip of Sumatra to beyond Java. There was room in this grand design for incidental swipes at other targets, including Midway and the British Force Z, the battle cruiser *Repulse* and the battleship *Prince of Wales*.

The only place the Japanese planners erred was in their time table; everything came to them far earlier than planned, with the exception of Bataan and Corregidor, of which more later. The speed was an occasion for concern for Emperor Hirohito, who cautioned that "The series of victories are too much, too fast."

Malay Peninsula

The fighting actually opened with multiple landings on the Malay peninsula and Thailand by the Japanese Twenty-fifth Army. A fierce opposition was overcome as two detachments of the 18th Division swarmed ashore at Kota Baharu at 1145 hours on December 7, 1941 (0545 December 7, Hawaiian time), roughly 340 road miles north of Singapore, and began their journey down the eastern coast. The 5th Division, highly mechanized for a Japanese unit, landed at Singora, and by 0410 on December 8 had secured the beachhead. It moved quickly across Thailand to descend down along the west coast of Malaya, followed much later by the 18th Division.

Japanese forces in Malaya were commanded by Lieutenant General Yamashita Tomoyuki, who would earn the nickname "Tiger of Malaya" before falling into disfavor with Tojo. An ultranationalist, Yamashita was also one of the most widely traveled of the Japanese generals, having held attaché positions in Switzerland, Germany, Austria, Italy and Hungary. Considered a friend of rebellious junior officers, he had been "exiled" to Korea; subsequently, he fought against both the Chinese and the Russians. His brilliant offensive in the Malay peninsula was later matched by equally brilliant defensive tactics in the Philippines. (Generally considered to be the finest Japanese general of his time, he was ultimately captured, tried as a war criminal—on hotly contested grounds—on 123 counts involving 57,000 deaths and hanged at Bilibid Prison in Manila, on February 23, 1946.)

Yamashita commanded about 42,000 troops supported by eighty tanks and forty armored cars. The key to his victory, in addition to the ferocious fighting capacity of his troops, was the superior Japanese air power based in Formosa and Indochina, which consisted of more than 1,000 aircraft, 682 provided by the army and 409 by the navy. The army fighters were the Nakajima Ki 43 *Hayabusa* (Peregrine Falcon, but later called "Oscar" by the Americans), which resembled the Zero and was only slightly inferior to it.

Yamashita's counterpart in Malaya was Lieutenant General Arthur E. Percival, an intelligent man who had served bravely in World War I but made a complete botch of his service in the second. In the debacle in France in 1940, he had declined to take the necessary measures to prepare defenses for retreating British soldiers on the grounds that it would be bad for morale. In Singapore, as the General Officer Commanding Malaya, he failed to fortify the northern defenses of the city for the same reason. A weak man who vacillated, he was the worst choice to command the motley mix of Allied ground forces, strong in number though they were. If Yamashita had been able to pick his opponent, Percival would surely have been his choice.

Percival ultimately had 138,000 troops at his disposal; when the battle began he also had 155 operational aircraft and eighty-eight in reserve. The RAF was equipped with the rotund Brewster Buffalo, the U.S. Navy's first monoplane shipboard fighter. Although rugged, it was slow and unmaneuverable compared to Japanese fighters.

In Singapore, however, the British felt confident that the Japanese would not be able to negotiate the seemingly impenetrable jungle to the north, and posted their men in small units to defend crossroads and the several airfields, most of which lacked aircraft after the initial Japanese air attacks.

But the jungle was penetrated as the Japanese introduced low-technology blitzkrieg, using bicycles to traverse the narrow paths used by planters and natives. Where they met strong British resistance, they simply melted into the jungle and bypassed it. Small craft were used to transport troops down the coast for unopposed landings, leapfrogging defended positions. In short, the Japanese forces, not specially trained for jungle warfare as was later reported, simply fought harder and smarter, keeping Allied forces off balance and never relinquishing the initiative. It was no different at sea.

TOM THUMB TO THE RESCUE

One of the most controversial admirals in the always turbulent politics of the Royal Navy, Admiral Thomas Phillips, was known as "Tom Thumb" to his sailors because of his diminutive stature. He was the protégé of Admiral Dudley Pound—almost an indictment in itself, given Pound's growing unpopularity with the fleet. Phillips was castigated as having a "storekeeper mind," rigid in his planning and insisting on managing even the smallest details, yet he was aggressive, and thus inevitably a favorite of Winston Churchill—until Churchill disagreed with him. Others attributed his pugnacious attitude to his small stature, an assessment reinforced by his aloof manner. He was sniped at by Admirals Cunningham and Lord Louis Mountbatten as well; it can be hell to have friends in high places.

It fell to Phillips to command Force Z, the hopelessly inadequate reinforcements sent to the Far Eastern Fleet, consisting of the *Prince of Wales*, notorious as a "jinx ship," having had a number of mishaps on trials and failing to distinguish herself in the fight with the *Bismarck*, and the *Repulse*, a 1916-vintage battle cruiser of 37,400 tons, fully loaded. Neither of the ships was adequately equipped with antiaircraft weapons.

Dispatched at the insistence of Winston Churchill, who further lowered Dudley Pound's standing in the Royal Navy by again overruling his objections, Force Z was a wistful attempt to impress the Japanese with the same fleet-in-being effect that the *Tirpitz*, *Gneisenau* and *Scharnhorst* had on the British. Air cover was to have been provided by the new armored-deck carrier *Indomitable*, but she ran aground in Jamaica and was unable to participate.

Admiral Phillips was perhaps not as concerned about having air cover as he should have been, believing as he did that a well-fought capital ship, fully equipped with antiaircraft guns, should be able to fight off an air attack. He sailed from Singapore on December 8 with his two capital ships and four destroyers, the *Electra*, *Express*, *Tenedos* and the Royal Australian Navy's *Vampire*, hoping to catch the Japanese invasion fleet at Singora and sink the transports. He requested air cover, but the Japanese air force had already eliminated that possibility, occupying airfields in the area, destroying most of the RAF aircraft on the ground and suppressing those that did get into the air to engage. At midday on December 8, Lieutenant Commander Harada Hakue in the submarine *I-65* spotted Force Z and radioed the information to Vice Admiral Kondo Nobutake, commander of both the Southern Force and the Imperial Navy's Second Fleet. Along with his cruisers *Atago* (flag) and *Takao*, and ten destroyers, Kondo had two older battleships, the *Haruna* and the *Kongo*, the latter ship designed by England's Sir George Thurston and launched in 1912. Both were extensively rebuilt in the 1930s, but Kondo knew that their eight 14-inch guns were no match for the ten 14-inch guns of the *Prince of Wales* and the eight 15-inch guns of the *Repulse*. He nonetheless called in the 7th Japanese Cruiser Squadron, and planned a night engagement in which the Type 93 Long Lance 24-inch oxygen-propelled torpedoes, with their phenomenal 40,000-yard range and 36-knot speed, would redress the balance of firepower.

At 0050 on December 10, however, Admiral Phillips received word—incorrect as it turned out—that the Japanese were landing at Kuantan, midway between Kota Baharu and Singapore. He ordered his ships to turn to the southwest, determined to attack and destroy the transports. As Saigon was 400 miles away, he probably felt himself safe from airborne torpedo attack, and confident about his ability to outmaneuver any high-level bombers.

Admiral Kondo gave the 22nd Air Flotilla at Saigon orders to make a torpedo attack at dawn. The 22nd, commanded by Rear Admiral Matsunaga Sadaichi, mustered over 100 aircraft, including Zero fighters and the Mitsubishi G3M and G4M bombers (later respectively called "Nell" and "Betty"), which had both a high-level and torpedo capability—and, with rigorous cruise-control methods—the range to reach out and strike Force Z.

To Admiral Phillips's intense disgust, reconnaissance revealed that there was no invasion at Kuantan, so he again turned south toward Singapore. Unfortunately, his time had run out. Eleven Japanese reconnaissance planes, nine Nells and two sleek Mitsubishi C5M2s, were tracking Phillips's fleet. At 0625, Admiral Matsunaga ordered the launch; thirty-four G3Ms carrying either two 250-kilogram or one 500-kilogram armor-piercing bombs; then twenty-five G3Ms and twenty-six G4Ms carrying the 21-inch Type 91 torpedoes. It was a long and dangerous flight, out more than 500 miles from Saigon.

While the Mitsubishis were searching for him, Phillips now made his greatest error. When a signal was received at 1030 from the destroyer *Tenedos*, already en route home to Singapore, that she was being attacked (unsuccessfully) by bombers, Phillips failed to ask for the air support that could have been provided him.

The G3Ms were sighted by a Supermarine Walrus reconnaissance plane from the *Repulse;* when it returned to the ship to make a report (being forbidden to break radio silence), the G3Ms followed it to their targets.

The G3M level bombers then did what had proved so difficult to do in other air forces—hit a moving ship at sea. The *Repulse* moved out of a shower of splashes, burning amidships, but still making 25 knots.

Strangely, Phillips still did not call for fighter cover now that there was no longer a reason for radio silence; at least ten Buffalos were available an hour's flight away, and they might have made a difference, for the bombers were unescorted.

The first torpedo attack on the *Prince of Wales* was by nine G3Ms flying in groups of two or three. Flying at 150 knots at a height of 100 feet above the water, they moved through what appeared to the British to be an impenetrable wall of flak, then dropped eight torpedoes at the distance of a mile from their target. Two hit home, striking the port side and damaging steering, propellers and electric-generating equipment. Despite her modern armor and the bulges designed to stop torpedoes, the *Prince of Wales* was mortally wounded, more damaged than the *Bismarck* had been by the initial Swordfish attacks. Within moments, the *Prince of Wales*'s speed had dropped to 15 knots, and 13-degree list to port developed. The list, combined with a power outage, deprived the *Prince of Wales* of more than half her antiaircraft guns. Several of the Nells were damaged and one was shot down.

Eight G3M2s of the Genzan Kokutai (Genzan Naval Air Corps) led by Lieutenant Takai Sadao, launched the next attack. Camouflaged wavy green and brown on top and painted light gray underneath, the slender, midwing Nells flew at almost sea level on their run in to the *Repulse,* which turned to "comb" the oncoming torpedoes and sustained no hits. In his excitement, Lieutenant Takai forgot to release his torpedo and circled around for a second attack, alone this time. He missed. The *Repulse* shook off a level bombing attack without damage and was then boxed in by Nells attacking from port and starboard, but still managed to avoid being hit. Her captain, W. G. Tennant, was an able man at the con, avoiding no fewer than nineteen torpedoes and multiple bombs.

Captain John Leach of the *Prince of Wales* must have mentally hearkened back to the previous May, when he had witnessed the stricken *Bismarck* lurching in circles. Now his own ship was out of control and vulnerable.

The next attack came from twenty-six of the portly Bettys. Four torpedoes blasted the *Prince of Wales*, the first blowing an enormous hole entirely through the dying warship. The tremendous inflow of water temporarily righted the list, but the ship was clearly sinking.

The Bettys assaulted the *Repulse,* coming in from all sides to divide her fire and scored four hits, the last jamming her rudder. The *Repulse* began circling; a fifth torpedo in the E boiler room was the coup de grâce, for the old ship did not have the modern compartmentalization of her companion. Tennant gave the order to abandon ship, and most of the crew, even from the lower compartments, plunged into the oily waters before the *Repulse* capsized and sank, stern-first, at 1223.

The last attack came at 1246, when seventeen G3Ms made a level bombing attack on the *Prince of Wales.* One 500-kilogram bomb struck amidships, imparting savage damage in a makeshift casualty station. The destroyer *Express* came alongside to rescue crewmen. At 1320, the *Prince of Wales* turned on her back, rocking the *Express* in the process, then sank, carrying with her both Captain Leach and Admiral Phillips.

After the Japanese bombers had gone, four RAF Buffalo fighters arrived to witness the slow death of the *Prince of Wales,* which lost 327 officers and men. The *Repulse* lost 513 officers and men. A total of 2,081 was saved. The Japanese lost three Bettys and one Nell—four aircraft exchanged for two of the world's most powerful capital ships.

The battle was the first instance in which aircraft had sunk a battleship under way at sea; it was also the last time Britain would lose a capital ship. (The hulls of the *Repulse* and the *Prince of Wales* are now officially designated war graves, and, being only about 150 feet down, can be reached by scuba divers.)

The news of the double tragedy shook the Western world; coming on the heels of the debacle at Pearl Harbor, it began to look as if the Japanese were truly invincible on land, sea and air.

HONG KONG

The Japanese 38th Division crossed from occupied China into Hong Kong at 0800 on December 8; five days later they had occupied the New Territories, including Kowloon. On December 18, they jumped across to the island of Hong Kong and forced the remaining British forces into a pocket on the west side of the island. Surrender was inevitable, and took place on Christmas Day.

GUAM AND WAKE ISLAND

Guam was indefensible; 1,500 miles from Manila and 3,000 miles from Hawaii, it was the southernmost of the Marianas Islands and Japan already had strong forces on neighboring Saipan. Air attacks began on the first day of the war, but it was not until December 10 that the Japanese Fourth Fleet, under Vice Admiral Inouye, put 5,000 men ashore to overwhelm the 365 Marines and 308 armed Guamanians. After a brief resistance, the island surrendered.

Wake Island was a tougher nut for the Japanese to crack. It had gained attention when the tiny atoll of three low islands was selected by Pan American as a refueling stop for its Clipper flying boats in the mid-1930s. Its defensive importance was obvious, for it was only 1,300 miles from Guam and 1,025 miles from Midway. The Japanese were closer, however, with a major base at Kwajalein only 620 miles away.

Admiral Kimmel had anticipated that the Japanese would attack Wake, and sent reinforcements to help defend it. A marine defense battalion that was to make real and popular history began arriving in mid-August 1941. Its commander, Major James P. S. Devereux, arrived in October. The principal armament was six 5-inch guns removed from old battleships and twelve 3-inch antiaircraft guns. A flight of twelve Grumman F4F Wildcats of VMF 211 arrived on December 4, having flown off the carrier *Enterprise*, the delivery thus saving her from being in port at Pearl Harbor three days later.

Thirty-six Bettys bombed Wake on December 8, destroying seven of the Wildcats on the ground, killing twenty and wounding eleven. Three pilots were dead and four more wounded. The two large 12,500-gallon gasoline tanks were destroyed. This loss would not matter. The bombing continued for two days, and the invasion began on December 11, the Japanese making the same mistake they would subsequently make on Guadalcanal—sending a boy to do a man's job.

The defenders on Wake fought back desperately. Major Devereux waited until the flagship, the cruiser *Yubari*, and two destroyers closed to 4,500 yards before opening fire with Battery A's 5-inch guns, hitting *Yubari* three times and forcing her to depart. Two destroyers were holed, and the destroyer *Hayate* blew up after six hits, breaking in half and sinking in two minutes. Her companion ships steamed away, leaving the crew to drown. It was the first Japanese surface warship to be lost in the war. Captain Henry Talmadge Elrod, who had scored two aerial victories earlier, dropped a 100-pound bomb on the destroyer *Kisaragi*, which blew up shortly thereafter, almost certainly from the explosion of the depth charges it carried. Elrod, badly injured, flew back to crash-land his Wildcat on the beach. He was later awarded the Medal of Honor for his heroism.

The landing was called off, costing Rear Admiral Kajioka Sadamichi considerable loss of face; Yamamoto later removed him from command.

The exultation felt by Wake's defenders was amplified in an America desperately in need of good news; the media capitalized on a phrase used as padding in a coded message, "Send us more Japs," and the country buzzed with excitement and martial spirit. Like Colin Kelly's "sinking of *Haruna*," the phrase was invaluable propaganda. The first genuine good news for Americans, however, was to be four months away.

The exhilaration felt on Wake was pumped up by the word that a relief expedition was on its way. Unfortunately, the confusion endemic at Pearl Harbor after the attack upon it, and ill-considered delays in assembling the relief force caused it to wither on the vine; the carrier *Saratoga*, with eighteen more Wildcats for Wake in addition to her own air group, was delayed for refueling, and a dawdling relief force under the command of Rear Admiral Frank Jack Fletcher got to within only 425 miles of Wake by December 22, when he was ordered to return to Pearl Harbor.

Keenly conscious that his was the only element of the Japanese attack to be turned back, or to have lost a major ship, Admiral Inouye sent back the original invasion force, moderately reinforced and still under the command of Admiral Kajioka. This time it was backed up by four heavy cruisers, the *Aoba*, *Furutaka*, *Kako* and *Kinugasa*, but more importantly by a detachment from Nagumo's Pearl Harbor striking force, the carriers *Hiryu* and *Soryu*, along with the redoubtable heavy cruisers *Tone* and *Chikuma*. Inouye now provided a sledgehammer to swat a fly.

The island had been worked over almost every day, twice a day by bombers from Kwajalein hitting it about noontime and four-engine patrol bombers bombing either in the early morning or late afternoon. Carrier planes took over the task on December 21, hammering aircraft, artillery sites and any other visible target. The last Wildcat was shot down the next day, and the marine aviators reverted to their traditional role as infantry troops.

Early on the morning of December 23, about 1,000 men of the Naval Special Landing Force landed on Wake; they were immediately engaged by marine defenders for the next thirty hours until the inevitable surrender occurred. The Japanese captured 470 officers and enlisted men and 1,146 civilians; the Japanese suffered 1,155 casualties, including 820 killed. The American prisoners were taken to Japan in mid-January, except for 100 civilian workmen who were kept back to work the island's facilities. The latter were all executed in 1943 in reprisal for a U.S. Navy strike on the island.

THE PHILIPPINES

The American decision to reinforce and hold the Philippines had been made in reliance on General MacArthur's assurance that, suitably reinforced, he could defeat the Japanese on the beaches, and on the naive faith that thirty-five Boeing B-17s would constitute a formidable offensive weapon which would keep the Japanese navy at bay.

This was a wildly optimistic assessment, considering that the Imperial Navy had provided for the invasion of the Philippines the Second and Third Fleets, consisting of one carrier, two battleships, nine heavy cruisers, six light cruisers, forty-one destroyers, 120 transports and eighty-three other vessels—minelayers, patrol craft and similar smaller ships, all buttressed with hundreds of aircraft. It was an overwhelming force, for the U.S. Asiatic Fleet at Admiral Thomas Hart's disposal in the Philippines consisted of one heavy cruiser, one light cruiser, twenty-seven submarines and twenty-four smaller vessels. Hart had an additional light cruiser and ten destroyers in Borneo. Of these, the Japanese were concerned principally about the submarines, which were supposed to have been designed, built, trained and tested to halt invasion fleets.

The primary Japanese goal in seizing the Philippines was to make use of the naval base at Manila as a means of protecting their trade routes to the East Indies from American interference. As always, the Japanese sought to secure immediate air superiority by a surprise air attack.

The American forces had had a series of warnings about an impending attack, for weather had prevented the Japanese air forces from coordinating their efforts with the Pearl Harbor strike. A commercial Manila radio station had broadcast the news of the attack on Hawaii at 0330 local time December 8 (0830, December 7, in Hawaii) and all American and Filipino military units were placed on the alert.

Admiral Hart had responded to the first warning with this message to the Asiatic Fleet: "Japan started hostilities. Govern yourself accordingly." This was followed fifteen minutes later by a rephrase of Admiral Stark's order: "Execute unrestricted air and submarine warfare against Japan." Initially, the submariners received little chance to do so, but the message proved to be of immense importance in securing the final victory, for U.S.

submarines began their war without any reservations. After many false starts and weapons failures, the U.S. submarine force would fight well.

In a pattern that would be typical of all of the Japanese advances in the south, there had been a series of early morning air attacks; eighteen planes from the 10,000-ton *Ryujo* bombed and strafed the naval base at Davao on southern Mindanao. General MacArthur's headquarters made no response to this attack, nor to another smaller one three hours later. Twenty-five Japanese army air force Kawasaki Ki-48 ("Lily" to the Americans) bombers from Formosa struck the Tuguegarao airfield in northern Luzon at 0700, while another eighteen Mitsubishi Ki-21 Sallys attacked Baguio.

The U.S. Far Eastern Air Force's commander, Major General Lewis H. Brereton, went to General MacArthur's headquarters at Fort Santiago to ask permission to launch his thirty-five B-17s against Formosa as soon as possible. For reasons still unknown, the request was denied and fortune smiled on the Japanese as long-range bombers and Zero fighters caught most of the American war planes on the ground at Clark Field on Luzon.

The American high command thus made it possible for the Japanese to compensate for the delays due to fog and the long overwater hop, so that twenty-six Mitsubishi G3M Nells, twenty-seven G4M Bettys and thirty-six A6M Zeroes could decimate the U.S. Far Eastern Air Force. About sixty American fighters were lost, thirteen of them shot down. Twelve of the precious B-17s were destroyed, and two more damaged. Another thirty aircraft of miscellaneous types were also demolished. All hope of repelling the invasion by suppressing the Japanese navy was eliminated, and a psychological pall was cast over the American military forces.

Over the next several days, Japanese aircraft systematically eradicated American resistance by attacking airfields. All remaining B-17s were sent to Australia by December 16, and the surviving American fighter pilots were evacuated on December 31, since there were virtually no planes left to fly.

With air superiority established, the Japanese ground and naval forces moved accordingly, invading Luzon at three points without any preliminary bombardment. Airstrips were quickly acquired to cover troops pushing onward toward Manila. Later, the Japanese navy would act as a shuttle service, bringing forces around American lines in short jumps.

General MacArthur was forced to withdraw his forces to defend the Bataan peninsula, using Corregidor as a command post. He had originally hoped to hold Manila for as long as six months until an American relief expedition arrived.

Although the widespread Japanese attacks were difficult to counter, the American and Philippine forces fought well, particularly when the odds were relatively even and the Japanese were unable to provide immediate air support. The limited number of defending troops and the vast expanse of territory involved enabled the Japanese troops to bypass well-defended areas; this, coupled with their growing aura of invincibility, forced MacArthur to withdraw to Bataan, which had always been described as a defender's paradise, with its rugged mountains, jungles and limited roads.

At Bataan, however, MacArthur found himself encumbered with 63,000 more people than he had provisioned for, including 26,000 civilians, and the entire military and civilian population of 106,000 immediately had to go on short rations. Malaria raged on the peninsula and both armies soon were wasting with the disease, the Japanese being afflicted worse because of their inadequate medical services. The Japanese forces under Lieutenant General Honma (Homma) Masaharu actually grew so weak that he had to cease offensive operations on February 8 and withdraw to a defensive line that would not have been able to withstand an American counterattack had one been launched. Honma called for reinforcements, so great a loss of face that the Emperor, outraged at the failure to keep to the time table, reproved him, and allowed his command authority to be taken over by young Turks willing to attack regardless of losses. Although no longer in command when the events occurred, after the war Honma was tried, convicted and shot for brutal treatment of prisoners and civilians.

SUBMARINES UNDER FIRE

With air superiority lost, most of Admiral Hart's surface ships were ordered south, running away to fight another day. This left the bulk of naval fighting to the twenty-eight submarines (one having been sunk at Cavite), two destroyers (one under repair), six motor torpedo boats, two tenders, three gunboats and various small craft. The submarines' performance was abysmal while that of the smaller ships was often brilliant, perhaps because of the fact that they knew they were expendable and thus took wild risks.

The U.S. submarine fleet proved to be more a threat to itself than to the Japanese, never managing to inhibit any of the multiple invasion forces in the slightest. The hard light of war exposed the submarine element of the Asiatic Fleet for its lack of rigor; there was a serious shortfall in planning, training and maintenance. Even after Admiral Stark's alert of November 27, the submarines were not deployed for wartime operations. When they got under way, at last, they often failed even to observe, much less interdict, the Japanese invasion forces. Many of the commanding officers were not aggressive enough, and those that were found their torpedoes faulty, running too deep and hampered by malfunctioning magnetic detonators. (In an air attack on Cavite Naval Base on December 10, the Japanese had blown up 233 of the Mark XIV torpedoes, irreplaceable even if unreliable.)

The difference in peacetime training and wartime operations became evident on December 13. Lieutenant Commander Morton C. Mumma, one of the most highly regarded commanding officers in the submarine force, had been made captain of the *Sailfish* because of his leadership qualities and the premium he put upon discipline. It was felt that strong leadership was needed because the *Sailfish* was formerly the *Squalus*, sunk in 1939 with twenty-six dead, then salvaged and refurbished. Mumma took the *Sailfish* (dubbed *Squailfish* by the irreverent among her crew) to oppose the Japanese landing at Vigan, in northern Luzon. After a brush with Japanese destroyers in which he claimed one sinking, the *Sailfish* was subjected to a depth-charge attack. Mumma became so unnerved that he turned over command to his executive officer and asked to be locked in his tiny stateroom. The sinking was never confirmed. However, it was not the time for antiheroes, so Mumma was given the Navy Cross for his heroism and simultaneously relieved of command. The *Sailfish*, under new commanders, subsequently had a productive wartime career, by 1944 sinking seven Japanese cargo vessels totaling 45,029 tons.

The U.S. submarine effort reached its nadir in the Japanese invasion of Lingayen Gulf on December 21. Three groups had sailed, two from Formosa and one from the Pescadores; seventy-six transports carried two infantry divisions and all the specialized equipment to mount a drive direct to Manila. It was without doubt the juiciest target to be found so far in the war, the submariner's dream.

The *Stingray*, commanded by Ray Lamb, saw the invasion force and sent a message to Admiral Hart, but Lamb made no attack on the force. Six additional submarines were dispatched to the area, but only a minelayer and a freighter were sunk, an irrelevantly small fraction of the invasion force.

General MacArthur declared Manila an open city on December 25, and by January 1 a decision was made to evacuate all submarines (except for *Sealion*, which was scuttled after being damaged in an air attack) from the Philippines, south to Surabaya. A postwar analysis of the submarine effort showed ninety-six torpedoes fired in forty-five attacks; only three Japanese vessels were sunk. It was a pitiful effort, but the tide of war would shift dramatically in the next years, when the American submarine force would cover itself with glory in a series of actions that would decimate the Japanese merchant marine and navy. By a twist of fate, U.S. submarines did distinguish themselves in the same clandestine supply and evacuation role into which Japanese subs were forced later in the war. The *Seawolf* delivered thirty-seven tons of .50-caliber ammunition to Corregidor and evacuated twenty-five pilots, and went on to become the fourteenth ranking U.S. submarine for tonnage sunk, with eighteen vessels and 71,609 tons. The *Trout* delivered 3,500 rounds of 20mm ammunition and departed with twenty tons of Philippine gold. The *Swordfish* evacuated President Manuel Quezon and his party of nine, then took the American High Commissioner, Francis B. Sayre, and his party of twelve to safety. There were eight other similar missions, the forerunners of many that would be conducted throughout the war.

SMALL CRAFT ACTIONS

As the Japanese army pressed the defenders of Bataan slowly back toward Corregidor, the navy supported the American force by using motor torpedo boats (the famous PT boats) and other small craft to protect its flanks.

One of the great figures who emerged was Commander Francis J. Bridget, who created his own "scratch battalion" of available troops and threw them, virtually untrained, into combat, stopping Japanese units infiltrating behind the lines. The Japanese were shoved back over the ridge of cliffs bordering the sea, where they took refuge in caves.

Three motor launches from the submarine tender *Canopus* (taking the role of repair ship when the submarines departed) were provided with boilerplate armor, machine guns and a 3-inch fieldpiece and sent along the coast to pick off the Japanese troops, firing point-blank into the caves. Called "Mickey Mouse Battleships," they were tasked to do the job again on January 23; they succeeded, but this time Japanese dive-bombers attacked and forced them to beach.

The PT boats were called on to break up the continual end runs around the successive U.S. defense lines drawn across the Bataan peninsula, achieving some successes; their claims for sinkings made good reading, but like many wartime claims, these were largely the product of young men's imaginations heated by combat. The most publicized mission of the PT boats in the Philippines was the evacuation of General MacArthur, his family and senior members of his staff. Ordered personally by President Roosevelt to depart, MacArthur turned command over to Lieutenant General

Jonathan Wainwright, who would endure three years of captivity and emerge whip-lean to stand proudly behind MacArthur at the September 2, 1945, surrender ceremonies on the USS *Missouri*.

MacArthur's party embarked on the evening of March 11, 1942, in the four surviving motor torpedo boats. The plywood PT boats (in the press "mosquito boats") were seventy-eight feet long, powered by three Packard V-12 engines of 1,500 horsepower each, giving a nominal top speed of 45 miles per hour when hulls were clean and the sea was calm. Crewed by three officers and fourteen men, they carried four torpedoes and two .50-caliber twin machine-gun mounts.

MacArthur stepped aboard *PT-41* and told her skipper, Lieutenant John D. Bulkeley—soon to be famous in book and film as the hero of *They Were Expendable*—to cast off. The flotilla of four (including *PT-32*, *PT-34* and *PT-35)* slipped through the Japanese blockade, the enemy so confident there was no naval opposition that its guard was down. The trip would have been hazardous enough even had there not been a war on, but the stakes were high. A scheduled rendezvous with a submarine did not materialize, so Bulkeley pressed on in an arduous 600-mile journey to deliver MacArthur to Cagayan, Mindanao. On March 16, two B-17s took his party on to Australia, where MacArthur assumed command of Allied forces.

Bataan fell on April 9, 1942, after a long, hard fight that contrasted sharply with the abysmal performance of the British army and its colonial forces in Malaya. Corregidor, crowded with 15,000 troops, was pounded by 16,000 shells a day. Its stout resistance cheered everyone, but the Japanese inevitably managed to get a foothold on the island, which surrendered on May 6, 1942.

General Wainwright, the new American commander, was forced by the Japanese to order a general surrender for the entire Philippines. It was the worst defeat in American military history, with 100,000 Filipino and 30,000 U.S. troops surrendering. The Japanese, weak and exhausted themselves by the campaign and malaria, found the surrender of numerically superior forces contemptible and treated their prisoners brutally, beginning with the infamous Bataan death march and continuing for the remainder of the war. In the first two months after the surrender, 28,000 American and Filipino prisoners died from maltreatment and starvation.

The Philippine campaign was the only one in which the Japanese fell behind their time table; they had expected to secure the harbor at Manila within forty-five days; the stubborn defense of the "Battling Bastards of Bataan" and Corregidor extended that to 150 days. The campaign was to have tremendous later influence in the war, determining at least one half—

MacArthur's half—of the U.S. Pacific strategy, for the general never wavered from his immortal message, "I shall return." MacArthur was subsequently criticized for the egoism implicit in the use of the first-person singular, but he knew the Philippine people, and his ringing promise was a singular boost to morale during the occupation.

With the surrender, the Japanese gained the best harbor in Asia, along with the resources of the Philippine nation. Proud of their achievements, they had no premonition that in just over two years the Philippines would be the scene of far greater battles on land, sea and air that would herald the end of their empire.

THE END IN SINGAPORE

Although the United States was shocked and angry at the loss of the Philippines, it did not have to bear the humiliation faced by the British empire in the catastrophic fall of Singapore. Its defenses recently modernized at the cost of £60 million, Singapore was designed entirely to defend against an attack from the sea; the British had stocked only armor-piercing shells which were largely ineffective against infantry.

After their meteoric swing through the Malay peninsula, the Japanese laid siege to the city, its propagandists proclaiming that "There will be no Dunkirk at Singapore." With the Japanese in complete control of the sea, evacuation was out of the question. Winston Churchill demanded that "every inch of ground be defended . . . and no question of surrender to be entertained until after protracted fighting among the ruins of Singapore City."

The Japanese, at the limit of their resources, nonetheless began a heavy bombardment by aircraft and artillery, much of the latter the British's own. One of the consequences was the loss of Singapore's water supply. General Percival was overwhelmed, fearing the outbreak of disease and disheartened by the native populace, which had little sympathy for the British and no interest in the war. Percival, tall, slender, with rabbitlike teeth and a Bertie Wooster manner, surrendered on February 15, 1942, without having put up much of a fight. Yamashita had been bluffing; his small army had already suffered 9,500 casualties, including 3,500 killed, and was down to about 35,000 troops. Had Percival followed Churchill's injunction and conducted house-to-house fighting, the Japanese would have had to break it off, for they were at the end of their supplies. General Percival marched under a white flag to surrender 70,000 British, Australian and Indian troops. A further 68,000 had been lost earlier in the campaign, most taken prisoner. One third of the prisoners taken would die in Japanese prison camps. Many of these were in forced labor camps immortalized—and highly sanitized, for the truth defied telling—in books and films such as *The Bridge on the River Kwai*.

ABDACOM DISASTER

Reorganization has been the recourse for troubled organizations through the centuries, and the Allied powers desperately sought a combination that would slow the Japanese juggernaut. On January 2, 1942, the ABDACOM (American, British, Dutch, Australian Command) was established under Field Marshal Sir Archibald Wavell as Supreme Commander, with General Sir Henry R. Pownall as his Chief of Staff. An accomplished pilot, Lieutenant General George H. Brett, United States Army, was deputy commander. Admiral Hart, spirited out of the Philippines aboard the submarine *Shark*, was made Commander Naval Forces (ABDAFLOAT). Lieutenant General Hein ter Pootren, Netherlands East Indies Army, was made Commander Ground Forces (ABDAARM). Air Chief Marshal Sir Richard E. C. Peirse, Royal Air Force, was Commander Air Forces (ABDAAIR).

This complex organization is itself sufficient to convey the impossibility of the arrangement; officers from widely separated areas were thrown together on the basis of availability and given precedence by virtue of their rank. Wavell had been dismissed by Churchill in anger over his failure to contain the Germans in either Africa or Greece; the action may have been unfair, but it did not engender confidence. An austere intellectual but uninformed about the Far East, Wavell lacked all the qualities necessary to weld his disparate group into an effective fighting force.

The more able Hart, still stung by the defeat in the Philippines, had a very unbalanced force at his disposal to face the Japanese. The four ABDA nations could provide only two heavy cruisers, seven light cruisers, twenty-two destroyers and forty-six submarines. There was no time to work them up in maneuvers, develop common procedures, merge their codes, or even for officers to come to know their counterparts. Logistics support was a nightmare, for each navy had particular requirements, and there was little in the way of repair facilities.

Against this motley crew, Admiral Kondo had brought together for the

Southwest Pacific Force two battleships, five carriers, fourteen heavy cruisers, five light cruisers, forty-three destroyers and large numbers of submarines, transports, minelayers, minesweepers, antisubmarine craft and tankers. It was also a homogeneous force, bound by the same language and sailing with the wind of continual victories behind it.

THE EAST INDIES FALL

The Japanese navy now turned to conveying the Sixteenth Army in three elements to the East Indies. Staging out of the Philippines, the Center Force was to reach into Dutch Borneo and seize oil fields and airfields, including Tarakan Island (where the oil was sufficiently pure to be piped directly into ship fuel tanks without any processing), Balikpapan, Andang and Bandjarmasin. The Eastern Force, also from the Philippines, was to seize Celebes, Ambon and Timor. The Western Force embarked from a place that was to become hauntingly familiar to another generation of Americans, Cam Ranh Bay in Indochina, to attack the west coast of Borneo and southern Sumatra. When these had been brought under control, effectively severing communications between Australia, Singapore and the Philippines, the primary target, Java, would be taken in a pincers movement.

The attacks of Lieutenant General Imamura Hitoshi's Sixteenth Army followed the pattern evolved in Malaya, but moved even faster over larger areas thanks to the mobility provided by the Imperial Japanese Navy and the inability of the ABDA powers to react. (Imamura was one of the few Japanese commanders to use the carrot rather than the stick approach with conquered territories; he treated the native populace well, and even released Achmed Sukarno from captivity, an action that would have tremendous import in the postwar years when Sukarno became head of state.)

In Indonesia the native population provided the Dutch with a far more critical situation than the merely indifferent Malays had given Percival. Rebellion was brewing, and the Dutch knew that there was no question of fighting a delaying guerrilla action—there was no popular support. The commanders of Dutch forces were also unsettled because the Nazi occupation of their homeland left them without direct guidance or support.

When the attack began, ABDA air power in the area was not inconsiderable. The Royal Netherlands Indies Army's Air Division was numerically strong, with fifty-eight bombers, 101 fighters and more than 100 observation and liaison craft. The bombers were semi-obsolete Martin 139s, a variant of the American B-10, while the fighters were a mix of Brewster Buffalos, Curtiss Wright CW-20 Interceptors and Curtiss Hawk 75A aircraft, none equal to the Zero. In the fighting in the air, as on the land and on the sea, the Japanese control of the initiative dictated events and Allied air power was whittled down.

The naval forces—first under Hart, and then, for reasons of national pride, under Vice Admiral Conrad E. L. Helfrich of the Royal Netherlands Navy—attempted to block the Japanese landing efforts, but with little success. Field Marshal Wavell and General Brett were recalled, effectively dissolving ABDACOM and leaving the Dutch in full control, supported by Allied ships.

Yet things began well, with the U.S. Navy winning its first surface engagement since the Spanish-American War in the Battle of Balikpapan on January 21, 1942. Four American "four-piper" destroyers, of the same World War I type that had been given to the British, raced into the Makassar Strait at 27 knots to strike at a Japanese force consisting of the light cruiser *Naka*, twelve destroyers and several armed auxiliaries, all covering the unloading of transports and cargo ships at Balikpapan, on the southwest coast of Borneo. Led by Commander P. H. Talbot of ComDesDiv (Commander Destroyer Division) 59, the four destroyers (*John D. Ford, Pope, Parrott* and *Paul Jones*) found the Japanese ships silhouetted against the burning refineries, blown up by the Dutch. Drifting smoke covered the approach of the destroyers; Talbot gave the order: "TORPEDO ATTACK, USE OWN DISCRETION IN ATTACKING INDEPENDENTLY WHEN TARGETS ARE LOCATED. . . . WHEN ALL TORPS FIRED, CLOSE WITH ALL GUNS. . . . USE INITIATIVE AND DETERMINATION."

The daring mission, worthy of John Paul Jones, was hampered by malfunctioning torpedoes but surprise aided the Americans, who were in so close that when the Japanese saw torpedo tracks, they assumed a submarine attack was under way, and deployed their destroyers accordingly. Working up and down the column of Japanese ships, the American "tin cans" sank four Japanese transports and a patrol craft, a total of 23,496 tons of shipping, and then, without any damage to themselves, sped out of the harbor to safety. The victory came at a time the Allies desperately needed it, but it was not given the full measure of acclaim it merited. It was to be the last such victory for a long time.

The Japanese moved quickly toward their main prize, the island of Java, once again applying overwhelming power. A two-pronged attack was made with the 48th Division and supplementary troops landing in the east, near Surabaya, and the 2nd Division in the west, to capture Batavia. Admiral

Kondo's entire fleet had been brought into position to support the invasion, along with almost 1,000 aircraft.

To oppose this juggernaut, the Dutch now had an Allied fleet of eight cruisers, twelve destroyers and thirty-two submarines, 25,000 regular and 60,000 not entirely reliable Home Guard troops, and about 100 aircraft. The area they had to defend was vast, their forces were small and their will beginning to crack.

BATTLE OF THE JAVA SEA

The Japanese had already retaliated for Balikpapan, severely damaging the U.S. cruiser *Marblehead* in a torpedo and bombing attack on February 4. The *Marblehead*'s captain, A. G. Robinson, fought his ship well, but the Japanese were incredibly persistent and the fourth attack wreaked havoc, the near misses doing almost as much damage as the hits. She limped away, steering by propellers, rudder control gone, eventually reaching the United States for repair. The Japanese also hit the cruiser *Houston* hard, knocking out her after 8-inch gun turret, but not impairing her steaming ability. Then, at Badung Strait, southeast of Bali, on February 18, the Dutch Rear Admiral K. W. F. Doorman, Commander of the Allied Combined Striking Force, erred. His hesitation and poor execution of the attack resulted in the loss of a destroyer in exchange for disabling one enemy vessel. The landing operation itself was not impeded.

A week later, Doorman was aware that three heavily escorted enemy convoys were closing in on Java. On the afternoon of February 27, he led his strike force to attack the enemy east of Baewen, about ninety miles due north from Surabaya. For cruisers, Doorman had his flagship *De Ruyter*, followed in line by the *Exeter* (victor over the *Graf Spee*), *Houston*, with her after turret still out of action, the Australian *Perth* and the Dutch *Java*. A mixture of British, Dutch and American destroyers screened the force.

Doorman sailed with no operational plan, hopelessly confused signaling procedures, no scout planes and no air cover. The battle began at 1616 with Admiral Takagi Takeo's heavy cruisers *Nachi* and *Haguro* opening up on the *Houston* and *Exeter* from 28,000 yards. The Japanese ships were heavy cruisers of 10,000 tons, each armed with ten 8-inch guns and eight torpedo tubes.

Next, one of the greatest fighting admirals in the Japanese navy made his fateful appearance. Flying his flag in the light cruiser *Jintsu*, Rear Admiral Tanaka Raizo led his destroyer column against the British destroyers *Electra* and *Jupiter*, hurling torpedoes at 18,000 yards, beyond the range of the British guns. When the battle was over, Tanaka's ships would claim three victories.

Admiral Doorman fought well, handicapped as he was, pressing to get within range of the Japanese warships, and then to break through to the transports. It was not to be; an 8-inch shell from the cruiser *Haguro* plunged into the *Exeter*, damaging her severely and cutting her speed by half.

The difficulties in communications were underlined when the *Exeter* swung hard left to avoid a collision with *Houston*, closing rapidly from behind. The other captains interpreted this as a general signal to turn, and Doorman's battle line disintegrated, each ship becoming a perfect target for the torpedo attack the Japanese immediately launched. The Dutch destroyer *Kortenaer* exploded, broken in half by a torpedo.

Doorman was game, rallying his ships for a counterattack, then slipping away for one last attempt at the transports, using only guesswork, for he had no reconnaissance planes to find them. Their torpedoes exhausted, he sent his destroyers back to base and proceeded with the four cruisers. All ship-to-ship communication was almost completely broken down; it was largely a case of "follow me and do as I do." Japanese scout planes kept his formation illuminated with their excellent flares as it proceeded.

At 2320, seven hours after the battle had started, Doorman experienced firsthand the high level of Japanese skill in night fighting. The enemy cruisers and destroyers launched their swift, powerful torpedoes from 8,000 yards to hit *De Ruyter* and *Java*, enveloping them in flames and stopping them dead in the water. Both Dutch cruisers sank within a few moments of the attack, Doorman signaling to the *Perth* and the *Houston* to depart without attempting to pick up survivors, then electing to go down with his ship.

LOSSES IN THE WEST

The first U.S. aircraft carrier, the *Langley*, had been converted from a collier; long obsolete, she was now converted to a seaplane tender. With thirty-two assembled Curtiss P-40s and thirty-three pilots aboard, she steamed in company with the freighter *Seawitch*, which carried another twenty-seven P-40s in crates, their destination Java. The value of the cargo was inestimable; only air power had a chance to repel the Japanese, and only the P-40 had a chance against the Zero. A series of communication mix-ups delayed the two ships en route, and at 1140 on February 27, they were sighted by Japanese reconnaissance planes. Land-based bombers followed, and despite excellent ship handling, the *Langley* took hits that left her aflame and drifting. Her crew was taken off by destroyers and the *Langley* was scuttled by torpedoes and gunfire. The *Seawitch* made it to Java, but had to leave port before unloading because of the advance of the Japanese.

On the following day the *Houston* and *Perth* made a pass at about fifty Japanese transports unloading in Banten Bay, on the north Java coast, when they were trapped by heavy Japanese forces, including the heavy cruisers *Mogami* and *Mikuma*. The Allied warships accounted for four transports and succeeded in blowing General Imamura himself into the water before being overwhelmed by shells and torpedoes. Imamura floated to shore on debris, none the worse for wear. The *Perth*, holed by four torpedoes and innumerable shells, sank at 0005, March 1. The *Houston*, once used by the President of the United States, became the immediate focus of all the Japanese guns and torpedoes, and she went down at 0045, flag still flying.

The remains of the ABDA striking force were finished off the same day when the crippled British cruiser *Exeter* and destroyer *Encounter* and the U.S. destroyer *Pope* tried to make it through the Sunda Strait for Ceylon (now Sri Lanka) and safety but were trapped by four Japanese heavy cruisers and five destroyers. Shells shattered the *Exeter*, and her captian, O. L. Gordon, gave the order to abandon ship. Before it could be carried out, a torpedo in the port side sank her.

The *Encounter* was smothered in shell fire and abandoned by her crew. In a battle that seemed to characterize the entire war to date, the *Pope* fought on, one old U.S. four-stack destroyer against the cream of the Japanese navy, until six dive-bombers from the *Ryujo* attacked her. A near miss blew a hole in the side of the *Pope*, damaged the propellers and started flooding that could not be contained. At 1250, Lieutenant Commander W. C. Blinn ordered abandon ship; moments later a hit from a salvo of 8-inch guns blasted the wounded ship, and she sank by the stern. In a few short weeks, Japan had turned ABDAFLOAT into ABDASUNK.

A BRIEF BURST OF SUNSHINE

Although U.S. carriers staged a series of raids on Japanese islands in February and March 1942, their principal value lay in the blooding of American pilots. President Roosevelt, well aware that the public was desperate for some good news, knew that bombing Tokyo was the best way to provide it. Two of Admiral King's staff officers, Captain Francis S. Low (later Commander of the Tenth Fleet) and Captain Donald B. Duncan, developed a proposal that army bombers be used to take off from a carrier and bomb Tokyo, then fly on to China to land, no navy bombers having the range to do so.

King discussed the matter with Lieutenant General Henry H. "Hap" Arnold, who immediately agreed, assigning the famous racing and test pilot Lieutenant Colonel James H. Doolittle to lead the operation.

The navy entrusted their part of the mission to Vice Admiral William F. Halsey's Task Force 16, increasingly famous for its hit-and-run raids on the outer islands of the Japanese empire. His *Enterprise* would provide cover for Captain Marc A. Mitscher's *Hornet,* which would carry the sixteen North American B-25Bs and their crews. The two ships rendezvoused in mid-ocean, between Midway and the westernmost of the Aleutians, and proceeded with four cruisers, eight destroyers and two oilers to a point 1,000 miles from Tokyo, where the last refueling took place on April 17, 1942.

The plan called for Doolittle's planes to take off when the task force reached a point 500 miles from Japan; the planes would bomb targets in Kobe, Osaka, Nagoya, Tokyo and Yokohama, then fly to China. Each plane carried three 500-pound bombs and one incendiary cluster. Everyone knew that the raid was a gesture and that the Japanese would recognize it as such. But it was worth doing as a morale builder and as a token of things to come.

The task force was detected by Japanese picket boats, and, 650 miles from Japan, Halsey had to make a tough decision. The 150 miles of extra travel might mean that the B-25s wouldn't be able to reach bases in China. In consultation with Doolittle, he nevertheless decided to launch the attack as soon as possible. Thirty-one minutes after the last picket ship had been sighted and sunk, at 0725 on April 18, 1942, Doolittle led the B-25s off the *Hornet*'s pitching deck.

The Japanese were aware of an impending raid from the picket boat reports, but they assumed it would be made by standard carrier planes, which would have to be brought in much closer to the coast, and thus offer an opportunity for a counterstroke.

The timing of the raid achieved total surprise, and although no B-25s were shot down, all were subsequently lost except one that landed at a Soviet airfield. A strong tail wind compensated for their early launch, but without the agreed-upon radio beacons to guide them to the Chinese bases, bailouts and forced landings were inevitable, except for the plane that went to Vladivostok, where the crew was interned. Three men were killed in crashes and eight were captured by the Japanese and subsequently tortured. Three of the captured prisoners were executed and one died in prison from maltreatment.

Doolittle, regarded as a renegade by regular Army Air Force officers because he had left the service to go into private industry before the war, was now catapulted into the limelight, receiving a promotion to brigadier general and the Medal of Honor from President Roosevelt, personally.

No one could have anticipated that his raid would have had the far-reaching political and military consequences that it did. The Japanese interpreted it as a continuing threat from U.S. carriers—which it was not—and influenced many to agree with Yamamoto that it was essential to bring the U.S. fleet to battle and destroy it. Nor could anyone have known the revenge the Japanese would exact from the Chinese people. In a savage reprisal for the assistance a few patriotic Chinese had rendered the Doolittle crews, the Japanese went berserk, destroying homes and villages and killing 250,000 Chinese, a scale of murder equal to that of the Rape of Nanking. Little was made of this after the war; nothing is made of it today.

Losses in the East

The Japanese staged a massive raid on Port Darwin, Australia, on February 19, 1942, sinking twelve warships, including the U.S. destroyer *Peary*. Two ammunition ships blew up, so devastating the port installations that they were of little use for the rest of the war. On March 7, the Dutch surrendered Java with as much protocol as they could negotiate from the stolid Japanese, who were willing to make concessions to get oil production going again. The last Dutch unit fighting surrendered on March 9.

The East Indies' flank had been secured by Vice Admiral Nagumo's businesslike ejection of the Royal Navy from the Eastern Indian Ocean, waters it had long regarded with a proprietary eye. Sir James F. Somerville, famous for his command of Force H in the Mediterranean and North Atlantic, was now given an obsolete fleet, based at Ceylon; with it he was supposed to keep the Japanese from the Burmese shipping routes and India. It was a hopeless task, for he had only five World War I battleships, so slow that they could not keep up with the two modern aircraft carriers, the *Indomitable* and *Formidable*. These, with the older, slower carrier *Hermes*, had only fifty-seven strike aircraft, mostly Swordfish and its would-be replacement Albacore torpedo planes and Hurricane and Fulmar fighters. In addition, he had seven cruisers and sixteen destroyers.

The Japanese General Headquarters was pleased and surprised by the rapid progress of its forces, and began to discuss what its next actions should be. In the meantime, Yamamoto wished to retain the initiative and ordered Nagumo to make a raid on the British fleet stationed at the naval base at Trincomalee in Ceylon. Nagumo's force consisted of the aircraft carriers *Akagi, Hiryu, Soryu, Zuikaku* and *Shokaku*, the battleships *Kongo, Haruna, Hiei* and *Kirishima*, the heavy cruisers *Tone* and *Imamura*, the light cruiser *Abukuma* and nine destroyers, far too strong a force for Somerville to battle.

Allied intelligence kept Somerville informed of the Japanese intentions, and he prudently removed his forces from the area before the April 2 attack on Ceylon by 200 planes. Somerville made a virtue out of necessity by dividing his forces into Force A, of the faster vessels, and Force B, of the old war horses. Force A consisted of the carriers *Indomitable* and *Formidable*, the cruisers *Cornwall, Dorsetshire, Emerald* and *Enterprise*, and the battleship *Warspite*. The latter had a fantastic combat career, which included attending the surrender of the German High Seas Fleet in 1918 and the Italian fleet in 1943; she absorbed thirteen hits at Jutland, damaged the *Giulio Cesare* in the Mediterranean, and would survive a hit by the German Fritz-X guided missile before bombarding the Normandy coast on D-Day. (There is little sentiment in peacetime, and the *Warspite*'s reward after thirty years of service was to be broken up and sold for salvage soon after the war.)

Force B comprised the battleships *Resolution, Ramillies, Royal Sovereign* and *Revenge* (all sister ships of Prien's Scapa Flow victim, the *Royal Oak*); the carrier *Hermes*, ordered in 1917, and the first warship in the world designed from the start to operate aircraft; the cruisers *Caledon, Dragon* and *Jacob van Heemskerck* (Dutch); and eight destroyers.

Somerville played a waiting game, trying to keep his fleet out of reach during the day, but moving his carriers close enough for an attack during the night. In the meantime, Nagumo launched a heavy raid against Colombo, sending ninety-one bombers and thirty-five fighters. The British reacted strongly and in the ensuing fight lost nineteen Hurricanes and Fulmars and six Swordfish, while shooting down only seven Japanese aircraft.

Doing better reconnaissance work than usual, an Aichi E13A1 Jake from the *Tone* spotted the *Cornwall* and the *Dorsetshire*, steaming at 27 knots to join up with Somerville on April 5, Easter Sunday. Caught without air cover, the two cruisers quickly succumbed to the attack of fifty-three dive-bombers, the *Dorsetshire*, the ship that had administered the coup de grâce to the *Bismarck*, sinking almost immediately. Destroyers picked up more than 1,100 survivors, but 425 officers and men drowned, sacrificed to the folly of deploying ships without air cover.

While Nagumo's force was savaging Somerville, Vice Admiral Ozawa Jisaburo's 2nd Expeditionary Force was prowling the Indian Ocean, in a single week sinking a total of 135,869 tons of Allied shipping, more than German warships or armed merchant cruisers could do over a period of months. Ozawa was unusually tall for a Japanese, and was widely regarded as his navy's premier tactician. A fighting admiral, he distinguished himself in the losing battles Japan was forced to fight for much of the war, and demonstrated his humility by declining promotion to the rank of full admiral.

The litany of British and American naval disasters continued; on April 8, eighty Japanese dive-bombers sank the *Hermes*, a destroyer, a corvette and two tankers, but allowed a hospital ship to proceed without attacking it. Somerville was ordered to remove the remnants of his fleet to Kilindini on the east African coast, and the Indian Ocean became a Japanese lake. Two years would pass before Somerville would be able to take the offensive again. In the meantime, he would fall into disfavor with Churchill, quarrel with Admiral Lord Louis Mountbatten and have to play second fiddle in the only successful major British operation of the period, the seizure of Madagascar.

If the Japanese were disappointed that their foray into the Indian Ocean did not achieve another Pearl Harbor in terms of warships sunk, they did not reveal it. More importantly, they did not draw the essential conclusion that the reason they could not bring the entire British fleet to battle was that the enemy had been forewarned by a leak in security. Not realizing that their security had been compromised, they saw no reason to suspect that their naval codes had been broken, and thus set themselves up for defeat at Midway.

8.

BATTLES OF THE CORAL SEA AND MIDWAY

THE OUTBREAK OF THE VICTORY DISEASE

Corregidor surrendered on May 6, 1942, completing Japan's conquest of the Philippines; it had already secured Hong Kong, Malaya, Singapore and the Dutch East Indies. The Japanese navy escorted scores of transports loaded with troops from Singapore to Rangoon without incident; there, the troops began a brilliant land campaign, advancing 300 miles in eighteen days to close the famous Burma Road to China and drive the British out. Besides Wake Island and Guam, Japan had seized a host of smaller islands. In their almost flawless campaign, Japanese forces had added 20 million square miles (mostly ocean) and some of the richest raw resources in the world to their empire.

All these triumphs were greeted with public celebration; newspapers and magazines outdid themselves in extolling the virtues of the Japanese military and the Japanese nation. After all the years of considering themselves have-nots, the Japanese suddenly controlled riches beyond their imagination, the most important of which was the intoxicating psychological value of the one-sided victories over the Anglo-Saxon countries. That these riches did not translate into any amelioration of the hardscrabble poverty gripping the nation did not seem to matter, for in apparent fulfillment of its destiny of *hakko ichiu*—to bring all the corners of the world under one roof— Japan had also turned the globe upside down. All of Asia could see that the white man was no longer to be feared, still less admired.

The speed and relative ease of the conquest blinded Japan's leaders to the hazards ahead, and they could not see that the massive new empire they had acquired had to be defended in depth, nor that what they had done to the Allies could someday be done to them. They had fallen victim to what became known as *shoribyo* (victory disease)—supreme overconfidence.

One symptom of the disease was the grandiose debate Japan's leaders had been conducting as to what should be their next step. One faction argued for an invasion of India, to link with German forces in the Middle East. Another opted for the seizure of New Britain, New Guinea and establishing bases in the Solomons, preparing the way for an invasion of Australia. The army was acutely aware that it had only seventy-four divisions; of these, twenty-six were required in China and fifteen along the Soviet border. When divisions needed for the occupation of the newly conquered territories were deducted from the total, there were not enough left to embark on too ambitious an offensive. They agreed, grudgingly, to the second option; in pursuing it, another symptom of the victory disease would be unmasked. Contemptuous of their enemies, the Japanese would regularly send forces too small to do the job expected of them.

Yamamoto objected to both plans, insisting that the correct strategy was to undertake an action that would bring the American fleet to battle, and, implicitly, to destruction. He proposed an attack on Midway Island, and threatened to resign if his recommendation was not adopted. The Naval Staff objected, feeling that the United States could retake Midway eventually, and that supplying it would be a logistical nightmare. Opposition also was voiced within Yamamoto's command structure, where it was argued that his plan was risky and perhaps impossible to execute. All objections were swept away by Doolittle's raid. Yamamoto was obviously right once again: the American carriers had to be destroyed to protect the homeland. Yet the move from New Guinea to the Solomons was too attractive, and the confused military bureaucracy eventually settled on four widely spread objectives. In the east, Port Moresby in New Guinea was to be taken, along with the Bismarck Archipelago; to the southwest, the islands comprising New Caledonia, Fiji and Samoa were to be occupied; to the northwest, Kiska and Attu islands in the Aleutians were to be invaded; in the middle, Midway would be captured to force the showdown battle with the still weakened U.S. fleet. The strain of the complex venture was the first in a series of fatal mistakes.

THE ODDS BEGIN TO SHIFT

Not quite one month after the sinking of the *Hermes* came the Battle of the Coral Sea, signaling a change in the tide of the war.

Characteristically, Yamamoto developed an intricate plan, with heavy emphasis on timing, coordination and absolute security. Although the first two elements were at least possible for him to control, he had already forfeited the security factor, thanks to the American code breakers who were becoming increasingly proficient in reading Japanese military traffic.

Yet there was good reason for his confidence. His strength was overwhelming, his aircrews highly trained and the morale of his forces superb. He knew that the best the Americans could oppose him with would be two aircraft carriers and a mixed fleet of Australian and American cruisers.

What he did not reckon on was the cool determination of his opposite number in the Pacific, Admiral Chester William Nimitz. Nimitz was a man of extraordinary capability whom the navy had tested in a variety of roles. In 1907, at twenty-two, he was given command of a destroyer, an almost unheard-of responsibility for so young a man in Teddy Roosevelt's Great White Fleet. Two years later, he was on the cutting edge of warfare, commanding submarines, and doing it so well that at twenty-seven he was invited to lecture at the U.S. Naval War College, another unprecedented honor for a junior officer. Because he knew firsthand the hazard of gasoline engines in submarines, he campaigned for the substitution of diesel engines, and became an expert on the subject, going to Germany to study them. Nimitz was one of the first to conduct studies in the under-way refueling that was to be invaluable to the United States, and, with King, became the advocate of circular battle formations with carriers placed at their center, a tactic the war would prove essential.

Unlike many of his colleagues, Nimitz was not a harsh disciplinarian, but a man who knew how to lead by example, and by the judicious selection of his subordinates. His ability to remain calm under the most adverse circumstances was contagious and amplified his effectiveness. Properly confident in his abilities, he astounded his colleagues in early 1941 by asking to be excused from accepting the post of Commander-in-Chief, U.S. Fleet (CINCUS—an unfortunate acronym Admiral King later changed to COM-

INCH). He reasoned that he was too junior, and that his promotion would antagonize the men over whom he was selected. A cultured man, who liked reading and classical music, at the age of fifty-six Nimitz was at the peak of his professional skills. After assuming command of the Pacific Fleet on December 31, 1941, he sent notice through the fleet of his managerial style by retaining all of Kimmel's staff. It was an astute move that prepared the way for the almost slavish devotion to him that followed.

Nimitz followed King's order to hit the Japanese as soon as he could by dispatching the carriers to make hit-and-run raids, striking Japanese bases at captured Wake, the Gilberts, the Marshalls and Marcus Island. It made good newspaper copy, lifted morale and created a new hero for the American public, Vice Admiral William F. "Bull" Halsey, whose nickname came not from the apt description it was, but from a serendipitous typographical error.

One of the most important, if least attended to, members of the departed Kimmel's staff was Lieutenant Commander Joseph Rochefort, who though unorthodox in appearance, dress and attitude was one of those geniuses to whom cryptanalysis was not so much a profession as a religion. In Rochefort's own words, "I took as my job, my task, my assignment that I was to tell the Commander-in-Chief today what the Japanese were going to do tomorrow."

Rochefort was the officer-in-charge of the 14th Naval District's Combat Intelligence Unit, known locally as Station Hypo; the operators monitored enemy radio traffic, becoming so familiar that they could identify an individual operator's sending technique—his "fist" in their jargon. His boss and good friend, Lieutenant Commander Edwin T. Layton, was the chief of the Pacific Naval Intelligence staff and had been enjoined by Nimitz to think like the Japanese Commander-in-Chief. With his broad experience, Layton was able to do just that, piecing together Rochefort's analysis of radio traffic with other information and his basic intuition.

The complexity of the Japanese Naval JN-25B code, compounded by the complexity of the Japanese language, meant that only about 15 percent of any given message could be interpreted; however, Rochefort and his men worked with lapidary skill to add the newest 15 percent to all the 15 percents of the past, so that the intent as well as the content of the messages became meaningful, especially within the context of known events like ship sightings, news reports and other non-radio-derived information. When Rochefort relayed information on current Japanese radio traffic, Layton was able to forecast that Yamamoto was going to attempt to strike Port Moresby in New Guinea and then move on to a larger operation in the Pacific.

More importantly, Nimitz *believed* him and acted upon the information. (Rochefort has been described by no less a historian than Captain Edward L. Beach as being the man who made more difference at a more important time than any naval officer in history. For his contributions, he received the usual reward the establishment bestows on the outsider: stepping in and stealing the credit for his actions. Rochefort was castigated for his manners, relieved of his command and assigned to trivial duties for the rest of the war. He never complained, then or later.)

Nimitz assembled a makeshift force composed of seven American and Australian cruisers and two American aircraft carriers, the *Lexington* and *Yorktown*, under the command of Rear Admiral Frank J. Fletcher. Nimitz's support of Fletcher, whose reputation had suffered when Wake Island was not relieved, is typical of his ability as a leader to worry about getting the most out of the people on hand rather than being concerned about covering his flanks and rear.

The need to meet the Japanese threat also enabled Nimitz to make lemonade from the lemon that was the American command system, which had arrived at the same dichotomy by accident that the Japanese armed forces had achieved on purpose. Admiral King would not allow the navy to be subordinate to General MacArthur, and MacArthur would not be subordinate to anyone. A dual-track command system was developed in which the Pacific theater was divided into four sections—north, central, south and southwest. The first three were largely open ocean areas dotted with small islands; the southwest area included the great land masses of Australia, New Guinea, the Bismarcks, the East Indies and the Philippines. In addition to his role as Commander-in-Chief, Pacific (CINCPAC), Nimitz was appointed Commander-in-Chief, Pacific Ocean Areas (CINCPOA), comprising the north, central and south of the Pacific; MacArthur became Commander-in-Chief, South-West Pacific Area (CINCSWPA). Each man commanded all American and Allied forces in his area, whether land, sea or air; the only, but major, exception was that Nimitz retained control of the Pacific Fleet, no matter where it was steaming.

Only the United States could have afforded such a system, and it was a beneficent accident of the war that the two-command system turned out to be, in the main, mutually supportive rather than destructively competitive.

THE BATTLE OF THE CORAL SEA

Yamamoto's plan was far too elaborate. While the main part of his fleet was refitting after four months of hard sailing and tough fighting, he sent Vice Admiral Inouye Shigeyoshi with the Fourth Fleet to cover the operation in New Guinea at Port Moresby and the Tulagi operation in the Solomons, code-naming it Operation MO. Operation MI, the attack on Midway, would take place later, after all the ships undergoing refit were ready.

Inouye was one of the coolest heads in the Japanese navy; if he had had Yamamoto's influence, it is unlikely that there would have been a Pacific war, for he recognized that Japan's best interests lay in an accommodation with Britain and the United States.

Using their usual modus operandi, the Japanese split their forces, but Inouye's was nonetheless powerful. About 150 land-based aircraft were ferried down through Rabaul under the command of Rear Admiral Yamada Sadayoshi. The carrier striking force consisted of the heavy cruisers *Myoko* and *Haguro* (which had dispatched the *Exeter*), the big 30-knot carriers *Shokaku* and *Zuikaku*, six destroyers, including the veteran *Akebono*, and an oiler, all under the overall command of Vice Admiral Takagi Takeo; Rear Admiral Hara Tadaichi was his choice for carrier commander. Of these three leaders, Takagi had the most distinguished career, but both Yamada and Hara were highly regarded by Nagumo.

An invasion force followed the strike force through the Bismarck Sea toward Port Moresby. Commanded by Rear Admiral Kajioka Sadamichi, who was eager to recover the face lost in his first attempt at Wake Island, this force consisted of the light cruiser *Yubari*, still bearing the marks of Wake's five-inch guns, eleven transports, six destroyers, two oilers, a minesweeper and a repair ship, an early version of the fleet train the Americans were going to perfect within eighteen months. The transports carried the tough 3rd Kure Special Landing Force and the South Sea Detachment, the Japanese navy's equivalent to the U.S. Marines.

Backing up Kajioka was the Support Force of two cruisers, an aircraft depot ship and three gunboats, and protecting all was Rear Admiral Goto Aritomo with the Covering Force of four cruisers, the aircraft carrier *Shoho* and a destroyer.

Little trouble was expected at Tulagi in the southern Solomons, where a much smaller force was sent under Rear Admiral Shima Kiyohide. This consisted of two destroyers, a transport, a minelayer, eight auxiliary minesweepers and some auxiliary ships.

Against these dispositions, Nimitz deployed his two carrier groups—Task Forces 17 and 11—with Fletcher in overall command. The former consisted of the *Yorktown* (Fletcher), with the cruisers *Astoria*, *Chester* and *Portland* and four destroyers. In Task Force 11, the *Lexington*, under Rear Admiral Aubrey W. Fitch, was supported by the heavy cruisers *Minneapolis* and *New Orleans* and five destroyers. General MacArthur's "private navy" provided Task Force 44, under the Australian Rear Admiral J. G. Crace. Crace had three cruisers, the Australian *Hobart* and *Australia*, and the USS *Chicago*, along with two destroyers. In a fateful addition, the oilers *Neosho* and *Tippecanoe* were also deployed, along with two destroyers and eleven submarines.

The two opposing fleets sought each other out, but a combination of poor reconnaissance and bad weather kept them at a distance. Both sides began the search for the enemy on May 5 and continued through May 6—the bitter day of Corregidor's surrender. The fluid reconnaissance would suddenly jell into a ferocious battle in which each side would find, fix and strike the other simultaneously in the first battle in history in which neither fleet came in sight of each other, all offensive action being conducted by aircraft.

The Japanese landed on Tulagi without opposition on May 3. On May 4 the *Yorktown* sent ninety-nine aircraft against the Tulagi task force, sinking the destroyer *Kikuzuki*, a veteran of the Guam, Wake and Rabaul operations, and three minesweepers.

On May 5, the Japanese Carrier Force entered the Coral Sea, just as the U.S. carrier force sortied in that direction; visibility was bad as the two fleets came within seventy miles of each other.

Like many great moments in war, the real battle opened with a mistake. On May 7 the *Shokaku* and *Zuikaku* had run south in the Coral Sea to a point about 250 miles due south of Guadalcanal, where they received a report locating an American carrier and a cruiser. Lieutenant Commander Takahashi Kakuichi, who had led the attack on Wheeler Field only six months before, was dispatched with thirty-six Vals, twenty-four Kates and thirty-six Zeroes. Instead he found and attacked the oiler *Neosho* and the destroyer *Sims*. The *Sims* took three hits, broke in two and sank immediately. The *Neosho* (called the "Fat Lady" by the ships she nurtured), hit by bombs and a crashing plane, was a ravaged and floating derelict for four days before the destroyer *Henley* arrived to take 123 of the crew off and pick up the fourteen surviving crew members of the *Sims*. In one of the typical sad footnotes to battle, sixty-eight of the *Neosho* crew members had abandoned ship on four lifeboats lashed together. When the destroyer *Helm* found them ten days later only four were still alive.

At 1100 the same day, Douglas SBD Dauntless dive-bombers from the *Lexington*, looking for the two big carriers, found and dove on the *Shoho*. A bomb destroyed her steering, setting her up for attacks from more SBDs and Douglas TBD Devastator torpedo-bombers that hit her with more bombs and several torpedoes, leaving her burning for the *Yorktown* attack force to finish off. The first of many Japanese carriers to be sunk, *Shoho* slipped beneath the water at 1136 with almost 700 men. An exuberant radio call went out, one that ranked with the reported Wake Island call of "Send us more Japs." Lieutenant Commander Robert E. Dixon radioed: "Scratch one flat-top! Dixon to Carrier. Scratch one flat-top." The call marked a fundamental change in the war. Japan was no longer just giving blows; it was now going to take some.

That evening, Japanese planes, mistaking the *Lexington* and *Yorktown* for their own carriers, attempted to come on board; driven off by antiaircraft fire, they were followed by radar, which disclosed that the *Shokaku* and *Zuikaku* were less than thirty miles away. Admiral Aubrey Fitch, an experienced carrier airman, proposed a night attack by cruisers and destroyers, but Fletcher vetoed it, ordering instead an early morning attack. His judgment was confirmed by the Japanese, who also contemplated a night attack but decided against it. The two forces moved away from each other, the Americans to the southeast, the Japanese first to the north, then to the southwest.

Rarely have two forces been so evenly matched; the Japanese had 121 aircraft, with Zeros and Kates in the majority, while the Americans had 122, mostly SBDs and Grumman Wildcats, with a smaller number of the Devastators. But Fletcher had radar and better homing devices, equipment the Japanese lacked, which cost them heavily. In compensation, Fletcher had detached Admiral Crace's cruisers and destroyers, and consequently had far less antiaircraft protection.

Neither fleet could make a dawn attack; the Americans located the Japanese by 0815 and thirty minutes later got off an attack of forty-six SBDs, twenty-one TBDs and fifteen F4Fs. The Japanese fleet had the weather advantage, hiding under an undercast, but the American SBDs and TBDs, working without any fighter cover, caught the *Shokaku* in a clear patch. The Devastators, surely the unluckiest American aircraft of the war, launched nine torpedoes, and scored no hits. Part of the problem was the typical American torpedo malfunction, but part was the fact that they were launched from too great a distance and the torpedoes were so slow that the Japanese ships could turn and run from them.

Fifteen SBDs evaded fighters and antiaircraft to score two hits, which left the *Shokaku* burning but still able to recover aircraft. An attack by *Lexington*'s SBDs added another hit. *Shokaku* got her fires under control and departed for home, some of her aircraft landing on the *Zuikaku*. Admiral Hara's sixty-nine-aircraft strike, launched almost simultaneously with the American attack, hit the *Lexington* with professional élan at 1100, the defending antiaircraft fire having to contend with dive-bombers peeling off from above while torpedo planes poured in from all sides. The Japanese torpedoes worked, and the "Lady Lex" caught two torpedoes in the port side, setting up an immediate list; three more torpedoes and several bombs followed.

Meanwhile, the attack on the *Yorktown* began with a bomb penetrating four decks, killing or wounding sixty-six crew members, but not inhibiting flight operations. Damage-control work was outstanding, and the *Yorktown* was able to withdraw under her own power.

The listing *Lexington*, once captained by Admiral King, was righted by shifting fuel oil, and air operations were resumed until a massive aviation fuel explosion set fires that soon were out of control. Captain Frederick C. Sherman was forced to give the order to abandon ship. An American destroyer, the *Phelps*, put five torpedoes in her to prevent possible capture by the Japanese. She still lies in the Coral Sea, 2,400 fathoms down. Of her crew, 216 lost their lives, while 2,735 were saved, as was the captain's dog.

There was sufficient glory in the battle for Japan to overlook its implications. The Japanese had sunk the fabled *Lexington* as well as the *Neosho* and the *Sims*, and damaged the *Yorktown*. They had lost the much smaller carrier *Shoho*, one destroyer and several lesser vessels. The *Shokaku*, however, was far more severely damaged than the *Yorktown*, and the *Zuikaku*'s air complement had suffered heavy losses. The *Yorktown* would return in time for the next big battle, but neither Japanese carrier would, and that difference proved to be immensely important.

The strategic significance, while lost on the Japanese at the moment, was much greater, for the attempt to take Port Moresby, so vital to both sides, was stopped, the first time that any Japanese advance had been halted.

Merely listing ships' names—*Yorktown, Shokaku, Lexington*—cloaks the immensity of their size and power just as it conceals the essential humanity of the sailors operating them. Each ship came into being as a result of careful thought and planning, sometimes with more than a dollop of duplicity, to achieve what the strategists intended in terms of speed, armor and armament. Take the *Lexington* as an example. The size of the ship remains unappreciated until one walks upon the 888 foot-long deck or plumbs the cavernous depths of the hull, or mingles with the 1,730 men and 169 officers, each one with a life and dreams. The mass of a such a ship is staggering—at full speed of 33.25 knots and at a standard 33,000-ton displacement, the *Lexington* would turn sharply in battle, but took long minutes to get under way or to stop. But no matter what the size of the ship, from a *Yamato*-class battleship to the E-boats churning up the English Channel, every ship in every navy had its own personality, traditions and customs. Each one had its portion of luck, sometimes good, sometimes bad. Ship names necessarily evoke an image of purposeful, often lethal hardware, but to the men who designed and built them, and especially to the men who served on them, they were far more than iron and steel—they were home and safety and even in the darkest moments, hope.

Japanese Forces and Strategy for the Midway Operation

Midway atoll had been claimed by the United States since 1859, but its remote location and lack of fresh water inhibited its use until 1903, when President Theodore Roosevelt sanctioned it as a station on the telegraph cable line connecting Manila and Honolulu. (The cable would be of immense importance in 1942, for it permitted preparations for the coming battle to be made without recourse to the radio.) Considered the farthest outpost of the Hawaiian chain, 1,135 miles west-northwest of Pearl Harbor, it consists of two little islands, Sand and Eastern, a barrier reef around them, a lagoon and a harbor. Only six miles in diameter, the atoll had one 5,300-foot landing strip and two smaller ones that occupied virtually all of Eastern Island, a seaplane hangar, fuel dumps and the water distillation plant that was later used in a clever deception.

For this intrinsically worthless but strategically invaluable target, Admiral Yamamoto mustered impressive forces: four heavy and two light carriers; seven battleships, including the *Yamato*, the world's most powerful, and Yamamoto's flagship; ten heavy cruisers; four light cruisers; forty-four destroyers; sixteen submarines; twelve transports and host of oilers, seaplane carriers, minesweepers and other auxiliary craft.

It was an overwhelming force. But Yamamoto proceeded to dilute its strength by dividing it into five separate groups:

1. The Advance Expeditionary Force, consisting of four groups totaling sixteen submarines, which were to be posted north and south of Frigate Shoals and thus cordon off Hawaii. Rear Admiral Fukudome protested that some of the submarines assigned to the task were over twelve years old, and too slow; none could dive below 200 feet: they were not equal to the task being assigned them. He was overruled, but events would prove him correct. The submarines were only twenty-four hours late, but it was enough: the American forces had passed. Had they been there in time, the surprise the Americans were planning would have been ruined, and the outcome of the Battle of Midway might have been far different.

The Japanese had used the lee of the French Frigate Shoals, 490 miles west-northwest of Oahu, as a site for positioning submarines to refuel the magnificent four-engine Kawanishi H8K Emily flying boats when they had bombed Honolulu on the night of March 3, 1942. They intended to use it again for reconnaissance, but the Americans, using a combination of SIG-INT (signals intelligence) and intuition, forestalled their efforts by mining and guarding it. These two occurrences shifted the odds against Yamamoto, who had made no alternative plans.

2. The Striking Force, consisting of *Soryu, Kaga, Akagi* and *Hiryu* and commanded by Admiral Nagumo; all four ships had been at Pearl Harbor. They were denied the addition of *Shokaku* and *Zuikaku* because of the Battle of the Coral Sea. The carriers had seventy-three fighters, eighty-six dive-bombers and ninety-three torpedo planes, and the best naval aircrews in the Japanese navy, which at the time meant the best in the world.

3. The Military Occupation Force, commanded by Admiral Kondo, CINC of the Second Fleet. He had twelve troop transports to deliver a force of 5,000 officers and men to take Midway and hold it. The transports were heavily screened by destroyers, probably the best in the world.

4. The extraordinary Main Body, with seven battleships, the *Yamato, Mutsu* (paid for by Japanese schoolchildren's contributions), *Nagato, Ise, Hyuga, Fuso* and *Yamashiro*. The last four were detached for the jab at the Aleutians, which was intended to send the American fleet scrambling northward. Curiously, given the comparative weight of importance of the two combat areas, the Main Body was theoretically positioned so that it could go to the assistance of either the Midway or the Aleutian force. Events would prove that in fact it could do neither. The Main Body also included the carrier *Hosho*, normally used for training in the Inland Sea, as well as a complement of destroyers.

5. The Northern Area Force with two light carriers (*Ryujo* and *Junyo*) and two heavy cruisers, and the occupation forces for Attu and Kiska in the Aleutians.

Yamamoto left nothing obvious to chance, including planning what the American reaction ought to be. In essence, he sought to divert attention to the Aleutians, then quickly capture Midway Island. When the frustrated Nimitz would come to recapture it, the Combined Fleet would annihilate the American Pacific Fleet. His planning was terribly flawed because Nimitz not only knew what was going to happen, he was willing to risk his precious carriers to stop it.

The Japanese threw 165 ships into the operation, and prepared their usual complex time tables and operation orders, consuming enormous quantities of fuel. Yamamoto enjoyed the notorious comfort of the *Yamato*. While good for morale, Yamamoto's sailing with the fleet effectively took him out of the command role, for radio silence was essential.

Yamamoto's views were reinforced by the pessimist Nagumo's appreciation of the situation. According to Nagumo, the American navy would be surprised but would fight to retake Midway. He did not believe there were any carriers in the area at the moment, but even if they arrived, there would still be sufficient strength to deal with them despite any losses sustained in conquering Midway.

Rarely have two such distinguished admirals been so wrong.

AMERICAN FORCES AND STRATEGY FOR THE DEFENSE OF MIDWAY

Admiral Nimitz reacted in the way Admiral King knew he would— promptly and aggressively. He reinforced Midway with as much strength as he could muster, and insisted that the three months' repair work required by the *Yorktown* be done in three days. It was. With huge scab patches of steel on the outside and timber reinforcements like a mine shaft inside, she sailed from Pearl Harbor at 0900 on May 31, with hundreds of workmen still on board.

Nimitz established a carrier striking force under Fletcher consisting of his own Task Force 17 (*Yorktown*) and Halsey's Task Force 16 (*Enterprise* and *Hornet*). The three ships provided him with seventy-seven F4F Wildcats, 112 SBD Dauntlesses and forty-two TBD Devastators; it was not much, especially since the Devastators were hopelessly inadequate. He would have been delighted to have the *Saratoga,* but she had just finished undergoing repairs for the torpedo she had taken in January and did not reach Pearl Harbor until after the battle.

Bull Halsey had missed the Battle of the Coral Sea because he was returning from the Doolittle raid. To his intense chagrin, a severe case of exhaustion and dermatitis forced him into the hospital in late May and he would also miss Midway. To take his place, Halsey recommended Rear Admiral Raymond A. Spruance.

Spruance was almost fifty-six years old; among his many distinctions was Admiral King's evaluation that Spruance was the smarter of the two, an admission King never made about anyone else. Spruance had made the trip around the world with Teddy Roosevelt's Great White Fleet as a midshipman, and moved quickly and quietly upward, leading by example. Unlike many naval officers, his interests were wide-ranging, and reflected in his avid reading. After a series of increasingly important positions, he finally obtained his real desire when he became Commander, Cruiser Division Five, with the cruiser *Northampton* flying his flag. He worked with Halsey in a number of the fast carrier raids. He was not, however, an aviator. Therefore Spruance was more surprised than anyone when Halsey nominated him to succeed him. But Halsey knew his man.

In addition to the carriers, Fletcher had six cruisers, fifteen destroyers and nineteen submarines to face Yamamoto's overwhelming forces. For the first time, the American navy called upon its submarines to support fleet operations en masse, a departure from its usual sink-and-destroy raiding missions. Like Yamamoto, Nimitz wanted to use his submarines for a fleet alarm, a trip wire to find the enemy, report him, then attack.

Rear Admiral Robert H. English, the new Commander Submarines Pacific (COMSUBPAC) was a true veteran, having reported for submarine duty in 1914 aboard the gasoline-engine-powered *D-3,* and serving in the field for most of his career. (He was killed in a plane crash in January 1943.) English had twenty-nine submarines under his operational control, with twenty-five ready to fight and nineteen dedicated to the Midway battle. He put twelve in Task Group 7.1 to form the Midway patrol group; he placed three in Task Group 7.2, to cover the area northeast of Midway, about halfway to Oahu; the four submarines of Task Group 7.3 were stationed 300 miles north of Oahu. It was a splendid group of ships, well manned, but handicapped by faulty torpedoes; although the air power dictated most of the battle, the submarines would have one decisive success and be influential in a post-battle action.

While Yamamoto was dividing his forces, hoping that his opponent would subdivide his own, the flaxen-haired, pink-cheeked Nimitz concentrated the moderate strength he had to gain both tactical and strategic advantages. At Midway, the Marine Corps garrison was reinforced, raising the total to 2,000 troops. The 2nd Marine Air Wing had VMF-221's twenty Brewster F2A Buffalos and seven Grumman Wildcats, while VMSB-241 had eleven obsolete Vought SB2U-3 Vindicators and sixteen SBD-2 Dauntlesses. (V stands for heavier-than-air; M stands for Marine; F stands for fighter and SB stands for Scout-bomber.) There were also thirty-two Consolidated PBY Catalinas for patrol duty, and six newly arrived Grumman TBF Avengers, the airplane that would ultimately prove to be as excellent as the Devastator was deficient—but not in the coming battle. An army air force detachment had nineteen Boeing B-17 Flying Fortresses and four Martin B-26 Marauders fitted to carry torpedoes.

Nimitz wanted Midway to be an oceanic Verdun, sucking the enemy forces into a battle of attrition when attacking the unsinkable island. With Nagumo preoccupied by Midway, Fletcher's carriers would make their rapier strokes. Intelligence was of course the key, and once again Rochefort and Layton had done what proved to be battle-winning work. Random bits of chatter—a request for a large quantity of refueling hoses, a regretful notice that a battleship would not be ready for the campaign, a requirement for maps of the Aleutians—all meant something to Commander Rochefort. A breakthrough came through when Rochefort determined that a *koruaku butai*, an invasion force, was headed for AF—but where was AF?

All during this crucial period, Rochefort had been under attack from Naval Intelligence in Washington, which, for reasons of turf, chose to disagree with his prediction that the Japanese were going to attack Midway. To prove them wrong, he arranged via the secure communications cable for the Midway garrison to make a plain-language emergency request for water by radio, reporting an explosion in the water distillation system. The Japanese promptly noted that AF had sent a message on the water problem, giving proof that AF was Midway.

From his bits and pieces, Rochefort also elicited the projected dates for the attack on Midway, June 2 or 3. In Washington, his intelligence rivals, forced now to agree the target was Midway, were convinced that it would be June 15.

THE BATTLE OF MIDWAY

Nimitz ignored the Japanese attack on Dutch Harbor on June 3, safe in the knowledge that it was a feint. The first intimation that the Japanese invasion force was approaching Midway was a report from Ensign Jewell "Jack" Reid in a Catalina at 0925; Reid continued to shadow the force for two and one half hours.

Neither side was yet aware that Nagumo was fatally handicapped not only by the break in security but by the fact that he had been assigned two incompatible tactical missions. He had been asked to attack Midway on June 5, in preparation for the landing operations, which confined him to a small area of the sea and reduced his flexibility; he was also tasked to destroy the American Pacific fleet, which required absolute freedom of movement.

The first action came at 1640 when six American B-17 bombers from Midway made an attack on the transport force almost 600 miles west of the island; no hits were scored. The appearance of the bombers should have sent a spasm of fear through the entire Japanese fleet, not because of American bombing prowess, but because it was obvious that surprise, the element that Yamamoto and Nagumo most valued, was lost.

Just after midnight, four slow Catalinas, fitted overnight with makeshift torpedo release mechanisms, found the invasion fleet with their radar and made a torpedo attack—the first ever for their pilots or the Catalinas. Emerging from an undercast to catch the fleet illuminated by a patch of moonlight, Ensign G. D. Propst hit a tanker, the *Akebono Maru*. It was a splendid bit of flying and put the lie to Nagumo's assumption that the Americans would not want to fight. It also demonstrated the already widening gap in American and Japanese technology—there was no radar with the invasion force.

Nagumo moved through the Pacific, cloaking his striking force in bad weather until June 4 when he reached his launch point, 240 miles northwest of Midway. He was undoubtedly sustained by the knowledge that the Imperial General Headquarters had such confidence in victory that they had already renamed Midway: it was to be called "Glorious Month of June" after the occupation. (The Japanese must have had an officer-in-charge of hubris; prior to each operation, dates and places were selected for the receipt of the enemy's surrender.)

Tracking Nagumo by intuition, Fletcher's force hastened to the southwest, ready to launch just over 200 miles north of Midway. At 0603 a positive sighting was provided by a Catalina, which radioed the position of two carriers to Midway. *Yorktown* heard the report as well. Three minutes later Fletcher ordered Spruance to proceed to the southwest and attack the enemy carriers when they were definitely located. Fletcher's own dive-bombers had been on patrol and were being recovered. His own attack would follow.

The decision to split his forces was a brilliant gamble, like Lee at Chancellorsville; totally outnumbered, unable to endure a full-scale enemy attack with all its power, Fletcher diluted his defensive antiaircraft and combat air patrol capability to slip the twin swords of his air attack into Nagumo's flank. With this single decision, not immediately appreciated for either its courage or its intelligence, Fletcher bolstered his later reputation.

In conformance with Nimitz's plan, the fighters from Midway began to act as the picadors to Fletcher's matador. At 0616 they took off to intercept the incoming force of 108 aircraft, equally divided among Vals, Kates and Zeros, from the carriers *Hiryu*, *Soryu*, *Akagi* and *Kaga*. The marines were mauled, their Brewster Buffalos and Grumman Wildcats no match for the experienced Japanese pilots in their superb Zeros, who shot down fifteen and damaged seven more American planes.

By 0630 the attack on Midway was under way; fortunately it was no Pearl Harbor. An American sailor had taken care of one target during a drill a few days previously, burning up 400,000 gallons of gasoline by accident; the Japanese did not do much more damage on purpose, being too few in number and carrying bombs of too light weight. They hit the laundry and hospital, then the power house, knocking out electrical power. Hits on the seaplane hangar, oil tanks and some storehouses followed, but the damage was insufficient to soften up the island for invasion. A second attack would be necessary for the landing to take place.

The Americans reacted to the raid, making up in bravery what they lacked in coordination. At about 0710 four Martin Marauders of the army air force's 69th Bombardment Squadron (Medium) and six navy Grumman TBF Avengers attacked, scoring no hits, their torpedoes letting them down. Only one TBF and two Marauders got back, both badly shot up. Four minutes later, fourteen B-17Es dropped bombs, claiming hits that were later discounted.

Nagumo's Poor Reconnaissance

Just as at Pearl Harbor, American carriers were going to reap the benefit of Nagumo's failure to make the full use of his reconnaissance capability. Reconnaissance was regarded as basically defensive, and thus anathema to the offensive-minded Japanese. The single phase reconnaissance plots laid out did not cover the entire area, nor was any follow-up planned. At first light, seven reconnaissance planes (six Aichi E13K Jakes from his cruisers and a single Nakajima E8N2 Dave from the *Haruna*) had been sent out to cover all quadrants. The seventh plane, from the cruiser *Tone,* had as its search area the precise spot where Fletcher's task force lurked, but its takeoff was delayed for thirty fateful minutes by catapult problems.

Nagumo, perhaps mindful of the criticism that followed his previous failure to make a follow-up attack, agreed to a request from the leader of the *Hiryu*'s air unit, Lieutenant Commander Tomonaga Joichi, that a second strike be made on Midway. Tomonaga, Fuchida's replacement, had been wounded and his radio shot out; his message to Nagumo had to be relayed by a wingman. At 0715, the same moment when the all-clear was sounded at Midway, Nagumo ordered the deck cleared of the ninety-three aircraft he had ready to go for an anticarrier strike so that he could recover returning aircraft. He ordered that the airplanes in the carriers' hangar deck were to be rearmed for a ground attack, an involved operation requiring the off-loading of torpedoes and armor-piercing bombs and their replacement by ordnance appropriate for land targets. Even though each carrier's two elevators could be raised or lowered in fifteen seconds, it took another sixty seconds at least to move the aircraft on board, restrain it, then lower the elevator and move it off; handling ninety-three aircraft, even allowing for those who had their armament loads changed on deck, would take at least an hour.

At 0728, Admiral Nagumo was shaken by a message from *Tone*'s scout, reporting ten enemy surface ships bearing 10 degrees, distance 240 miles from Midway. This was totally unplanned for; the American fleet was not supposed to emerge from Pearl Harbor until after Midway was taken. Nagumo knew at once that he had to make an agonizing decision. As many as 100 of his first-line planes and aircrews were returning from Midway, some of the planes damaged, some with wounded aboard. If he reversed his decision and ordered the planes prepared to attack the newly found enemy fleet, the airplanes from Midway would be lost, and perhaps many of their crews drowned. Time hung heavily, and his subordinates agonized as he weighed the alternatives for a precious seventeen minutes. At 0745, he changed his mind, ordering the rearming stopped and an antishipping strike prepared.

A series of communications with the *Tone*'s scout plane heated the already boiling pot. At 0809, the scout plane pilot reported "Enemy is composed of five cruisers and five destroyers." This should have been warning enough to Nagumo; the Americans would certainly not have let a light force like this one blunder within range of Japanese carriers unless they too were protected by aircraft. Then at 0820 the *Tone*'s plane radioed "The enemy is accompanied by what appears to be a carrier."

The import was horrendous. Nagumo's attack aircraft were not yet ready to go, nor had he recovered the planes from the Midway attack, and American planes might be en route at the very moment. Chaos raged above and below deck, the urgency to get aircraft rearmed resulting in sloppy armament procedures. Instead of bombs being stowed in magazines, they were left loose on deck to be dealt with later.

The American attackers would soon be in a position to clean up the loosely stowed bombs themselves, for Admiral Spruance had been better served by his reconnaissance; as soon as he had heard from the Catalina of Nagumo's whereabouts, he'd turned TF 16 on an intersecting course, determined to launch first and make the first strike. Then reports reached him of the air strike on Midway, and Spruance, on the advice of his chief of staff, Captain Miles Browning, decided to take a calculated risk and time the attack to coincide with the enemy's rearming and refueling of the planes back from Midway. It was pure intuition and it was genius—helped by a great deal of the luck that had deserted the Japanese. Just before 0700, Spruance ordered the *Enterprise* to send out thirty-three SBD Dauntless dive-bombers, fourteen TBD Devastators and ten F4F Wildcats, and the *Hornet* to send thirty-five Dauntlesses, fifteen Devastators and ten Wildcats. The pilots and their crews knew the gamble they were undertaking—their briefing had told them their enemy was 155 miles away, and their aircraft had an average radius of action of no more than 175 miles. The chances of making a strike and getting back were slim; if any kind of aerial combat ensued, chance no longer entered in—they were certain not to have enough fuel.

The *Yorktown*'s launch was delayed until 0838 because of the need to recover aircraft. Because only two of the four known Japanese aircraft carriers had definitely been found, Fletcher sent off only part of his force—seventeen Dauntlesses, twelve Devastators and six Wildcats.

In the meantime, Midway's naval commander, Commander Cyril T. Simard, kept up the pressure, retaliating this time with sixteen marine SBD dive-bombers of VSMB 241, led by Major Lofton R. "Joe" Henderson. Most of his men did not have dive-bombing experience, having done glide-bombing attacks in the older Vought SB2U Vindicators; as a result Henderson led them in a gliding attack that left them vulnerable to enemy guns for an extended period of time. Nagumo's Zeros shot down eight of them, including Henderson (who would have an airfield and a destroyer named after him). Ten minutes later, fifteen army B-17s once again littered the ocean with bombs, dropping from 20,000 feet and scoring no hits—Billy Mitchell must have been spinning in his grave. (During the Battle of Midway the B-17s dropped 322 bombs, none of which hit a target.)

Next, eleven obsolescent Marine Vindicators of VSMB 241 made the last land-based attack on Nagumo's ships, bulling their way in through intense antiaircraft fire to attack the battleship *Haruna.* Even though no hits were scored, they delayed the recovery of carrier planes coming back from the attack on Midway, many of which crashed into the sea.

As the Midway-based attacks on his carriers wound down, Nagumo at last began recovering some of his planes, finishing by 0917 and ordering a change of course for his formation, which by chance took him out of sight of thirty-five Dauntlesses from the *Hornet.* They missed a majestic sight, for his four carriers were protected by a screen of sixteen ships—two battleships, three cruisers and eleven destroyers. To the starboard, the flagship *Akagi* (Red Castle), Yamamoto's old command, was followed by *Kaga* (Increased Happiness), a little over a mile astern. Three miles to port, in similar formation, were the *Hiryu* (Flying Dragon) and *Soryu* (Green Dragon). Their poetic names belied their sinister appearance; the flat, yellow-varnished decks with disproportionately small islands, their smokestacks projecting horizontally athwartship; to the American eye, they completely lacked the familiar graceful lines of carriers of their own navy. But taken as a whole, the formation was a powerful offensive force; it was not yet evident that it was woefully vulnerable defensively, for the Japanese formations lacked radar to pick up the enemy aircraft coming in or to guide the inadequate number of antiaircraft guns the fleet possessed. Less apparent, but even more deadly, was the lack of emphasis on damage control. The carrier's aviation fuel tanks were vulnerable, as were the fuel lines; fire-fighting equipment was insufficient, and so was the training in its use. These problems were compounded by a general lack of awareness of the looming hazard of gasoline fumes in a damaged ship and the absence of tight internal discipline required to prevent accidental ignition. And while U.S. ships suffered some of the same problems, the Americans were quick to learn and adopt new designs and techniques to overcome them; the Japanese did not.

GO IN AND GET A HIT

Fate intervened in the unkindest possible way for both the Japanese and the Americans. The previous day Lieutenant Commander John C. Waldron, leading VT-8 (Torpedo Squadron 8) from the *Hornet,* had run off mimeographed copies of his before-battle thoughts, attaching them to the orders issued to his men. Waldron told them that they were as well trained as possible under the circumstances, and that if worse came to worse, each man was do his utmost to destroy the enemy; if only one plane was left to make a final run-in, that plane was to go in and get a hit. VT-8 would follow his advice almost to the letter.

Waldron's fifteen Douglas TBD Devastators were barely able to make 100 knots with their torpedoes. Flying without any escort fighters, the TBDs were slaughtered as the Zeros came down from their CAP (Combat Air Patrol—the defensive formation maintained over the carrier force) to a veritable shooting gallery of targets. Finally, as Waldron had inadvertently predicted, there was just one plane left, piloted by Ensign George Gay. Gay got close enough to drop his torpedo, then roar up over the *Akagi*'s bridge before crashing, wounded in his foot and arm. The torpedo did not hit. Gay, the only man from VT-8's fifteen aircraft to live through the attack, floated in the middle of the Japanese fleet throughout the day's battle, hiding himself under a seat cushion from time to time, but surviving until he was picked up by a PBY the next afternoon.

The *Enterprise*'s torpedo squadron VT-6 suffered almost as badly; led by Lieutenant Commander Eugene E. Lindsey, it attacked the *Kaga.* Only four out of fourteen survived; no hits were scored. Then *Yorktown*'s VT-3 came in, twelve Devastators to attack the *Soryu;* they had six Wildcats as escort, but the Zero combat air patrol had descended, overwhelming the Grummans even as they devastated the Devastators, shooting down seven immediately. The squadron commander, Lieutenant Commander Lance E. Massey, died, as had Lindsey and Waldron. In all, forty-one Devastators attacked and only six returned. Not one of their torpedoes struck an enemy ship. It was an appalling price to pay for prewar economy measures, when the United States considered itself too poor to fund airplanes, training or torpedoes that would work.

And yet the portly Douglas torpedo planes had served in a way never intended; they had been sacrificial lambs for the Zeros, which had deserted the sky from whence now came the dive-bombers.

Lieutenant Commander Clarence "Wade" McClusky, leading thirty-two SBD Dauntlesses from both *Yorktown* and *Enterprise,* was disappointed in his search—the Japanese fleet had not been where it was supposed to be. Unwilling to admit defeat, he flew on for ten more minutes, then turned right, knowing that as he did so he was consuming all his fuel reserves. At 0955, the wake of the Japanese destroyer *Arashi* caught his eye; he turned to follow it, putting aside the knowledge that it was probably going to be a one-way trip.

At 1001, McClusky saw the diamond formation of carriers in the distance and reported the position of the enemy fleet to the *Enterprise.* At 1022 he led his flight of SBDs tumbling down to bomb the *Kaga,* while five other Dauntlesses attacked the *Akagi,* Nagumo's flagship. (The Japanese carriers, obviously more concerned about being mistakenly attacked by their own forces than by those of the enemy, were marked with bull's-eye aiming points, a fifty-foot red sun, enclosed in a five-foot band of white, giant *hinomarus* at bow and stern.) The first bombs missed the *Kaga,* but Lieutenant Wilmer Earl Gallaher put a 500-pounder into airplanes parked aft; it pierced the deck, leaving behind exploding planes and bombs. Two more bombs struck forward, starting gasoline-fed fires that turned the ship into an oven so hot that paint burned and peeled on its sides. Eight hundred men were trapped below decks, unable to get through the wall of flames.

Lieutenant Dick Best led four other SBDs in an attack on the *Akagi,* which strangely was neither taking evasive action nor firing antiaircraft guns. The *Akagi* was wracked by explosions from one 1,000-pound bomb smashing through the flight deck amidships and two more hits aft, among the parked planes.

Next, the *Yorktown*'s Dauntlesses took the *Soryu* as their target, with Lieutenant Commander Maxwell Leslie leading VB-3 (Bombing Squadron 3). The *Soryu* was vulnerable, her decks crowded with planes intended to do to the American ships what was about to be done to her. The SBDs attacked from three different directions, spacing three 1,000-pound bombs evenly along the deck—forward, midships and aft. Fires erupted with such fury that the crew was driven off within twenty minutes. Later, when the flames subsided and the hulk still floated, the Japanese tried to take her under tow.

Lieutenant Commander William H. Brockman, captain of the submarine *Nautilus,* had weaved his way through the heart of the Japanese fleet, ignoring a series of depth charges from air and surface ships. He came to periscope depth only to see the battleship *Haruna* fire a broadside at him. He fired three torpedoes at the battleship—none hit—then dove again; the next time he made contact, at 1145, he saw a burning Japanese carrier in his periscope—the *Soryu*. Brockman stalked the ship as it slowed to a stop, then prepared to be taken under tow. At 1359 he fired three torpedoes from the point-blank range of 2,700 yards. This time, all three hit and two exploded. Brockman took his boat down to 300 feet to wait out the depth-charge attack. The gallant *Soryu* sank at 1913, breaking in two; her skipper, Captain Yanagimoto Ryusaku, went down with her, singing the national anthem, "Kimigayo." Brockman and his crew could hear the sounds of her breaking up and exploding all the way down. More than 700 men died on board. (Despite Brockman's detailed reports, people now contend that the *Nautilus*'s torpedoes missed, and that *Soryu*'s sinking was due entirely to the bombing from the *Yorktown*.)

The diary of Rear Admiral Ugaki Matome reveals that Yamamoto was as far removed from reality as he was from the battle. (Ugaki, a heavy drinker, was a true hardcase; shot down in the same engagement with Yamamoto by P-38 Lightnings, he survived a crash landing and swam ashore with his arm broken. He became an advocate of kamikaze tactics, and proved it himself in a final but unsuccessful kamikaze attack, one of the last of war, on August 15, 1945. Like much of his service, the gesture was futile, for the plane crashed without causing any American casualties.)

Serving with Admiral Yamamoto aboard the *Yamato*, 500 miles from the carrier-versus-carrier battle, Ugaki wrote that the reports of the discovery of the American fleet west of Midway had pleased Yamamoto, who assumed it would be wiped out immediately by an attack from his carriers. His diary records that "a startling report came in from the Eighth Heavy Cruiser Division Commander: as a result of enemy carrier-borne bomber and land-based bomber attacks *Kaga*, *Soryu* and *Akagi* were set ablaze. *Hiryu* continued her attacks upon enemy carriers while the task force is going to withdraw to the north for a while to regroup."

Ugaki went on: "This sad report immediately changed the prevailing atmosphere in the operations room to one of deepest gloom." Well it might have; the on-scene commander, Nagumo, had just been forced, against his will, to flee from the blazing bridge of the *Akagi* to the destroyer *Nowaki*, and thence to the light cruiser *Nagara*.

Admiral Yamamoto refused to allow the *Akagi* to be finished off by her own people, hoping to salvage the ship and the situation by leading an attack on the Americans. Once the fleet gunnery engagement that he had always planned was concluded, he intended to tow the *Akagi* home. When reality sunk in, the valiant ship was finally sunk by torpedoes from the *Nowaki*. Yamamoto was furious with Nagumo, and ordered him relieved of command by Admiral Kondo.

In the heat of the battle, no one on the American side was yet sure of the extent of the victory. They knew losses had been heavy—seventy-four planes down and more damaged. Nor did they know that the Japanese still had a true samurai in the ring, Rear Admiral Yamaguchi Tamon, Commander of the 2nd Carrier Division, on board the *Hiryu*. A maverick, he had openly objected to Nagumo's planning, voicing his own views on three occasions, and then even committing the unpardonable sin of going over Nagumo's head to complain about it to his friend and Eta Jima military academy classmate Ugaki. Yamaguchi was absolutely opposed to the idea of dispersing carrier strength—a direct criticism of Yamamoto, a man he was rumored likely to succeed. Now, too late, his argument was unassailable; if they had had the carriers *Hosho*, *Ryujo* and *Junyo* there, the battle might still be won.

Bloody but unbowed, Yamaguchi launched a flight of eighteen Val dive-bombers and six Zeros, the size of the force indicating the growing weakness of the Japanese. The *Yorktown* came under attack at 1150. The Japanese pilots, having flown with the desperate knowledge that only they could salvage something from the defeat all around them, fought their way through the twelve Wildcats of the *Yorktown*'s combat air patrol. Seven Vals penetrated, and three put bombs directly into the *Yorktown*, bringing her to a halt, burning fiercely. Those of her aircraft still airborne went aboard the *Enterprise*, but many, out of fuel, were forced to ditch alongside American ships. Fortunately, the Pacific waters were warm, and a few hours or even days in the water were survivable.

Down to his last strength, Yamaguchi launched another strike of six Zeros and ten Kate torpedo planes. The *Yorktown*'s damage-control parties were doing a better job than their Japanese counterparts had done. The fires were out, and she was soon under way at 15 knots. Then the Kates came in and put two torpedoes in her. Once again she slowed to a stop, listing at a 26-degree angle, with her rudder jammed. By 1500, Captain Elliot Buckmaster, afraid that she would capsize, ordered her abandoned, and 2,270 crewmen were placed on board her screening destroyers.

Admiral Yamaguchi's run of luck was over. Simultaneously with his own torpedoes plowing into the *Yorktown*, the *Enterprise*'s VS-6 (Scouting Squadron 6) sighted the *Hiryu*. Some of the pilots from the successful attack on the *Akagi*, including Earl Gallaher, were mobilized into a pickup strike force on the *Enterprise*. VB-6 and VS-6 had only eleven SBDs, but *Yorktown*'s VB-3, now on the *Enterprise*, had fourteen ready. They would be joined by sixteen more from the *Hornet*, the force including eleven that had come from Midway to get in on the action. By 1600, forty-one SBDs (Slow but Deadly, as their crews affectionately called them) were on their way to attack the pugnacious *Hiryu*.

Somewhat full of themselves, the American pilots decided that one group, led by Gallaher, would attack the *Hiryu* while the rest would go after the battleships supposed to be in her company.

The six Japanese fighters on Combat Air Patrol (CAP) missed Gallaher's flight until he had begun his dive, leading his SBDs down from the sun against the *Hiryu*, which kept turning just enough to make the first wave miss. This brought the other SBDs back to the scene. Yamaguchi almost brought it off as the *Hiryu* curved away from most of the bombs. Finally, the last SBDs put bombs through the flight deck; *Hiryu* was finished and Yamaguchi knew it. A fatalist, he had warned his wife before the battle that he might not get back this time.

The *Hiryu* burned like a volcano, the flames force-fed by her still high speed; internally, she rippled with explosions from fuel tanks, bombs and torpedoes. Yamaguchi and the *Hiryu*'s commanding officer, Captain Kaku Tomeo, had a last ceremony, eating some hard naval biscuits, and toasting with water. They then had themselves tied to the bridge to go down with the ship. A tragicomic element was introduced when the *Hiryu*, like the *Akagi*, stayed afloat. Yamaguchi continued to refuse rescue, ordering the destroyer *Makigumo* to fire two torpedoes into her; the *Hiryu* did not sink until after 0900 on June 5. A valiant band of thirty-six sailors from the engineering division below deck had been abandoned; they fought their way through watertight doors and roaring flames to the deck of the carrier, then plunged overboard just before she sank. Truly survivors, they found a lifeboat, climbed aboard and were ultimately spotted by a PBY and rescued by the U.S. seaplane tender *Ballard*.

At 0255 on the morning of June 5, just barely able to digest the fact that his operation had gone from sure thing to sheer disaster with the loss of four carriers, Yamamoto gave the order for his still powerful fleet to withdraw. Operation MI was over. When concerned officers wondered how the news would be broken to the Emperor, he said "I'll apologize to the Emperor myself."

WITHDRAWAL AND PURSUIT

Assuming that Yamamoto would have liked nothing better than a night gunnery engagement, and correctly gauging that preserving the remaining

American carriers was more important, Spruance ordered his forces to withdraw to the east. (When *Yorktown* was hit, Fletcher graciously turned over command of the task force to Spruance.) Thus buoyed by their victory, but eager to make it even more decisive, the U.S. fleet turned to the pursuit of the enemy. At 0215 on June 5, the submarine *Tambor*, under Lieutenant Commander J. W. Murphy, picked up a formation of Japanese ships only eighty-nine miles from Midway. Murphy kept the *Tambor* on a parallel course, identifying the heavy cruisers *Suzuya*, *Kumano*, *Mikuma* and *Mogami*, then considered the most powerful of their class in the world. The cruisers sighted the submarine, and made an emergency turn to port; the post-battle tension was high, and *Mogami* rammed *Mikuma* in its port aft quarter. A patrolling Catalina spotted the two cruisers as they fell behind, and, feeling secure that Yamamoto's battleships were not lurking nearby, Spruance ordered an attack at 0800 on June 6, when the *Hornet* put up twenty-six SBDs and eight Wildcats. They were followed by a second wave from the *Enterprise* at 1045, consisting of thirty-one SBDs, three of the remaining Devastators—one can only wonder at the state of mind of their crewmen—and twelve Wildcats. At 1330, the *Hornet* launched a third flight of twenty-four SBDs and eight F4Fs.

This was a new kind of warfare for the veterans of Midway; here there were no Zeroes to flash through the formation, no wall of antiaircraft fire; instead there were two virtual sitting ducks. The pilots took their time and set up proper bombing tactics. *Mogami* took five hits, but somehow survived, making it back to Truk. *Mikuma* took a number of hits, including one that detonated torpedoes; she sank that night. Photos purportedly showing the dying *Mikuma* were released to the press (some were actually of the *Mogami*), a refreshing change from the images of Pearl Harbor.

YORKTOWN'S LAST GASP

To Captain Buckmaster's chagrin, the tough *Yorktown* continued to float and was taken under tow by the minesweeper *Vireo*, which tugged it along at about 3 knots. At 1200 on June 5, Buckmaster reboarded with twenty-nine officers and 141 men to set about salvaging the ship. The destroyer *Hammon* was transferred to her side to provide power and pumps, and the list was gradually corrected.

The *I-168*, the Japanese submarine that had bombarded Midway, now received information on the *Yorktown*'s position. Its skipper, Tanabe Yahachi, spent six hours working his way through the *Yorktown*'s escorts, getting so close to his target that he had to make a wide hour-long circle to gain enough distance for his torpedoes to run. By 1300 on June 6, Tanabe, his presence shielded by the thick layer of oil from the *Yorktown*, which interfered with sonar operation, fired four torpedoes. The first missed; two went beneath the destroyer *Hammon* to strike the *Yorktown;* the fourth blew the *Hammon* in half, sinking her within four minutes. Tanabe, exulting in the sounds of the explosions he had caused, then dove straight ahead to pass under the *Yorktown* in an attempt to avoid detection. The destroyers were on him immediately and he endured an intense twelve-hour depth-charge attack before finally surfacing in the hope that he had evaded his pursuers. Three destroyers immediately shelled him and he dove again. This time he got away, one of the few successful Japanese heroes of the Battle of Midway. The tough old *Yorktown* did not sink until 0600 on June 7.

FIASCO IN THE ALEUTIANS

The only place where things had gone well for Yamamoto was his diversion to the Aleutians, the bait Nimitz had rejected. In this he was assisted by American Rear Admiral Robert A. Theobald, who had been sent to protect the Aleutians as best he could with a force of two heavy cruisers, three light cruisers and ten destroyers. Theobald rejected information provided on the intent of the Japanese forces, and, acting on his own reasoning, positioned himself 500 miles south-southeast of the Japanese forces. It was perhaps just as well, for the Japanese air power might have sunk his cruisers and thus in part have mitigated the defeat at Midway.

The Japanese administered some sharp air raids on Dutch Harbor and occupied Attu and Kiska during the week of June 7. The islands were to have been the northernmost part of the Japanese defensive line; without the linchpin of Midway, however, they made no strategic sense. There was a prestige factor, however: Japanese troops had occupied American soil. There followed a long and dreary war in which the Japanese on the islands did little harm to the United States, but the atrocious weather did.

THE TURNING TIDE

The Japanese navy maintained strict secrecy on the extent of its defeat at Midway, informing only the very top-ranking members of the army in General Headquarters. Surviving crew members were enjoined to secrecy, and even the wounded were brought secretly into hospitals. The Emperor was reported to have taken the news with some equanimity, commenting that such setbacks were to be expected in the war. But the import of the defeat must have been crushing to Yamamoto, who had suffered a parasitic infection during the battle and was already enervated. It may have been this fact that prevented him regrouping and attacking Midway with the full force of his fleet after his two Aleutian carriers had joined him. He had already gambled and lost one throw, but he might have recovered all with the next. But, more likely, it was his realization that he had indeed seen the first part of his prophecy fulfilled: he had run wild for six months. Now he saw that the United States was rebounding far faster than the year or two respite he had hoped for, and the concept of a negotiated peace with a war-weary America was clearly out of the question.

Back in harbor in Japan, there was an orgy of apologies; Nagumo, his *eminence grise* Kusaka, Genda and others apologized not only for losing but for coming back alive, rather bad form considering that it was the first Japanese naval defeat in 350 years. The captains of three of the carriers, Kaku Tomeo (*Hiryu*), Okada Jisaku (*Kaga*) and Yanagimoto Ryusaku (*Soryu*) had gone down with their ships, as had Yamaguchi, the feisty commander of the 2nd Carrier Division. It was also evident to the Japanese from Yamamoto (who Ugaki noted to be "brooding over something and losing spirit") down that any misconceptions concerning the willingness of the Americans to do battle had to be changed. The army would soon find out how true that was in the Battle of Guadalcanal, where it would be supported to the hilt by the navy, but still go down to grinding defeat.

The Americans accepted the victory gratefully but cautiously at first, until a full determination was made that Yamamoto was indeed retiring, and an assessment of relative losses was calculated. The United States had 307 casualties, lost one carrier (which, with more aggressive damage control, might have been saved), one destroyer and 158 aircraft; the Japanese had more than 3,000 casualties, lost four carriers, one heavy cruiser and 332 aircraft. The Japanese lost over 100 of their best pilots, whose experience could not be replaced; it was the beginning of a fatal process of attrition for the Japanese air forces.

If only one man were to be credited with the success of the battle on the American side, it would be Admiral Nimitz, who was smart enough to believe the intelligence estimates provided him, and courageous enough to act upon them, for the odds were such that he could not have been faulted if he had declined combat. He displayed the most elusive of all qualities of a great military leader, the delegation of both responsibility and authority for the execution of his plan. And he delegated it to at-sea commanders who worked well together, Fletcher and Spruance. Fletcher had the courage to divide his forces in the face of the enemy, and the grace to turn command over to Spruance after *Yorktown* was hit; a lesser man would have continued to exercise command by insisting on bringing his flag to either the *Enterprise* or the *Hornet*. Spruance, for his part, had the wisdom to listen to Miles Browning, and once victory was achieved, did not allow vainglory to lure him into an attempt to finish off Yamamoto's main fleet, which might have been a tragic error.

The effect of the victory on Admiral King, President Roosevelt and the rest of the Amerian high command was electric. They saw at once that a new weapon had evolved to restore the balance of naval power in the Pacific, the carrier task force; more importantly, they knew that they would be able to vastly increase that force and they now had tremendous confidence in the commanders who would employ it. With Hawaii no longer threatened, full attention could be paid to ejecting the Japanese from the South Pacific.

9.

THE EARLY
EVACUATIONS AND
INVASIONS

With the victory at the Battle of Midway in June 1942, the tide of the Pacific war turned irrevocably in favor of the Allies. The change was not dramatic at first; for most of the rest of 1942 the United States and the Japanese were about equal in strength, slugging it out like two well-matched antagonists in the ring. It was not yet obvious that the Japanese strategy for offensive warfare had become a handicap: the seizure of the barrier of island outposts rapidly turned out to be far beyond its resources to defend, much less exploit. Japan didn't have the merchant shipping to support both its military adventures and its vital imports to the homeland, and it lacked the men and planes to garrison the widespread bases with anything approaching adequate strength.

The Japanese empire was now a swan's neck laid across island chopping blocks, positioned perfectly for the axe the Americans would swing as their power grew. The long, fierce Japanese resistance was sustainable only because the concept of dying for their country was so immutably ingrained in the psyches of its soldiers and sailors. What Goebbels and Hitler tried to do with their Nazi propaganda had been accomplished in Japan's homes, schools and services. The message to the armed forces was cast in lofty tones of giving their lives for the Emperor; those who sent the message lived rather comfortably in Tokyo until the bombing came, and, except for a few executed for war crimes, survived to enjoy Japan's postwar recovery.

In Europe, Germany was on the march everywhere, and the Allies were at low ebb. Nonetheless, 1942 saw a similar trend reversal, with the battle of El Alamein heralding a heady series of triumphs in 1943 that included Stalingrad, the Battle of the Atlantic, Kursk, Tunisia and Sicily.

This global tilt in fortune was a direct result of the Allies at last being able to mobilize their economies for a total war effort, one effect of which was a gargantuan increase in their naval strength, which grew steadily in both numbers and technology at a rate its opponents were unable to match.

This preponderance of power, totally beyond the imagination of those who had conducted war plans over the years, naturally had complex and varied impact upon naval operations, including how invasions and evacuations were conducted. It is instructive to reach back to the beginning of the war and compare the early efforts with the growth in scale, technology and technique of invasions conducted later in the war. Evacuations are in many ways the reverse of invasions, so it is particularly interesting to note the difference in techniques and the psychology of evacuations over the years, especially between the Axis and the Allies. Although both the early invasions and evacuations were executed by scratch forces made up of regular navy personnel using peacetime training methods and standard types of ships, they were carried off successfully. In very short order, however, the scale of invasion went rapidly from the relatively small forces used by the Japanese to gobble up the Southwest Pacific to the armadas involved in the invasions of North Africa, Sicily, Italy and Normandy. As with the air war, the numbers of men, ships, guns and airplanes increased by more than an order of magnitude in many instances, with a wide variety of specialized ships, aircraft, radars, communications links and weapons all tailored to the task. That this happened is perhaps not remarkable, given the resources invested; what is astounding, however, is how short a time period in which it was accomplished, for it was but two and a half years from the small wooden Japanese landing craft in Malaya to the myriad types of specialized landing ships and craft, artificial harbors, artillery support ships and headquarters ships of D-Day.

The early pattern of Axis invasions and Allied evacuations was reversed after 1942. In Europe, the German invasions had been, with the exception of Norway and continental excursions, beyond the scope of this book. In the Pacific, the pattern varied in that Japanese invasions were usually planned so that the invading forces were protected by land-based air power wherever possible. When the United States began its push, it followed the same pattern initially, but soon had established such predominance in the air that it was able to do what had previously been considered impossible, sending ship-based air power to defeat land-based air power.

THE EARLY YEARS OF GIVE-AND-TAKE IN THE WESTERN HEMISPHERE

The Allies rapidly became expert in evacuations, having to endure the humiliation of forcible ejection in Norway, France, Greece and Crete. In each instance, evacuation was possible only because of British naval power, supplemented at Dunkirk by a slim margin of air power.

Norway

When the British evacuated Norway, they did it in the manner in which they had invaded, a helter-skelter assemblage of ships, men and supplies, but now operating from inadequate ports and under savage attack from superior German air power. The task was made somewhat easier by the totally inadequate resources that Great Britain and France had landed in the first place—there were not great numbers to move. Nonetheless, the Germans, flushed with the prospect of victory, threw all their available resources into thwarting the efforts of Admiral John Henry Dacres Cunningham, who steamed from Scapa Flow with three cruisers, five destroyers and three transports to take off survivors from Namsos, in central Norway. Cunningham's ships acted as a covering force while the redoubtable Captain Phillip L. Vian took a cruiser, three French auxiliary cruisers and four destroyers into the harbor.

Vian, whose stony, angular face gave him the appearance of Buster Keaton in a bad mood, was a favorite of Churchill and was called both "a fighting sailor" and a "tricky rascal" by his colleagues, the latter name a favorite of those he overhauled on his rapid rise to the top. Reported to be cruel to his subordinates to the point of sadism, it was he who had led the assault on the *Altmark*, then went on to fight in most of the British naval engagements of the war. In Namsos on May 2, 1940, he brilliantly improvised the evacuation, embarking 5,700 men directly from the docks or from small craft onto his ships. The Germans reacted the following day, with dive-bombers sinking two destroyers, the British *Afridi* and the French *Bison*.

Totally out of synchronization with the dramatic May 10 escalation of the war from sitzkrieg to blitzkrieg, the Allies had continued the fight for Norway at Narvik, finally forcing a much smaller German force out on May 28—two days after the evacuation began at Dunkirk. The triumph was short-lived, however, as the disasters in France, Belgium and the Netherlands swelled to catastrophic proportions. In one of the ironies in which the war was so rich, Churchill, newly named Prime Minister, had been the advocate of the invasion of Norway when First Lord of the Admiralty. Now events forced him to decide that Narvik, captured at last, had to be evacuated immediately. The aircraft carriers *Ark Royal* and *Glorious* were sent to provide air cover, exposing them to submarine and air attack. Evacuation began in orderly fashion on June 7, with equipment being given first call for shipping space, although 15,000 troops were also evacuated. By June 9, another 10,000 were on board. Port facilities, while damaged, were usable.

The loaded ships were a ripe target for the German navy, which was thirsting for revenge for its heavy ship losses in the Norwegian operation. The battleships *Gneisenau* and *Scharnhorst*, with the heavy cruiser *Admiral Hipper* and four destroyers, wanted to catch the evacuation fleet and slaughter the troopships. They succeeded in sinking the empty troopship *Orama* (19,480 tons); a tanker, the *Oil Pioneer* (5,666 tons); and a trawler on June 8. The following day they fell upon the *Glorious* and sank her, with two destroyers, as has been earlier related.

As disheartening as the loss of the *Glorious* was, it still was not the horror that the drowning of 25,000 troops would have been, if the German ships had had better reconnaissance. Many of the soldiers who survived Norway would later find themselves in Greece and Crete, there to undergo further retreats and evacuations.

Dunkirk

Churchill was beset on all sides; some of his most trusted advisers in his Cabinet were suggesting that Great Britain accept Mussolini's offer to negotiate a peace settlement with Germany; his stricken ally, France, produced one dismaying surprise after another, their frequency surpassed only by the ensuing demands for assistance; worst of all, Germany was in the process of driving the British Expeditionary Forces (BEF) into the sea at Dunkirk.

Churchill's penchant for diverse operations had embroiled Britain in the invasion of Norway. It also stimulated the foresight that—as early as May 20—had him task the navy to prepare for the evacuation at Dunkirk by assembling a great fleet of small vessels for what became known as Operation Dynamo, under the direction of Vice Admiral Sir Bertram H. Ramsay.

Like so many of the Royal Navy's leaders, Ramsay was cantankerous. In 1937 he had taken the unusual step of resigning his commission, when, as Chief of Staff to Admiral Sir Roger Backhouse, he found that he wasn't being delegated a sufficient amount of responsibility. With the war he returned to service, and was serving as Vice Admiral in command at Dover in the spring of 1940. Highly intelligent, he was often remote with his subordinates, and had the reputation of being a "brutal mimosa," a martinet who was extremely sensitive about his personal feelings. He was also unquestionably the man for the job, able to delegate, to summon up endless energy, and open to suggestion.

Operation Dynamo was the kind of stirring challenge that appeals to the British soul. The evacuation was unorthodox in the extreme, with every kind of vessel, from destroyers to cross-Channel ferries to fireboats to passenger-liner lifeboats, combining with yachts, fishing boats, trawlers and everything else in the southeast of England that would float. Sailors who normally never left their home harbors became expert in embarking grimy, exhausted soldiers in their tiny boats, all the while being drenched by the spray from German near-misses. There were many hits as well, making the odds very much against the English, the way they seem to like their first battles, if not their last.

Just when the Germans had backed 400,000 British and French troops into a pocket at Dunkirk, ready for the coup de grâce, Hitler—influenced by General Gerd von Rundstedt's concerns—got cold feet. Worried about the nonexistent French threat to his flank, concerned that the ground was not suitable for tanks (it was), he called the German army to a halt even though his generals on the scene were lunging like Dobermans on a weak leash. Goering pompously volunteered to complete the liquidation of the troops with his Luftwaffe, the first of a series of unfulfilled promises that would see him end the war stripped of his offices and a prisoner of the SS.

A more hands-on commander would have known that his Luftwaffe was exhausted from its whirlwind tour through Norway, Denmark, Holland, Belgium and France, where losses reached 28 percent of its frontline strength. But his aircrews gamely took on the task, while the German tank commanders fumed impotently.

Despite their long retreat, British morale was still high, and the troops were handled with surprising brilliance by the former Chief of the Imperial General Staff, General John Gort. Lord Gort, commanding the BEF, had never been accused of being an intellectual, but he was courageous and hardworking, and determined to maintain the defensive perimeter until his troops were evacuated. His reward for being successful in this was to be made a scapegoat for the larger fiasco in France.

An impromptu evacuation had begun as early as May 23, when 5,768 troops were brought home while under heavy German air and artillery attack. Operation Dynamo began officially on the evening of May 26, when about 1,500 soldiers were brought home. The work continued slowly the following day, with another 7,700 soldiers returned. But Ramsay was reinforced by the appointment of Captain W. G. Tennant (who would later survive the sinking of the *Repulse*) as Senior Naval Officer ashore. As the docks within Dunkirk harbor had been destroyed by the Luftwaffe, Tennant worked night and day to get troops out onto either the east or west moles, which stretched like narrow stepladders out into the sea, or on the open beaches. The troops were orderly, almost benign, queueing up for removal like tourists in the Underground, although they grew increasingly hostile to the apparent absence of the Royal Air Force (RAF). The RAF was too weak to maintain a constant air cover, and usually fought at altitudes too high to be seen. The Luftwaffe, in contrast, was seen far too close up, the Stukas peeling off incessantly to hit the mobs of troops on the beach, or, with less success, the ships darting to and from England. For months after Dunkirk, jeers and jibes were thrown at RAF personnel by army men, even though the Luftwaffe had, in fact, been given its first defeat.

Even in the compressed time available, an expertise was established. Larger ships—destroyers, passenger ferries and the like—came to the moles to embark the hungry troops, who, bereft of equipment, had bellies full of war and not much else. The destroyers would pack several hundred men on board like open-air sardine tins, crowding the upper decks as if on a red London double-decker bus. The loads made the destroyers top-heavy and hard to handle in evasive actions. The soldiers on the beaches had to wade out to the small craft, which were powered by everything from outboards to steam to sail, and which carried them out to the larger ships waiting offshore. Loading went on despite bombs dropping all around.

The Luftwaffe and German artillery attempted to suppress the evacuation, but two circumstances worked against them. First, the RAF was focused on the task of covering the evacuation, and, though its fighters were limited in number and at the limits of their range, was determined to protect the troops. Second, the sandy beaches swallowed up the bombs as they dropped, minimizing their effect. Still, the Luftwaffe scored heavily; of a total of 861 vessels participating, 243 were sunk, including six destroyers. The

Luftwaffe's biggest day came on June 1, when it sank thirty-one ships and craft.

The tempo of the evacuation grew until May 31, when 45,072 were evacuated from the moles while another 22,942 were brought off from the beaches. As the troops left, the defensive perimeter was allowed to shrink, French and British troops fighting valiantly to hold their new positions.

The "Mosquito Armada," as Churchill termed it, finally evacuated 98,780 from the beaches while the larger ships took 238,446 from the moles at Dunkirk. When Dynamo came to an end at 1423 on June 4, Churchill knew that the total of 337,226 soldiers saved would make all the difference in the months to come.

There were other evacuations as well, from Cherbourg, Saint-Malo, Brest, La Pallice and Saint-Nazaire. From these an additional 192,000 British, French, Czech and Polish troops were taken, in addition to some 23,000 civilians from the Channel Islands, which were abdicated to the Germans. Vice Admiral Ramsay's reputation was made, and he would be given greater responsibilities as the war went on.

The entire evacuation operation had been improvised from the start; hard work and truly brilliant leadership on the part of the British combined with an irrational hesitation on the part of the Germans to allow the deliverance Churchill would soon give thanks for, even as he made sure that it was not interpreted as a victory.

Greece

The British were overdue for a victory when Field Marshal Archibald Percival Wavell conducted two, sequential offensives with minimum forces in Africa. On December 9, 1940, he sent Major General Sir Richard O'Connor sweeping west from Sidi Barrani, Egypt, while on January 24, 1941, he sent Lieutenant General Sir William Platt against Italian East Africa.

O'Connor gained the more spectacular success, pulverizing five Italian divisions in a raid that turned into a drive. He took the British army to the Libyan border by December 17, ready for a march to Tripoli. Bardi fell on January 5, followed by Tobruk on January 21. By February 6, O'Connor had closed the trap on the Italians retreating to Tripolitania. In a 500-mile thrust, the British had killed or wounded 20,000 Italians and taken 130,000 prisoners at a cost of 500 dead and 1,400 wounded.

The Italians were dazed by their series of defeats, which forced Mussolini to accept further German aid. The situation was compounded by the fiasco in Greece, where the tough Greek troops had driven the Italians to a defensive line fifteen miles inside the Albanian border. Things were no better in Ethiopia and Eritrea, where the unfolding disaster would end in total Italian surrender on May 19, two weeks after Emperor Haile Selassie was returned to his throne. The Italian Empire, literally built on sand, had collapsed.

The glow from these triumphs inflamed Winston Churchill's desire for a Balkan Front consisting of Greece, Turkey and Yugoslavia. Supported by Great Britain, this coalition was to resist German intrusions into the area, and perhaps provide entrance to Europe's "soft underbelly." More and more information was being gathered on Hitler's determination to assist his Italian ally, as indicated by the arrival in Tripoli of Lieutenant General Erwin Rommel and the first units of what would become the Afrika Korps, and by the increasing German buildup in the Balkan states friendly to Germany. Churchill made a decision to call a halt to O'Connor's advance, and begin sending troops and equipment to Greece. This three-cushion strategic billiard scratched, leading as it did to the loss of the gains in North Africa, a debacle in Greece and Crete, and the endangerment of Egypt.

The Greeks had long refused active British military involvement, not wishing to bring the Germans in against them. But as intensely satisfying as their successes against the Italians were, they had exhausted their strength. It was evident that the Germans were coming in any event, so they now acquiesced and Churchill funneled men, tanks and planes to Greece. In the general Allied manner of the time, however, the reinforcements were far from sufficient.

Over the next month Admiral Cunningham would again show himself a man of courage, not afraid to lose ships if he had to, as he had during the convoy battle Operation Tiger. Although he knew reinforcing Greece was politically necessary, it was militarily dangerous, for England lacked the resources to carry out Churchill's plans. Nonetheless, he sent his ships in without air cover and without regard to losses to remove troops in two evacuations brought on by operations he had heartily advised against. His message to his sailors was that "the Navy must not let the Army down." Cunningham actually began planning the evacuation simultaneously with the execution of Operation Lustre, the convoying of 68,000 troops and their equipment to Greece. Cunningham knew that he would be severely attacked by the Luftwaffe; the big question mark was whether the Italian navy would sortie after its defeat at Matapan.

Things had seemed to begin well for the Allies. On March 27, 1941, a coup d'état in Yugoslavia had ousted the pro-Axis regime and begun mobilization (never completed) of no fewer than 1.4 million men, but this silver cloud's dark lining was an angered Hitler's vow of vengeance. He set his staff planners to work shifting forces gathered for the attack on the Soviet Union, and on April 6, 1941, he went fifty-one divisions crashing into Yugoslavia and Greece, attacking from Germany, Hungary, Romania and Bulgaria. Even the Italians mustered strength to strike from Albania. The hastily planned operation was masterfully executed. Although the terrain in Yugoslavia was unsuited for the usual blitzkrieg, the Germans adapted their tactics to it. Hitler took his revenge with Operation Castigo (Punishment), the terror bombing of Belgrade, which resulted in 17,000 deaths. The Yugoslavs capitulated on April 17. The Germans had lost only 558 men.

In eastern Greece, eight German divisions quickly drove three weaker British divisions back; on April 19, the British guard took up positions at historic Thermopylae to allow the next evacuation to be organized. When Greece surrendered to the Germans on April 21, its soldiers were treated with the greatest respect and dignity, in honor of their heroic resistance. Mussolini, furious at not being party to the surrender, but not without his usual chutzpah, insisted on a second ceremony that included the Italians, on the twenty-third.

The evacuation problem was far more difficult than that at Dunkirk, for the RAF was not there as air cover, nor was an 800-vessel Mosquito Armada available. The difficulty had been compounded earlier, on April 6. The great maverick of the Luftwaffe, Major Hajo Hermann, and his observer, Lieutenant Heinrich Schmetz, the men who would later sink the Italian battleship *Roma* with a Fritz-X missile, swooped down in their Junkers Ju 88 bomber to the harbor at Piraeus and blew up the merchantman *Clan Fraser*. The 7,259-ton vessel had 250 tons of dynamite on board with another 100 tons on the dock. The resulting explosion sank thirteen ships of 41,942 tons, sixty lighters and twenty-five motorships as it obliterated the only harbor adequate for landing or embarking troops.

Nonetheless, Cunningham had brought the troops and matériel in unscathed. Getting them out would be a different story. The Luftwaffe was in full ascendance, and on April 21 and 22 sank twenty-three ships, including two hospital ships and a Greek destroyer. The British soldiers, weary and discouraged from weeks of rear-guard fighting, had to be picked up on the seven beaches selected for embarkation and ferried out to the ships. Most of the British forces were embarked from beaches near Raphina and Porto Raphti in Attica, and at Nauplia, Monemvasia and Kalamata. Vice Admiral Pridham-Wippell was given command of Operation Demon, with four light cruisers (his flagship *Orion*, *Ajax* of *Graf Spee* fame, *Phoebe* and the Australian cruiser *Perth*, doomed to die with the *Houston* in the South Pacific the following year). There were also three antiaircraft cruisers, *Coventry*, *Calcutta* and *Carlisle*. The latter were 1918 vintage cruisers of 4,190 tons, modernized in 1934 with heavy antiaircraft weaponry, including ten 4-inch Mark V guns and two of the soon-to-be-famous eight-barrel pom-pom guns. The ships were handicapped by a peacetime Admiralty decision to use the High Angle Control System, which still relied on classic eighteenth-century gunnery estimates for range and altitude, and was very inaccurate. In addition to the cruisers, Pridham-Whipple had twenty destroyers, twenty-four troopships or their equivalent, and miscellaneous lesser vessels.

If Pridham-Wippell, commanding from Crete, was the Admiral Ramsay of this evacuation, then Rear Admiral H. T. Baillie-Grohman was its Tennant, controlling operations on shore. He had British sailors brought in to act as beach parties and to man the local fishing boats and other small craft that Commander K. Mitchell had chartered. They fully loaded the ships, packing 3,500 into the merchantmen, 2,500 on the cruisers and up to 850 on each of the destroyers.

Cunningham had ordered that the men be given precedence over matériel; 50,672 troops were brought off from April 24–29, aided by the fact that the Luftwaffe did not bomb at night and the Italian navy did not intervene. It was a long 400-mile trip home to Alexandria, however, and in the process planes from the German VIII Air Force sank the destroyers *Diamond* and *Wryneck*, and four large transports, *Pennland* (16,381 tons), *Slamat* (11,636 tons), *Costa Rica* (8,672 tons) and *Ulster Prince* (3,791 tons). During the course of the evacuation, the Luftwaffe sank twenty-six vessels, including five hospital ships.

Crete

It was apparent from Ultra intercepts that Crete was next on the German list, and Churchill demanded that it be defended. The Germans made an airborne assault that wavered on the brink of failure for days, but the British forces, under Major General Bernard Freyberg, never realized the importance of holding the airfields; the Germans did, and ultimately were able to overwhelm their opponents.

By putting his ships to great risk and taking losses, Cunningham had allowed no reinforcement by sea for the Germans. On May 27, 1941, it was decided to evacuate Crete, and he was tasked with the job, which had to be carried out between midnight and 0300 to avoid air attack. Once again it was a contest between the Royal Navy, weakened, but by force of reputation still able to keep the Italian navy in port, and the daylight operations of the Luftwaffe.

Experts in their field now, Cunningham's ships steamed to Heraklion on the northern coast and Sphakia on the southern coast of Crete. The destroyers went into the harbors to stand by the jetties and board troops for ferrying back and forth to the larger ships offshore, leaving finally with their own heavy loads. The Luftwaffe would reach out to them when dawn broke, the Ju 87 Stukas dive-bombing until the limits of their range, followed by level bombing from Ju 88s. By May 31, 16,500 troops had been returned, but the Mediterranean fleet had suffered heavily. Three cruisers, the *Gloucester, Fiji* and *Calcutta*, and six destroyers, the *Greyhound, Hereward, Imperial, Juno, Kashmir* and *Kelly*, were sunk. The last, with Lord Louis Mountbatten commanding, floated for almost thirty minutes, the survivors clustering around a man who would ascend to high rank. The battleships *Warspite* and *Barham*, the aircraft carrier *Formidable*, the cruisers *Orion* and *Dido* and the destroyers *Nubian* and *Kelvin* were damaged beyond the capacity for repair in Egypt. More than 2,000 sailors and merchant seamen had lost their lives. When asked whether it was wise to risk his ships, Cunningham had replied "It takes three years to build a ship but 300 years to build a tradition."

This time there was again deliverance, but there was no victory concealed within it. Yet within eighteen months, the men who had suffered the humiliation at Crete would be in command of vastly greater operations from which the light of Allied victory would shine, never to be extinguished. Fittingly enough, the first of these was Operation Torch.

OPERATION TORCH: A COSTLY COMPROMISE

Operation Torch was the first of the major Allied invasions; as a benchmark, it deserves a broader treatment than will be given some of the later invasions.

Churchill, quite wisely, wanted to avoid invading Europe and placing the Allies in direct contact with the elite of the German army. The Americans, from Chief of Staff General George C. Marshall down, wished to invade the continent as soon as possible, drive into Germany, defeat the German army and end the war. Marshall thought that an army of fifty-eight divisions and an air force of 5,800 planes could do this in 1943; as events would prove he was naive. For all his varying enthusiasms, the Allies could be grateful that Churchill was *politically* astute enough to prevent an invasion of Europe in 1942 or 1943, despite the genuinely desperate cries from the Soviet Union for a second front. Had Churchill been overruled, and an invasion made before 1944, the Germans almost certainly would have thrown the invaders back into the sea. The probability of this was demonstrated later in Operation Jubilee, the ill-named, ill-fated raid on Dieppe, France, on August 19, 1942, where the Germans inflicted a heavy defeat on 6,500 Allied troops.

The Methodology of Invasion

On July 30, 1942, Roosevelt overruled his staff and agreed with Churchill that the target should be North Africa. Even after agreement on an invasion area had been reached, there were far more unknowns than knowns. Fortunately, the Allies evolved a methodology of both command and operation that would serve them well in subsequent actions.

Political Hazards

The biggest hazards were political: the unknown reactions of Vichy France and Spain. There was, in addition, the problem of what the Germans would do to metropolitan France if the North African French were seen to be co-operating with the Allies.

The Vichy French forces were formidable, with 120,000 troops, 500 airplanes, of which perhaps 300 were first-line, and a navy that was still first-rate, despite its inactivity and the English preemptive strikes.

There was also a genuine concern that Spain might honor its agreements with the Axis and intervene to seize Gibraltar, long an object of Spanish revanchist desire. This would seal off the Mediterranean at a stroke and put the entire invasion force in peril.

Logistical Challenges

The practical hazards were unprecedented, dwarfing anything ever encountered in the past. Three mighty invasion forces were going to sortie in secret and slip past the German submarine forces, then at the height of their power. The task was facilitated by excellent work with both Enigma and HF/DF detection, which located the submarines and routed the convoys around them. The Central and Eastern Forces stopped at Gibraltar to refuel, completely jamming the harbor within sight of Axis spies. All three forces were to make simultaneous landings on a front that spread around the coast of Africa from south of Casablanca to east of Algiers. It was an incredible gamble that bespoke the growing Allied confidence, particularly since the time allotted to planning and training was very short, D-day having been set for November 8, barely three months after Roosevelt's decision.

Command Decisions

In Operation Torch, the enormous combined operation was under a unified if sometimes complicated command at all times. In part because of the sensitivity of the French, in part as a payoff for Roosevelt's acquiescence, all ground commanders in the operation were to be American, and Lieutenant General Dwight D. Eisenhower was picked to be Commander-in-Chief Allied Expeditionary Force in Africa. Eisenhower's velvet-glove stroking of important figures to preserve political alliances was complemented by his iron-handed exaction of working harmony at the lower levels of command. Admiral Sir Andrew Cunningham, newly made Baronet, was selected as Allied Naval Commander; after the vicious battering his convoys had taken on the runs to Malta in 1942, ABC Cunningham was doubtless delighted to have a chance to take revenge. With his extensive, almost continuous command battle experience, he was an excellent choice to "stiffen" Eisenhower, who was still a little overwhelmed by the magnitude of his assignment, and who had no previous combat experience. Both men were favorably impressed with each other, a circumstance unusual enough to comment upon, especially since Cunningham was a man capable of gundecking so tough a nut as Admiral King when the situation demanded it.

Cunningham would call on the services of Admiral Sir Bertram Ramsay, architect of the Dunkirk evacuation, to supervise the planning of the British portion of Torch. For the U.S. Navy, the task fell to Rear Admiral Kent Hewitt, who would also command what became known as the Western Naval Task Force (Task Force 34). Hewitt worked closely with another soldier about to become a public figure, Major General George S. Patton, Commander of the Western Assault Force, who would assume command of his area once ashore. Some of the reasons for the later success of the Allies were beginning to emerge as potentially great leaders came to the fore, and concomitantly, weaker men were jettisoned.

Key Objectives

The primary objectives for Operation Torch were to secure a lodgment on the North African shore, help the British Eighth Army defeat the Germans in North Africa and open the Mediterranean to Allied shipping. Because of the number of troops that were going to be put ashore, it was essential that serviceable ports be secured, and these had to be outside the range of German and Italian bombers, a factor that ruled out a landing in Tunisia. Five landing sites were originally planned. A shortage of shipping and a concern about the German air power at the easternmost sites reduced this to three invasion points: Casablanca, in French Morocco on the Atlantic Coast, and Oran and Algiers in Algeria on the Mediterranean coast.

The Forces

Operation Torch was the first manifestation of the much greater scale of the war that the Allies intended to wage. In the past paltry forces had been sent to Norway and to Greece, but the invasion of North Africa would provide forces far stronger than any seen before, so strong in fact that Hitler took it as a personal compliment that his war had elicited such a mammoth undertaking.

Casablanca

Hewitt's Western Naval Task Force was composed entirely of U.S. Navy ships. He had three battleships (*New York, Texas* and *Massachusetts*), one fleet carrier (*Ranger*), four escort carriers (*Sangamon, Chenango, Suwannee* and *Santee*), three heavy cruisers (*Wichita, Tuscaloosa* and *Augusta*), four light cruisers (*Savannah, Brooklyn, Cleveland* and *Philadelphia*), thirty-eight destroyers, three minelayers, eight minesweepers, four submarines, twenty-three troop transports, eight supply ships, five tankers and some miscellaneous vessels. These were to land Patton, with 37,000 men, all their equipment and fifty-four medium and 198 light tanks, to take Casablanca.

Oran

The Central Naval Task Force, under Commodore Thomas Troubridge, a protégé of Cunningham, had the innovative headquarters ship *Largs,* which was to perform brilliantly and become the pattern for future invasion headquarters ships, two escort carriers (*Biter* and *Dasher,* built on American cargo-ship hulls), two cruisers (*Aurora* and *Jamaica*), two antiaircraft ships, thirteen destroyers, six corvettes, eight minesweepers, eight trawlers, ten launches, two submarines, nineteen landing ships and eighteen supply transports. These were to land the 39,000 troops of Major General Lloyd R. Fredendall, who was to take Oran.

Algiers

The Eastern Naval Task Force, under Vice Admiral Sir Harold Burrough, comprised the headquarters ship *Bulolo;* an ancient monitor with a 15-inch gun, the *Roberts;* three antiaircraft ships, eight destroyers, three sloops, six corvettes, seven minesweepers, eight trawlers, three submarines, seventeen landing ships and sixteen supply ships. This task force was backed up by Force O, commanded by Rear Admiral C. H. J. Harcourt with the old carrier *Argus* (the first in the world to have a flight deck from stem to stern), the escort carrier *Avenger;* three light cruisers (*Sheffield,* which had escaped the Swordfish torpedoes in the *Bismarck* chase, *Scylla* and *Charybdis*), five destroyers and some lesser craft.

Burroughs was to land Major General Charles W. Ryder with 23,000 American and 10,000 British troops, who were to take Algiers.

The two Mediterranean forces had Force H, under Vice Admiral Sir Neville Syfert, consisting of three battleships (*Duke of York, Nelson* and *Rodney*), the battle cruiser *Renown,* three fleet carriers (*Victorious, Formidable* and the elderly *Furious*), three light cruisers and seventeen destroyers.

Deployment

Admiral Ramsay—working in concert with Admiral Hewitt—developed a schedule that routed the ships from the various ports on courses to deceive watching U-boats so that they could rendezvous and be ready to launch a simultaneous invasion on the three widely separated beaches.

Security was a tremendous concern, for the information on the invasion had been distributed far too widely, and young officers, drunk in the streets at Gibraltar, were leaving little doubt about where the invasion forces were going. The Spanish and Italian intelligence services both correctly guessed an invasion of North Africa; this was rejected by the German high command, which preferred to believe the disinformation spread to the effect that the landings would be in Sardinia or Sicily.

Operation Torch was to prove to be a great training ground for invasions, and the lessons of commission and omission learned during its execution would pay off many times in actions to come.

The process of getting men from ship to shore was a difficult one, made more so if the seas were rough and the surf high. In addition, the plans for the process were overly elaborate. Involved were the landing *ships*, the vessels capable of a transoceanic journey, which carried both troops and landing *craft*, the smaller craft used to ferry from ship to shore.

The planners called for the landing ships to home in on infrared beacons from submarines stationed eleven miles off shore; the landing ships would then anchor at a release point, two miles out from the submarines, and undertake the difficult task of placing the heavy landing craft into the reinforced davits for loading, then lowering them to the surging ocean. Alternatively, the heavily laden troops had to scramble down nets to the bobbing boats below.

At each of the major objectives, Casablanca, Algiers and Oran, landing areas were identified so that troops could be put ashore to take their objectives from the rear. Each of the landing areas was further divided into specific sectors that were identified for each of the landing units. These were to form up in their landing craft at individual rendezvous points, usually a destroyer acting as a control ship. On signal, they would then proceed to shore in waves. The sectors were further subdivided into beaches marked out by scout boats anchored near the beach, using flashlights and flares to signal through the pitch-dark night. On paper, it was a logical pyramid-tree approach, designed to get the right troops and the right equipment to the right spot with minimum effort. Once the troops were ashore, the landing craft were to shuttle back for another load.

However, the time between the July 31 decision to proceed and the November 8 landing date did not allow for adequate training for the coxswains of the landing craft. Most were young sailors inexperienced at their job and totally unfamiliar with operating in conditions where the wind, current and surf were all strong. Fortunately, the resultant confusion as landing craft went ashore at the wrong spots was not fatal because for the most part there was little or no opposition on the beaches.

Because the ports were so essential (Allied divisions each required about 700 tons of supplies a day, far too much to bring in over a beach), special task forces were developed to race in and seize each of the port facilities to prevent their being sabotaged.

The Landings

Casablanca

All of the Allied forces had been heartened by the good news of the advance of the British Eighth Army at El Alamein. The information was especially welcomed by the Western Naval Task Force, the first of its 102 ships having been at sea since the October 23 departure from Hampton Roads, Virginia, in the longest, largest ship-to-shore invasion in history. Despite weather predictions that the surf could rise to twenty feet, far too high for the landings, Admiral Hewitt ordered everything to proceed according to plan, all too conscious that the rocky coast of Morocco, with its long sloping beaches, would keep the troop ships far distant from the shore.

CENTER GROUP

The most critical landing was at Fédala, a port twelve miles north of Casablanca; it was heavily defended by four batteries of guns ranging in caliber from 75mm to 138.6mm. Just before H-hour, a small Vichy French convoy escorted by a corvette steamed right into the invasion force. A British destroyer had to machine-gun the French corvette to keep it from alerting shore batteries, then board and take the ship in classic pirate style. The first mix-up came offshore, where the landing ships were unable to anchor at the proper positions. Then it was found that the pitching ocean slowed the loading process, as the soldiers, encumbered with 60-pound packs, reasonably took care about climbing down nets or ladders to the landing craft below.

Only 50 percent of the landing craft were filled when it came time to go in; they were met first by searchlights and then by fire from the French batteries, who didn't know or care who the invaders were, but were determined to fight. Their fire was returned, and at 0620 Admiral Hewitt sent out the signal "Play Ball," meaning to commence offensive operations.

The invasion forces were badly scattered by an offshore current, and some of the young coxswains lost control, either colliding with other boats, hitting rocks or broaching in the surf to spill the helpless, heavily laden soldiers to drown in the sea.

Nonetheless, the majority made it ashore, and the quick-thinking American sailors soon hired enterprising Arabs to carry supplies to the beaches, cigarettes becoming the medium of exchange.

The French army continued to resist, awaiting news of the events taking place in the harbor at Casablanca, where the incomplete but still formidable battleship *Jean Bart* lay, along with the light cruiser *Primauguet*, the super-destroyers *Albatross* and *Milan*, four lighter destroyers, eleven submarines and twenty other smaller warships.

The *Jean Bart*, although not yet mobile, had four 15-inch guns and became the main target of the newly commissioned battleship *Massachusetts*, which fired her nine 16-inch guns in salvos, the fifth salvo knocking the

Jean Bart's single operational turret temporarily out of action. The French naval forces, led by Vice Admiral François Michelier, put up a spirited resistance by sallying forth and approaching the American forces under cover of a smoke screen. The combination of aircraft from the carrier *Ranger* and the accurate, intense naval gunnery was too much, however, and all of the French surface ships were damaged, beached or sunk. Of the eleven submarines, seven were sunk.

SOUTHERN GROUP

On November 7 at 0600, Rear Admiral Lyal A. Davidson led his Southern Attack Group south to the port of Safi. Davidson, who flew his flag in the cruiser *Philadelphia,* was accompanied by the escort carriers *Sangamon* and *Santee.* At Safi, he was to put 6,500 troops and ninety medium and light tanks ashore for a march north to Casablanca, under the command of Major General Ernest N. Harmon.

Two old razeed destroyers (masts, stacks and most of the superstructure removed) were assigned the task of capturing the port area and the sea wall before the amphibious assault began. The four-stackers *Cole* and *Bernadou,* manned by 200 volunteers, were challenged as they entered the harbor and then fired upon.

In response to the fire from the 75mm batteries, the destroyers flashed the agreed-upon signal for resistance, "Play Ball," and with the covering force, began shooting back. Counterfire from the cruiser *Philadelphia* was to be excellent throughout the invasion, suppressing French batteries with 6-inch rifle fire almost as soon as the French opened up. The movement from ship to shore started at 0400 without any previous naval bombardment. The landing craft were a mixture of many of the smaller thirty-six-foot Higgins boats, powered by gasoline engines, and a few of the LCM (Landing Craft, Mechanized), fifty feet long and capable of carrying a tank. (By the time the war ended, the United States would possess more than 82,000 landing ships and craft in eight principal categories.)

Once ashore, the troops rapidly overcame resistance and moved out toward Casablanca. All in all, Safi was the best of the Allied landings during Torch.

NORTHERN GROUP

The Northern Attack Group ran into trouble from the start. Its five landing beaches were widely separated and few of the landing craft made it to the correct spot. The famous Casbah was stoutly defended and French colonial troops counterattacked the American forces with considerable vigor. Meanwhile, repair crews had put the *Jean Bart*'s guns back in action and it took a dive-bombing attack from the *Ranger* to silence her again. The airfield at Port Lyautey wasn't taken until November 10, by which time Vice Admiral Michelier had received orders to cease resisting.

Inside the Mediterranean—Algiers and Oran

The Eastern Task Force, under Admiral Burrough, reached the Algiers landing sites without opposition. It was hampered by the same sort of confusion that had characterized the American landings, and for the same reason: inexperienced coxswains trying to deal with a strong breeze, surf and current. Fighting broke out within Algiers proper when two destroyers, *Broke* and *Malcolm*, were badly damaged by shore batteries, but Algiers was secured by 1900, and with it the key to the political situation—Admiral of the Fleet Jean François Darlan, who by chance was visiting a sick son.

At Oran, things did not go so well with the Western Task Force in two out of three of the landing sectors. There was little or no opposition, but sea conditions and ordinary disembarking problems delayed much of the force. Had there been stout enemy resistance, the invasion probably would have failed there.

The real problem, as at Algiers, had occurred earlier, when two English ships—the *Walney* (ex–U.S. Coast Guard *Sebago*) and the *Hartland* (ex–U.S. Coast Guard *Pontchartrain*)—were caught in a cross fire by French ships and badly damaged, the *Walney* sinking later and the *Hartland* blowing up.

Over the next two days French resistance increased steadily, with ships and planes attacking vigorously until the surrender on November 10, this the product of a political deal.

Dangerous Politics

To persuade the French not to resist, U.S. Ambassador Robert Murphy had sought to bring General Henri Giraud to Algeria to serve as a rallying point for pro-Allied forces. Unfortunately, he meant nothing to the French authorities, who instead looked for leadership to Admiral Darlan, head of the French armed forces and High Commissioner for French North Africa. Eisenhower, distressed at the delays at the various landings, and eager to press on to Tunisia, made a unilateral decision to deal with Darlan, securing the surrender of the French forces on November 10.

On November 11, Hitler ordered the occupation of the rest of France, and on November 27 attempted to seize the French fleet at Toulon. Admiral Jean de Laborde ordered the scuttling of sixty French ships.

A political firestorm broke out over Eisenhower's having worked with Darlan, but the general stuck to his guns, and the situation was relieved on December 24 when a French monarchist assassinated Darlan.

The invasion of North Africa was a complete success; German submarines had not seriously interfered until the French had surrendered. Eventually, some twenty-five U-boats came to graze at the huge shipping concentration that had to disperse itself and return to other duties.

In the meantime, Hitler began pouring reinforcements into Tunisia at a rate that infuriated Rommel, who knew that if he had been similarly provided, he could have conquered Egypt. A long land struggle developed in which the Afrika Korps was bottled up in Tunisia and finally forced to surrender on May 13, 1943, with more than 240,000 prisoners taken, 130,000 of them German. It was a disaster of Stalingrad proportions, without, however, the subsequent ghastly cost in prisoners' lives.

OPERATION HUSKY: ALLIED INVASION, GERMAN EVACUATION

With North Africa secured, the Allies had to decide what to do next, for they could not leave their armed forces unemployed until the proposed invasion of Normandy the following spring.

Churchill, who was determined to give the Soviet Union as much assistance as possible—short of a genuine second front in France—championed the invasion of Sicily at the January conference in Casablanca, where a number of vital decisions was made. Some of these were excellent, including the acknowledgment that the submarine war had to come first, that Germany would continue to be the primary target and that there would be round-the-clock bombing, the Eighth Air Force by day and Bomber Command by night. In an unexpected move, Roosevelt announced that no terms would be offered or received from the Axis. The policy he promulgated (and with which Churchill appeared to agree) was unconditional surrender, which, while it undoubtedly prolonged the war and increased casualties, was not complied with in the case of either Italy or Japan.

The selection of Sicily as the next invasion site was unnerving to the U.S. Joint Chiefs of Staff, who correctly saw it as a furtherance of Churchill's favorite soft-underbelly strategy, tying up manpower and shipping that would be needed for the invasion of France. In the end an old-fashioned horse trade was made: Sicily would be invaded in return for confirmation from England that there would be a cross-Channel attack in 1944.

Oddly enough, the Sicilian operation was viewed by everyone as an entity unto itself, and insufficient thought was given to what must come after. A command team similar to that created for Torch was established, with four-star General Eisenhower as Supreme Allied Commander. Admiral of the Fleet Sir Andrew B. Cunningham was back as Commander-in-Chief Mediterranean; Admiral Hewitt reported to him as Commander, Western Naval Task Force and the U.S. Naval Forces Northwest Africa; while the master administrator Admiral Ramsay commanded the Eastern Naval Task Force. General Sir Harold R. Alexander controlled all ground troops, if anyone could be said to control his two land commanders, Lieutenant General Patton and General Bernard L. Montgomery. Air Chief Marshal Sir Arthur W. Tedder commanded the Allied Air Forces. Tedder believed more than anyone in interservice cooperation, but failed to provide the close support that the navy and the army required during the invasion, preferring instead to follow his doctrine of "sealing off the battlefield." As a result, no precise air plan was developed, forfeiting one of the great Allied advantages.

The Opposing Forces

The relative importance of Sicily to the Germans may be inferred from the overall distribution of their forces. They had one division in Sicily, five more in Italy, seven in Finland, twelve in Norway and Denmark, fourteen in the Balkans, thirty-eight in France and the Low Countries, and 175 in the Soviet Union, where they had launched a major offensive at Kursk—their last on the Eastern front.

Supplementing the single German division in Sicily were four Italian field and five coastal divisions. Most of the Italian forces were second-rate troops, ill-fed, ill-equipped and badly led. Many had no shoes, and it was common for them to beg for bread from civilians. Most of the troops were Sicilian reservists Mussolini hoped would defend their homeland to the death. In fact, most of them hated Fascism and the Germans with equal intensity and regarded the Americans as liberators. They were not alone. The loss of 75 percent of the men of the Italian Eighth Army at Stalingrad had soured Italy on Mussolini and Fascism. After the defeats in Africa culminated in the surrender in Tunisia, Italy itself was ripe for surrender.

Neither the Italian nor the German high command felt that Sicily was a logical choice for the Allies. Sardinia was less well defended and would provide air bases to strike northern Italy or southern Germany as well as a launching point for invasions of either Italy or southern France. This pre-conception, combined with a disinformation plan, convinced Hitler that the next Allied attacks were coming against Sardinia and Greece, and he rein-forced the Balkans with troops and aircraft.

In Sicily, the defenders numbered about 55,000 German and 300,000 Italian troops, supported by an estimated 500 aircraft within range of the battle. Allied air power soon drove Axis aircraft from the field.

Against this rather motley collection, so different from the panzer armies that had flashed through France, the Allies mustered 470,000 troops, more than there would be in the D-Day assault on France. To carry them from their embarkation points in the United States, England, Tunisia and Egypt, more than 3,000 ships were assembled, including 1,225 landing craft. The latter were to carry the initial invasion force of 115,000 British Com-monwealth and 66,000 American troops with their equipment, in an inva-sion plan similar in method to that of Torch. The Allies also had about 4,400 aircraft, of which 700 were fighters operating out of Malta and the newly conquered island of Pantelleria, between Tunis and Sicily, the first island ever to surrender to enemy air power.

The amphibious forces had grown in strength, sophistication and train-ing. There were now oceangoing LSTs (Landing Ship, Tank), 328 feet long and with shallow draft, with a bow ramp designed to land waterproofed tanks on a beach with a 1 to 50-degree slope; these could carry up to 2,160 tons of vehicles. These were supplemented by LCTs (Landing Craft, Tank); the Mark 5 models were 117.5 feet long and looked like wheelless open railroad freight cars. Some of the LCTs had hinged sections cut into their tops so that they could be mated to LSTs to permit tanks to be driven across the LST to yet another LCT for transport ashore. The LCIs (Land-ing Craft, Infantry [large]) were 158 feet long and could carry 200 men. New landing craft types were quickly developed, including the LCVP (Landing Craft, Vehicle and Personnel), carrying thirty-six troops or a 6,000-pound vehicle; the LCM (Landing Craft, Mechanized), fifty-five feet long and capable of carrying a single 30-ton tank. The DUKW, the amphibious version of the ubiquitous standard General Motors 2.5-ton truck, was an outstanding success. (DUKW was the most awkwardly derived acronym of the war, the D standing for its year of procurement, 1942, the U for "Util-ity," the K for its drive train, and the W for six wheels.) Inevitably called the "Duck," given its acronym and its mission, it could carry twenty-five armed troops or a 105mm gun or 5,000 pounds of cargo. It could disembark from an LST, using its propeller drive to get to the beach; if a sand bar intruded, as it did so often in the Mediterranean, the DUKW would use its six-wheel drive to roll right over it to the beach and beyond. Like the Jeep and the C-47 Gooney Bird, the Duck was invaluable.

Over time, landing craft ("the flat bottom navy" as their crews proudly called them) became ever more specialized. Six launch racks were placed on LCIs to lay down blankets of rockets with the explosive power of a 5-inch shell; other LCIs were modified with three 4.2-inch mortars and still others with six 40mm antiaircraft guns; a flight deck was built on an LST to launch Piper Cub liaison planes; and there were even LBKs (Landing Boat Kitchens), floating diners distributing food to the hard-pressed crews of other landing craft. The LCIs and LCTs were given alphabetic suffixes to designate their specialties: (R) for rocket, (G) for gunboat, (H) for headquarters, (K) for kitchen or (C) for control. All these grew up at a time when the Japanese were reduced to securing oil drums to palm logs to drift to shore and the German navy was forced to scuttle along inshore island barriers.

Supporting the amphibious fleet were cargo ships tailored to special missions like the APA attack transport and AKA attack cargo ship. These carried LCVPs for direct ship-to-shore operation.

A destroyer veteran, Rear Admiral Richard L. Conolly, was chosen by Hewitt to train, organize and lead the amphibious forces; he did so with exceptional imagination, overcoming the hazards of the "false beaches" with the mating of LSTs and LCTs, by building pontoon bridges to shore and by seeing that aluminum beach mats were laid down on the soft sand to create roads. Under Conolly, hundreds of young lieutenants, many who had never even seen an ocean before entering the navy, now commanded their own LCIs or LCTs, small craft, but nonetheless, a command!

The Attack

The obvious Allied target should have been the Strait of Messina, the two-mile-wide artery between Sicily and the tip of Italy's toe, indeed possibly an attack on the tip of the Italian boot itself, to quickly trap the German and Italian troops. Instead, after bitter opposition by General Montgomery, it was decided that the American task force should land on the southwest side of the triangular island in the Gulf of Gela, while the British forces would land on the southeast side, south of Syracuse. Montgomery had argued against an earlier plan that he said dispersed the forces, and landed the Americans nearer Palermo. He demanded concentration when he really meant that he wanted the freedom to race to Messina and cut the Germans off.

Never was the maritime aphorism "red sky at night, sailor's delight" so wrong; the sky had been red on the night of July 8, but the seas were high in the morning, so much so that it seemed improbable that the invasion could be launched. The trip across the normally placid Mediterranean was a nightmare for troops crowded not only into the holds but into the LCVPs and LCMs on the davits. The meteorologist who had fearlessly predicted acceptable landing conditions for Operation Torch, Lieutenant Commander R. C. Steere, did so again, and Admiral Hewitt believed him.

He was again correct, and this time the more experienced forces moved to their appointed places with greater precision than during Torch. The American Western Naval Task Force arrayed itself in the Gulf of Gela, with three attack points spread over the forty-mile arc of shore: Licata (JOSS force), Gela (DIME force) and Scoglitti (CENT force). As in Torch, each force had beaches identified as their initial objectives, after which they were to push inland and establish a beachhead deep enough to prevent enemy artillery from shelling the transports bringing in reinforcements.

Landing Techniques

Landing techniques varied with the available shore facilities; if docks and jetties could be seized, the APAs and AKAs would unload directly in the harbor. When objectives had to be reached less directly, techniques developed and refined after Torch were used.

For the troop landings, Royal Navy submarines acted as beacons after having sent teams ashore in folbots (folding boats) to reconnoiter. Destroyers were positioned five miles from each submarine, and used searchlights to indicate their positions. Patrol craft then positioned themselves latitudinally on the destroyers, but only 6,000 yards from shore.

The LSTs then arrived, anchored and began off-loading troops. As few as two and as many as eight attack groups were then assembled at each of the main points. These were led to a line of departure, about 2,000 yards from shore, and then given the signal for the run-in, that last minute, dry-mouthed, fear-laden stretch where enemy guns could do the most damage.

American Landings

By July 9, the enemy was fully aware of the invasion and began marshaling forces against it, handicapped, however, by a shortage of artillery and transport. The limited number of aircraft remaining to the Luftwaffe made themselves felt, for the air coverage over the invasion forces was minimal until July 13, due to the centralized control RAF Air Marshal Tedder had insisted upon. Requests for air cover were sent from Sicily to Malta to Tunis;

by the time action was taken, the need had passed, but not the navy's bitterness. The only offsetting factor was the introduction of proximity-fused antiaircraft shells, whose uncanny accuracy made the enemy wary.

At Licata, JOSS force shot it out against heavy automatic weapon fire from shore and forced its way in. The support from naval gunfire was outstanding from the very beginning, intervening with crushing accuracy wherever enemy artillery manifested itself. Allied interservice cooperation had reached a new high; the army called for the fire it wanted and the navy complied, a process employed with even greater effect in subsequent invasions. If the time was passing when the big guns of ships were dedicated against enemy ships, they now had become indispensable floating artillery, totally demoralizing enemy resistance with their weight of fire. At 0458, off Gela, a German Ju 87 Stuka put a bomb into the U.S. destroyer *Maddox*, sinking it in two minutes, and signaling that the landings were going to be fiercely contested. At 0830 the next morning, a counterattack by Italian tanks was stopped by salvos from the light cruiser *Boise* and the destroyer *Shubrick*. The navy used both land-based controllers and Curtiss SOC scout float-planes for artillery spotting. German Messerschmitt Bf 109s were quick to attack the vulnerable biplane SOCs, bravely flying without air cover, and drove them from the area.

On June 11, tanks of the Hermann Goering Division stormed within four miles of the beaches at Gela until the *Boise* began dropping salvos of 6-inch shells, halting the tanks literally in their tracks. A coordinated effort of naval ship gunfire and army artillery batteries managed to hold them off. The DIME force continued unloading and secured its beachhead for the sweep inland.

At Scoglitti, CENT force encountered greater problems unloading from the transports. The landing boats had trouble identifying landmarks on the essentially featureless beaches; only the first wave landed in the right spot. In the dark, several landing boats piled up on the rocks with a heavy loss of life. The result was a greater scattering of forces and losses almost equal to those of the Torch landings.

When the Germans saw the size of the assault forces, they knew that there was no way to halt the invasion on the beaches, and began plans for retiring.

British Landings

Admiral Ramsay of the Eastern Naval Task Force put the Eighth Army ashore on a 100-mile front between the southwestern tip of Sicily and Syracuse. Some of the larger British landing ships ran into trouble and were unable to get in a position to off-load; the situation was saved here as on the American side by using the capable DUKWs for the task. Resistance was light, but a new peril of war developed: some Italian units were so eager to surrender that they stampeded to get into the prisoner-of-war compounds hurriedly established on the beach, nearly trampling some British soldiers.

The British landings went off well, and Montgomery began his race for Messina—one he was destined to lose.

Enemy Reaction

The Germans began the war by making other people evacuate; in Sicily, they learned the technique themselves in a brilliant defensive operation that is often overlooked. A quick assessment of the overwhelming strength of the Allied effort and the underwhelming level of Italian resistance caused the Germans to began planning for an evacuation on July 14, four days after the invasion. It was extremely successful because the German forces had some outstanding leaders.

Rommel, after his recall from North Africa in March 1943, was now the Commander of Army Group B in Italy. He had selected General of Panzer Troops Hans Valentine Hube to command in Sicily, instructing him to ignore orders from his nominal Italian commander. Assisting Hube was Colonel Ernst-Guenther Baade, appointed Commander of the Strait of Messina. Baade was given unconditional authority over all artillery, antiaircraft guns and naval units in the area. Among his subordinates was Commander Baron Gustav von Liebenstein, who would turn out to be an evacuation specialist.

Hube saw at once that the Italian forces were not reliable, and began a planned withdrawal to buy as much time as possible while striving to get the maximum number of his troops to Messina for evacuation. On July 24, Mussolini was given what amounted to a vote of no confidence by his own Fascist inner circle, which included his son-in-law, Count Galeazzo Ciano. The following morning Mussolini supinely allowed the diminutive King Victor Emmanuel III to force him to resign and be placed "in protective custody." Thus the Sicilian campaign suddenly assumed vital importance to the Germans, for every day that Hube hung on gave Hitler more time to complete the transfer of his troops, disarm the Italian army (whose soldiers promptly became forced laborers in the Reich) and take up defensive positions. Hube took full advantage of the mountainous terrain, which lent itself to defense, his troops fighting dozens of mini-Thermopolaes as they tenaciously dug in.

Hube then implemented a plan for three concentric lines of defense in the northeast tip of Sicily; as the Allies drove him back, his line contracted, freeing up troops for evacuation.

While this was going on, Baade, a tough, no-nonsense leader, acquired thirty-three naval barges, twelve Siebel ferries borrowed from the Luftwaffe, and almost 100 other boats for use in the evacuation.

The Siebel ferry was designed and manufactured by the Siebel *Flugzeugwerke,* which built light aircraft for the Luftwaffe. The pontoon ferry, originally intended for Operation Sea Lion, the aborted invasion of England, was now to be the savior of the evacuation. Eighty feet long and fifty feet wide, it could carry 450 men or ten loaded trucks or sixty tons of cargo. Double-ended and of light draft, it could be loaded or unloaded in twenty minutes.

In planning the evacuation, known as Operation Lehrgang, Hube had begun sending not only noncombatant troops but also workshops, supplies and equipment across the Strait of Messina to Italy in late July. He had assembled almost 200 pieces of heavy artillery to protect the strait from Allied naval incursions, along with more than 300 antiaircraft guns.

The actual mechanics of the evacuation fell under the control of Baron von Liebenstein, who had devised the first "roll-on-roll-off" method of loading trucks, and who saw to it that supplies were funneled to Hube's troops right to the very end. Liebenstein anticipated air attacks by changing the place and time of his crossings while still maintaining a steady flow of traffic.

Hube encouraged Italian evacuation before his own troops left. His allies began their own ferry service on a rather laissez-faire basis, using a large train ferry, the *Villa,* as their principal lift vehicle. Ultimately, 62,000 Italian troops and a minimum amount of equipment was saved, including troops and equipment transported by the Germans. Unknown to the Italians, Hube planned to charge a toll: all of the evacuated Italian transport and weapons were requisitioned by the Germans.

The German evacuation took place August 11–17, under the most rigid discipline. No soldier was allowed aboard the ferry without his rifle. No Italian units were allowed to be evacuated without Hube's express permission.

Baade's antiaircraft guns kept Allied aircraft at bay, and the evacuation was conducted brilliantly. In six days, almost 40,000 German troops, 9,600 vehicles, forty-seven tanks and hundreds of tons of supplies were carried safely to the mainland in addition to the 12,000 troops and 4,500 vehicles evacuated earlier. Only six boats were lost to Allied air attack. With the acquisition of Italian stores, the German divisions found themselves better equipped in Italy than they had been in Sicily.

The invasion of Sicily had enormous repercussions in Russia. Hitler's generals believed (wrongly) that they were just about to break through to win the battle of Kursk when the Fuehrer suddenly lost his nerve; citing Sicily as an excuse, he called off the offensive. For the Western Allies, the most useful thing about Sicily was the polish it put on their invasion techniques, which were used later at Salerno and Anzio. The later decision to invade Italy at the south and work up the length of the boot has been rightly criticized, for it suited German needs perfectly.

SALERNO

From the very beginning of the Mediterranean campaigns, Germany, using a minimum of resources, had managed to tie down enormous Allied forces. The Allied decision to invade Italy at the tip of the Italian boot permitted Hitler to continue this strategy, made all the more necessary by the death struggle being conducted on the Eastern Front.

The Allies wished to speed their progress up the Italian peninsula, and on September 9, 1943, made large-scale landings at Salerno, a port about fifty miles south of Naples. The intent was to make an end run on Field Marshal Albert Kesselring's flank, but instead, the action almost resulted in an humiliating Allied evacuation.

The Allied forces followed the now tried-and-true invasion tactics, but their choice of landing sites was limited by the combat radius of their fighter aircraft cover. Kesselring's defensive skills presented the Allies with unexpectedly heavy German resistance. Known as "Smiling Albert" from the almost perpetual wide grin that appeared in his photographs, Kesselring was tough and resourceful, and had he been able to reinforce his troops at a greater rate, he would have inflicted a decisive defeat on the invaders.

Despite heavy losses to German bombing and to the new radio-directed Fritz-X guided missiles dropped by the Luftwaffe (which damaged the battleship *Warspite* and two cruisers, the USS *Savannah* and HMS *Uganda*), the Allied navies eventually determined the outcome of the battle, as reflected in Kesselring's memo to this effect: "On September 16, in order to evade the effective shelling from the warships, I authorized a disengagement from the coastal front."

Anzio: The Flopping Tail of a Whale

The Anzio campaign, which began on January 22, 1944, was intended to prevent the withdrawal of German troops to reinforce the Eastern front and to hasten the capture of Rome. As at Salerno, the aim was to turn the enemy's flank, but once again unexpectedly tough German resistance put the issue in doubt. The battle lasted until June 2, 1944, and was the only instance in which an Allied army was pinned to the beachhead by an enemy for so long a period of time. Of Anzio an exasperated Winston Churchill commented: "We hoped to land a wild cat that would tear the bowels out of the Boche. Instead we have stranded a vast whale with its tail flopping about in the water."

Ironically, the invasion had gone off very well, with little opposition and an efficient supply system established almost overnight. But American hesitation after landing allowed the Germans time to bring their own strength up to eight divisions, making it impossible for the four Allied divisions landed to break through the German lines. When the Germans counterattacked, the big guns of the American fleet were decisive in preserving the Allied positions. The battle settled down into a slugging contest, with the Germans having the advantage of terrain and numbers, while the Allies had air and sea power to back them up. Eventually, the general Allied drive in Italy in June forced the Germans to give up their containment of the bridgehead at Anzio, but not before they had inflicted 59,000 casualties on the Allies.

10.

LATER INVASIONS
AND EVACUATIONS

INITIAL PLANNING FOR A CROSS-CHANNEL INVASION

Despite British reservations, planning for a cross-channel invasion began after the Casablanca summit of January 1943, with the selection of Lieutenant General Sir Frederick Morgan as Chief of Staff to the Supreme
Allied Commander (designate). Morgan, a man of wit, immediately chose
COSSAC as the acronym for his title. His personality was as friendly and al-
lies-embracing as Eisenhower's, and he soon built up a staff of almost 1,000
officers and men engaged in examining every possibility for an invasion.
Sites were studied ranging from Norway to Portugal (both favorites of
Churchill), including consideration of beaches, times, tides, weather, moon
phases, shipping, available forces, defenses, post-invasion breakout routes,
enemy transport, resupply requirements, communications, deception, security and available harbors; each variable came fully equipped with a dozen
variables of its own, so that the possibilities were astronomical.

Eventually, two main areas were considered most feasible. The Pas-de-
Calais, that area of France nearest to England and to Germany was the
shortest route, offered the quickest turnaround for loading and unloading
and thus reduced the number of ships required. The beaches were excel-

lent for landing, and it was closest to Belgium, Holland and the Ruhr. When the sites for launching the new V-1 and V-2 Vengeance weapons came into being, another reason was added to choose the Pas-de-Calais. But the Germans had taken all this into consideration, and it was by far the most heavily defended area on the French coast.

As planning progressed, it was evident that the very scale of the invasion made the absolute distance from England to the target area less important. The thousands of ships involved had to wait in ports all around England and Scotland; as D-Day approached, ship departure times would be conditioned on their distance from their assigned stations, and whether they spent two days or three at sea was a matter of indifference.

The Normandy beaches were almost as good as those at the Pas-de-Calais, and were well within the range of fighter aircraft from bases in England. Although the terrain immediately behind the beaches was difficult—bocage country of small fields surrounded by hummocks of shrubs and trees, easy to defend and impossible to bypass—there were good possibilities for the breakout from either flank. The defenses, while strong, were not as formidable as at the Pas-de-Calais.

LEADERSHIP

German

Curiously, the Germans welcomed the invasion, for it represented their one last chance at victory. If the invaders could be repelled on the beaches, the danger would be overcome, and many of the fifty-nine German divisions in the west, plus those in Norway, could be transferred to the crumbling Russian front.

The German leadership was of very high quality, but handicapped by dissension and Hitler's interference. Field Marshal Gerd von Rundstedt, Commander-in-Chief West and Army Group D, believed that the correct way to repel the invaders was to let them land and then make a massive counterattack with all the armored forces at his disposal. This was the correct way—had the Luftwaffe been up to the task. Field Marshal Rommel, Commander of Army Group B, was directly responsible for repelling the invasion. He had experienced the Allied air dominance over the Luftwaffe in Africa and fervently believed that it was necessary to repel the invasion on the beaches, knowing that mobile reserves would be interdicted by tactical air power before they could reach the battle. He wanted to mass his armored divisions within five miles of the coast. His subordinate, Chief of

Panzer Troops General Geyr von Schweppenburg, disagreed; he felt the effect of Allied naval gunfire on panzers close to the beach would be even more lethal than air attack.

Hitler, although absorbed in the Eastern front, agreed in principle with Rommel, but diluted both the leadership and the power of the army by assigning him only three panzer divisions. Three others were assigned to the south of France, and four were kept as a theater reserve under Hitler's personal control. This had the effect of excluding Rundstedt from the command process, for Rommel had direct access to the Fuehrer. Later in 1944, Rundstedt and Schweppenburg would both be relieved by Hitler for "defeatism."

When D-Day came only one panzer division, the 21st, was within reach of the beaches; Allied air power prevented the rest from arriving in a timely manner. Had Rommel prevailed and been able to place two or three more panzer divisions directly behind the Normandy beachheads, it is probable that the invasion at Omaha, at least, would have been repelled, and very possibly those at the other beaches as well.

Rommel did a brilliant job of reinvigorating German defensive efforts, filling the beaches with obstacles and mines, using French tank turrets as instant pillboxes, and siting an assortment of guns to rake the beaches. Simple stakes of concrete or timber, called "Rommel's asparagus," their ends sharpened and pointed outward, would prove to be especially effective against landing gliders. Only material shortages and a lack of time kept Rommel from his goal of laying an impenetrable barrier of mines by the millions. And yet there was an almost pathetic difference in the level of technologies between the combatants. While the Allies were planning technological marvels like the Mulberry artificial harbor, underwater fuel pipelines and specialized landing craft, the Germans were reduced to planting wood and steel obstacles that differed only in size from those used in the Middle Ages.

Allied

The British wanted the man considered to be the doyen of British generals, General Sir Alan Brooke (later Field Marshal Viscount Alanbrooke) to be Supreme Commander for the invasion. Yet the relative strengths showed clearly that an American would have to be chosen, for while the British contribution had peaked and could only decline thereafter, American strength was already double it, and still growing at a rapid rate. By January 1, 1944, almost 1,700,000 Americans were in Great Britain, "over paid, over sexed and over here" in the memorable, accurate and, in retrospect, affectionate phrase of the time.

President Roosevelt wished General George C. Marshall to be the Supreme Commander, in part because he would do the job well, but also because he deserved it for all he had already done. In testimony to his high standing, Admirals King and Leahy and General Arnold all pleaded with Roosevelt to keep Marshall on as Chief of Staff. Marshall keenly wanted the Normandy assignment, but, the quintessential selfless officer, made no suggestion of this even though it meant he would be denied the most important military command in history—and subsequently, possible election to the presidency.

On December 7, 1943, Roosevelt casually informed Eisenhower that he was to be Supreme Commander. One can imagine what the man millions came to like as "Ike" must have thought. He had no direct combat experience. It had taken him twenty-four years to progress from 2nd lieutenant to colonel, and less than two years (March 1941 to February 1943) to go from colonel to full general. More pointedly, his subordinates would be men of great seniority and enormous battle experience. (One of the most capable as well as most troublesome, General Bernard Montgomery, the victor of El Alamein, had been made a brigadier general in 1937 and had fought in France in both World Wars I and II, as well as in Africa and Sicily. He seldom let Eisenhower forget his superior experience.)

But as so many of Roosevelt's personnel decisions were, Eisenhower was exactly the right choice, and the British had to be content with filling most of the important subordinate positions on his staff. In recognition of the importance of air power, as well as of his agreeable personality, Air Chief Marshal Sir Arthur Tedder was chosen as Eisenhower's Deputy Supreme Commander—a classic good cop–good cop approach. Tedder, who had aggressively integrated air and land operations in Africa, would fail to do so during the invasion, where the primary air leaders, as in Sicily, resolutely forgot all that had been learned about combined planning and operations. Although 13,000 aircraft would be used in the preinvasion attacks and during the invasion, there were never enough to meet the needs of the troops or the egos of the commanders. The Allies were fortunate that the combined bombing offensive had already ground the Luftwaffe down, while the systematic bombing of transportation to isolate the front, which they had opposed so bitterly, turned out to be very effective.

Part of Tedder's problem was the appointment of Air Chief Marshall Sir Trafford Leigh-Mallory to be Commander, Allied Expeditionary Air Forces. The at times insufferable Leigh-Mallory would prove to be as troublesome in this position as he had been during and after the Battle of Britain. Montgomery, an even more difficult personality than Leigh-Mallory, was Commander of the Twenty-first Army Group in England, and the overall ground commander during the actual landing.

The key appointment for Operation Neptune (the maritime first phase of Overlord)—and consequently for Operation Overlord (the invasion of France itself)—was that of Admiral Sir Bertram Ramsay as Allied Naval Commander Expeditionary Force. Ramsay was considered somewhat infra dig in the Admiralty because he was a retired officer. He had, however, distinguished himself in the planning and execution of the Dunkirk operation, as well as in Operation Torch and Operation Husky. (The one blot on his escutcheon was the escape of the *Gneisenau* and *Scharnhorst* from Brest to Germany via the English Channel on February 12–13, 1942, a masterful plan, well executed, that caught the British off guard, but its effect on anything but English pride was minor.)

Ramsay was not a fighting admiral, but there was little naval fighting to be done in Overlord. The German navy, like its air force, was already beaten, its submarines suppressed and its capital ships either sunk or confined to harbor. He was, however, what was needed: a master planner possessing what Thomas Carlyle defined as the transcendent capacity to take trouble first of all. Although Eisenhower thought him "ritualistic" in his regard for protocol, Ramsay was nonetheless a likeable man. Stern and demanding of his subordinates, he recognized their limitations and worked within them. His style was not the American style, for he directed every detail from the top; American commanders tended to create the broad outlines of a plan and leave it to their subordinates to flesh out. As a measure of his thoroughness, the operations order he issued for Neptune, with its annexes, ran to more than 1,000 pages. It detailed the who, what, where and when for every cog in the gigantic invasion machine; the whys and hows were not always as carefully explained.

PLANNING AND LOGISTICS

Ramsay's orders were to secure a position on the European continent with sufficient port facilities to maintain a force of twenty-six to thirty divisions, these to be built up at the rate of three to five per month thereafter. A tall order, considering that the Germans had fifty-nine divisions in Western Europe, twenty-five of these first-line.

Even though the Allies had air and sea superiority, the success of the invasion was not a sure thing, for they were opposed on land by an army considered to be the best in the world, even by its opponents. Many factors were beyond Allied control, particularly the weather. The first part of Neptune's task, putting enough troops on shore to break into fortified Europe, would be difficult; the second part, maintaining a faster rate of buildup than the Germans, would be even more so.

It was essential that absolute security be maintained, and the most elaborate spoof in history, Operation Fortitude, was mounted. Fortitude was designed to make the Germans believe that the attack was coming on the Pas-de-Calais, and involved the creation of a fictitious army, with Patton, whom the Germans regarded with the highest respect, at its head. The deception required the Allies to make even more reconnaissance and bombing missions in the area behind the Pas-de-Calais than they did at Normandy. In England, dummy encampments were built with dummy tanks and landing craft assembled where they could just be seen by the rare German reconnaissance plane. Elaborate radio traffic, dwarfing that for the actual Overlord force, was spewed into the air; security leaks were faked and those responsible "punished." The Germans fell into the trap, keeping nineteen divisions out of action for six critical weeks.

For the invasion itself, Admiral Ramsay followed past practice. He orchestrated a vastly expanded version of the techniques used successfully in North Africa and the Mediterranean, improved by the new and more plentiful equipment, and by months of practice. More than 7,000 ships, 5,300 of them in the invasion fleet itself, were to be involved in an intricate series of movements that followed a precise schedule in order to place five divisions ashore in France. Three airborne divisions—22,000 men—would already have landed behind enemy lines.

The Americans were to land farthest to the south, at two beaches: Utah at the base of the Cotentin peninsula, and Omaha, between the tiny towns of Vierville-sur-Mer and Sainte-Honorine. The British Empire Force were to land farther to the north, at three beaches, Gold and Juno, which were between Arromanches and Saint-Aubin, and Sword, between Lion-sur-Mer and Ouistreham at the mouth of the Orne. The British beaches were separated by reefs. The straight-line distance from Utah's right flank to Sword's left flank was about forty miles.

Ramsay followed the same procedures as before in bringing the troops and equipment in larger ships to be off-loaded and guided to a line of departure for the assault. In Neptune, however, his planning task was complicated by a series of requirements not found in previous invasions, where the landing force was the total force to be committed to the endeavor. This time, the initial five divisions were to be followed as quickly as possible by others to match and exceed the German buildup and to prepare for subsequent operations on the continent. Inasmuch as an Allied division required 600 to 700 tons of supplies daily (compared to about half that for a German division), this meant that Ramsay had to oversee a supply buildup to 35,000 tons daily by the time fifty divisions were ashore.

Although there was some hope to capture the port of Cherbourg quickly, the Germans were such experts in demolition that it was probable that the port could not be used for several weeks. Therefore two artificial harbors were planned, an undertaking that Ramsay pursued wholeheartedly, but in which he did not have much faith.

Designated Mulberry A and Mulberry B, for the American and British beaches, respectively, the artificial harbors had humble origins stemming from an original requirement for mounting piers on fixed legs so that they could float up and down with the tide. Flexible steel bridges mounted on pontoons provided a route from ships tied up to the pier to shore.

Like so many great ideas, the concept took on a life of its own, for the likely tide and surf conditions at the selected beaches threatened to make unloading impossible. It was suggested that the piers might be protected if large hollow steel structures, made in the form of a cross, were anchored offshore as a breakwater to reduce wave action. Called Bombardons, they were 198 feet long and twenty-five feet high.

Commodore J. Hughes-Hallett next suggested that concrete caissons be placed inshore of the Bombardons. Code-named Phoenix, these were massive concrete structures 400 feet long and displacing 4,000 to 6,000 tons. Two hundred thirteen of them had to be built, tested, towed in place and sunk to form a sea wall on two sides of what was now an artificial harbor.

Rear Admiral W. G. Tennant, another veteran of Dunkirk (and of the *Repulse*), lacked faith in Phoenix and suggested that the concrete caissons be reinforced by sinking old ships parallel to the shore in a more conventional breakwater. Fifty-five ships, mostly old freighters but including one obsolete French battleship, the *Courbet* of 1912, were reluctantly provided by the Admiralty; the individual ships were code-named Corncob, while the line of sunken ships was called a Gooseberry.

All of the Corncobs except the *Courbet* were brought into place under their own power, but towing the Phoenixes and the Bombardons required about 200 tugboats.

In modern warfare, having a good acronym is almost as important as having luck. So it was with Pluto (pipeline under the ocean), a concept of running a flexible pipeline, uncoiled from a reel like telegraph cables, from England to France to supply fuel to the hundreds of thousands of vehicles and aircraft being sent there. The product of the fertile Combined Operations staff, Force Pluto supervised the building, testing and installation of flexible pipelines of several varieties. In addition, other pipelines were used to replenish storage facilities ashore from tankers.

The Allied preparations buttressed ingenious ideas like Mulberry and Pluto with the application of basic methods on the largest conceivable scale. Unlike previous operations, where mines had been only a minor threat, Ramsay assumed that the Germans would have sown thousands of them, and consequently he created an elaborate minesweeping plan using hundreds of minesweepers to carve out routes for the invasion boats and areas where his naval gun support ships could move in safety. As the landings unfolded, the attackers found that mines had not been laid on the scale imagined, nor was there as great a proportion as feared of the latest time-delay or pressure mines. Nonetheless, mines would cause the most damage to the invasion fleet.

Twenty-one American and thirty-eight British and Canadian convoys were scheduled to depart from ports around the southern coast of England. Seven channels, wide enough for two convoys to sail side by side, were swept from the English coast to a point thirteen miles southeast of the Isle of Wight, known as Picadilly Circus or Area Z. There, like an English traffic roundabout, almost every convoy passed to turn into a "spout" of five parallel mine-swept channels, one for each task force. Halfway across, these five were further divided into two lanes, one for fast convoys and one for slow. Charts (called Mickey Mouse diagrams) showed where each convoy would be every hour.

An abbreviated chronology gives but a hint of the depth and breadth of the 7,000-ship, 250,000-man operation. (D for D-Day, the day of the invasion; H for H-hour, the hour of the attack; M for minute, the moment the invaders touched shore):

D minus 45: Mineclearing operations begin
D minus 21: Supply ships begin loading
D minus 7: Minesweeping operations begin
D minus 3: X-craft (two-man submarines) depart for marker duty
D minus 2: Transports start loading
D minus 1: X-craft arrive offshore
         Transports, gunnery support ships sail
         Minesweeping intensified

D-Day: June 6, 1944

D-Day 0135: First paratroops start landing

D-Day 0200: Fire support ships anchored

D-Day 0200: Minesweeping off beaches

D-Day 0230: Attack transport *Bayfield*, headquarters ship, anchors off Utah

D-Day 0230: Western Task Force begins loading landing craft

D-Day 0250: Command ship *Ancon* anchors off Omaha

D-Day 0430: Western Task Force begins journey to beach

D-Day 0530: Eastern Task Force begins loading landing craft

D-Day 0530: British bombardment of beaches begins

D-Day 0530: American bombardment of beaches begins

D-Day 0600: U.S. medium bombers attack beaches

D-Day 0630: U.S. LCTs with rocket launchers bombard beach

D-Day, H-Hour: 0630: Landing on Omaha and Utah Beaches

0725: Landing on Sword and Gold Beaches

0735: Landing on Juno Beach, right wing

0745: Landing on Juno Beach, left wing

D-Day 0745: (all beaches) LCTs with self-propelled artillery and mortars arrive

D-Day 2359: More than 155,000 men, thousands of vehicles and tons of supplies landed by this time

D-Day plus 3: Gooseberrys sunk in place

D-Day plus 18: Mulberry A and Mulberry B completed

D-Day plus 18: Ship-to-shore pipelines in place

D-Day plus 20: First cross-Channel pipeline in place

D-Day plus 75: Tenth cross-Channel pipeline in place

D-DAY

The airborne operations required a moonlit night for success. The seaborne operations required the initial landings three hours before high water; if too low, the distance in was too long on the shallow slope of the beaches; too high, and the underwater obstacles, most of them mined, would destroy the landing craft. To get the proper combination of moonlight and tide conditions meant that D-Day had to be either June 5, 6 or 7, or two weeks later, on June 19, 20 or 21. Eisenhower selected June 5, but terrible weather forced a postponement. At 0415 on June 5, the Supreme Commander gambled on a forecast that there would be a window of good weather and decided to make an attempt on June 6, saying, "O.K. We'll go."

Ramsay had called upon two stalwarts, neither of whom he liked very much, to command. Rear Admiral Alan G. Kirk, in the cruiser *Augusta*, headed the Western Task Force, covering the American beaches. Vice Admiral Sir Philip Vian, in the cruiser *Scylla*, commanded the Eastern Task Force, covering the British sector.

Western Task Force

Utah

Neither German radar nor surface ships picked up the invasion fleet, the former because they had been systematically bombed out, the latter because Admiral Theodore Krancke had decided that the weather was too foul for an invasion attempt, and so gave some respite to his hard-pressed motor torpedo boat crews.

Rear Admiral Don P. Moon, U.S. Navy, headed Task Force 125, which was to disembark the Utah assault force, consisting of the 4th Infantry Division and units of the VII Corps.

By accident, the entire assault force was displaced about one mile south of the designated points; this turned out to be fortunate, for the new areas were less well defended. The beach was flat and featureless, and the navy's Underwater Demolition Team (UDTs) had little difficulty removing the obstacles. Intermittent German fire was suppressed by naval gunfire support under the direction of Rear Admiral Morton L. Deyo. Deyo had at his disposal the battleship *Nevada*, a veteran of Pearl Harbor, and the U.S. heavy cruisers *Tuscaloosa* and *Quincy*, plus the Royal Navy monitor *Erebus* and cruisers *Hawkins*, *Black Prince* and *Enterprise*. Working so close inshore that their keels often scraped the bottom were eight Allied destroyers, two destroyer escorts and the Dutch gunboat *Soemba*.

Gunfire was directed by flights of fighter planes, Supermarine Spitfires and North American Mustangs, flying out of England, with pilots who were trained for the exacting task of spotting the fall of shells, as a mistake could be catastrophic. The *Nevada*, refurbished after Pearl Harbor, could elevate her ten 14-inch guns 30 degrees, and Spitfires guided her in furnishing artillery support for American paratroops well inland. On June 8, one spectacular shoot proved Schweppenburg's contentions regarding the threat of naval-based guns when the *Nevada* destroyed 110 German vehicles with seventy 14-inch shells at a range of thirteen miles.

By 1800, 21,238 troops, 1,742 vehicles and 1,695 tons of supplies had been landed and a tenuous perimeter six miles deep established. Mines had accounted for the sinking of two minesweepers, two U.S. destroyers (the *Corry* and *Rich*), a destroyer escort, two LCIs, a patrol craft and three LCTs. There were only 197 casualties, about half that suffered when the German E-boats had pounced upon a landing exercise off Slapton Sands earlier in the year.

Omaha

Things did not go so well at Omaha. Rear Admiral John L. Hall, on board the command ship *Ancon*, commanded TF 124, the assault force O (for Omaha), embarking regimental combat teams of the 1st and 29th Divisions, two ranger battalions, and support units of V Corps. Naval gunfire support was provided by Rear Admiral Carleton F. Bryant, with the oldest battleship in the fleet, the 1912 *Arkansas*, and the 1914 *Texas*. These ships were hard to handle and bad sea boats, but they came into their own off Omaha, with the *Arkansas*'s twelve 12-inch and the *Texas*'s ten 14-inch guns hammering German emplacements. Bryant also had four light cruisers, HMS *Glasgow* and *Bellona* and the French *Montcalm* and *Georges Leygues* (inevitably known to U.S. sailors as "George Legs"). Inshore, nine American and three British *Hunt*-class destroyers served as field artillery, firing from as close as 800 yards when the DUKWs carrying the army's guns couldn't reach the beach because of rough seas. One of the destroyers, the *O'Brien*, was captained by the man whose ship had sunk the midget submarine at Pearl Harbor, Commander W. W. Outerbridge.

Omaha was far better defended than Utah, both in the depth of the defenses and the number and quality of the German troops. The terrain was also more difficult, the sandy beaches terminating at the base of tall, fissured cliffs that the rangers had to scale and take in hand-to-hand combat.

The first intimations of trouble at Omaha came with the loss of twenty-seven out of thirty-two of the DD (dual-drive) tanks. Launched from LCTs and fitted with canvas water wings, these tanks were swamped by the rough water, and the crews drowned inside the tanks.

The Germans were waiting with intense automatic weapons fire, and caught the troops wading in, burdened with their rifles and 68-pound packs; a wound or a fall often meant drowning. A 10-knot wind swamped many of the landing craft and the entire plan began to collapse. Despite the long experience and training, a paralyzing confusion occurred among the landing craft. Some LCIs were jammed up against underwater obstacles or other landing craft, blocking the routes in and causing confusion to the incoming assault waves, which began to mill around offshore. Eventually, there was no choice but to simply run straight ahead through the obstacles, beaching where they could, and taking losses.

With no sensible orders to follow, the situation was ultimately resolved only by the individual initiative of the young men guiding the landing craft. Most had seen neither a ship nor a foreign shore until the year before, but at Omaha Beach, when the plans went awry, they used common sense and courage to get troops and supplies on the beach despite gunfire, underwater obstacles, knocked-out tanks and landing craft, traffic jams and a rampaging surf. Their random individual efforts eventually created a strange sort of order out of the chaos. The supply depots, planned to be placed on land in a logical sequence, were forgotten; materials were simply dropped ashore, and the requirements of the battle drew down upon them as needed. It was messy, but it worked so well that the first message Lieutenant General Omar N. Bradley, Commander of the American First Army, received from his commander on shore, General Leonard T. Gerow, was "Thank God for the United States Navy."

By nightfall, the Allied beachhead was limited to a front five miles in width and one mile in depth. As night fell it was here that Rommel's plan might have succeeded—a panzer division might well have been able to split the front, then deal with each part separately, protected from naval gunfire by the proximity of the troops. Almost 34,250 troops had been landed at the cost of 2,000 casualties; long before new panzer divisions would arrive there would come more Allied troops, naval gunfire and air support—the invasion had succeeded.

Eastern Task Force

Vice Admiral Vian allowed his transports to run five miles closer in than the Americans had, cutting down on the troops' travel time from ship to shore and relying on the ships' guns to suppress any German artillery. On board the cruiser *Scylla*, Vian had an operations room unique in British history, where the radar picture of the landing area was converted to a surface plot, enabling him to control the action to a degree that satisfied even him.

The invasion of the beaches assigned the British was delayed because of tidal conditions, which permitted a much more intensive preliminary bombardment. Given Churchill's penchant for the unorthodox, it is not surprising that the British forces were equipped with far more imaginative equipment to penetrate the obstacles and minefields than the Americans. These included armored bulldozers to muscle obstacles out of the way; landing craft equipped to clear underwater hazards; "Crocodiles," Churchill tanks with a 120-yard-range flamethrower; and "Scorpions," Sherman tanks fitted with flails to detonate mines. The latter beat their way up the beach, chains rotating, mines exploding, and then proceeded to engage the Germans with their 75mm cannon.

The British landings at Sword and Gold went off well, with the Nazis seemingly stunned by the vast amount of artillery support, and not responding with much counterfire. The reason was soon discovered—the Germans had built their casemates with a solid face to the sea, with the guns angled to fire on the beaches instead of out to sea. The British pressed forward, and by nightfall had secured their position.

At Sword, Rear Admiral A. G. Talbot, in one of the two prototype command vessels used in Torch, HMS *Largs*, controlled 285 vessels, including a strong bombardment group. The warhorse *Warspite*, still not recovered fully from the hit by the Fritz-X glide bomb at Salerno, plied her operational 15-inch guns, as did the equally venerable if less combat distinguished *Ramillies* and the antique monitor *Roberts*. This heavy firepower proved not to be necessary, for the big guns they were intended to suppress were either unmanned or had been removed. Five cruisers and thirteen destroyers added to the weight of fire. For close-in support, Talbot had twenty-three armed landing craft. Sword Beach was not heavily defended, but the large number of Allied ships resulted in traffic jams that impeded progress during the morning. Seven landing craft were lost to mines or mortar fire.

Enemy opposition at Gold was particularly unspirited—the German troops were the 716th "static division," which had no mobile transport and had a strong component of less than enthusiastic Poles and Ukrainians. Force G, under Commodore C. E. Douglas-Pennant in HMS *Bululo*, the other prototype command ship in Operation Torch, used 243 amphibious ships for the attack. His heavy fire support came from the veteran of the *Graf Spee* affair, the *Ajax*, plus three other cruisers, *Argonaut*, *Orion* and *Emerald*. In addition, there were eleven British and one Polish destroyers and a Dutch gunboat. For close-in support, Gold relied on an unusual hybrid, twenty-one armed landing craft and sixteen armored LCTs that carried Centaur tanks equipped with 95mm "bunker-busting" howitzers.

Commodore G. N. Oliver positioned 187 amphibious ships for the Juno landings, commanding from the *Hilary*. His naval gunfire force was comparatively light, consisting of the cruisers *Belfast* and *Diadem* and eleven destroyers. Landing support was heavier with forty-three armed landing craft of various types.

The German defenses were found to be strongest in the area of the Juno Beach landings, with mines so plentiful that almost a third of the landing craft were sunk or damaged. The fabled 88mm antitank guns waited until the tanks hit the beach, then opened up at almost point-blank range, stopping many of them in their tracks. These wrecks contributed to a massive traffic jam on the beach as the incoming tide reduced its width to less than thirty feet.

By nightfall the British had penetrated an average of six miles, but their hold on Juno was as tenuous as the American hold on Omaha; had Hitler listened to Rommel, here again a couple of panzer divisions might have changed history with a night assault. But he had not, and the Allies were there to stay.

The Race to Buildup

As the Germans began to react to the Allied invasion, Ramsay concentrated on maintaining a continuous flow of men, vehicles and supplies to the beachheads. Although the bridgehead was very shallow and the weight of the German counterattack had not yet been felt, Ramsay and Eisenhower crossed the Channel on June 7 to view the situation for themselves. The two artificial harbors were begun, a time-consuming and difficult project, for both the Bombardons and the Phoenixes were intractable, their huge steel hulks tossing in the wind and current, threatening to crush the tugs that valiantly held them while the caissons were sunk into place.

By June 13 the process of supplying the beach had become relatively orderly, and a cumulative total of more than 370,000 men, 64,000 vehicles and 120,000 tons of supplies was delivered. By the eighteenth, the numbers had increased to 629,000 troops, 95,000 vehicles and 228,000 tons of supplies; the Germans, with their rail lines and roads continuously interdicted, could not compete.

Nature intervened against the Allies on June 19 (which had been one of the alternate landing dates), just as the Mulberrys were being completed. A "forty-year" storm blew up with a Force 8 wind velocity the next day, with waves reaching eight and a half feet in height. Tossed on the ocean like Ping-Pong balls on a lake, the huge steel Bombardons were flung against the concrete caissons, destroying most of them.

By the morning of June 22, Mulberry A was completely devastated, littering the beaches with its debris, while Mulberry B was heavily damaged.

A decision was made not to repair Mulberry A; ironically, the amount of men and matériel then handled over the beaches by the original floating pier concept rose to new levels.

Only the Allies could have afforded a concept like the Mulberrys, a logistics overkill that cost more than $200 million, took hundreds of thousands of man-hours and then, in the official British assessment, was probably not essential.

German Counterattacks by Air and Sea

German air and naval counterattacks were bravely done, but of limited effect, given the overwhelming Allied superiority. The richest target system in history in terms of sheer numbers of vulnerable vessels encompassed within a small area went virtually unscathed.

It had been feared that the Luftwaffe might put up 1,750 sorties during the first day of the invasion; in fact, it did less than a third of that number, and with little effect. Subsequently, the headquarters ship *Bulolo*, at Gold Beach, was hit by an incendiary bomb on June 7. The U.S. destroyer *Meredith* was either hit by one of the new Henschel Hs 293 radio-controlled glide bombs or struck a mine, and was severely damaged. Damage-control parties halted the list and took her under tow. The next day another German plane dropped a heavy bomb, a near miss that broke the *Meredith*'s back and she sank. (*Meredith* must have been an unlucky name—her predecessor was blown to bits in the Solomons.) The following day, the British frigate *Lawford* (a Lend-Lease destroyer escort) was sunk by a bomb, and on June 13 the British destroyer *Boadicea* was torpedoed.

The comparative level of Allied and German strength is well illustrated in the manner in which the S-boat problem was handled. On D-Day, the Germans had only twenty-nine *Schnell* boats operational. These corresponded to the famous American PT boats, and were called S-boats by the Germans and E-boats by the Allies. Built in a number of series, an S-boat of the invasion period was typically of 112 tons' displacement, 105 feet long with a 16-foot beam, and powered by three Mercedes-Benz MB501 diesel engines with a total of 6,000 horsepower. Manned by a crew of twenty-four, they had a top speed of 39 knots and carried two torpedo tubes and four torpedoes along with light guns. They had a long history of gallant operation, dating back to World War I, and had done signal service in the English Channel, the North Sea, the Baltic and Norway, and even in areas remote to Germany, like the western Mediterranean and the Adriatic, Aegean and Black Seas.

Although Vice Admiral Theodor Krancke had called off the alert on June 5, the German 5th Torpedo Flotilla, operating out of Cherbourg, and led by Commander H. Hoffman, made a daring run-in on June 6, firing fifteen torpedoes and sinking the Norwegian destroyer *Svenner*. After the landings, the S-boats, along with aircraft, began to lay the pressure mines that Hitler had delayed putting into use. The S-boats attacked every night, but were usually driven off by the destroyers, managing to sink only two LSTs on night of June 8. The following night, S-boats from Boulogne's 4th Flotilla, commanded by Lieutenant Commander Anhalt, blew the bow off the British frigate *Halstead* and sank four tugboats, two of which were struggling with a Mulberry caisson, which promptly ran amuck.

Concerned by the attacks, Admiral Ramsay asked Bomber Command for assistance and it was promptly rendered. On June 14, 335 Lancasters and thirteen Mosquitoes ravaged Le Havre with more than 1,000 tons of bombs. The Lancasters of No. 617 Squadron dropped twenty-two of the 12,000-pound Tallboy bombs, which broke up the pens shielding the S-boats. In all, three destroyers, ten S-boats and twenty other vessels were sunk and another sixteen damaged. The S-boat was eliminated as a threat, minor as it was.

German destroyers made two sorties, both repelled. The first had been a surprise, but Ultra had learned of the second sortie and the Royal Navy's 10th Destroyer Flotilla was sent to intercept it. In a long-running battle, two German destroyers were sunk, one beached and another severely damaged. So advanced was the British radio intelligence system that the German talk-between-ships network was monitored, and when the German commander called for a turn, the British anticipated it with a spread of torpedoes. The destroyers made no further efforts during the invasion.

The U-boat threat failed to materialize primarily because the deception on the date of D-Day had caught them in port, unable to intercept the vast invasion fleet. Heavy Allied air and sea patrols kept the U-boats suppressed; of the nine snorkel boats that put to sea, only two scored, one sinking an LCT and the other damaging the British destroyer escort *Blackwood* (a U.S.-built ship supplied under Lend-Lease), which later sank. One of the snorkel boats was sunk and two others were damaged. Of the seven standard U-boats that sortied, four were sunk and three were damaged.

The measure of German desperation was evident in the special weapons it deployed, all with a kamikaze tinge. Called the Kleinkampfverbände (K-verband), or Small Battle Unit Command, the concepts derived from the successful Italian use of "pigs" in Alexandria, the Japanese midget submarines and the British use of X-craft to damage the *Tirpitz* in September 1943.

The Neger (Moor) was a manned torpedo developed by Richard Mohr, whose last name in German also means "moor." It was twenty-five feet long and first saw action at Anzio. A follow-on, the Marder (Marten), was developed to obtain a diving capability, which the Neger lacked, and was a little over two feet longer. Essentially, both weapons were powered by torpedo motors and each carried a 21-inch G7e torpedo. They had a maximum speed of 10 knots and a range of forty-eight miles. They usually operated on the surface with the plexiglass dome awash, and were so dangerous to operate that Doenitz would not allow his submariners to crew them. Of the total of 500 built, 400 were lost, many due to the asphyxiation of the pilot.

In an attack on July 5, twenty-six Marders attacked the fleet supplying the invasion, and the minesweepers *Cato* and *Magic* were lost, at a cost of fifteen Marders. Another attack, on July 18, sank another minesweeper, the *Pleiades*, and damaged the Polish-manned cruiser *Dragon*, which was subsequently sunk as an addition to the Gooseberry line of blockships.

The *Linsen* were fast motorboats operating in pairs; one boat served as a control boat, the other, packed with explosives, operating by remote control. On August 2, sixteen control and twenty-eight explosive Linsen, with fifty-eight Marders, attacked ships approaching the beachhead, sinking the British destroyer escort *Quorn*, a trawler and an LCT, and damaging three transports. Twenty-four Linsen and forty-one Marders were lost, a costly exchange.

The Biber was a true one-man submarine, but so difficult to control that it was normally operated on the surface. With the Marder and Linsen, it continued operation for months, but the entire K-verband operation can only be considered a dismal failure. The time and resources expended upon them would have been far better spent on minelaying operations.

German mines were effective on the invasion beaches, and continued to be until the end of the war. At Normandy, the Americans lost three destroyers, *Corry*, *Glennon* and *Meredith*, the destroyer escort *Rich*, and two minesweepers, *Osprey* and *Tide*, to the silent, unseen enemy. The British lost eleven vessels, including seven warships, to mines, the most significant of which was Admiral Vian's *Scylla* and the destroyers *Wrestler*, *Swift* and *Fury*. The French destroyer *Mistral* also was lost to a mine.

The German sailors, like the Luftwaffe airmen and the soldiers, were brave. The Allies simply deployed too much matériel and firepower for them to contend with.

OPERATION DRAGOON — THE INVASION OF SOUTHERN FRANCE

The invasion of southern France on August 15, 1944, came as an anticlimax. Originally intended to take place simultaneously with the invasion of Normandy—Operation Anvil to Overlord's hammer—it was renamed Dragoon because Churchill felt he was dragooned into the operation.

The invasion of southern France was provoked by the Allied requirement for an additional port, Marseilles, despite the fact that by the end of August, more than two million men, 425,000 vehicles and three million tons of supplies would be landed across the Normandy beaches.

The Western Naval Task Force was commanded by Vice Admiral Henry Kent Hewitt, who had begun American amphibious operations in Operation Torch and now presided over the most perfectly executed invasion of the war. Hewitt, in the command ship *Catoctin*, was to land Major General Alexander Patch and the Seventh Army, along with the U.S. VI Corps under Major General Lucian Truscott and the French II Corps under General Jean de Lattre de Tassigny, between Cannes and Toulon. After a heavy bombardment by 1,300 aircraft and a paratroop drop of 5,000 men of the 1st Parachute Division, Hewitt followed the tried-and-true tactics of assigning numbered task forces to particular beaches and backing them up with heavy naval gunfire support.

For the most part it was no contest; more than 2,000 transports and landing craft and 310 warships were able to dispose of the single instance of German naval opposition—the patrol boat *Escaburt*, which managed to sink the destroyer *Somers* before being sunk itself.

Hewitt landed 95,000 men the first day at a cost of only 183 casualties. The American troops fanned out to capture Toulon and Marseilles, often allowing the French forces to pass through to enter the cities of their homeland first. All of the objectives for the first month of the invasion were obtained within two weeks. German resistance was meager; instead Germany extricated its troops for a return to the homeland. By September 15 Operation Dragoon was over.

THE LAST EVACUATION

One of the least well known naval operations in the European theater came at the very end. The war had been hard on the German navy; its surface ships were sunk or bottled up, and its submarines, after their initial period of ascendancy, were suppressed. Yet in the final months of the war, operating under the greatest difficulties, devoid of air power, short on fuel and ships, the German navy pulled off its greatest triumph: the largest and most comprehensive evacuation in history. If Dunkirk had been a deliverance, then the German navy's Baltic operation was an epiphany to the 2.3 million soldiers, sailors and civilians who escaped the ravages of the Soviet army.

The Germans had started the war with 4.3 million tons of merchant shipping and added another million to the total with new construction and requisitioned vessels from captured territories. The Allied air and naval campaign subtracted 2.7 million tons by the end of the war, but many of the surviving ships did remarkable service in the Baltic. Approximately 1,100 ships of all sizes, in even greater variety than the Mosquito Armada at Dunkirk, worked unceasingly even after the official May 8 end of the war. The fleet consisted of remainders of the once great German passenger liners, including the specially built "Strength Through Joy" ships (originally designed to provide one-class, low-cost cruises for the average German worker), as well as tramp steamers, icebreakers, fishing trawlers, barges, whaleboats and sailboats. From January through May 1945, refugees flocked from cities with famous names—Danzig, Kolberg, Koenigsberg, Pillau, Revel and Riga—as well as from tiny fishing ports and beaches, a desperate tide of humanity taking the only chance remaining: escape by sea. The roads to Germany were clogged with other refugees, as rail and truck movement was no longer available for them. Those caught by the Russians were gunned down and driven over by tank columns.

The refugees trekked to the ports to be fed from navy soup kitchens, if they were lucky, then sent aboard the first vessel available. Oddly enough, coal was in shorter supply than oil, so oil-burning ships were used wherever possible. One account relates how babies became valuable as priority tickets onto the ships—so much so that they were sometimes passed back to shore for another member of the family to use. In other instances, babies were thrown from shore to departing ships in the hope that someone would take pity and care for them.

In many cases, the ships shuttled back and forth until they had consumed all the fuel they had on board, and were then laid up, no more fuel being available. Their route ran between the Baltic coast and the northern German ports at first, but these quickly became overcrowded, vulnerable to enemy land attack and subject to almost continuous bombing. It was soon obvious that it was time and fuel well spent to go the extra distance to Copenhagen, still occupied by the Germans.

Hitler had refused to evacuate his soldiers in Courland and in East Prussia, demanding that they hold their ground or die. Yet the Soviet forces, not to be denied, steadily compressed the German army into rings around the Baltic ports. Because the departing ships carried a mixture of soldiers and civilians, they were legitimate military targets subjected to continuous attack by aircraft and submarines, and exposed to the threat of the hundreds of thousands of mines lurking in the Baltic. The exact numbers will never be known, but only about 34,000 persons were lost in the evacuation. More than half the casualties occurred in the three greatest sea tragedies in history: the sinkings of the *Wilhelm Gustloff, General von Stueben* and *Goya.*

In its former capacity as a cruise ship, the 25,000-ton *Gustloff* normally carried 1,465 passengers and a crew of 400. On January 30, 1945, the twelfth anniversary of Hitler's ascension to power, she put to sea with a smaller crew but with *8,000* passengers. Sailing without escort, she was an easy victim for the Russian submarine *S-13*, commanded by Captain Third Class Alexander Marinesko. Marinesko put three torpedoes into her side and she sank in the bitter cold water with at least 6,000 casualties, most drowned.

On February 9, the former transatlantic liner *General von Steuben* sailed from Pillau. Built as the *München*, the 14,690-ton ship had survived a fire, a rebuilding, a renaming and service as a Strength Through Joy cruise ship. Marinesko was waiting to hit her with two torpedoes. This time more than 3,000 drowned, many of them wounded soldiers believing they were heading for safety.

The third major tragedy was the 5,230-ton *Goya*, a small but modern freighter packed to the wales with as many as 7,000 refugees and soldiers, the latter mostly wounded, all elated to have escaped the hated Russians. The Soviet submarine *L-3* lay in wait. The *L-3* was a 1,355-ton minelayer built in 1929, of a class notorious for its poor construction. Her commander, Captain Third Class Konstantinovich Konovalov, put two torpedoes into the *Goya* on April 16, 1945. Only about 100 persons were saved.

In three sinkings, more than 16,000 lives had been lost, ten times the toll of the *Titanic.* Little moment was made of the deaths in this time of Germany's *Gotterdamerung,* where one horror followed another in rapid succession. Yet of all of the many iniquities of that terrible period, none seems to capture the war's futility and inequity more than the loss of these three ships.

INVASIONS AND EVACUATIONS IN THE PACIFIC

During the first 100 days of the war, Japanese invasion forces went about their business as if they were peacetime maneuvers, following the policy of making small leaps well covered by air power. The Japanese had long experience in the process, having built the world's first specially designed landing ship, the *Shinshu Maru*, in 1937. It could carry twenty fully loaded Daihatsu landing craft, and unload them two at a time through stern doors. (The *Shinshu Maru* had an eventful career, being torpedoed three times, sunk twice and raised once during the war. The final sinking was in 1945.)

The Japanese use of both landing ships and landing craft at Tientsin, China, in 1937 was a model for the 1941 aggression in Southeast Asia. The technique for most of the invasions was the same: an assault force of transport ships would be accompanied by a striking force to put down artillery fire on the beaches, if necessary, and both units would be protected by a covering force consisting of heavy ships and usually an aircraft carrier.

With Japan in control of both the sea and the sky, Allied forces were unable to do much in the way of evacuations, and large numbers of troops were trapped in the Philippines, Singapore and the Netherlands East Indies. The few who did get away, did so covertly on PT boats, submarines or destroyers.

As will be seen in the following chapters, the changing circumstances of war forced the Japanese to become adept at resupplying their garrisons at night by means of destroyers, barges and submarines. When it became necessary, they used the same methods to evacuate island garrisons to defensive positions on the next island up the chain. Thus, when things finally turned against them on Guadalcanal, they evacuated 13,000 men in secrecy in a single week. Rear Admiral Koyangi Koniji used about twenty destroyers in three separate nighttime operations between February 1 and 7.

They used the technique again in the Aleutians; on May 11, 1943, American troops invaded Attu for a bitter eighteen-day battle. When it was over, only twenty-nine Japanese surrendered out of 2,500. The Americans lost 561 killed and 1,136 wounded, a high price to pay. On August 15, a joint

Canadian-American amphibious force invaded Kiska; they found it deserted, the entire garrison having evacuated under cover of fog and night on July 29, thus ending the Japanese occupation of U.S. territory in World War II.

Later in the war the Japanese found themselves defending islands without any means to either supply or evacuate; on the islands that were invaded, the garrisons had to fight to the death. On the islands that were bypassed, the soldiers withered away from starvation and disease, the glorious 100 days of the war's beginning long forgotten.

11.

GUADALCANAL AND THE GROWTH OF AMERICAN POWER

The Battle of Guadalcanal (August 1942 to February 1943) was a searing rite of passage that saw the U.S. military services transformed from amateur to world-class status on land, sea and air. The naval experience was particularly difficult, for the navy fought six major and many minor battles in the shark-, iron- and blood-steeped waters around Guadalcanal. The United States was victorious in only two of these battles; in two it suffered catastrophic defeats, one the worst in its history; the others were less determinate if no less savage. The Japanese navy won more often because of its superior training and because it had retained the initiative for eight months. The battles of the Coral Sea and Midway were primarily carrier conflicts and the American surface fleet still had much to learn in the bloody battles that raged for so long around an island few Americans had ever heard of before 1942.

Even as the requirements for the Battle of the Atlantic and Operation Torch were soaking up most of the available supplies and shipping, Admiral King remained determined to undertake offensive action in the Pacific. Not noted for his diplomatic skills, but expert in playing the military system, he funneled strength to the South Pacific, where more than 250,000 troops and an increasing number of aircraft were gathered. Relying on the Royal Navy in the Atlantic, Admiral King sent four fleet carriers to the Pacific, along with ten battleships, thirteen heavy cruisers and many light cruisers and destroyers. American naval strength did not yet match that of the Japanese, but the new emphasis on fast carrier strikes, combined with increasingly potent intelligence work, leveled the playing field.

The battle for Guadalcanal began accidentally, and on land was fought on American terms from the start. At sea the Japanese initially held the initiative until a combination of American land- and sea-based air power gradually seized control. (The Japanese had used both army and navy land-based air power in conjunction with carrier operations from the start of the war. Such coordination was new for the Americans.) In the air, the battle began on a fairly even basis, but the sharp twin blades of attrition and American buildup scissored Japanese strength away.

THE GEOGRAPHY OF THE BATTLE

Those young soldiers who had read Nordoff and Hall's rhapsodic descriptions of the beauty of South Pacific islands were bitterly disappointed in Guadalcanal's overwhelming odor of decay. The Solomons are a combination of coral reefs and the tips of mountains sunk long ago into the Pacific. One hundred inches of rain a year assures both verdant growth and rotting vegetation as well as ample breeding grounds for malarial mosquitoes. The islands are inhospitable, with little in the way of edible flora or fauna, but rich in insects and reptiles. A few thousand Melanesian natives scratched out an existence on British coconut plantations; the natives soon became rabidly anti-Japanese and pro-American, giving information to the Allies and aiding downed Allied pilots.

A glance at a map shows how New Guinea was plucked from Australia eons ago as the continents drifted, but only by referring to the scale can one understand how great are the distances involved in the islands that would soon become battlegrounds. Six hundred fifty miles to the east-northeast of New Guinea lie the Solomons, first Buka, then the largest of the group, Bougainville. Farther to the south, the islands are arranged in parallel chains to form an amphitheater for naval warfare. The western chain consists of Vella Lavella, Kolombangara, New Georgia and Guadalcanal, 1,000 miles from New Guinea. The eastern chain includes Choiseul, Santa Isabel and Malaita. At the southern end, like a stopper in a bottle, lies San Cristobal. Thousands of islets dot the area.

The war made these names familiar and American sailors' slang humanized them. The channel between the islands became known as the "Slot," through which Japan would run the "Tokyo Express," while the waters between Guadalcanal and the smaller islands of Savo and Florida were soon called "Ironbottom Sound," because of the many sunken ships that came to rest there.

An Accidental Beginning

Although heavily engaged on New Guinea's Papuan peninsula the Japanese army also decided to build an airfield on Guadalcanal, not bothering to inform the navy of its decision. This division of Japanese resources between Papua and Guadalcanal was to prove disastrous to both enterprises.

But the American side was also riven by dissension even as it moved toward objectives comparable to those of the Japanese. General MacArthur was determined to return to the Philippines by driving the Japanese out of New Guinea and then New Britain. Admiral Nimitz, anticipating that carrier air power would burgeon in the next year, wanted to take the Central Pacific route, through Micronesia, capturing the Gilberts, the Marshalls, the Carolines and the Marianas. Unspoken but implicit was each man's determination not to serve under the other. No country other than the United States could have willingly submitted to a divided command in planning two such monumental efforts, and it was only by the good fortune and geography that the two offensives were mutually supportive and prevented the Japanese from concentrating against one thrust at a time.

The same July 2, 1942, directive from the Joint Chiefs that apportioned the Pacific between General MacArthur and Admiral Nimitz assigned the two commanders three tasks.

Admiral Nimitz was given Task I, Operation Watchtower, the capture of the Santa Cruz Islands by August 1, 1942, in preparation for an attack on Tulagi. Tasks II and III were assigned to General MacArthur. Task II was to be done simultaneously with Operation Watchtower: drive the Japanese out of New Guinea. In Task III, MacArthur was to invade New Britain and take Rabaul, the main Japanese base. Each leap forward was to be about 300 miles in length—the effective range of fighters at the time.

As things developed, Japanese actions preempted both Tasks I and II. FRUPAC, the Fleet Radio Unit Pacific, under Commander Rochefort, discovered the airfield being built by the Japanese army on Guadalcanal before the Japanese navy did. The Japanese landings near Buna on the Papaun peninsula anticipated MacArthur's Task II. Countering it took so long that the war situation changed drastically and made Task III redundant; the ultimate objective, Rabaul, with 100,000 troops, was bypassed, deemed no longer worth the effort.

The bitter battle of Guadalcanal, which changed from an accident to a question of national prestige, lasted from August 7, 1942, to February 9, 1943. The Japanese had an excellent chance of overpowering the Americans during the first weeks of the battle, but a combination of hubris and poor planning caused them to consistently underestimate both the numbers and the fighting qualities of the Americans on Guadalcanal. When they at last realized the truth, all chance for victory was gone.

GUADALCANAL, BATTLE BY BATTLE

The struggle for Guadalcanal was dominated by air power during the day, the respective navies risking their carriers while the Americans made excellent use of Henderson Field, named after a hero of the battle of Midway. By night it was a question of surface warfare.

Thanks to the unequivocal courage of Admiral King, who ruthlessly overrode the properly cautious responses of his commanders in the field, the Americans moved swiftly on Guadalcanal. On August 7, the Allies' seventy-six-ship invasion force attacked Tulagi, Tanambogo, Gavatu and Guadalcanal Islands. Under the overall command of Vice Admiral Richard L. Ghormley, Commander South Pacific Force (COMSOPAC), Vice Admiral Frank Jack Fletcher, with Task Force 62, cautiously committed three aircraft carriers—*Saratoga, Enterprise* and *Wasp*. These were to provide air cover for Task Force 61, under Rear Admiral Richmond Kelly "Terrible" Turner, so called for his foul mouth and temper. Turner was the Amphibious Force Commander, tasked to put ashore the 19,500 men of Major General Alexander Vandegrift's 1st Marine Division for their initiation into battle. Vandegrift was the finest sort of professional officer, one who wanted to fight and knew how to, and could cajole the necessary support from his superiors.

The 1,500 Japanese on Tulagi, a tiny islet 23 miles north of Guadalcanal, put up a desperate resistance, symbolic of all the fights to come; only twenty-three surrendered, none voluntarily. Seven Kawanishi H6K Mavis four-engine flying boats and nine Nakajima A6M2-N Rufe float planes were destroyed, the latter by an earlier B-17 bombing raid. On Guadalcanal, the 600 soldiers and 1,500 men of the 11th and 13th Construction Groups, the Japanese equivalent of the American Seabees, fled into the jungle, some to be hunted down, some to join the reinforcements that soon appeared, but few, if any, ever to see Japan again.

General Vandegrift recognized that the airfield was key, and set up a perimeter defense around it. Fletcher's carrier planes fought off the quick response by Japanese bombers on the day of the landing, detected both by radar and by the "Coastwatchers." These were planters, natives, retired servicemen and others hidden on the islands, reporting Japanese naval and air activity. Their work was invaluable, but dangerous.

Admiral Fletcher, overly sensitive because of the loss of the *Yorktown* and *Lexington*, was worried both about air attacks and the enemy's surface fleet. Over the violent objections of Turner and Vandegrift, he withdrew his carriers on August 8 at 1810, twelve hours before they were scheduled to leave, lamely and inaccurately claiming a shortage of fuel and fighters. This precipitated Turner's decision to withdraw his transports, leaving Vandegrift with less than a month's supply of food, and short on ammunition, artillery and supplies.

THE BATTLE OF SAVO ISLAND

Turner's apprehensions were well founded, for Vice Admiral Mikawa Gunichi had hastily assembled a pickup force to attack the transports. Yamamoto had written Mikawa that the situation at Guadalcanal was as serious as it had been in 1904 when the Japanese had to seize Port Arthur to deny its use to the Russian fleet. Now Guadalcanal had to be denied to the Americans, and at once.

Few men had concentrated as much experience in warfare as Mikawa had in the last eight months, from Pearl Harbor to Ceylon to Midway, nor were any as expert in night fighting. Although many of the ships in Turner's force had worked together previously, the Americans were still inexperienced and unaware of war's real demands; the enemy force, while not used to operating together, was so well trained and experienced that it functioned flawlessly in the unfolding chaos of battle.

Mikawa led with his flagship, the heavy cruiser *Chokai*, followed in column behind him by the heavy cruisers *Aoba*, *Kako*, *Kinugasa* and *Furutaka*, the light cruisers *Tenryu* and *Yubari*, and the destroyer *Yunagi*, all stationed at 1,300-yard intervals. In that force were thirty-four 8-inch guns, thirty-seven of smaller caliber and sixty-two torpedo tubes, the latter firing what Samuel Eliot Morison called "the equalizer," the 24-inch-diameter Long Lance torpedo.

The Allied forces guarding the approaches to Guadalcanal around Savo Island were under the command of Rear Admiral Victor A. Crutchley, a Royal Navy officer commanding the Australian squadron. Crutchley's bright red beard and mustache hid the wounds he had suffered at Jutland; he had won the Victoria Cross in two attempts to block the harbors of Zeebruge and Ostend. As Mikawa's force approached, Crutchley, in his cruiser *Australia*, had gone to meet with Admiral Turner to discuss Fletcher's withdrawal (viewed as little short of traitorous) and future plans.

It has been reported for years that an Australian Lockhead Hudson saw Mikawa's fleet and failed to report it for eight hours. Later investigation has shown that the pilot, Sergeant Bill Stutt, sent several reports that were received by both the Japanese and the Americans, but not acted upon by the latter. Because the sighting had reported "seaplane carriers" in the formation, Turner was convinced that the Japanese were going to establish a seaplane base, and ruled out the possibility of a night surface attack. Terrible Turner, despite being the author of many a war plan, made the classic mistake of assuming what the enemy *would* do instead of preparing for what he *could* do. He had to learn the hard way how to make war.

Crutchley had arranged his forces to block all approaches around Savo Island. The Southern Force, between Savo and Guadalcanal, consisted of the Australian cruiser *Canberra* and the U.S. cruiser *Chicago*, steaming in column formation, 600 yards apart, with the U.S. destroyers *Patterson* and *Bagley* as escort. The Northern Force, between Savo and Florida Islands, consisted of three U.S. heavy cruisers, the *Vincennes*, the *Astoria* and the *Quincy*, plus the U.S. destroyers *Helm* and *Wilson*. The eastern approaches were covered by the U.S. light cruiser *San Juan* and the Australian cruiser *Hobart*, and the U.S. destroyers *Monssen* and *Buchanan*. Offshore from Guadalcanal were nineteen transports and cargo ships, Mikawa's primary target.

Once again, the ships' names alone can convey little of the fatigue, the tension, the anxiety of the men waiting for combat, just as they do not tell of their unique combination of power and vulnerability that puts such a premium on leadership.

Crutchley, somewhat diffident because he was an Englishman in an Australian ship commanding American forces, had not provided a plan of action. Two picket ships, the U.S. destroyers *Ralph Talbot* and *Blue*, were equipped with the relatively ineffective model SC radar, intended to provide early warning. As events transpired, the two destroyers were at opposite ends of their beats, their radars unable to detect the Japanese, when Mikawa burst through their center. Allied inexperience allowed Japanese scout planes to be ignored as they circled overhead for more than an hour, their blinking navigation lights seeming to assure their friendly status. After almost forty-eight hours of continuous alert, many of the Allied sailors were sleeping, as were some of the captains of the Allied cruisers.

Reality broke at 0143 on August 9, 1942, when the Japanese illuminated the HMAS *Canberra* and the USS *Chicago* with their excellent pyrotechnics—air-dropped flares and starshells—as well as searchlights. Mikawa quickly reduced the *Canberra* to a wreck by sending two torpedoes and twenty-four 8-inch shells into her, while the *Chicago* lost a portion of its bow from a torpedo. The *Chicago* limped off in pursuit of one of its own destroyers, neglecting even to radio the presence of the Japanese; her skipper, Captain Howard D. Bode, subsequently committed suicide in remorse for his failures.

Swinging north like a roundhouse right from the floor, Mikawa's ships accidentally moved into two columns to sandwich the northern force between them. On the starboard side the *Chokai*, leading four cruisers, commenced the engagement at 0148 with torpedoes and shells fired at the *Astoria*. On the portside were three cruisers, led by *Yubari*. The *Astoria* responded with shell fire, getting off twelve salvos before the action passed her, leaving her to sink ten hours later, victim finally of a magazine explosion after a heroic attempt to save her by her crew. The *Quincy*, her guns still trained fore and aft, was caught in the cross fire and riddled with shells, but soon fought back bravely, the best of all the American ships by Japanese reports. Before capsizing and sinking at 0235, her shells had killed thirty men on board the *Chokai*.

Incredibly, the officers on the *Vincennes* had interpreted the gunfire, dimly seen through the rain, as antiaircraft fire. The first shells to hit her set the scout planes on her catapults on fire; then she was hit by three torpedoes from the *Chokai*. A fourth torpedo, from the *Yubari*, left her dead in the water; she sank at 0250. Ironbottom Sound was beginning to fill up.

Mikawa wanted to turn in and attack the transports, the object of his mission, but was persuaded not to by his staff, which feared an attack by carrier planes when dawn broke. The Japanese were unaware that Fletcher was long since out of range. The Japanese force withdrew, shells from the *Yubari* badly damaging the destroyer *Ralph Talbot* as the ship tried to intervene.

The Japanese celebrated their stunning victory, which seemed to prove to them that Midway had been a fluke, not realizing that Mikawa's withdrawal had guaranteed the loss of the battle of Guadalcanal. If he had returned and destroyed the transports, the invasion probably would have failed, and prompt Japanese reinforcement would have made a U.S. second try costly.

Japanese enthusiasm was dampened when the old American submarine *S-44*, captained by Lieutenant Commander J. R. "Dinty" Moore, stalked the cruiser *Kako*, firing four torpedoes "up her skirt" from only 700 yards, so close that Moore reported seeing the Japanese crew on the bridge using binoculars. The *Kako* broke up and sank in five minutes, the first major enemy naval vessel of the Pacific war to be sunk solely by the action of a submarine. (On September 26, 1943, the *S-44* would in its turn be sunk in a surface action with a destroyer; the two survivors of her sinking would also survive Japanese prisoner-of-war camps.)

Savo Island was the worst defeat in a surface engagement in American naval history, with 1,979 casualties, including 1,270 killed and four cruisers sunk and one badly damaged. The latter, the unlucky *Chicago*, was fitted with a new bow, only to be torpedoed and sunk the following January.

The engagement serves as a baseline for evaluating later battles. Outnumbered sixteen ships to eight, the Japanese had the advantages of surprise, skill and weapons. Included in the last were better night-vision equipment, better pyrotechnics and the superb oxygen-fueled Long Lance torpedoes, fired from both destroyers and cruisers. The rapid improvement of American radar could have negated most of these advantages in the coming months had there been sufficient time for U.S. commanders to learn and depend upon radar's true capabilities. It would take several months to develop a proficiency in the use of radar; when learned, however, the new technique would enhance the inexorable increase in American battle skills.

Among the more basic lessons learned were that peacetime luxuries like flammable furniture and wall decorations had to be removed, paint had to be chipped off so it would not burn when the steel turned red-hot, and communications had to be improved. The last was a long time in coming. In terms of basic errors, the Allied force had no flag commander on the spot, no plan of battle and was poorly disposed, with three separate units operating in close proximity at night, with no plan of battle.

For the next eleven days, as the Japanese mustered the strength to react, the marines prepared an airfield. On August 20, the first aircraft of what came to be known as the Cactus Air Force arrived—nineteen Grumman F4Fs of VFM 223 led by Major John Smith and twelve Douglas SBDs of

VSMB 232 led by Lieutenant Colonel Richard Mangrum. Captain Dale W. Brannon brought five Bell P-400s of the 67th Fighter Squadron on August 22. This slender air force, reinforced scantily from time to time, was just sufficient to win and maintain daylight air superiority over Guadalcanal. It gave the battle a characteristic not seen before or since, swing-shift superiority at sea, the Americans ruling the area waters during the day, the Japanese at night.

THE BATTLE OF THE EASTERN SOLOMONS, AUGUST 24, 1942

Admiral Yamamoto was more interested in engaging the American carrier task forces, and decided to mobilize his Combined Fleet and the land-based 11th Air Fleet in a major effort to reinforce Guadalcanal, supplementing the great Rear Admiral Tanaka Raizo's efforts in ferrying in troops to the island in his destroyers—the operation called the Tokyo Express by the Americans. Arriving off Guadalcanal around midnight, his ships would offload to small boats, fire a few shells at Henderson Field, then hurry back to reload, getting out of range of Guadalcanal-based aircraft by daylight.

(Tanaka was perhaps the most brilliant Japanese flag officer of the war; slight of build and shy, he was tenacious in battle, determined to complete his mission regardless of odds. But he was outspoken, and when he eventually told his superiors that the cost of the operation was not worth its results, he was removed from sea command in late 1942, proving that in war as in peace, no good work goes unpunished.)

Yamamoto named his late August operation KA, and placed Admiral Nagumo in command of a force consisting of the two large carriers, one light carrier, three battleships, nine cruisers, thirteen destroyers and no fewer than thirty-six submarines to cover a troop reinforcement of 1,500 men. This single operation epitomizes the disjointed nature of Japanese planning. A mammoth naval effort expending a considerable percentage of Japanese fuel stocks was made to support an insignificant troop movement. Yamamoto did hope to ambush Fletcher, but his approach was hardly subtle.

The fleet carrier force, commanded by Vice Admiral Kondo Nobutake, consisted of the new but now veteran large carriers *Shokaku* and *Zuikaku*, two battleships and two cruisers. It positioned itself in the waters northeast of the Solomons. Rear Admiral Hara Chuichi's light carrier *Ryujo*, the heavy cruiser *Tone* (whose ineptly flown scout plane was the villain of the drama at Midway) and two transports were to act as bait. When Fletcher's aircraft attacked it, planes from the *Shokaku* and *Zuikaku* would strike the *Enterprise, Wasp* and *Saratoga*. Unknown to Kondo, Fletcher had detached the *Wasp*, commanded by Captain Forrest P. Sherman, to refuel, a decision he would regret, and one that would have an impact on his already somewhat shaky record as a carrier task force commander.

American reconnaissance was excellent. The *Ryujo* was located twice by PBY Catalinas and once by a flight of two SBD scout bombers, 220 miles north of Malaita, and 280 miles northwest of the American carriers. The Dauntlesses also spotted the two big carriers sixty miles farther north, and with enormous courage, four men against a wall of flak and Zeros, bombed the *Shokaku*, damaging her slightly.

At 1345, following Kondo's script, Fletcher launched twenty-nine SBDs and seven Avengers, which hit *Ryujo* with four bombs and a torpedo. The *Ryujo* burned fiercely and had to be abandoned, drifting for seven hours before sinking. Her crew was taken aboard some destroyers and the ubiquitous cruiser *Tone*.

Sticking to the storyline, Vice Admiral Nagumo, both the lion and the lamb at Pearl Harbor, launched sixty aircraft in two waves from the *Shokaku* and the *Zuikaku;* these encountered fifty-four Grumman Wildcats of the U.S. Combat Air Patrol. Enough Vals broke through to place three hits on the *Enterprise*, commanded by Captain Arthur C. Davis. The first 1,000-pound bomb came through the right corner of the aft elevator, blowing holes below the waterline; thirty seconds later, the second bomb struck within twenty feet of the first, setting off ammunition stores. A minute later, a 500-pound bomb detonated on impact, blasting a ten-foot hole in the flight deck, but not penetrating to the lower decks. As the "Big E" took on a list, well-trained damage-control crews put the fires out, and within an hour the ship was making 24 knots and recovering her aircraft. But seventy-four men had been killed and the *Enterprise* eventually had to return to Pearl Harbor for repairs.

In the meantime, the *Saratoga*, commanded by Captain DeWitt C. Ramsey, launched five Avengers and two Dauntlessness, which failed to find the big carriers but made a successful strike on the seaplane carrier *Chitose*, severely damaging her. (During its subsequent repairs, *Chitose* was converted to an aircraft carrier, only to be sunk on October 25, 1944, by U.S. carrier planes in the Battle of Leyte Gulf.)

The *Saratoga* had been struck by a torpedo on January 10, fired from the submarine *I-6* some 500 miles off Oahu. On August 31, she was torpe-doed in her stout side again, this time by the *I-26*, captained by Comman-der Yokota Minoru. With both the *Enterprise* and the *Saratoga* sidelined for repairs, the American carrier forces in the Pacific dwindled to the *Wasp* and the *Hornet*. (The *I-26* was a killer—a year later she would sink the cruiser *Juneau*.)

Admiral Fletcher was another casualty of the battle, literally and figura-tively. Slightly wounded, he was relieved and assigned to duty in the back-waters of the North Pacific. He had been under fire because of his failure to get relief to Wake Island in time, and his removal of his carriers from Guadalcanal after the landing; his detachment of the *Wasp* to refuel at a cru-cial moment was the last straw. The criticism was not entirely fair. Fletcher was by nature cautious and he was experienced in cruisers; his less-than-dashing use of carriers should have been expected.

On September 15, *I-19*, under the top Japanese submarine commander of World War II, Commander Kinashi Takachi, popped its periscope up in the midst of twenty-three American warships. Kinashi fired the most cost-effective salvo of torpedoes in history with a spread of six Long Lances. The first three smashed into the thin side of the *Wasp*, tossing planes on the flight deck into the air and starting fires that would doom her; five hours later, the American destroyer *Lansdowne* had to sink the three-year-old ship. The second three torpedoes went beyond the *Wasp*, the first of these hitting the *North Carolina*, tearing a thirty-six-foot-wide gap in her bow and killing five men. The second torpedo of the second group so damaged the de-stroyer *O'Brien* that she broke up and sank on the way home for repairs. The effects of a torpedo hit on any ship could be devastating, but when a destroyer took a hit racing in the pounding ocean, her entire structure was affected; the combined forces of the explosion and the stress of high speed could tear a destroyer into shards of steel confetti.

(Some American accounts credit the *North Carolina* and the *O'Brien* to the *I-15*, but Japanese accounts agree that it was *I-19* alone that did the damage. *I-15* fired at the *Hornet* in the same engagement, but missed.)

Aircraft from the *Saratoga* left the damaged ship and joined those from the *Enterprise* at Henderson Field, where a handful of pilots maintained air superiority, helping the marines hold the perimeter as the Tokyo Express continued to bring troops (usually about 900) and supplies down the Slot at night.

The Battle of Cape Esperance, October 11–12, 1942

The Americans revenged Savo Island at Cape Esperance in a battle that was not neat but satisfying nonetheless. Rear Admiral Norman Scott, commanding Task Force 64, code-named Task Force Sugar, was ordered to escort 6,000 troops to Guadalcanal. This accomplished, Scott sought combat with the Japanese fleet that used the Slot like a commuter rail line.

A B-17 from the army's 11th Bombardment Group caught sight of Japanese ships slashing down the Slot. By 1800 on October 11, they were less than 100 miles from Savo Island. Under the command of Rear Admiral Goto Aritomo, on board the flagship *Aoba*, the bombardment force also had the heavy cruisers *Kinugasa* and *Furutaka* and the destroyers *Hatsuyuki* and *Fubuki*, the last the namesake of a destroyer class notorious during its early days for its instability. Goto guarded a reinforcement group of two seaplane carriers, the *Chitose* and the *Nisshin*, which carried personnel and equipment, and six destroyers, *Akizuki, Asagumo, Natsugumo, Yamagumo, Murakumo* and *Shirayuki*.

Scott was waiting with two heavy cruisers, the *San Francisco* and *Salt Lake City;* two light cruisers, the *Boise* and *Helena;* and five destroyers, the *Farenholt, Buchanan, Laffey, Duncan* and *McCalla.* Scott had radar. Goto had none. And Scott had learned from the Savo Island battle, catapulting off two Vought OS2U Kingfishers, handsome float plane scouts, to track Goto.

Following some extensive preliminary maneuvering, Scott's ships caught the Japanese fleet with their guns trained fore and aft; the *Helena* opened fire at 2346 followed by the rest of the American force, shooting point-blank from 4,000 yards. The Japanese responded, but in an incredible coincidence both sides almost immediately stopped firing, each convinced that they were shooting at friendly forces.

Goto then made a fatal error by ordering a column right turn to reverse course that presented his ships as serial targets to the American guns. Firing resumed almost at once and when Goto was killed on board the *Aoba* the Japanese resistance lost cohesion, if not ferocity. When the battle ended at 0020—thirty-four minutes after it began—the Japanese had lost the cruiser *Furutaka* and the ill-starred *Fubuki.*

The *Farenholt* and the *Boise* were badly damaged. The destroyer *Duncan* had in error fought the battle on its own. Detached from Scott's battle line, she bravely assaulted the *Furutaka* and another destroyer even as she was being struck by both American and Japanese shells. Badly damaged and burning, she careened out of control in circles at 15 knots. When she finally lost power and the crew was able to abandon ship, they were assaulted by hordes of sharks. Only the arrival of small boats from the *McCalla* averted a complete disaster. The burning *Duncan* did not sink until noon the next day, by which time SBDs from Henderson caught the destroyers *Natsugumo* and *Murakumo* and sank them.

ANOTHER ATTEMPT AT HENDERSON FIELD

The Japanese had always recognized the significance of Henderson Field and decided to make it the focus of another major attack. General Hyakutake Seikichi, in personal command of the Japanese force on Guadalcanal, now assumed that there were 7,500 Americans on the island—and concluded that two infantry divisions would be an adequate force to wrest control of the island—if Henderson Field were knocked out. That his estimate was 12,000 short is sufficient commentary on the intelligence information available to him.

Yamamoto agreed, and sent four carriers, five battleships, fourteen cruisers, twenty-eight destroyers and a host of auxiliaries in support; for the first time, battleships were assigned to an artillery support role. That Yamamoto committed so many vessels is a testament to the effort's importance, for it cut deeply into Japan's dwindling fuel reserves.

On October 13, the Japanese followed a bombing attack with an intensive bombardment from the 14-inch guns of the battleships *Haruna* and *Kongo*. In one hour, the World War I–era battleships pumped 918 shells into Henderson, destroying the gasoline supplies but leaving seven SBDs, six P-400s and twenty-nine F4Fs intact. The adverse effect on morale was considerable; forever afterward, "the bombardment" meant the visit by the *Haruna* and the *Kongo*. The following night, two victors of Savo Bay, the cruisers *Chokai* and *Kinugasa*, finished the work on Henderson with 752 8-inch shells, destroying most of the remaining aircraft. Twelve miles from the field, the Japanese unloaded tanks, heavy artillery and enough troops to build their numbers to 20,000. Even though Japanese surface naval fire had temporarily suppressed Henderson Field, it had not destroyed the artillery and the automatic weapons fire of the marines, who beat off the ill-coordinated banzai charges of Hyakutake's troops, forcing them to retreat for yet another try. Japanese troop commanders had a persistent tendency to commit their troops in small detachments allowing them to be easily defeated in detail.

Another event transpired that would add to the Japanese difficulties. Nimitz, weary of Admiral Ghormley's poor performance and growing defeatism, replaced him with Vice Admiral Bull Halsey. Halsey was not politically correct: his unabashed slogan was "Kill Japs, Kill Japs, Kill More Japs." This was not mere rhetoric; Halsey believed in the slogan and wanted to boost morale by reversing the idea that the Japanese were invincible. There was a Napoleonic touch to his leadership—the men he commanded were ready to die for him, and many did.

THE BATTLE OF SANTA CRUZ, OCTOBER 26, 1942

So far in the battle for Guadalcanal, the Japanese had sunk the *Wasp* and sent the *Enterprise*, *Saratoga* and *North Carolina* home for repairs. Admiral Nagumo, with the carriers *Shokaku*, *Zuikaku*, *Zuiho* and *Junyo*, now planned the fourth major carrier battle in six months between the two navies. His aim was to sink the *Hornet*, then use shipborne air power to help Hyakutake in his final drive to capture Henderson Field.

Work on the *Enterprise* had gone swiftly, however, and she rejoined the *Hornet* along with the battleship *South Dakota*, which had already acquired several nicknames. Called "Sodak" in the fleet and "Battleship X" in censored press reports, the crew affectionately referred to her as "the Big Bastard." While undergoing repairs for an accidental grounding at Pearl Harbor, she had been equipped with sixteen 40mm Bofors and twenty 20mm Oerlikon antiaircraft guns. This formidable array was supplemented by radar-directed 5-inch guns using proximity-fused antiaircraft ammunition for the first time.

Determined to erase the shame of Midway, Nagumo launched a first wave of thirty-three fighters, thirty-eight dive-bombers and twenty torpedo planes from the *Shokaku*, *Zuikaku* and *Zuiho* at 0710 on October 26. It was one of the last times that the Japanese forces would have such a tremendous advantage in experience over their opponents, who were learning fast. One untoward lesson came later that very day, as the green air controllers aboard *Enterprise* and *Hornet* did poor work positioning aircraft and giving bearings, resulting in far fewer interceptions than should have been made.

At 0730, the American response began. Once again supplied with intelligence on Japanese strength and location, Rear Admiral Kinkaid launched seventy-three aircraft in three batches over a forty-five-minute period from the *Enterprise* and *Hornet*. The Japanese and American airborne forces passed each other, wary gladiators en route to their separate combat rendezvous. The carrier duel began at 0840 with an attack on the *Zuiho* by sixteen SBDs. Two 500-pound bombs struck the light carrier, blowing a huge fifty-foot hole in the rear of her flight deck, leaving her a minimum capability to launch aircraft but unable to recover them.

The sharp contests since the Coral Sea had proved that carrier battles were like a barroom brawl—getting in the first punch was half the battle. Once a strike force was launched, the heaviest combat air patrol and most intense flak could not turn all the attackers away; here British Prime Minister Stanley Baldwin's 1932 prediction was right again—the bomber always did get through.

At 0910 a fortuitous rain squall sheltered the *Enterprise* as Captain C. P. Mason of the *Hornet* tried to fight off a simultaneous dive-bombing and torpedo attack. Three bombs and two suicide crashes set the *Hornet* afire even as two torpedoes slammed into her hull. By 0920 the remaining Japanese planes were heading home to their carriers as the flames on the *Hornet* grew intense and she began to list. But even as she burned, she counterpunched, her SBDs hitting the *Shokaku* with four 1,000-pound bombs at 0930, knocking her out of the war for nine crucial months.

Nagumo's second strike of twelve Kates, thirty-eight Vals and twenty-eight Zeros then put three bombs into the *Enterprise* and knocked out the *South Dakota*'s number-one turret. Captain Osborne B. Hardison, the *Enterprise*'s skipper, skillfully avoided repeated torpedo attacks (one of which so badly damaged the ill-starred destroyer *Porter* that she had to be sunk later), but took one more bomb hit. The damage to the *Enterprise* was hastily repaired, and she began recovering an amazing ninety-five of her own and the *Hornet*'s planes. Fifty-four aircraft had to be ditched in the ocean because there was not space for them on the *Enterprise*.

The *Hornet* went through hell; just as the fires had been almost contained, another attack from *Zuikaku*'s Kates forced her to be abandoned again, this time around 1400. American destroyers attempted to sink her, but she drifted on despite sixteen hits by the subpar torpedoes. Eight hours later, a Japanese submarine put four of their potent torpedoes in her and she went down, protesting to the end. Controversy still swirls around the *Hornet*'s abandonment—was it too soon? Could more have been done? But it is easy to second-guess when you don't have a red-hot deck under your feet.

The Battle of Santa Cruz was another cause for celebration by the Japanese; they had reduced U.S. carrier power in the Pacific to a single ship, the damaged *Enterprise*, at the cost of heavy damage to two of their own.

But even this exchange rate was insufficient. The ways of the new ship-yards in America were crowded with ships racing toward completion; in Japan, resources were straining just to replace losses. In addition, another facet of the criminal inadequacy of Japanese planning was being exposed: it was sufficient to have a small air force of highly trained pilots *only* against light opposition. Against the grim tenacity of American flyers, who seemed to relish battle, losses were mounting at a rate that could not be sustained, more than 100 aircraft being destroyed in this battle alone. No large Japanese carrier appeared again in operations in the South Pacific.

Yet with monotonous ferocity the Japanese high command mounted further major air, land and sea attacks on Guadalcanal, adding the army's second-rate 38th Division strength to the troops already ashore, supported once again by the firepower of the Combined Fleet. Imperial General Headquarters refused to accept that their efforts were doomed by a lack of air superiority and their inability to match American firepower on the island with sufficient tanks and artillery.

THE BATTLE OF GUADALCANAL, NOVEMBER 11–12, 1942

The battle for Guadalcanal had reached yet another crisis point, and as both sides sought to reinforce, a two-day long brawl erupted that proved to be decisive. The Tokyo Express had been running with its customary regularity and by November 11 the Japanese at last outnumbered the Americans on Guadalcanal, having more than 30,000 troops, many of them, however, not in condition to fight. This time the Japanese believed they could not fail, for they mustered two carriers, four battleships, five heavy cruisers and forty-two destroyers against Halsey's five cruisers and twelve destroyers.

Work was rushed on the battered *Enterprise* at Nouméa, where the re-pair facilities that would come to characterize the wealth and mobility of the American fleet were beginning to form. Seabees and civilian contractors worked from the repair ship *Vulcan* (which forty-nine years later served a similar function in Operation Desert Storm) to get the *Enterprise* marginally ready to sortie on November 11, three weeks of repairs done in eleven days. She was more vulnerable than ever before. Unrepaired damage below decks prevented closing the watertight doors that subdivided the ship into many smaller watertight compartments. The forward elevator was secured in the up position for fear that it might jam when lowered and render the flight deck unusable.

Because the Big E was so precious, Halsey devised a new strategy, stationing her well southwest of Guadalcanal, using Henderson as a staging base. She was joined by the *South Dakota* and the *Washington* (the latter with over 100 antiaircraft guns besides her nine 16-inch-gun main battery), along with the cruisers *Portland* and *San Juan*, and eight destroyers. With the exception of a few elements, like the vitally important torpedo, the American fleet had already surpassed the Japanese navy in the quality of its technology; it was now beginning to approach it in quantity as well.

COMMANDERS MAKE THE DIFFERENCE

The Americans were becoming more professional, adapting their tactics to reflect their growing resources. The Japanese continued with tactics that had failed in the past, apparently believing that, in spite of evidence to the contrary, persistence paid off. The differences would be played out in a vicious battle that began on November 12, 1942.

Admiral Turner, terrible still, but given a second chance by Admiral Nimitz, moved with Task Group 67.1 to reinforce Guadalcanal with 6,000 men carried in four transports and supported by TG 67.4, with three 8-inch heavy cruisers, the *San Francisco*, *Pensacola* and *Portland*, the light cruiser *Helena* and the antiaircraft cruiser *Juneau* and ten destroyers. A "fast burner," Rear Admiral Daniel Callaghan, a former naval aide to President Roosevelt, commanded TG 67.4. Callaghan was a man of utmost decorum and a devout Catholic, but believed he was in the navy to fight, first seeing combat in Nicaragua in 1912, where he participated in the capture of Coyotepe Hill. Since then he had had a model career, culminating in his appointment as commanding officer of the *San Francisco*, a beautiful 9,950-ton cruiser with nine 8-inch guns. If "Uncle Dan" Callaghan had a weakness, it was his unfamiliarity with radar as reflected in the disposition of his ships and the faulty execution of his battle plan. The U.S. Navy's new SG radar represented a major leap forward in reliability, and, much like today's radar sets, it featured a Planned Position Indicator (PPI) scope with the ability to display targets with each rotation of its beam; the screen now portrayed a map of the ships and shore features within the illuminated area. Bearing and range to friendly ships and enemy targets were immediately evident.

The older, less reliable, SC radar portrayed a "pip" that illuminated only when the beam was directly focused on the target, and it was far more difficult for the operator to interpret range and direction. When Callaghan went into battle, he placed the three cruisers and two destroyers with SG radar in the rear of his formation, forfeiting in large measure one of the most sensational technical advantages in naval history.

TG 62.4, commanded by Rear Admiral Scott of Cape Esperance fame, would join Callaghan before the battle with the antiaircraft cruiser *Atlanta* and two more destroyers. Scott was by far the more experienced of the two, but was junior in rank; it is possible that the battle might have gone better if Scott had been in command.

Turner had a double task: to land reinforcements, including heavy artillery, and at the same time prevent an exceptionally heavily protected Japanese convoy, far larger than the usual Tokyo Express, from landing troops and equipment. His cruiser/destroyer forces were to be backed up by Task Force 16, under "Fighting Tom" Kinkaid (the Americans put a premium on combative leaders and on nicknames), with the patched-up *Enterprise* supported by the heavy cruiser *Northampton* and the antiaircraft cruiser *San Diego*, and six destroyers. Also in support, but ordered to operate independently if the situation called for it, was Task Force 64, under Rear Admiral Willis A. Lee, with the fast battleships *Washington* and *South Dakota* and four destroyers.

The American fleets were not concentrated, however, and when word came down of an immense Japanese armada north of Guadalcanal, the ball fell into Callaghan's court.

It was a very large ball in a small court. The Japanese Advanced Force, under Vice Admiral Kondo Nobutake in the heavy cruiser *Atago*, had a raiding group out in front commanded by Vice Admiral Abe Hiroaki.

Abe's force was formidable, with the battleships *Hiei* and *Kirishima*, the light cruiser *Nagara* and fourteen destroyers. Behind Abe the main body under Admiral Kondo consisted of a bombardment unit of two heavy cruisers, the *Atago* and *Takao*, which, with the *Kirishima*, were to blast Henderson Field into submission. Kondo also had the light cruiser *Sendai* and eleven destroyers.

Kondo planned that when Henderson Field was suppressed, Vice Admiral Kurita Takeo, with the converted carriers *Junyo* and *Hiyo*, was to establish air superiority once and for all, their efforts buttressed by additional fire support from the battleships *Kongo* and *Haruna* and the heavy cruiser *Tone*. The support group, under Vice Admiral Mikawa, included the heavy cruisers *Chokai* and *Kinugasa* and light cruiser *Isuzu*, along with two destroyers.

Mikawa, the victor of Savo Island, had his own bombardment unit, with the heavy cruisers *Suzuya* and *Maya*, the light cruiser *Tenryu* and four destroyers. There was going to be hell to pay on Guadalcanal.

These mammoth forces were intended to permit Tanaka's eleven destroyers and eleven transports to put enough men on the island to decide the battle. But the Japanese had not reckoned with Callaghan's bravery or Abe's timidity. Totally outnumbered, Callaghan immediately decided to attack, ordering his ships to adopt the time-honored battle disposition B-1, a long column of ships—but again with his best radars in the rear.

GUNFIGHT AT THE GUADALCANAL CORRAL

The Japanese had ruled the seas around Guadalcanal so long at night that Abe assumed this would always be the case. With the light cruiser *Nagara* and nine destroyers acting as an advance screen, he sailed his battleships in with their guns loaded with high-explosive shells intended to wreak havoc on Henderson Field.

Despite its location as eighth in Callaghan's line of battle, the cruiser *Helena*'s superior SG radar picked Abe's fleet up at 0124 on the morning of Friday the thirteenth. The import of the sighting was lost on Callaghan, who engaged in too cautious maneuvering, delaying his attack until 0151, by which time Abe's alerted ships had been able to change over to armor-piercing shells.

As this was transpiring, a second American technical advance was creating another problem. A new *single-channel* Talk-Between-Ships (TBS) system had been installed, and free access to the airways exerted its usual fatal fascination. The TBS frequency was jammed with multiple requests for direction, information on targets, permission to fire, warnings about potential collisions and simple calls for information. As the two forces closed at a combined speed of 40 knots, Callaghan was as uncertain of the whereabouts of either his ships or the enemy's, and he delayed giving the order to fire. Despite an almost unbearable tension, the American ships displayed good fire-control discipline, keeping their guns and torpedo tubes trained on the passing enemy ships, now clearly visible, even as American voices battered the airways with radio chatter.

The battle opened at 0150 with the usual Japanese searchlight precision in spotting ships followed by an exchange of fire at less than a mile's distance between the battleship *Hiei* and the antiaircraft cruiser *Atlanta*.

The unequal contest ended quickly with *Atlanta*'s bridge wiped out and Admiral Scott killed. One or more destroyer torpedoes blew the *Atlanta* out of the battle, leaving her drifting, to be scuttled the following day after her survivors were removed.

Against the wishes of both commanders, the two fleets had merged, each ship firing wildly at one target after another, not always an enemy. Callaghan wished to "cross the T." (Crossing the T is the classic surface engagement tactic in which one battle line [the line of capital ships] crosses the van [leading ships] of the opponent, upon which it concentrates its fire. Admiral Togo Heihachiro did this to the Russians in the 1904 Battle of Tsushima in the Yellow Sea, and the British did it no fewer than three times to the Germans at Jutland in 1916. The Germans, fortunately for them, had drilled on course-reversal tactics, which extricated their forces.) Instead, he had managed to plunge his ships into the midst of the Japanese force and now gave a strange order: "Odd ships commence fire to starboard, even ships to port."

Callaghan's confusion was matched by Abe's distress. Abe could only attribute sinister intent to the sudden appearance of American cruisers and destroyers so close to his main units. It was too unorthodox, and even as his ships fought back, he turned away, trying to remove the *Hiei* and *Kirishima* from the battle.

The destroyer *Cushing* increased the pressure with a salvo of six torpedoes fired at the *Hiei*, none of which hit. Japanese discipline and training paid off as their counterfire knocked out the *Cushing* and the *Laffey* in quick succession, blasting their thin hulls and superstructures with both main and secondary armament as well as torpedoes.

The engagement degenerated to a naval knife-fight as the *San Francisco* and the destroyers *Sterett* and *O'Bannon* next took on the *Hiei*, setting her superstructure ablaze and destroying her fire control for the main and secondary batteries. The battleship's steering gear room was also hit and flooded.

In the confusion, the *San Francisco* shifted fire from the *Hiei* to the helpless *Atlanta*, prompting an amazing—and not universally obeyed—order from Admiral Callaghan: "Cease Firing Own Ships."

The order was catastrophic, for the as-yet-undamaged *Kirishima* then opened up with her 14-inch shells, shattering the *San Francisco* and killing Callaghan with his ship's captain, Cassin Young. As the *San Francisco*, already damaged at Cape Esperance, reeled away, the *Portland* took a torpedo hit that blew her hull plates out to form an accidental rudder that sent her into endless circles. But "Sweet Pea" was tough, and Captain Laurance Du-

Bose kept her firing from the circle whenever a target came under her guns; much later, still circling, she gave the coup de grâce to the damaged destroyer *Yudachi* with a salvo from her 8-inch guns. The *Portland* would eventually make harbor in Tulagi almost twenty-four hours after she was torpedoed.

The slaughter went on; the Japanese, experts at infighting, slipped a torpedo into the *Juneau* that broke her keel and left her dead in the water. The destroyer *Barton*, just six months old, took two torpedoes that split her into equal halves that quickly sank. Her squadron mate, the *Monssen*, was illuminated by pyrotechnics and searchlights before being smashed by almost forty heavy shells.

Despite the unfolding American debacle, the pusillanimous Vice Admiral Abe had already ordered a withdrawal; the *Hiei* and the *Kirishima* steamed away from victory, leaving Henderson Field unshelled and American air power intact. Abe, perhaps too preoccupied that the *Hiei* was steering by his screws, had won a tactical victory in spite of himself, even while losing the strategic goal.

There were many heroes that night, and Dan Callaghan was one of them in terms of bravery if not in the skillful exercise of his ships. Even though he made a series of errors—not using radar effectively, not opening the battle swiftly enough, not crossing the enemy's T when the chance was there, ordering a cease-fire—his bold thrust intimidated Abe and that was enough. It was a time when the nation needed heroes, and his combative dash earned Callaghan a posthumous Medal of Honor.

The American ships retired at 18 knots, the best speed that their most battered ship, the *Juneau*, could maintain. With Callaghan and Scott dead, command passed like a bitter cup to Captain Gilbert C. "Gib" Hoover of the *Helena;* she led, followed by the *San Francisco, Juneau, Sterett, O'Bannon* and *Fletcher.* On the way back, the redoubtable *I-26* fired a spread of torpedoes at the group; one caught the *Juneau* amidships, detonating a magazine into a violent explosion; when the huge cloud of smoke cleared, *Juneau* was gone. In miraculous fashion, about 140 crew members survived, only to be left behind in shark-infested waters. Captain Hoover, shaken by the suddenness of the *Juneau*'s disappearance and convinced that there were no survivors, made the correct decision to go on, saving his battered force from another torpedo attack. Incredibly, no adequate search was made, and of those who had been blown into the water only eleven managed to survive endless days without water, broiling in the South Pacific sun, their wounds unattended.

Even in the midst of titanic events, human personalities intervened.

On the advice of Admiral Halsey's Chief of Staff, Captain Miles Browning, Hoover was made the villain of the incident, relieved of his command and sent home in disgrace. Hoover was an experienced combat veteran who had already won three Navy Crosses, and was destined for flag rank. Browning was a brilliant officer whose tactical genius had urged Spruance to take the gamble that won the Battle of Midway, but he was wildly unstable, so hot-tempered and held in such contempt by his peers that even the somewhat detached Secretary of the Navy, Frank Knox, tried to get him removed. But Halsey needed his intellectual qualities and effectively ruined Hoover's career. Upon later reflection, Halsey realized that Hoover had done the right thing; if he had returned to the scene he probably would have lost another warship. But Hoover's failure in not mitigating the circumstances as much as possible by ordering rafts, boats and other rescue equipment dropped over the side was amplified because all five Sullivan brothers were lost on the *Juneau*. This poignant event, later made into a film, had great impact and led to a change in rules about brothers serving together in the same ship.

Fate has a particular way of settling accounts in the military. Some sixteen months later, Browning would be captain of the new carrier *Hornet*, and his irascible nature would bring his crew to the boiling point. His boss, Rear Admiral Joseph J. "Jocko" Clark, realized that something had to be done. Cause came when a man was lost overboard and Browning did not take adequate rescue measures. Clark had Browning detached, and a new skipper, Captain William D. Sample, soon had the *Hornet*'s crew efficient and happy again.

*H*IEI'S AGONY CONTINUES

At first light the next day, November 13, 1942, Guadalcanal-based SBDs spotted the *Hiei* as it circled helplessly at five knots, five miles west of Savo Island, attended by a single destroyer. (Later two more destroyers arrived to assist in removing her crew.) The Cactus Air Force was determined to exact revenge for the horrendous bombardments Henderson Field had endured from Japanese warships. Planes from the *Enterprise* joined in a day-long series of dive-bombing and torpedo attacks that proved just how tough the *Hiei* was. After suffering damage from eighty-five hits, including naval gunfire, seven torpedoes, three 1,000-pound and one 500-pound bomb, she remained a testament to her British designer, Sir George Thurston, not sinking until Abe had three scuttling charges exploded deep in her hull. Destroyers took all of the survivors off the ship; 500 men had already perished. Eight Zero fighters sent to protect her had been shot down. Abe, who had been wounded in the battle, was relieved of his command and with an intolerable loss of face was retired in March 1943, so ill thought of that his suicide was *not* encouraged.

TENACIOUS TANAKA

Admiral Kondo persisted with classic surface tactics, which included the forlorn hope of saving the *Hiei* long after the waters had closed over her battered form. Once again the Japanese planned to suppress Henderson Field with a one-two punch. Kondo's fleet, reinforced by the still shocked remnants of Abe's raiding group, was to bombard Henderson Field on the night of November 13–14, thus allowing Tanaka's eleven slow transports and eleven fast destroyers to reach Cape Esperance and begin unloading. Mikawa, who had never lost a battle to American surface forces, planned to use two heavy cruisers, the *Chokai* and *Kunugasa*, the light cruiser *Isuzu* and three destroyers to intercept any American fleet that attempted to intervene while the Bombardment Unit, under Rear Admiral Nishimura Shoji, went in to bombard Henderson Field with the heavy cruisers *Suzuyu* and *Maya*, covered by the light cruiser *Tenryu* and four destroyers. On the night of November 14–15, Kondo in turn would bombard with his heavy cruisers *Atago* and *Takao*, reinforced with the *Kirishima* and *Nagara* while Tanaka unloaded. With Henderson Field at last suppressed, the Carrier Support Group, under Admiral Kurita Takeo, with the carriers *Junyo* and *Hiyo*, the battleships *Kongo* and *Haruna* and the ever-present heavy cruiser *Tone*, would provide air support.

Everything is relative, even naval bombardments. Nishimura's ships pounded Henderson Field with about 1,000 8-inch shells, but these lacked the awesome effect that the 14-inch guns of "the bombardment" had provided. The attack broke off after forty-five minutes when pugnacious U.S. PT boats began some harassing attacks. Only one dive-bomber and two fighters were destroyed with another sixteen aircraft moderately damaged at Henderson Field; the next morning, the Cactus Air Force was up, thirsting for revenge. As heavyweight champion boxer Joe Louis had commented about one of his opponents, Mikawa's forces could run but they couldn't hide. At 0800, a mixed group of marine and navy aircraft caught Mikawa's ships 140 miles from Guadalcanal and proceeded to torpedo the *Kinugasa* and dive-bomb the *Isuzu*. The flames and smoke towering up were a beacon for planes from the *Enterprise*, which sank the *Kinugasa* at 0950. Mikawa steamed on, unable to retaliate, and taking hits on the *Chokai, Maya, Isuzu* and a destroyer. The Japanese were stunned; they believed that their bombardment had wiped out the Cactus Air Force.

Serene in the same belief, Tanaka's force sailed to its slaughter; with no clear idea of the position of Mikawa's ships or of conditions on Henderson Field, he had no choice but to press on, presenting the Americans with an important, virtually undefended target. From 0830 until night fell, Tanaka's ships were attacked by planes from the Cactus Air Force and the *Enterprise*, which sank seven transports ranging from 5,425 to 9,683 tons; some of the troops were rescued, but many more were drowned.

The battle continued, unrelenting. Kondo sent in the *Kirishima*, the *Atago* and the *Takao*, still determined to cover Tanaka's four remaining transports and eleven destroyers. Moving in to intercept was Rear Admiral Willis Augustus "Ching" Lee with two battleships, the fast *Washington* and the *South Dakota* (their very presence in these shallow waters an indication of American resolve), and four destroyers. Like Callaghan's force, Lee's ships had never worked together before, the destroyers being selected for duty on the basis of their fuel levels; all units were insufficiently trained to take full advantage of their radar.

Kondo had, in typical fashion, split his fleet into three separate units as they sallied into Ironbottom Sound. Even though his keen-eyed scouts picked up the American fleet visually before Lee's radar had "painted" them, it was Lee's ships that fired first, at 2317 on November 14. The Japanese destroyers, savage pit bulls at night fighting, displayed all of their years of training and combat by drawing first blood, sinking the American destroyers *Preston* and *Walke* in short order, and damaging the *Gwin* and the *Benham*.

Lee pressed forward with his two battleships, even though an electrical power failure occurred on the *South Dakota*, blacking out its radar. Lee was now in the worst of all positions, fighting a battleship in the narrow waters off Guadalcanal, with his destroyers sunk or damaged and the Sodak useless. He pressed on to the north, nonetheless, just as Kondo swung in to bring the *Kirishima, Atago* and *Takao* into the battle—one of the three actions between battleships in World War II.

The *South Dakota*'s power outage had blinded it to the latest events, and it sailed forward through a hall of thirty-four torpedoes, all of which missed, directly into the heart of Kondo's bombardment force; the *Kirishima, Atago* and *Takao* opened up, shattering the *South Dakota*'s upper works, knocking out her communications and radar and causing heavy casualties from more than forty large-caliber hits.

But while the *South Dakota* was serving as a whipping boy, the *Washington* laid a seventy-five-shell barrage down on the *Kirishima*, so long unscarred by battle. Nine 16-inch shell hits destroyed her steering gear, killed 90 percent of her engine room crew and set her aflame from stem to stern, knocking her out of the battle. The *Washington* then switched targets, and, along with the *South Dakota*'s remaining armament, scored hits on the cruisers *Atago* and *Takao*.

With considerable courage, risking not just his own life, but the ships he commanded, Lee drove on to the northwest toward Tanaka's approaching convoy. Kondo ordered his ships to withdraw, and Lee subsequently did likewise, confident that he had delayed the arrival of the convoy until daylight, when planes from the Cactus Air Force and the *Enterprise* could attack.

Unwilling to repeat the indignities meted to the *Hiei*, the captain of the *Kirishima* joined 1,127 members of his crew on board attending destroyers and scuttled his ship early on the morning of November 15. In two days, the Japanese had scuttled two battleships and the destroyer *Ayanami;* like their battered hulls, Japan's world was turning upside down.

That November 15 morning, Tanaka also sent his four remaining transports to ground themselves on Guadalcanal, a brutally primitive way of insuring that the men and supplies were not sunk. The transports immediately became the stranded targets for every American plane in the area, and for U.S. Army and Marine artillery on Guadalcanal. The destroyer *Meade* came in close offshore to polish them off with gunfire before swinging out to sea to rescue 266 survivors from the American destroyers *Walke* and *Preston.*

The battle had begun as a race to reinforce: Admiral Turner successfully landed all his troops and equipment, but despite Tanaka's desperate efforts, the Japanese landed only about 2,000 troops (much the worse for wear), 260 cases of ammunition and 1,500 bags of rice. The Japanese navy, once the most professional fighting group in the world, had made mistake after mistake, most especially failing to bring their aircraft carriers *Junyo* and *Hiyo* into battle. The United States lost two cruisers and eight destroyers, while the Japanese lost two battleships, a cruiser, three destroyers and the object of the battle, ten transports.

TANAKA'S REVENGE AT TASSAFARONGA

While the Japanese commanders seemed to vacillate feebly from one plan to the next, Rear Admiral Tanaka Raizo maintained his usual high standards of efficiency. On November 30, he inflicted a humiliating defeat on another American group commanded by a newcomer, Rear Admiral Carleton H. Wright, who was briefed on November 29, 1943, of a plan drawn up by Rear Admiral Thomas Kinkaid, and ordered to execute it the following day. He was to intercept yet another Tokyo Express, whose tactics had been reduced to dropping drums of provisions or supplies overboard, to be collected by small boats from shore.

Tanaka had eight destroyers completely laden with supplies to the point that guns on only two of the ships, the *Takanami* and the *Naganami* (his flagship), could be brought immediately to action. Wright's force was overwhelmingly powerful, with four heavy cruisers, the *Minneapolis*, *New Orleans*, *Pensacola* and *Northampton*, the light cruiser *Honolulu* and six destroyers.

American radar conferred the advantage of surprise, detecting the Japanese at 2306. Once again two columns of hostile ships streamed into Ironbottom Sound, the Japanese from the left, the Americans from the right. But, as in the past, the American commander vacillated, delaying the order to open fire for four minutes, allowing the range to open. When Wright at last gave the word, the American torpedoes were unable to reach the enemy ships. Wright then ordered the guns to open fire, revealing their position to the Japanese, who responded with a fusillade of Tanaka's torpedoes.

The Japanese destroyers struggled to jettison their cargo and to fire their torpedoes, getting off twenty Long Lances in the first few minutes of battle even as American guns battered the *Takanami* into submission. Twenty-one minutes after the battle opened the *Minneapolis* was hit by two torpedoes, which slowed her so rapidly that the *New Orleans*, following behind, had to swerve sharply out of line—straight into the path of another torpedo that blew 120 feet of her bow off. Despite their serious damage, both the *Minneapolis* and *New Orleans* kept firing, but with as little accuracy as before.

Another salvo of Long Lances flashed toward the *Pensacola*, hitting her almost dead-center on the port side, causing such destruction that she had to head immediately to Tulagi to avoid sinking. Tanaka was not finished; two torpedoes smashed into the port side of the *Northampton*, setting her on fire as water rushed through the entire ship.

Despite their damage, the *Minneapolis* and the *New Orleans* also made it safely to Tulagi; at 0304 the *Northampton* joined the growing fleet on the bottom of Ironbottom Sound.

The battle at Tassafaronga was the last major naval engagement of the Guadalcanal campaign, which can be regarded as a rigorous tutorial for the American navy. Under the hard fire of Japanese guns and the explosive power of their torpedoes, the American navy at last learned just how serious the war was, and that intensive training was necessary to wage it successfully.

There were many lessons, including:

1. The classic disposition of ships in column was no longer satisfactory in battle. The ships with the most modern equipment should be placed in the van.

2. Commanders needed to learn how to use the new types of radar, the most difficult task being learning how to visualize the battle in terms of the glowing radar screen.

3. Destroyers should not be tied to cruisers, but should operate independently, as the Japanese destroyers did.

4. Carrier aircraft effectiveness is amplified if they can be routed to a land base to refuel and rearm during the battle.

5. Effective communications require an iron discipline.

6. Ships had to work together for an extended time to become effective teammates. Pickup formations were almost certain to be ineffective.

7. Better methods of rescuing survivors had to be introduced.

These lessons coincided with the tilt in relative strength. The land, sea and air forces of the United States were growing steadily stronger, permitting a policy of spending virtually unlimited matériel and firepower in the interest of saving lives. The Japanese were forced to an exactly opposite course; unable to match the American growth in strength or technology, they were forced to attempt the substitution of human lives for adequate firepower, a policy that played into American hands and ensured Japan's eventual defeat.

CONCLUSIONS

The battle of Guadalcanal marked the high tide of the Japanese offensive in the Pacific; from then on, it was the Allies who were inexorably on the move. The drain of supplies to Guadalcanal from Papua had resulted in a

Japanese defeat there as well. Much bitter fighting was to follow, but on January 4, 1943, General Tojo Hideki, the Prime Minister, ordered the evacuation of Guadalcanal. Tanaka's destroyers then reversed their role, successfully evacuating more than 11,000 Japanese troops from the island without the Americans being aware of it. By February 9, Major General Alexander M. Patch, the army commander whose troops had relieved the marines in December after their long fight, was able to wire Halsey that "Tokyo Express no longer has terminus on Guadalcanal."

Neither Admiral Yamamoto nor Admiral King had ever imagined just how high the cost would be. The Japanese lost two battleships and the United States lost two of its precious carriers; both sides each lost an additional twenty-two combat ships. The Japanese lost 900 land- and carrier-based aircraft. The Americans lost about 200 planes both land- and carrier-based.

Until the very end, the Japanese fought with tenacity. The amateur qualities of some American commanders lingered on, as when the unfortunate USS *Chicago* became the hapless victim of two successive torpedo attacks by Betty bombers, the second one while under tow. It sank on the afternoon of January 30. Many other lives would be lost in engagements between the two navies, but nothing could disguise the fact that the back of the Japanese effort had been broken on November 15.

The balance scales of warfare, which had edged precariously upward from Japanese dominance to American parity, now shifted abruptly as the weight of American production, technology and training grew at a prodigious rate. Even more surprising to the Japanese was the similar increase in American ferocity and combativeness. The Japanese had taught their enemy to fight; in the learning process, the Americans used their growing wealth of weapons to create new combat rules that their enemy could not match. The Japanese formula for victory had been the use of a relatively few weapons by fierce experts; the American equation was use of massive quantities of heavy weapons by increasingly professional warriors exercising a newly learned savagery. The result was a bitter contest, the issue of which was never in doubt.

If, like some sports, battles had "most valuable player" awards, the man most deserving to win would be the courageous Tanaka Raizo, whose administrative and logistic genius was exceeded only by his mastery of destroyer tactics. His removal from sea duty at least allowed him to survive the war; he died in 1969 at the age of seventy-six, a true hero.

12.

SINKING AN
EMPIRE

The relative strength of Japanese and American forces had altered drastically in the first eighteen months of the war. In the beginning, surprise, training and concentration had enabled the Japanese to appear almost invincible; for a long period of time at Guadalcanal, there was a rough parity in power. By the end of the battle for Guadalcanal, it became obvious that American forces were growing at an amazing rate. By mid-1943, ships, planes, men and matériel were flowing to every theater of war in quantities beyond the scope of Japanese imagination.

Despite maintaining the commitment to finish the war in Europe first, and following up the invasion of North Africa with the invasions of Sicily, Italy and France, the United States still had the capacity to fight two major (and accidentally complementary) campaigns in the Pacific. It also continued to furnish both the Soviet Union and the British empire, along with the many Allied nations now involved in the war, with incredible quantities of munitions, supplies and raw materials.

The increase in strength in the Pacific came in part due to the astute political maneuvers of Admiral King, who, with the support of General Marshall, was able to convince President Roosevelt and the British Chiefs of Staff at the Casablanca conference in January 1943 that the existing ratio of

85 percent of resources going to the European theater and 15 percent to the Pacific was inappropriate, and that a 70/30 division would be more productive. To achieve this new distribution, the Americans agreed to delay the invasion of Europe until 1944—much to Churchill's relief.

The following table of comparative strengths as of January 1 of each year reveals how quickly and decisively the United States outstripped Japan.

PACIFIC THEATER							
	1942		1943		1944		1945
	Japan / U.S.		Japan / U.S.		Japan / U.S.		Japan / U.S.
Fleet Aircraft Carriers	6	3	4	2	4	7	2	14
Light Aircraft Carriers	4	0	3	4	4	22	2	65
Battleships	10	2	10	9	9	13	5	23
Cruisers	38	16	36	25	30	37	16	45
Destroyers	112	40	99	146	77	245	40	296

The sheer number of warships was only a part of the equation, as there was an even greater buildup in submarines, cargo ships, tankers, amphibious craft and every other type of ship. Moreover, air power had become the dominant factor; no major issue would ever again be resolved by an engagement solely between surface vessels. Japan had bet its fortune on small, highly expert air forces that had in fact made air power the dominant factor in naval warfare, only to have them consumed in a battle of attrition.

The steady loss of Japanese pilots in air battles over both land and sea was matched by a corresponding decline in the quality of their replacements, as new pilots with inadequate training were thrown into the fray. American pilots received 300 or more hours of intensive training before entering battle, but Japanese pilot training was continually reduced, so that by the end of the war, novices with perhaps forty hours crammed into two months' training, unable to do more than take off and land, were thrust into combat.

Equally important, with each carrier lost and each island evacuated, invaluable ground crews were lost, men who were almost as difficult to replace as pilots, and were just as essential in maintaining an effective air force.

After Guadalcanal, Japan still possessed a powerful navy in the absolute sense, with excellent ships and brave and dedicated sailors, and the national will to use both at any cost. Relatively, however, Japan had been eclipsed; the main elements of her strength were no longer relevant to modern sea warfare, and could prolong the war but not change its outcome.

Yet the United States's dual strategy in the Pacific might have been disastrous had it failed to allocate sufficient resources to make it successful. General MacArthur and Admiral Nimitz pursued their separate paths to a common goal with a frenetic energy that left the Japanese gasping for breath, unable to recover. The dual strategy was facilitated by the brilliant orchestration of its components. MacArthur, fighting a bitter and unexpectedly long land campaign in New Guinea on his way to returning to the Philippines, depended upon what amounted to his own navy, the Seventh Fleet and the VII Amphibious Force, to shuttle his troops from one amphibious landing point to the next.

The American success in breaking the Japanese codes gave them an overwhelming advantage, one never grasped by the Japanese as they continued to counter with "Tokyo Express" style operations. These were never able to match MacArthur's strength or mobility, and while always putting up a strong fight, they were unable to stop the advance. Admiral Nimitz had the Third and Fifth Fleets and the V Amphibious Force for his drive that would lead along the island chain from the Solomons to Okinawa. MacArthur's air power was supplied by the Fifth Air Force, augmented, as required, by the fast carrier task forces, which raced between the two commands.

American productivity was at least a year ahead of the Japanese, and the fast carrier forces began receiving new equipment in prodigious quantities in 1943. Roosevelt's demand for a two-ocean navy bore fruit as the *Essex*-fleet-class and *Independence*-light-class carriers, augmented by a horde of escort carriers, joined the fleet.

The design work begun on the *Essex* class in 1939 resulted in what many regard as the most influential carriers of the war. The basic design of the *Yorktown* (CV-5) was used as a starting point, but the *Essex* (CV-9) was larger, capable of operating as many as 100 aircraft and able to carry more aviation fuel. It had an armored hangar deck and at 15 knots could steam for 15,000 miles; top speed was 33 knots. In many other ways the *Essex* was not merely larger, but better, with vastly improved antiaircraft defenses, torpedo protection able to withstand the detonation of a 500-pound warhead, improved hull subdivision and a less vulnerable engine installation. The 27,100-ton *Essex* was commissioned on December 31, 1942; sixteen more of her class would follow before the end of the war, reinstating in combat such illustrious names as the *Yorktown* (CV-10), *Lexington* (CV-16), *Hornet* (CV-12) and *Wasp* (CV-18), while introducing future legends—the *Ticonderoga* (CV-14), *Bunker Hill* (CV-17) and *Franklin* (CV-13). (Another seven *Essex*-class carriers were commissioned after the end of the war. Some were later reconfigured with angled decks and saw further combat service in the waters off Vietnam. Two survive as floating museums, the *Yorktown* in Charleston, South Carolina, and the *Intrepid* in New York City.)

The year 1943 also saw the commissioning of nine light carriers of the 11,000-ton *Independence* class. Built on hulls originally intended for *Cleveland*-class light cruisers, these carriers were the result of an emergency program advocated by President Roosevelt, ever eager to dabble in naval affairs. Although they carried only thirty aircraft, they proved to be invaluable, seeing action throughout the Pacific. Only one, the *Princeton*, was lost. (Because of their relatively small size, most of the remaining eight carriers were decommissioned soon after the war; only the *Bataan* saw combat again, in the Korean War. Several were operated by foreign navies.)

To this flood of new floating airfields must be added the seventy-eight escort carriers (CVEs) that were commissioned before the war's end. There were several classes, the most numerous of which was the *Casablanca* class, built on the Kaiser shipyard's S4 hulls; fifty were commissioned by July 1944. Relatively slow at 19 knots, the 8,331-ton ships carried twenty-eight aircraft. The largest ships were in the 19,211-ton *Commencement Bay*–class, built on tanker hulls and carrying thirty-three aircraft. (None of this class saw combat.) The very number of escort carriers, if not their individual capabilities, revolutionized warfare at sea for they provided both a depth and breadth of air cover never before possible.

The power of the new carriers, large and small, was enhanced by the new aircraft reaching the fleet, including the Grumman F6F Hellcat (especially designed to combat the Zero), the Vought F4U Corsair, used initially by the marines from land bases, and improved versions of the Grumman TBF Avenger (TBM when built by General Motors), which was increasingly used for level bombing, reconnaissance and antisubmarine warfare. In aircraft as in aircraft carriers, the Japanese were unable to compete in numbers, types or quality.

MONDAY MORNING QUARTERBACK STRATEGY

In recent years, the point has often been made that after 1942, the United States could have followed a totally different policy against Japan. Instead of conducting an island-hopping campaign, during which the lives of thousands of Americans and hundreds of thousands of Japanese were lost, some contend that the United States should simply have intensified the unremitting economic warfare already under way. Rather than invading the Philippines, taking the Marianas and undertaking the B-29 bombing campaign with its atomic denouement, the argument is made that Japan could have been blockaded so effectively by surface ships, submarines and carrier-based air power that her war-making capacity wold have evaporated, and she would have had to surrender, thus sparing the lives of hundreds of thousands of fighting men and Japanese civilians.

Accurate in that Japan could have been starved into submission, this contention ignores other factors, the most important being time. The dedication of the Japanese people is impossible to overestimate. They would have endured starvation, disease and suffering for as long as their Emperor and military masters told them to do so. The pattern of their stubborn resistance on bypassed islands was a harbinger of what might have been. On those lonely island outposts, cut off from food, medicine, ammunition and any other supplies, the Japanese army maintained its fighting integrity even though it was reduced to grubbing roots and even cannibalism. The Japanese homeland might have held out for five years or more before succumbing, even though millions of civilians would in all likelihood have died of starvation and disease, hardly a better fate than bombing.

Then the question must be raised as to the fate of the populations of all the territories Japan still occupied—Indochina, Malaya, the Dutch East Indies, the Philippines and enormous areas of China. It defies both experience and belief to think that the Japanese would not have exploited these captive populations to the greatest possible degree, and that their suffering would have been less than that of the Japanese people. Five more years of the ruthlessly exploitative occupation of those countries would certainly have resulted in additional tens of millions of civilian deaths, as well as the deaths of thousands of Allied prisoners of war.

Another important factor is the mood of the American people at the time. Japan had started a fight; it was the American inclination to finish it, particularly when it was so obvious that victory was just a matter of time.

Revenge is not always a dish best eaten cold; it was sweet in each of the hot battles that led to Tokyo Bay, despite the losses on the way.

Finally, no one knows what the Soviet Union might have done after the Germans were defeated. It is difficult to believe that it would have opted out of the war with Japan to await the success of the blockade. More probably, it would have conducted an active military campaign in Manchuria, China and Korea, and might even have undertaken its own invasion of Japan.

Rather than blaming the leaders of the United States for not having the compassionate vision to step back from the war with Japan and ask themselves how it could be most humanely ended, it is more sensible to ask why the Japanese leaders persisted with the fight long after Yamamoto's rueful predictions had been fulfilled, and all hope of winning was gone. The war might have been stopped in mid-1943 if the Japanese leadership had drawn the obvious conclusion and surrendered. Like the Nazi hierarchy, however, the leaders preferred to play for time and chance, meanwhile maintaining their positions of privilege.

MacArthur's Advance

It is beyond the scope of this book to relate the American land and air campaigns in detail, but it must be noted that the inexorable American advance along the New Guinea–Mindanao axis was slow and expensive in matériel, but most economic in terms of American blood. In the Papuan campaign in New Guinea, only 930 Americans were killed from all causes with almost 2,000 wounded; malaria took a heavy toll. In the advance from Hollandia all the way to Morotai in the North Moluccas, the army had only 1,618 killed. These impressively low numbers are a tribute to General MacArthur, who used his advantage in intelligence gained from the code breaking to follow a prudent policy of applying overwhelming strength in each operation, isolating Japanese forces and eliminating them before pushing on.

MacArthur's advance from the tip of the Papuan peninsula through Lae, Wewak and Hollandia to the Vogelkop, the western extremity of New Guinea, with side trips to New Britain, the Admiralty Islands and Biak, was concluded on August 31, 1944. One of the most important joint objectives of both MacArthur and Nimitz had been the Japanese base at Rabaul, at the western end of the island of New Britain. The occupation of the Admiralty Islands effectively isolated Rabaul, and on July 21, 1943, the army's Chief of

Staff, General Marshall, suggested to MacArthur that Rabaul be leap-frogged, cutting 100,000 Japanese soldiers out of the war. At first taken aback by having his previous goal suddenly removed, MacArthur quickly re-covered, realizing that the decision speeded the schedule for his return to the Philippines. MacArthur was ably aided by the versatile Vice Admiral Thomas C. Kinkaid who would win his fourth Distinguished Service Medal in the Philippines. Kinkaid, in turn, was well served by his amphibious commander, Rear Admiral Daniel E. Barbey, who would command fifty-six landings, becoming ever more expert. Barbey had been a pioneer in am-phibious tactics, and created much of the doctrine that proved so successful. A natural leader of men, he was also a skilled engineer who personally de-signed the DUKW, and supervised the design of the LCI and many other amphibious craft.

Leapfrogging cut off Japanese garrisons by bypassing them, and in-stead seized less well defended but strategic positions ever closer to Japan. After the war, Tojo himself told General MacArthur that the three most de-cisive elements of American strategy were the leapfrogging tactics, the fast carrier forces and the submarines.

The victory in New Guinea had been immensely facilitated by Lieu-tenant General George Kenney's Fifth Air Force. Kenney had raised the Fifth from a defeated ragtag collection of airplanes evacuated from the Philippines into a powerful, innovative force with complete air superiority over New Guinea and the surrounding waters. The quality of Kenney's ef-fort is encapsulated in the Battle of the Bismarck Sea. Despite the humilia-tion of Guadalcanal and the continual erosion of its sea power, on March 1, 1943, Japan dispatched the 51st Infantry Division to reinforce New Guinea, hoping that bad weather would conceal from Allied eyes the five-day jour-ney of the convoy of seven merchant ships and eight destroyers through the Bismarck Sea.

Intercepted Japanese radio intelligence and vastly improved American reconnaissance had tracked the fleet despite the weather. On March 2, Ken-ney's planes sank all of the transports and four of the destroyers, moving General MacArthur to call it "the decisive aerial engagement" in the Pacific theater of war. The Japanese lost more than 3,000 troops, most of them to drowning, but an unfortunate few to the headhunters on New Guinea. Ulti-mately, the Fifth Air Force's aerial blockade condemned the hard-fighting Japanese troops on New Guinea to slow starvation on rations brought in at night by submarines or small barges. Kenney's depredations so weakened the Japanese air forces that they were less able to resist the concurrent ad-vance from Guadalcanal by Admiral Nimitz's forces.

NIMITZ'S THRUST

Even as MacArthur and Kenney were destroying or isolating Japanese forces in New Guinea, and (under Admiral Nimitz's direction) Admiral Halsey was pursuing his own course in Rabaul, Nimitz was preparing a bold new advance along the central axis from the Solomons to Okinawa. At the time, naval strategists were contemplating another five years of hard fighting, culminating in an invasion of Japan in 1948. Within months new concepts would telescope that schedule.

General MacArthur, as Supreme Commander Allied Forces in the Southwest Pacific Area, was nominally responsible for the move on Rabaul, but Halsey, Commander South Pacific Area, was ready at Guadalcanal with land, sea and air forces that could not be left unemployed. The arrangement required some organizational finesse, and, to smooth the command lines, Halsey was placed under General MacArthur for general directives, but in fact would operate independently.

(It should be noted in passing that the navy, more than any other American service, was absolutely riven with disagreement at all levels—from Secretary Knox through Undersecretary James V. Forrestal to Admirals King, Nimitz, Halsey, Spruance, Mitscher and on down through the various commands to the ship captain level. Only the force of his extraordinary personality enabled Admiral King to ride herd on his cantankerous subordinates. Reassignment became an art, moving individuals into positions in which their worth could be demonstrated—or their dissident views quashed. In addition to the flying/nonflying split [worsened by an increasing concern about the *postwar* division of the budget], there were numerous personality clashes, some with histories dating back to Naval Academy days. Even so formidable a personality as Vice Admiral John H. Towers, Naval Aviator No. 3, was deprived of a combat command almost until the end of the war despite his years of experience and his stature in the aviation community. In the interval, Towers had to endure seeing combat commands going to "JCLs" [Johnny-come-latelys, senior officers who entered flying school late in life] and, even worse, to nonflyers like Spruance. Tower rose above the slights from Admiral King to become one of the guiding lights of the fast carriers. In many ways it was a miracle that the navy was able to achieve its great successes, given the intricate fabric of discord among its top commanders.)

Halsey's drive through the Central Solomons, starting with New Georgia, began on July 2, 1943. The man who was fast becoming the most proficient commander of amphibious forces in history, Rear Admiral Turner, applied overwhelming force with twelve destroyer transports, ten large transports, nine LSTs and eleven LCIs, the latter two miserable craft to be aboard on long journeys. Turner was backed up by a huge support force including battleships.

New Georgia was even worse than Guadalcanal in terms of its terrain, and the 9,000 Japanese estimated to be on the island had lost none of their determined fighting spirit. Before the fighting ended more than 50,000 American troops were committed in bitter bunker-by-bunker battles; of these, more than 1,100 were killed. The main objective, the airfield, was not secured until August 5. This time the remnants of the Japanese escaped to join a force of 10,000 others on Kolombangara Island. (Lieutenant John F. Kennedy's famous *PT-109* was lost off Kolombangara.)

The way to the future was pointed by a decision to leapfrog to the virtually undefended island of Vella Lavella, leaving the Japanese on Kolombangara isolated and effectively removed from the war.

On to Bougainville

Unable to halt the unrelenting American advance, Admiral Koga Mineichi denuded the Third Fleet of aircraft and pilots taken from the *Zuikaku*, *Shokaku* and *Zuiho*, flying them in to Rabaul to operate from land bases. It was a costly substitution; carrier-qualified navy pilots were better trained and fewer in number than their army counterparts. (Koga, who had violently opposed the war with the United States, had succeeded Admiral Yamamoto as Commander-in-Chief of the Combined Fleet. Koga began the reorganization of the Combined Fleet along American lines, but died when his plane crashed into the sea during a storm on March 31, 1944.)

Lieutenant General Kenney's Fifth Air Force broke the back of these reinforcements with a series of raids in preparation for the invasion of Bougainville. The most successful of these was on October 12, 1943, when the Fifth Air Force launched the largest air strike of the Pacific war so far— 349 aircraft sent against Rabaul. Hundreds of enemy aircraft were destroyed on the ground, and fuel and ammunition storage dumps were blown up. Twenty-six of the thirty-five Japanese aircraft that rose to oppose the attack were shot down.

Admiral Halsey's objective was to establish airfields on Bougainville in preparation for capturing Rabaul. The Japanese had 40,000 troops and

20,000 sailors on the island when Halsey began the invasion on November 1, 1943, at Empress Augusta Bay. The U.S. III Amphibious Force, under Rear Admiral Theodore S. "Ping" Wilkinson, landed 14,321 men of the 3rd Marine Division plus more than 6,000 tons of supplies, at Cape Torokina.

It was a logical site in terms of position; in terms of terrain, it was a disaster, for the surrounding area was so swamp-ridden as to be virtually impassable.

Koga reacted immediately with air strikes, and sent 1,000 troops to counterattack, convoyed by a powerful force of warships to attack the American transports and bombard the troops already ashore. Rear Admiral Omori Sentaro led the Japanese 5th Cruiser Squadron. The heavy cruisers *Myoko* and *Haguro* were in the center with the veteran light cruiser *Sendai* and three workhorse destroyers, the *Shigure, Samidare* and *Shiratsuyu*, 5,000 yards to port; 5,000 yards to starboard were the light cruiser *Agano* (Rear Admiral Osugi Morikazu) and the destroyers *Naganami, Hatsukaze* and *Wakatsuki*.

The Japanese hoped for a reprise of Savo Bay, but time and technology had changed. Task Force 39, commanded by Rear Admiral A. Stanton "Tip" Merrill was outgunned, for it consisted only of four light cruisers, the *Montpelier, Cleveland, Columbia* and *Denver*, and eight destroyers. The latter were in two divisions, DesDiv 45, commanded by the soon-to-be-legendary Captain Arleigh A. Burke, and DesDiv 46, commanded by Commander Bernard L. "Count" Austin. Burke's nickname, "31-knot," bestowed for his speed and dash, was yet to come. (He'd earned an earlier sobriquet, "the biggest son of a bitch in the harbor," by his demanding training requirements.)

Burke was an ardent advocate of the independent employment of destroyers; to realize the destroyer's true potential, he wanted to throw his ships upon enemy ships as soon as they were sighted, without waiting for permission to fire.

Merrill's intent was to seal off Empress Augusta Bay from any Japanese intrusion. Burke's destroyers were disposed in a column to starboard; the cruisers steamed in column in the center, while Austin's destroyers followed in formation to port. The American fleet was outnumbered and outgunned, but the "Sugar George" (SG) radar on Merrill's cruisers picked up the Japanese fleet at 0230 on November 2, and the American destroyers began the battle with a torpedo attack that failed to score. The tactics were correct; the torpedoes were faulty.

The four-hour melee that followed, deadly serious and bloody, nevertheless opened with a Keystone Kops quality. The *Sendai* and a destroyer collided immediately before shells from Merrill's cruisers shattered the *Sendai*, exploding her magazines. The cruiser turned abruptly, causing a full-speed collision between the destroyers *Samidare* and *Shiratsuyu*, forcing both to retire. At 0300 the flagship *Myoko*, desperately seeking an American target, smashed into the *Hatsukaze*, tearing off a portion of her forward section, which remained balanced precariously on the *Myoko's* bow like an improbable hat throughout the fight. To keep pace, the American destroyers *Claxton* and *Stanly*, moving on reciprocal courses, sideswiped each other at high speed and both were then fired on by the *Charles Ausburne*, Burke's flagship. The U.S. destroyer *Foote* was hit by a Long Lance in the stern, taking her out of the battle. The *Spence* then sideswiped the *Thatcher*, but without serious damage. The *Spence* next took a hit in a fuel bunker but, with the *Converse*, went on to fire eight torpedoes at the damaged *Sendai* before pursuing the battered *Samidare* and *Shiratsuyu*. In reprisal, an 8-inch shell from the heavy cruiser *Myoko* slammed into the *Spence*, almost disabling her, and moving her into the line of fire from Burke's column of destroyers. Over the TBS, the *Spence* radioed, "WE'VE JUST HAD ANOTHER CLOSE MISS HOPE YOU ARE NOT SHOOTING AT US"; when assured that no hits had been scored, Burke displayed both his composure and his sense of humor by replying "SORRY BUT YOU'LL HAVE TO EXCUSE THE NEXT FOUR SALVOS THEY'RE ALREADY ON THE WAY." The valiant *Spence* then engaged the rammed *Hatsukaze*, hammering shells into the blazing wreckage, which soon came under fire from Burke's entire division and sank.

The tempest raged on within the teacup area of Empress Bay, all pretension to doctrine and tactics thrown to the wind as twenty-four ships maneuvered and fired at high speed, as much at risk to collision and grounding as to shell fire and torpedoes. In effect, the destroyers were fighting their separate battles as Merrill's cruisers set up a figure-eight pattern, firing salvos from their 6-inch guns while undertaking with high-speed maneuvers to evade incoming shells from Omori's 8-inchers. The radar-directed 6-inch shells finished off the *Sendai*, whose battle honors had included Malaya, the Dutch East Indies, Ceylon and Guadalcanal. At 0337, Omori declared victory and retired, convinced that he had sunk two cruisers, but ignoring the fact that his target was the transports. Merrill's smaller, lighter squadron had won, sinking one cruiser and one destroyer, and damaging two cruisers and one destroyer, at the cost of damage to two cruisers and two destroyers. It was a rarity for the time, an American-Japanese naval battle in which the United States didn't lose a single ship. Times had indeed changed.

Once again, a Japanese admiral lost the opportunity to intervene in a decisive manner because he lacked the courage to risk his ships. His penalty was to be relieved of his command, small comfort indeed to the men of the *Sendai* and the *Hatsukaze,* which had been sunk by American destroyers, and even less to the beleaguered Japanese troops on Bougainville.

Koga had already dispatched seven heavy cruisers from Truk to exploit Omori's victory; Halsey answered by using his carrier aircraft in concert with Kenney's Fifth Air Force to attack the Japanese fleet in the harbor at Rabaul on November 5 and November 11, mauling it so severely that Japanese heavy cruisers never again ventured into the area. Shaken by the continual loss of planes and aircrew, the Japanese pulled the survivors back more than 600 miles to the north, to Truk.

The genius and primal energy of American Seabees converted the dank miasma of Bougainville swamps into bustling airfields for the further prosecution of the war, while a lack of supplies forced the Japanese on the defensive. By the end of the war, the enemy troops were more interested in growing food to survive than in engaging the Americans. Just as General Marshall had predicted, Japan wrote off Rabaul and its 100,000-man garrison, unable either to reinforce or evacuate it.

OPERATION GALVANIC: THE ATOLL WAR

After long months of buildup, the time had now come for the prosecution of Nimitz's central thrust, where the fighting in the air and on the sea became increasingly one-sided while the hand-to-hand combat on the ground became ever more costly.

Coincident with the explosive growth in American strength was the development of a mammoth logistics network, a "fleet train" of unprecedented extent. In military service, victorious combat admirals and generals go up in rank and down in history, while the architects of the victory—in terms of training, procurement and logistics—are often overlooked. Nowhere was this more true than in the creation of the Service Force Pacific Fleet under Vice Admiral William Calhoun, an organization that began on an improvised basis and grew into one of the greatest industrial facilities in history. Where navies had traditionally returned to port for provisioning and repair, the American concept of the fleet train brought the port to the navy.

Under Calhoun, a system of reprovisioning and repair evolved and grew, with the net effect of doubling the size of the combat fleet, for it removed the need for long weeks of travel to and from home ports for refitting for all but the most major repairs. Every need, from new guns to ice cream machines, was available from the Service Force, as was every skill: machinist, welder, electronics expert, aircraft mechanic, diver—the list was comprehensive. The single most critical element, refueling, which hobbled both the Japanese and British navies, was solved by a roving fleet of oilers that rendezvoused with warships in the combat area; the oilers in turn were kept filled by merchant tankers transporting hundreds of thousands of barrels of fuel every month.

An incredible variety of vessels was assembled, from refrigerator to hospital ships. Each one was the access point for a supply network that ran back through Hawaii to the Pacific coast to every factory and farm in the United States. The days of salt beef and lime juice were long gone; now fresh and frozen meat and vegetables poured through the system in a torrent, sufficient to feed not only the hundreds of thousands of servicemen, but also the natives on the islands being taken. It was a munificent undertaking, far beyond the ken of the other combatant nations.

All of these efforts made Operation Galvanic possible. Galvanic began on November 13, 1943, with seven days of air bombardment of Makin and Tarawa atolls by B-24 Liberators from the Seventh Air Force. The string of islands, roughly 750 miles east-northeast of Guadalcanal and stretching both north and south of the equator, were part of the Gilberts, which Japan had seized from Great Britain in establishing its chain of "unsinkable aircraft carriers." War had transformed virtually unknown coral atolls, scant necklaces of islands and reefs, into America's first rung on the central Pacific ladder to Japan.

The Fifth Fleet, under Vice Admiral Spruance, was comprised of more than 200 ships, with 27,600 army and marine assault troops and 7,600 garrison troops, 6,000 vehicles and 117,000 tons of cargo. (The Gilberts in all their history had not seen more than 500 vehicles of all types; now 6,000 were bearing down on them, an interesting comparative measure of the way the two combatants waged war.) Vice Admiral Towers would, with just a touch of sour grapes, describe the assemblage as "a sledgehammer to drive a tack."

Task Force 50, under Rear Admiral Charles A. Pownall, included TG 50.1, a Carrier Interceptor Group, with the new *Lexington* and *Yorktown* and the light carrier *Cowpens*, all supported by the battleship *South Dakota* and six destroyers. The Northern Carrier Group, TG 50.2, was under Rear Admiral Arthur W. Radford, a future Chairman of the Joint Chiefs of Staff, and comprised the Big E (*Enterprise*) and the new light carriers *Belleau Wood* and *Monterey*, with the fast battleships *Massachusetts*, *North Carolina* and *Indiana* for antiaircraft protection along with six destroyers for screening. The Southern Carrier Group, TG 50.3, under Rear Admiral A. E. Montgomery, had the fleet carriers *Essex* and *Bunker Hill* and the light carrier *Independence*, with four cruisers as antiaircraft protection and six destroyers for screening.

In addition there was TG 50.4, the Relief Carrier Group under Rear Admiral Frederick C. Sherman, who had distinguished himself at Rabaul and would again at Leyte and Okinawa, with the old *Saratoga* and the new light carrier *Princeton*, two cruisers and four destroyers. If this were not enough, Spruance also disposed of two air support groups, with eight escort carriers for direct air support, and ninety Liberators, along with assorted patrol and rescue aircraft.

The massive fleet, beyond Japan's capacity to imagine, much less duplicate, carried 369 F6F Grumman Hellcats, 168 Douglas Dauntlesses, 237 Grumman Avengers and thirty-two of the new and still problem-ridden Curtiss SB2C Helldivers, nicknamed "the Beast." The pilots were a mix of veterans and well-trained newcomers.

In addition, there was an armada of transports and assault ships augmented by seven older battleships, six heavy cruisers, two light cruisers and eighteen destroyers.

Japan, its air power neutered by the losses at Midway, Guadalcanal and Rabaul, its navy in no condition to intervene against so powerful a fleet, had no alternative but to concede the Gilberts while trying to make their capture as costly as possible.

A commando raid had been made on Makin by the marines' 2nd Raider Battalion on August 17, 1942. Colonel Evan S. Carlson had led 220 men on a hit-and-run raid in which Major James Roosevelt, the President's eldest son, distinguished himself as the raiders' executive officer. Not much was achieved but to spur the Japanese to begin extensive fortification of the Gilbert Islands. Fifteen months' work by hundreds of laborers and the hard-working, hard-fighting men of the 7th Sasebo Special Landing Force had turned Makin and Tarawa into a rat's nest of 400 interconnected bunkers, tunnels and pillboxes, a fortification system extending over more than 300 acres of desolate ground. Light tanks were dug in, and a large number of cannons, from 37mm to 203mm, were well sited to repel an invasion. Rear Admiral Shibasaki Keiji took over command in September 1943. He boasted that "It would take a million men fighting for a thousand years to capture this island." He told his 4,835 men on Tarawa and 830 on Makin that they would earn their pay by fighting until they died—not much of an incentive program for a private making 6 yen, or about $1.38, per month. Somehow, it worked.

For a week prior to the invasion, carrier- and land-based air strikes were made over the length and breadth of the Gilberts; the B-24s alone dropped seventy-five tons of bombs on Makin and Tarawa. Immediately before the landings, the naval bombardment began, so heavy that the commanders believed that the landing would be a walkover. The well-trained, experienced amphibious forces had confidence in their 125 LVTs (Landing Vehicle, Tracked), watertight hulls propelled on land or water by cleated tracks able to climb over coral reefs right up onto the beach. Early experiments at Guadalcanal and in Morocco had been less than successful, but improvements had been made. One hundred of the new LVT-2 were available; these "amtracs" were twenty-six feet long, eleven feet wide and eight feet high; powered by Continental radial engines of 200 horsepower, they had a speed of 25 miles per hour on land and 5.4 knots on water, carrying twenty-four armed men or 6,500 pounds of cargo, and a crew of three. In the fierce fighting, ninety would be lost, but their contribution proved to be an invaluable forecast of the future.

Despite air and naval bombardment, the amtracs and a three-to-one American numerical superiority, the Japanese resisted fiercely on both islands. On Tarawa the assault craft grounded on the inner reef, and the troops had to wade through several hundred yards of waist-deep water in a withering cross fire, taking so many losses that the ominous signal, "Issue in doubt," was sent by Major General Julian Smith to Major General Holland "Howling Mad" Smith on the first afternoon.

The marines held on and were reinforced; of the 5,000 landed by the end of the first day, 1,500 were casualties. At tremendous cost, the following day the Japanese defenders were pushed back yard by yard. The principal target was Betio, where the Japanese had an airfield. An estimated 3,000 tons of 5-inch to 16-inch shells fell on the fortifications even as adverse tides prevented adequate reinforcement. Heavy fighting ensued for the next three days; Tarawa was secured on November 23 at a cost of 985 dead and 2,193 wounded. Japanese resistance ended with a futile banzai charge. Fighting on Makin was concluded on the same day, at less cost, with sixty-four Americans killed and 150 wounded. Admiral Shibasaki had kept his word in regard to his men dying to earn their pay; only 122 Japanese prisoners were taken, and of these only seventeen were combat soldiers.

The central ladder to Japan suddenly seemed very long indeed; the American public was shocked at the cost of taking Tarawa, and the commanders analyzed the battle to make sure the mistakes were not repeated.

Brave Japanese aircrews had made night raids in small groups all through the invasion, using the very effective technique of dropping flares to light up the targets. A raid by GM4 Betty torpedo bombers succeeded in hitting the *Independence* on November 20, forcing her to retire for repairs, an event that had more impact on American carrier strategy than on the invasion of Tarawa, for it led to a better method of deploying carriers. On November 24, the submarine *I-175* put a torpedo into the bomb storage area of the escort carrier *Liscome Bay;* in just over twenty minutes the ship sank with 644 of her crew. (The *I-175*, a large KD6A type submarine of 2,564 tons, met its fate off Kwajalein on February 5, 1944, at the hands of the destroyer escort USS *McCoy Reynolds*. The captain, Lieutenant Commander E. K. Winn, used five salvoes of the relatively new Hedgehog depth-charge system to sink the *I-175*.)

OPERATION FLINTLOCK: MITSCHER MAKES HIS MARK

Operation Flintlock was designed to capture the Marshall Islands, 500 miles to the northwest of the Gilberts. The Japanese had ten mutually supportive airfields or seaplane bases on seven islands in the Marshalls, some only 125 miles apart, some as distant as 360 miles. Japanese defensive forces were spread out, with the majority at Kwajalein, the world's largest coral atoll. As a first step, the undefended island of Majuro was occupied by U.S. forces and turned into a first-class harbor. In contrast to so many previous conquests, it was an almost idyllic island paradise. The decision to take Majuro was gutsy, for it was only 100 miles from Jaluit, seventy-five miles from Mili and 125 miles from Maloelap, all heavily defended Japanese bases. Majuro, one of the best harbors in the Pacific, became the advanced base of the Fifth Fleet and Task Force 58.

The task of suppressing Japanese air power in the Marshalls fell to Rear Admiral "Oklahoma Pete" Mitscher, who was the archetypal carrier commander—a graduate of the Naval Academy (1910); early naval aviation (Pensacola, 1916); pioneer pilot of the Curtiss NC-1 flying boat on its 1919 transatlantic attempt; carrier pilot on the *Langley* and the *Saratoga;* and captain of the *Hornet* on the Doolittle raid. All of this plus a remarkable command personality qualified him for the premier naval aviation job of the Pacific war, Commander of the Fast Carrier Task Force. Mitscher was a small man, but so rough-and-tumble and quick with his fists in his youth that it took him six years to get through the academy, earning his cowboy-like nickname in the process. Now a workaholic and not of robust health, he was quiet and unassuming, filled with compassion, willing to take on any assignment and inevitably inspiring his people to excel just to live up to his expectations. He had demonstrated his fighting ability as COMAIRSOLS (Commander Air Solomons) as he battered the Japanese back toward Rabaul. If he had a fault, it was ruining his health by overwork.

The aviator-nonaviator feud was finally tipped in favor of the flyers when Mitscher was recommended by Vice Admiral Towers to become Commander of the Fast Carrier Air Force, succeeding Rear Admiral Charles Pownall, who had not demonstrated sufficient aggressiveness in handling the fast carriers in the post-Tarawa raids on the Marshalls. Towers became deputy to Nimitz, a clear statement that the day of the old "Gun Club" battleship admirals had passed, and that air power was the key to victory.

Mitscher selected the new *Yorktown*, commanded by Captain "Jocko" Clark, as his flagship and divided TF 58 into four task groups, each with three carriers. (The Fast Carrier Task Force was designated TF 58 when part of Spruance's Fifth Fleet, and TF 38 when part of Halsey's Third Fleet.) TF 58's striking power rested on four *Essex*-class carriers, six light carriers of the *Independence* class and the old tried-and-true *Enterprise* and *Saratoga*. In addition, there were numerous battleships (including the new *Iowa* and *New Jersey*), cruisers and destroyers to provide an effective antiaircraft defense and screen against submarines.

Mitscher proceeded to devastate Japanese air power at Kwajalein, paving the way for one of the most extensive amphibious operations in history, one third again as large as that used in the Gilberts, and one that had learned much from Tarawa. At Kwajalein, Japanese aerial resistance was completely suppressed and naval gunfire was laid on in unprecedented quantity at very short range. The extremely complicated amphibious operation was spread over a number of islands and islets from January 31 to February 7, and resulted in the death of 7,870 Japanese of their total force of 8,675. Only 375 American troops were killed out of the 41,000 invading.

Eniwetok atoll fell next; 326 miles to the west-northwest of Roi, the northernmost point of the Kwajalein atoll, Eniwetok was defended by 2,200 Japanese troops, all of whom were killed at a cost of 339 American dead. Tarawa's lessons had been learned.

A series of small operations followed to secure most of the remaining islands in the Marshalls; those that contained significant numbers of Japanese troops, like Wotje, Mili, Jaluit and Maloelop, were bypassed and used as bombing ranges by both navy and air force planes. By the end of the war, the garrisons, which gamely repaired the airstrips after every raid although no Japanese plane would ever land there again, were reduced to a subsistence existence, living off the food they raised and the fish they caught. Toward the end of the war, the U.S. Navy occasionally rescued natives from the Japanese occupation, ferrying them to other islands.

TF 58 TAKES ON LAND-BASED AIR POWER

Truk, "the Gibraltar of the Pacific" to the American press at the time, was a valuable harbor for the Japanese, for its outer ring of coral reefs prevented naval gunfire from striking ships within the anchorage. Only air power could penetrate, and landing craft would have a difficult time entering the four passes into the harbor. Mitscher's TF 58 attacked Truk on February 17, 1944, eliminating its air power, and sinking 200,000 tons of merchant shipping in a two-day rampage. The original target, the Japanese fleet, had already left, permanently deprived of yet another anchorage. A few days later, on February 22, TF 58 attacked the Marianas, destroying more than 150 aircraft and sinking a number of ships. In less than a week, Mitscher had demonstrated that carriers could take on land-based aircraft and win; his attacks confirmed a decision to bypass Truk in favor of an attack on the Marianas, where the Japanese lacked time to prepare an adequate defense. There the Japanese would once again spend the lives of their soldiers to buy time.

THE INVASION OF THE MARIANAS: OPERATION FORAGER

So great had American strength become that a reorganization was necessary. Admiral Halsey was given the title of Commander, Third Fleet, and thus placed on a par with Admiral Spruance, both men reporting to Nimitz. To speed up the tempo of the war, Halsey's fleet would plan and train while Spruance's fleet was conducting an operation, and vice versa.

Each invasion taught the Americans lessons, one of the most important being that there was no such thing as too much power. To invade the Marianas, a reach of 1,000 miles that bypassed Truk and the Carolines, Admiral Spruance's Fifth Fleet brought seven battleships, twenty-one cruisers and sixty-nine destroyers, augmented by Mitscher's TF 58 with fifteen aircraft carriers and 956 aircraft plus its battleships and cruisers. In addition, nineteen of Vice Admiral Charles Lockwood's submarines and nine submarines under Rear Admiral Ralph W. Christie of the Seventh Fleet were deployed throughout the areas of the Japanese approach, and did remarkable work, not only accurately reporting the movement of the two Japanese fleets as they headed for a rendezvous, but turning Japan's war plan against itself by reducing its strength by submarine attack. Vice Admiral Turner had three marine divisions for the assault and two army divisions in reserve.

The Japanese had stationed 18,000 troops on Guam, 32,000 on Saipan and 9,000 on Tinian, for they recognized (as Nimitz did) that the three islands controlled the Central Pacific's sea lanes, and were the logical base for the planned Boeing B-29 attacks on the Japanese mainland.

The Japanese also felt that at last the Americans had moved to a position where the Imperial Navy, laboriously reconstituted over the past year, could bring about the only thing that could save Japan, a decisive naval engagement. After Admiral Koga's death, Admiral Toyoda Soemu had been named Commander-in-Chief of the Combined Fleet, and he adopted the A-GO plan of his hero, Yamamoto, which called for a combination of land- and sea-based air power to defeat the American navy. It would fall to Toyoda, known both for his sarcasm and for his preference for leading from behind, to preside over what proved to be the destruction of the Japanese navy in two engagements. Unfortunately for him, the solution he sought, a great fleet confrontation, was exactly what the American navy desired.

Toyoda gave at-sea command of the fleet to Vice Admiral Ozawa Jisaburo, while he remained at his command post in Tokyo. Only six months before, Ozawa's fleet would have been considered a formidable force, with five fleet carriers, four light carriers, five battleships, eleven heavy cruisers, two light cruisers, twenty-eight destroyers and fourteen other lesser ships. Japan's pride and joy, the two largest and most powerful battleships ever built, were the backbone of the fleet. The *Musashi* and *Yamato*, 74,000 tons, each carried nine 18.1-inch guns, the most powerful battleship armament in history, but design defects rendered them vulnerable to air attack. While they performed magnificently in the always-optimistic Japanese war games, they were already obsolete.

Frantic production efforts had provided Ozawa's carriers with 222 fighters, 113 dive-bombers and ninety-five torpedo-bombers, while his other ships carried forty-three float planes for reconnaissance. His greatest weakness was in aircrews, for fuel shortages had cut down training and most had no combat experience.

Operation A-GO planned to use 100 aircraft based in the Marianas. Because the lightly built Japanese aircraft had a greater range than their American counterparts, Ozawa hoped his "outranging tactics" would get in the first sighting and then deliver the first blow. He planned to have his flyers attack at very long range, then go on to land and refuel and rearm at airstrips on Guam, Saipan and Tinian. The next day they were to reverse the process, attacking the U.S. fleet en route back to their carriers, an excellent idea in principle, but riddled with hidden consequences.

Mitscher blocked the first part of A-GO planning with a massive pre-emptive strike by Task Force 58 on June 11. His gigantic fleet now had almost 900 aircraft at its disposal; he sent 219 of them against the enemy airfields on Guam, Rota, Pagan, Saipan and Tinian, destroying 110 Japanese aircraft at a cost of twenty-one Grumman F6F Hellcats.

Four days later, Rear Admiral Jocko Clark struck with planes from the *Hornet, Yorktown* (now called "The Fighting Lady"), *Belleau Wood* and *Bataan* at Iwo Jima and Chichi Jima, 635 and 735 miles north of Saipan, respectively, staging fields for aircraft en route to the Marianas. Twenty-eight Zeros were shot down, and the airfields, fuel dumps and shipping were worked over. The *Tatsutakawa Maru*, a 1,900-ton transport, was sunk off Chichi Jima, and American destroyers rescued 118 of its crew; another sixteen were rescued later. In the five days, more than 175 Japanese aircraft had been destroyed at a cost of eleven Hellcats; three of the American pilots were rescued.

The raid coincided with the first raid on Japan since Doolittle's attack; China-based B-29s bombed the steel mills at Yawata in an unimpressive performance, but a taste of things to come.

SAIPAN

In the famous comic strip *Li'l Abner,* cartoonist Al Capp created General Jubilation T. Cornpone, a mythical Confederate general immortalized for leading retreats at "Cornpone's Catastrophe," "Cornpone's Disaster" and "Cornpone's Humiliation." By the spring of April 1944, after the battles of Midway and the Solomons, Vice Admiral Nagumo Chuichi had fallen from the glory days of Pearl Harbor to Cornpone status, demoted to a command on Saipan. He had as his nominal subordinate an unimaginative cavalryman, Lieutenant General Saito Yoshitsuga, who was directly responsible for the island's defense. Saito was relatively inexperienced in combat, having risen from being commander of a horse procurement unit to command the 43rd Division. He was given to bold pronouncements: at the beginning of the battle for Saipan, he boasted that he would destroy the Americans at the beachhead; at the end, just before committing suicide, his message was "I will leave my bones as a bulwark of the Pacific."

Saipan's D-day was June 15, just nine days after the Allies had stormed ashore in Normandy. In his fifth amphibious operation, Admiral Turner brought 535 ships and 128,000 troops over 1,000 miles and more of open ocean from Eniwetok through waters made dangerous by Japanese submarines and, but for TF 58, land-based air power.

Amphibious landings were now choreographed with precision; there was little confusion as the myriad landing craft threaded their way around one another, shuttling between the beach and the transports, and cargo was off-loaded in the order that it was needed. Despite the overwhelming U.S. advantage in air support and in artillery, Saito's troops fought well, even though by the end of the first day the Americans had 20,000 troops ashore. Saito launched a counterattack the next morning, with 1,000 cheering soldiers—who had little to cheer about—and twenty-five light tanks, but was driven off. The Japanese then set a pattern for the future by retreating to the northern end of the island for an in-depth defense around Mount Tapotchau, taking comfort in the hope that Ozawa's fleet was on the way to defeat the Americans and relieve the island. The account of the Battle of the Philippine Sea that follows shows how futile that hope was.

Resisting fiercely, as they would do in every instance—General MacArthur spoke with enormous respect regarding the fighting qualities of the Japanese soldier—Saipan's defenders were gradually overwhelmed. The official resistance ended on July 6 after one final 4,000-man banzai charge that became mass suicide under the withering marine firepower. Saipan was not secured officially until August 10. Between those dates, individual parties of Japanese soldiers continued to resist, and, in one of the first of many grisly reminders of just how determined the Japanese were, thousands of civilians committed suicide on the northern Morubi Bluffs.

The Japanese lost 23,811 troops killed and 1,780 captured; of the latter, only seventeen were officers, most of them wounded. The Americans suffered a horrifying 24.5 percent casualty rate, with 3,426 dead and 13,099 wounded. The long-term prospects of an island-by-island battle leading to an invasion of the Japanese mainland became unspeakably grim.

JUNE 19–20, 1944: THE BATTLE OF THE PHILIPPINE SEA

Despite mounting evidence to the contrary, many Japanese firmly believed that the war could still be won. In *Fading Victories*, the annotated diary of Admiral Ugaki Matome, the admiral asks, "Can it be that we'll fail to win with this mighty force? No! It cannot be."

Both Nimitz and Toyoda had issued orders calling for the complete destruction of the enemy fleet. Nimitz instructed Mitscher that once the enemy carriers were knocked out, the surviving capital ships should be attacked. Admiral Toyoda asked Ozawa for a victory as significant as that of Tsushima almost forty years earlier. All four men were aware that the greatest carrier battle in history was about to take place; none suspected that it would also be the most one-sided.

Mitscher's TF 58 had seven fleet carriers and eight light carriers, steaming in five circular groups. In the rear, positioned line-abreast, twelve miles apart, were three Task Groups. Jocko Clark's TG 58.1 had the *Hornet, Yorktown, Belleau Wood* and *Bataan;* Rear Admiral John W. "Black Jack" Reeves's TG 58.3 had the *Enterprise, Lexington* (flag, with Mitscher), *San Jacinto* and *Princeton;* Rear Admiral Alfred E. Montgomery's TG 58.2 had the *Bunker Hill, Wasp, Monterey* and *Cabot;* each was surrounded by a screen of cruisers and destroyers. Admiral Spruance, Fifth Fleet commander, was on board the cruiser *Indianapolis* with TG 58.3. Spruance had overall command, but left the tactical decisions to Mitscher. Rear Admiral William K. Harrill, with TG 58.4, with the *Essex, Langley* and *Cowpens,* steamed twelve miles behind Clark, while Ching Lee's TG 58.7 Battle Line was positioned twelve miles to the south of Harrill and fifteen miles behind Reeves. Lee would have liked nothing better than a battleship-against-battleship confrontation, for he had seven of the best American capital ships, including the 58,000-tonners *New Jersey* and *Iowa.* The imposing formation, with its massive amounts of armor, firepower and unleashed horsepower, moved forward swiftly: the Americans intended to go in harm's way.

Ozawa had departed his Tawi Tawi anchorage in the southern Philippines early, then had to spend a day circling in the Philippine Sea, using up precious fuel and making himself vulnerable to U.S. submarines while waiting for confirmation that the land-based planes had been moved into position. (The Japanese were so short on fuel that some of his ships had unrefined and dangerously volatile crude oil from Tarakan in their bunkers.) When Ozawa finally moved on, he positioned Force C, three light carriers—*Zuiho, Chitose* and *Chiyoda*—and their supporting vessels in advance of his fleet to act as a decoy. These were under the command of Vice Admiral Kurita Takeo, one of the most pugnacious officers in the Imperial Japanese Navy—if one of the unluckiest, for it was his misfortune to participate in a series of losing battles. All three carriers were conversions. The 13,950-ton *Zuiho* had started life as the submarine tender *Takasaki*, and was a veteran of the battles of the Philippines, Midway, the Aleutians and Santa Cruz. The *Chitose* and the *Chiyoda* were converted from seaplane tenders; like *Zuiho*, they carried thirty aircraft. The three carriers steamed about six miles apart, and were inadequately defended by four battleships, the *Kongo*, *Haruna*, *Yamato* and *Musashi;* four heavy cruisers, *Atago* (flag), *Takao*, *Chokai* and *Maya;* and eight destroyers.

The rest of Ozawa's force was retained 100 miles behind the van, ready for the decisive attack. Ozawa's fast 33-knot battle group was designated Force A, and had the veteran *Shokaku* and *Zuikaku* along with the *Taiho*, the Japanese reply to the American *Essex*-class carrier. The *Taiho*, commissioned in 1944, displaced 34,600 tons and carried sixty aircraft along with a considerably heavier antiaircraft protection than the other carriers. Ozawa's screen was totally inadequate, with four heavy cruisers (the ubiquitous *Tone*, with *Chikuma*, *Kumano* and *Suzuya*) and seven destroyers. To Ozawa's port steamed Force B, under Rear Admiral Joshima Takaji. The perceptive Joshima had been convinced early on that the Americans were reading the Japanese code, and had flown to Yamamoto's headquarters and tried unsuccessfully to persuade him not to take his fatal flight on April 18, 1943. Under Joshima's command were three carriers, the old campaigners *Junyo* and *Hiyo* and the converted submarine support ship *Ryuho*. Protection was furnished by the 39,000-ton battleship *Nagato* (doomed to end its days in the atomic bomb tests at Bikini) and the bomb- and torpedo-magnet, the heavy cruiser *Mogami*, along with ten destroyers.

Although inadequate for screening, Ozawa's ships provided him with a large number of float planes to be used for reconnaissance; in this battle, Japanese reconnaissance, if little else, was superior to the American efforts.

The land-based air power that had been such a significant factor in the planning of Operation A-GO had already been destroyed on Guam by Mitscher's carrier-based planes. When the battle was joined, only a pitiful total of thirty fighters and five bombers reached Guam from Truk, and these were shot out of the sky. From that point on, everything depended upon Japanese carrier aviation.

At 0830 on June 19, Kurita launched the first strike from the van, with eight Jills with torpedoes, forty-three Zero fighter-bombers carrying single 251-kilogram bombs, and fourteen Zero fighters. The Zero fighter-bomber was an improvisation; there were no longer sufficient bombers to break through the American combat air patrol.

American radar and, more especially, the control of airborne fighters, had steadily improved; in this battle, the Americans monitored the frequency of the Japanese airborne controller, translating his instructions into English for precise guidance on the position and intention of incoming Japanese aircraft. More than 200 of the superb Grumman Hellcats scrambled from the *Essex*, *Cowpens*, *Bunker Hill* and *Princeton* to intercept. The Japanese were obviously inexperienced, and their flight leaders had to lead the loosely strung formation into a fifteen-minute orbit to regroup. One can imagine the frustration of the veteran Japanese pilots giving on-the-job training to amateurs—in combat. The perfectly positioned Hellcats had an altitude advantage when they began their field day with the incoming Zeros; some pilots ran up multiple kills on their first pass. The Japanese formation disintegrated, the bombers seeking their way out individually, the fighters using their agility to try to escape the Hellcats, who shot down forty-one. Only one aircraft scored a hit, a 551-pound bomb on the turret of the *South Dakota*, resulting in fifty casualties, with twenty-seven dead; the ship never left formation. At 0856, Ozawa launched the second raid, which included twenty-seven Jills, forty-eight Zeros, and fifty-three of the new Yokosuka D4Y Suisei (Comet) bombers. Called "Judy" by the Americans, the D4Y was a brilliant design capable of 343 miles per hour and possessing a range of 850 miles. (Admiral Ugaki would make his futile post-surrender kamikaze attack in a Judy.)

Disaster struck Ozawa's fleet even before his aircraft were engaged. The submarine *Albacore*, under her new captain, Commander J. W. Blanchard, fenced with Ozawa's fleet for more than an hour before sending a spread of six torpedoes at the *Taiho*. In some accounts of the incident, a Japanese Jill pilot, Warrant Officer Komatsu Sakio, saw a torpedo coming and dove his aircraft into it. He did not save the ship, for a second torpedo crashed into the port side of *Taiho*'s bow. Though she was flooded, *Taiho* was still able to make 30 knots, and her crew struggled to fix her forward elevator while damage-control parties fought the fires below. In a fatal move not unlike using a match to determine the quantity of gasoline in a tank, a sailor turned on all the ventilating fans, blowing the fumes of the Borneo crude throughout the ship so that it turned into a huge bomb. A spark ignited the fumes, resulting in an explosion so violent that the flight deck was blown up as the bottom was blown out. After seven hours of torture, the *Taiho*, the Imperial Japanese Navy's first armored-deck carrier on its first combat sortie, heeled over to its port side to sink almost horizontally, taking 1,650 men with her.

Sadly, the *Albacore*'s crew, victors over the *Taiho*, the light cruiser *Tenryu*, two destroyers and six other ships, would never know of their success, for the Japanese kept the sinking secret for several months, by which time the *Albacore* was lost in October 1944, probably due to hitting a mine.

Just as Ozawa's launch was concluded, Captain H. J. Kossler in the submarine *Cavalla* fired a spread of six Mark XIV torpedoes from a range of 1,200 yards, slamming three into the battered old veteran *Shokaku*. The *Cavalla*, on her maiden patrol, spent hours dodging depth charges—more than 100 were dropped—but had the satisfaction of hearing the shattering internal explosions on the *Shokaku* as it sank about three hours later with a loss of 1,270 lives.

Both carriers were lost in part because the Japanese shipyards failed to build in the necessary compartmentalization and fire-suppression equipment; additionally, the crews, while brave, were inexperienced in damage-control procedures.

While the subs were slaughtering the carriers, the second wave of Japanese aircraft flew on, as green and brave as the first. This time antiaircraft fire and Hellcats knocked down forty-one Judys, thirty-two Zeros and twenty-three Jills. Two Judys broke through to deliver near-misses on the *Bunker Hill*, causing minor damage.

The third raid was luckier, though no more successful; only seven out of forty-seven attacking aircraft were shot down, but the rest did no damage.

Ozawa's last gasp came at 1100, with a mixed grouping of nine Judys, twenty-seven Vals (an airplane obsolete at the time of Pearl Harbor), ten Zero fighter-bombers, six Jills and thirty Zero fighters. These made an inconsequential attack on American carriers, losing a dozen planes in the process and flying on, per plan, to land at Guam.

There, twenty-seven Hellcats caught forty-nine of them in the traffic pattern, some with gear and flaps down; thirty were shot down in short order, and the remainder badly damaged.

Ozawa's careful planning now brought him problems. With no knowledge of the extent of his losses, he believed in error that most of his aircraft must have landed at the island bases, and would return in the morning; he did not turn and run.

The great Marianas Turkey Shoot was over; the Japanese had lost 416 aircraft to air combat, antiaircraft, ground strafing, accidents, and on board the fleet carriers *Taiho* and *Shokaku*. With them had died 445 aircrew members, far more difficult to replace. But more was to come.

On June 20, Ozawa's fleet, having refueled while waiting for aircraft that would never return, was located by American reconnaissance planes

275 miles to the west. Mitscher made a late afternoon attack, launching 216 planes at 1620. Incredibly, Ozawa was complacent, convinced that his forces *must* have heavily damaged the American fleet, and so the Japanese defenses were not alert. Torpedoes from Grumman Avengers sank the light carrier *Hiyo* while direct hits were made on *Zuikaku, Junyo, Chiyoda, Haruna* and the cruiser *Maya*. Besides the aircraft on the *Hiyo*, Ozawa lost another sixty-five planes, most of them fighters. He then turned away to flee, having sustained the greatest naval defeat so far in the war.

Still exhilarated by the furious combat, the American flyers had to turn away as well, to face a long 335-mile night flight over a malevolent ocean. Pilots know that nothing is so lonely as an over-water flight at night in a single-engine airplane; the engine goes into automatic rough, the horizon disappears and minutes turn into attenuated Daliesque hours. Short on fuel and forced to maintain radio silence, the weary aircrews pressed on toward a blacked-out fleet. The smell of victory was in the air, however, and an ebullient Jocko Clark, part Cherokee Indian, wanted to save as many of his crews as possible. It was standard practice to have some lighting showing, but Clark ordered all his ships to turn all their lights on, and ordered the *Hornet* to turn on a vertical searchlight. Notified of his action, Mitscher concurred, and ordered the entire task force to turn on all its lights—in Clark's words, "one of the war's supreme moments." (Ironically, the profusion of light sources complicated the tired pilots' task of finding the carrier flight decks.)

The returning planes landed on the first available aircraft carrier, but it proved impossible to recover them all. Eighty aircraft were lost to fuel exhaustion or in landing accidents; the carrier crews were quick to shove damaged aircraft over the side to make room for the next one landing.

It was a crushing victory; by the end of the battle, at least 480 Japanese aircraft had been lost against 104 American. Only forty-nine American crewmen had perished in the assault on the Japanese fleet, but the Japanese had lost another generation of naval pilots, including some of their most famous aces.

Some later commentators have criticized Spruance for not completely fulfilling Nimitz's orders and for allowing the rest of the Japanese fleet to escape, particularly because Ozawa had lost all of his striking power—he had only about thirty-five planes left. Spruance rejected Mitscher's prodding to attack, believing his mandate was to defend the beachhead from attack. The same critics would have complained if Spruance had followed and his ships had fallen victim to land-based air power, Long Lance torpedoes and 18-inch guns in a night engagement.

Tinian and Guam

Tinian had been subject to naval and air bombardment for forty-three days, and saw the widespread use of napalm bombs. But the 9,000 Japanese on the island were not cowed, and when the invasion came on July 24, over narrow beaches on which it was difficult to land large numbers of troops, they fought with their usual fanaticism. The Japanese concept of individual sacrificial bravery in reckless banzai charges again proved costly as they were cut down by marine firepower. The marines were too experienced, too tough and too expert for such tactics. After the battle was over, the marines' legendary commander, General Howling Mad Smith, called Tinian "the perfect amphibious operation." It was finished by August 2, although individual Japanese held out for days.

Saipan and Tinian had been virtually anonymous islands in the American consciousness; in sharp contrast, Guam was U.S. territory, conquered and occupied by the Japanese, and coming back to it was sweet. The Japanese occupation troops had been particularly cruel to the native Guamanians. Males were impressed for military service as laborers while women and children were starved.

The U.S. naval and air bombardment softened the island for the invasion on July 21, and the amphibious operations went off like clockwork, as indeed they should have, given the training and experience of the sailors and the troops. The Japanese troops were of a higher quality than those on the two previous islands, and made good use of the difficult terrain. The island was not secured until August 10, after more than 18,000 Japanese had been killed, at a cost of 7,083 American casualties, including 1,435 killed or missing in action. With the Marianas secured, the army air force's B-29s now had a base from which to strike Japan.

Japan recognized the seriousness of its naval defeat and the loss of the Marianas. Premier Tojo Hideki, who had been so instrumental in driving Japan to war, resigned, but continued to be militantly opposed to an unconditional surrender. He lived out the war but was indicted on fifty counts as a war criminal, found guilty and executed by hanging in December 1948. Subsequently his ashes, with those of six other executed war criminals, were interred in a tomb that is inscribed "The Tomb of the Seven Martyrs." Tojo was not a martyr; instead he was a brilliant example of why all governments should insure that there is civilian control over the military.

LEYTE GULF AND THE LOGICAL SOLUTION

Events had carried the expensive U.S. dual marches across the Pacific to their common goal: the Philippine Islands. Any lingering thoughts of bypassing the Philippines or choosing Formosa as an alternative site were swept away by the force of General MacArthur's emotion and rhetoric. As the U.S. forces converged, they grew in strength on land, sea and air. Despite this convergence however, the concept of unified command was as remote as ever. Admiral Kinkaid and his massive Seventh Fleet remained under General MacArthur's control for the invasion, while Admiral Halsey and his Third Fleet reported to Admiral Nimitz. Halsey's Task Force 38 was positioned to assist either or both forces, as required. All of these powerful entities comprised the most powerful fleet in history, although possessing fewer vessels than assembled for the relatively short-distance invasion of Normandy.

The Battle of the Philippine Sea in June 1944 had reduced the Japanese navy to the same embattled state as the Japanese army. Both services now had to engage in combat with only a shadow of their formerly effective air forces. The Japanese navy felt it had to fight, that it would be a disgrace to have the fleet survive the defeat of the nation.

It now became obvious to some Japanese naval officers that their only remaining offensive capability was what became known in the United States as the Kamikaze Corps. The Japanese called the airmen who delivered suicide attacks the Kamikaze Toku-betsu Kogekitai, the Divine Wind Special Attack Corps.

As foreign as the concept was to Americans, it was perfectly logical to many Japanese, who recognized that the odds were now so heavily weighted against them that it was impossible to live through extended combat with the superior American forces. To the dedicated Japanese patriot, it was not difficult to decide that a suicide flight that destroyed an aircraft carrier was more desirable than merely being shot down in combat.

The movement began as a purely voluntary effort; later, many others were forced to "volunteer" by direct military orders and by peer pressure. The Japanese high command had initially been opposed to the concept on the grounds that it smacked of desperation and could be construed as evidence that the war was considered lost. But the defeat in the Marianas and the growing threat from B-29s combined with the hard economic facts of war to tip the scales in favor of suicide attacks.

Japanese aircraft production had reached its peak in 1944, and thousands of aircraft were on hand, even though most were inferior to their American counterparts. There was no longer time or fuel to train pilots to use the aircraft effectively, as the Marianas Turkey Shoot had demonstrated. In mass suicide attacks, however, even obsolete aircraft might slip through enemy defenses to crash into ships. Pilot training could be reduced to the minimum necessary for a pilot to take a plane off and dive it into a target.

The principal force behind the Kamikaze Corps was Vice Admiral Onishi Takijiro, an air power advocate generally considered, with Yamamoto, to have created the Japanese naval air arm. Onishi was rough-hewn and a fighter; a key to the samurai-sword toughness of his personality may be found in his death. After hearing the Emperor's broadcast of Japan's surrender on August 14, 1945, he committed traditional *seppuku* with a family heirloom, a *tachi*, a long-slung sword. Despite his agony, he refused a coup de grâce, suffering for twelve hours before dying.

Onishi personally disliked the idea of suicide attacks, but when given command of the First Air Fleet in the Philippines he realized there was little alternative if he was going to contribute to the islands' defense. And the Philippines were vital; if lost, Japan would be cut off from her South Sea territories and would have to rely solely on what could be imported through China and from Korea and Manchuria.

The Japanese again planned on the quick transfer of air power to land bases to supplement their naval actions. Even though the A-GO plan had failed, Admiral Toyoda now put forward the SHO-1 plan, a basically similar concept that would use land-based air power to assist the remnants of the Japanese surface navy to defeat the American fleet. It had the usual fillip of a decoy force; in this instance, Ozawa's Northern Force was to lure Admiral Halsey's carriers to the north, out of the main battle area. Then two heavy surface forces, the Center (Force A) and the Southern (Force C), were to drive into Leyte Gulf and destroy the transports.

The Japanese were able to muster four aircraft carriers, the tried-and-true *Zuikaku, Zuiho, Chitose* and *Chiyoda*, carrying eighty Zeros, twenty-five Jills, four Kates and seven Judys. The pilots were so inexperienced that Ozawa had ordered that after they were launched they would not attempt to recover on the carriers, but land instead in the Philippines. In addition, Ozawa had a detachment of two hybrid abominations, the *Hyuga* and *Ise*. These were 1915 vintage, 35,000-ton battleships converted in 1943–1944 to battleship-carriers, with their after guns removed and a flight deck installed from which aircraft could take off but not land. It did not matter, for neither ship had any aircraft, but did bristle with more than 100 antiaircraft guns and six rocket launchers.

Toyoda's plan was typically complex. Vice Admiral Kurita Takeo, with the Center Force (A), was to refuel at Brunei, Borneo, then move north through the Sibuyan Sea and San Bernardino Strait to burst into Leyte Gulf. Kurita had seven battleships, the *Yamato, Musashi, Nagato, Fuso, Yamashiro, Kongo* and *Haruna*. Kurita's flagship was the *Atago,* one of eleven heavy cruisers, supported by two light cruisers and nineteen destroyers. The van of this force was to be split off under Vice Admiral Nishimura Shoji, an old hand in the Philippines, having been with the December 8, 1941, attack force, and who fought subsequently at Balikpapan, the Java Sea and Guadalcanal. Nishimura with Force C was to take the *Fuso, Yamashiro,* the heavy cruiser *Mogami* and four ancient destroyers to enter Leyte Gulf from the south, trapping the American forces. Behind Nishimura sailed Vice Admiral Shima Kiyohide with the No. 2 Striking Force, with two heavy cruisers, the *Nachi* and *Ashigara,* the light cruiser *Abukuma* and four destroyers.

The elaborate plan—in which the four on-scene naval commanders had to coordinate primarily through communication with Admiral Toyoda in Tokyo—depended upon exquisite timing, and differed from past Japanese practice in one important detail: it almost worked. Only a failure of nerve on the part of Admiral Kurita at a decisive moment prevented its successful execution.

While Ozawa's considerable force of carriers acted as a red flag to Bull Halsey, luring him away to the north, the attack of Kurita and Nishimura on the American transports and amphibious craft were to be aided by land-based aircraft, including the Special Attack Force, adding weight to the attack.

A total of sixty-four Japanese ships were about to engage 219 Allied ships. Vice Admiral Mitscher's carriers were again designated TF 38, as they served under Admiral Halsey's Third Fleet. TF 38 was composed of sixteen fast carriers in four task groups: TG 38.1, under Vice Admiral John McCain, with the *Wasp, Hornet, Monterey* and *Cowpens;* TG 38.2 under Rear Admiral Gerald F. Bogan, with the *Intrepid, Hancock, Bunker Hill* and *Cabot;* TG 38.3 under Rear Admiral Frederick C. Sherman, with the *Essex, Lexington, Princeton* and *Langley;* and TG 38.4, under Rear Admiral Ralph E. Davison, with the *Franklin, Enterprise, San Jacinto* and *Belleau Wood.* A host of battleships, cruisers and destroyers served as antiaircraft protection and submarine screen.

The Fast Carrier Force had been wreaking havoc; as early as September 9, the carriers had ranged over the Philippines, striking as far north as Manila. In addition, the carriers were crucial in the capture of the Palaus and Ulithi in the Carolines; these would become the principal staging base for the navy's assault on the Philippines. Both were hard-fought battles, and the Japanese defenders at Peleliu inspired new and costly defense tactics. Japan henceforth would make only a minimum attempt to stop the Americans on the beaches, but would instead prepare the main defense lines in the toughest possible terrain, as far as possible out of the range of, or shielded by terrain from, naval gunfire. With this came the concept of keeping large reserve forces for counterattacks. The Americans had aerial superiority, but, because the islands were so small, the Japanese fought with what they had in place and without the transportation and mobility problems the Germans found in Europe.

In a preemptive strike reminiscent of those used before the invasion of the Marianas, the United States attacked Japanese airfields on Formosa, beginning with an October 12, 1944, strike by Mitscher's Task Force 38, in which almost 2,500 sorties were flown in three days. Army B-29s added another 109 sorties to the total. Admiral Fukudome Shigeru, commander of the Imperial Navy's Sixth Air Fleet, later reported the loss of 500 of his planes, saying that they had been shot down like "so many eggs thrown against the stone wall of indomitable enemy formations." Despite his defeats, Fukudome was intransigent, insisting long after the war that the Japanese had done the right thing—the only thing—in starting it. TF 38 also struck the Ryukyus, a portent of things to come.

October 20, 1944: MacArthur Returns/ Battle of Sibuyan Sea

General MacArthur kept his promise of two and a half years before, returning to the Philippines with overwhelming power on land, sea and air. The Americans landed on Leyte on October 20, to slight initial resistance.

At sea, submarines began the attrition of Japanese strength. At 0323 on October 23, Commander W. G. "Moon" Chapple in the submarine *Bream* closed to 800 yards to put torpedoes into the *Aoba*, knocking the veteran cruiser out of the battle and the war; she was later sunk while under repair at Kure, Japan. Next, a U.S. "wolf pack," the submarines *Darter* and *Dace*, operating in the Palawan Passage, which borders the South China Sea, further diminished the Japanese cruiser force. At 0532, the *Darter*, under Commander David McClintock, fired six torpedoes, five of them hitting and sinking the 13,400-ton cruiser *Atago;* one minute later, McClintock then fired his stern tubes, severely damaging the heavy cruiser *Takao*. At 0556, Lieutenant Commander B. D. Claggett heard his four torpedoes hit the heavy cruiser *Maya* and explode her magazines. Then, in a turn of fate, the *Darter* ran aground on the Bombay Shoal and had to be abandoned, her crew rescued by the *Dace*.

Kurita, already suffering from dengue fever and not improved by his dunking when the *Atago* went down, was picked up by a destroyer. He transferred his flag to the *Yamato*, to the discomfort of Admiral Ugaki. Ugaki had taken over temporary command of the fleet but now became immediately subordinate to Kurita on his own ship—and thus subsequently better able to second-guess him. Kurita was now separated from most of his senior communications officers and some vital code books, and was virtually cut off from communicating with either Ozawa or the Southern Force.

The Japanese opened the air battle on October 24 when a total of 150 aircraft operating from land bases in the Philippines made three separate raids on U.S. ships, demonstrating the low level of proficiency to which the Imperial Japanese Naval Air Force had fallen. Hellcats from the *Essex* intercepted one group, turning the attack into target practice; Lieutenant Commander David McCampbell, who would become the navy's leading ace with thirty-four victories, scored nine times, for which he was later awarded the Medal of Honor. Even though the Japanese attack was broken up, a single Judy bomber put a 551-pound bomb through three decks of the light carrier *Princeton* to start an aviation gasoline fire that exploded six torpedoes, causing the ship to be abandoned. When she was reboarded later and taken under tow, a second explosion fatally wounded her at 1523. The cruiser *Birmingham*, alongside assisting in rescue operations, was devastated by the explosion, with 229 killed and 420 wounded. The *Princeton* finally had to be scuttled by U.S. torpedoes, the first U.S. fleet carrier lost since the *Hornet* was sunk—also under tow—after the Battle of Santa Cruz on October 27, 1942.

Revenge for the *Princeton*: Exit *Musashi*

Halsey's planes found Force C at 0908 on October 24 to begin the Battle of the Sibuyan Sea, which in its own way was a laboratory experiment to settle the claims of airmen versus battleship admirals. The Japanese fleet sailed in two concentric circles, with the *Yamato* at the exact center. In a circle at two kilometers' distance were the *Musashi, Nagato* and three cruisers. The next ring consisted of seven destroyers, 3.5 kilometers from the *Yamato*.

If Force C's antiaircraft armament was not as sophisticated as the American navy's, it was nonetheless a formidable array. Primary reliance was placed on twin 12.7cm guns, of which the *Yamato* had twenty-four and the *Musashi* twelve. These guns could fire up to fourteen rounds a minute to an altitude of 31,000 feet. All of the ships were well endowed with numerous 25mm cannons; *Yamato* had 152, *Musashi* 130, the cruisers up to ninety and the destroyers up to forty. These were handicapped by a relatively slow rate of fire, but were supplemented by many 13mm machine guns. Even the battleship's 18.1-inch guns could be brought into play; the two huge battleships carried San Shiki shells, nicknamed "Beehive," each of which released 6,000 20mm steel balls when detonated by a time fuse. The 18.1-inch guns created their own problems, however; when fired, the overpressure from the muzzle blast could knock a man unconscious from a distance of fifty feet; consequently they were used only late in the battle when many of the other guns had been silenced.

The first American attack, a wave of forty-five aircraft at 1026, concentrated on the *Yamato* and *Musashi*, the latter taking two 1,000-pound bombs from Curtiss SB2C Helldivers, followed by a torpedo strike on the starboard side.

The torpedo hits would be critical; only 53.5 percent of the *Musashi*'s hull was armored, covering the most critical areas. Despite the care lavished on the ship by its principal designers, Hiraga Yazura and Fukuda Keiji, there was a basic design flaw in the size of the bulge used to detonate torpedoes and in the manner in which the 410mm-thick main belt of armor was attached to the ship's bulkheads by rivets. The system was not strong enough, especially since torpedo bulges on both of the big ships had been designed to withstand a blast of 500 pounds of TNT; the American torpedoes now had 600-pound warheads of Torpex, twice as powerful as TNT, and, as events would prove twice, too much for the super-battleships.

A second attack of thirty-five aircraft at 1207 put two torpedoes into the *Musashi*'s port side as two more 1,000-pound bombs knocked out one of her four main turbines. There were two side effects: the port-side torpedoes offset the list, and the bombs so damaged the ship's steam lines that her siren began a banshee wail that continued until she sank, unnerving her already shaken crew members.

But like all Japanese fighting ships, she was tough; prompt counterflooding and good damage contol kept *Musashi* under way at 22 knots, although slowly falling out of position. The next attack, also of thirty-five air-craft, came at 1331. It concentrated on the wounded ship, with four more bombs and three or four torpedoes striking home. *Musashi*, now well down at the bow, and her speed reduced to 16.5 knots, turned to flee westward. There was a two-hour respite before the next attack, and the *Musashi*'s skip-per, Rear Admiral Inoguchi Toshihara, slowed to 12 knots, aware that the forward momentum was forcing water into the ship at a fatal rate.

A final attack of sixty-five aircraft sealed the giant ship's fate; the Hell-divers put ten 1,000-pound bombs into her, totally destroying her super-structure, wounding Inoguchi in the shoulder and killing almost everyone else on the bridge.

At the same time the bombs were falling, the Avengers put from four to ten more torpedoes into her—the exact number is unknown because all Japanese records were destroyed and, in the heat of battle, the pilots were not able to tell whose torpedo hit.

As might be expected for such a magnificent vessel, the *Musashi*'s crew's damage-control efforts were excellent, but to no avail. By 1920 the list had increased to 30 degrees. At 1935 she rolled over and sank, carrying 1,023 officers and men down with her; 1,376 were saved. Inoguchi stayed on the bridge, insisting on going down with his ship.

The *Musashi*'s sacrifice served to spare the *Yamato* and the *Nagato*, which were only slightly damaged, the former by two bomb hits. Kurita be-gan a withdrawal that Toyoda curtly countermanded with a typically lyrical order: "Trusting in Divine aid, the entire fleet will attack." It was the right move, for if Halsey fell for Ozawa's ruse, Kurita would become MacArthur's worst nightmare. The entire invasion hung on the execution of Kurita's at-tack; if the transports and landing craft were destroyed, the Japanese could throw MacArthur's army into the sea. The ultimate resolution of the war would not be changed, but it would be delayed many months.

BATTLE OF SURIGAO STRAIT

Oil and debris were still rising from the *Musashi* as the most important por-tion of Ozawa's plan got under way. To ensure being noticed, Admiral Ozawa sent out an air strike of seventy-six aircraft, which, like earlier at-tacks, became an ace-maker for the American combat air patrol. The decoy force of carriers, now almost bereft of aircraft, was an intoxicating target for

Admiral Halsey, who at 2000 on October 24 ordered his TF 38 north into a stern chase 190 miles west of Luzon.

Halsey reacted aggressively and erroneously, for he could have detached at least one or perhaps two of his task groups to protect the Seventh Fleet in Leyte Gulf. Instead, he was determined to throw the full weight of his power, sixty-five ships and hundreds of aircraft, on Ozawa's virtually defenseless seventeen ships. In doing so, he threw over his duty to defend the Seventh Fleet and left the doors open for a Japanese attack.

At 0245, October 25, Admiral Nishimura slipped through the south door, Surigao Strait. According to some accounts, he was propelled by ego to engage in battle before his superior in rank but junior in age, Admiral Shima, came up. Nishimura, with four destroyers in his van, and the *Yamashiro*, *Fuso* and *Mogami* following in line of one-kilometer intervals, began his private Charge of the Light Brigade by shaking off determined but unsuccessful attacks by American PT boats. In this case there was no question of who had blundered; it was Nishimura, heading straight into a trap prepared by Rear Admiral Jesse B. Oldendorf, who had disposed his forces across the Leyte Gulf end of Surigao Strait. They were formidable, consisting of six veteran battleships, several of which had endured the Pearl Harbor attack, eight heavy cruisers and twenty-six destroyers, deployed so as to be the cross bar of the T for Nishimura.

The destroyers began with a slashing forty-seven-torpedo attack by DesRon (Destroyer Squadron) 54, which disengaged without being hit. Incredibly, Nishimura did not take any evasive action. The *Fuso*, launched in 1914, and the first battleship built in Japan with Japanese materials and guns, was mortally wounded by two torpedoes; enormous explosions ripped it into two burning halves, both of which continued to float. The destroyers *Yamagumo* and *Michishio* were also sunk.

Bull-like, Nishimura plunged on into a fusillade of torpedoes from DesRon 4; Commander H. G. Corey, skipper of the *Killen*, had been at Pearl Harbor and took pleasure in identifying the battleship and setting his torpedoes to run at a depth of twenty-two feet. They slammed into the *Yamashiro*'s hull, breaking her back. She kept under way however, directing inaccurate fire from her 14-inch guns at her tormentors.

Oldendorf's battleships had opened fire at 0353 at a range of 22,800 yards, their 14- and 16-inch shells pounding the wounded *Yamashiro* and the *Mogami* while the veteran *Shigure* zigzagged out of harm's way. The *Yamashiro* slowed, burning from stem to stern, and two torpedoes from the destroyer *Newcomb* finished her off. She sank at 0415. Some insight into

Nishimura's mental state can be derived from the orders he sent out just before the *Yamashiro* went down; one was to the *Fuso*, already sinking, asking her to come alongside as soon as possible; the second was to the other ships in his force: "YOU ARE TO PROCEED AND ATTACK ALL SHIPS." Only the *Mogami* and the *Shigure* remained to attack, and the *Mogami* was virtually dead in the water from shells fired by the cruiser *Portland*.

The battle of Surigao Strait was the last call for ship-of-the-line combat, ending an era that stretched back to the seventeenth century. Admiral Shima came upon the scene, assessed the situation and quite sensibly retired, but not before the heavy cruiser *Nachi* collided with the *Mogami*, under way again. Only the pursuit remained, in which the cruiser *Denver* sank the destroyer *Asagumo*. The gallant *Mogami*, after fighting off a series of attacks, was claimed to be sunk both by torpedo planes and by the *Akebono* the following day. Of Nimishura's force, only the indomitable *Shigure* survived. (She would live until January 24, 1945, when the U.S. submarine *Blackfin* sank her.) Shima's fleeing fleet did not escape further losses. Army air force bombers sank the light cruiser *Abukuma* off Negros Island on October 27, while navy planes sank the heavy cruiser *Nachi*. Shima lost everything except the *Nachi*'s sistership *Ashigara* and two destroyers. The Americans had suffered only seven hits, all on one ship, the destroyer *Albert W. Grant*, which ironically was also hit by friendly fire from the *Denver*, but fortunately did not sink.

It was a far cry from Pearl Harbor or Savo Bay.

THE BATTLE OFF SAMAR ISLAND: FROM SHO-GO TO TOGO TO NO GO

On the early morning of October 25, despite the almost total lapse in communications, Kurita slipped his force of four battleships, six heavy and two light cruisers and eleven destroyers through the completely unguarded but treacherous San Bernardino Strait where the 8-knot current made it hazardous to sail a formation at night. He moved to a point east of the island of Samar, heading straight for TG 77.4 under Rear Admiral Thomas L. Sprague.

Sprague's force consisted of three task units with operating areas about fifty miles apart. Sprague's Taffy 1, with the escort carriers *Sangamon*, *Suwannee*, *Santee* and *Petrof Bay*, was to the south, off the northern coast of Mindanao. Taffy 2, under the command of Rear Admiral Felix B. Stump, with CVEs (escort carriers) *Natoma Bay* and *Manila Bay*, was stationed in the center of the entrance to Leyte Gulf. Taffy 3, sailing to the north, off Samar, would take the brunt of the Japanese thrust. Under the command of Rear Admiral Clifton "Ziggy" Sprague, no relation to Thomas Sprague but a Naval Academy classmate, Taffy 3 had the *Fanshaw Bay* (flag), *St. Lo*, *White Plains* and *Kalinin Bay*.

Backing up this fleet of small, slow, thin-skinned but invaluable CVEs were Carrier Divisions 26 and 27 under Rear Admirals R. A. Ofstie and W. D. Sample, respectively. Ofstie had the *Kitkun Bay* and the *Gambier Bay* while Sample had the *Marcus Island, Kadashan Bay, Savo Island* and *Ommaney Bay*. Twenty-one destroyers and destroyer escorts were on hand as support, and they did so in such brilliant a fashion as to establish a naval tradition in a single battle.

The *Sangamon, Suwannee* and *Santee* were T-3 tanker conversions, displacing 23,875 tons fully loaded, with Allis-Chalmers geared turbines providing a cruising speed of 18 knots. Each carried twenty-eight aircraft and was 553 feet long overall, with a 495-foot flight deck. The rest of the escort carriers were all *Casablanca*-class ships, 10,900 tons fully loaded, 512 feet long overall, with 475-foot-long flight decks, capable of carrying twenty-eight aircraft, and powered by Skinner Uniflow reciprocating engines, giving them a 15-knot cruising speed.

These vulnerable CVEs, filled with aviation gasoline, bombs, torpedoes and depth charges, were jestingly called "Combustible, Vulnerable and Expendable" by their crews and were the only thing standing between Kurita and the helpless transports of the invasion fleet. In accidentally pulling off the most important part of Sho-Go, Kurita had the opportunity to become another Admiral Togo.

Both sides were surprised, the Americans by Kurita's sudden appearance, and the Japanese, unaware of the success of Ozawa's ruse, by what they presumed to be Halsey's fast carrier force. Kurita, whose personality seemed to be equally divided between timidity and rashness, was by now exhausted by the strain of battle and his illness. Confused, he hesitated, estimating that he faced no fewer than five to seven fleet carriers with many cruisers and destroyers.

His vacillation lasted long enough to be turned into a magnificent triumph by Admiral Ziggy Sprague, who pugnaciously ordered his ships to open fire with their puny 5-inch guns while launching his aircraft. He called for help and Taffy 1 and Taffy 2 responded. Within minutes, Kurita had to contend with attacks from Avengers and Wildcats. Ultimately, he would be engaged by no fewer than 253 fighters and 143 torpedo planes, the latter dropping Mark 13 torpedoes while the fighters used their .50-caliber machine guns and some rockets. Pilots of both types of aircraft continued to make feint attacks after expending their ammunition, and they made better use of the tactics the Japanese had planned for Guam, by landing, refueling and rearming at airfields in the Philippines.

The Japanese force included the battleships *Yamato, Nagato, Kongo* and *Haruna* and the cruisers *Suzuya, Haguro, Chikuma, Kumano, Yahagi, Chokai, Noshiro* and *Tone.* Opening fire at 0658, Kurita compounded his error in identification by giving the order "General Attack," i.e., each of his ships should choose its own targets. There was only one conceivable outcome for a fight between battleships and CVEs but Kurita's order gave Sprague the opportunity combat admirals fantasize about. His crews flew sortie after sortie, and as the larger Japanese ships closed, he ordered an all-out attack by his unarmored destroyers and destroyer escorts. These thin-skinned warriors, whose only chance for safety lay in their speed and maneuverability, raced in to launch torpedoes, then courageously duked it out with battleships and cruisers, firing their 5- and 3-inchers against broadsides from 6-, 8-, 14-, 16- and 18.1-inch guns. Each Japanese battleship used a different dye in its shells to mark their fall, and Sprague's destroyers sped through red, yellow, green and blue waterspouts, their very proximity making them difficult targets. No navy doctrine prescribed how destroyers should slug it out with battleships, but the U.S. destroyer crews were determined to save the carriers, and more importantly, the transports.

Sprague issued an order: "SMALL BOYS [destroyers] ON MY STARBOARD QUARTER INTERPOSE WITH SMOKE BETWEEN MEN [the escort carriers] AND ENEMY CRUISERS." The destroyers responded; then Sprague ordered: "SMALL BOYS FORM FOR SECOND ATTACK." The destroyers began a successful, if almost suicidal, charge.

At 0805, Commander Leon Kintberger, commanding officer of the USS *Hoel* (2,100 tons), first engaged the 32,000-ton *Kongo*, then the 14,000-ton *Kumano*, firing five torpedoes at each. More than forty shells, many of them 14-inchers, left the *Hoel* a shattered wreck; she sank at 0855 with a loss of 253 men. The USS *Samuel B. Roberts*, a 1,400-ton destroyer escort commanded by Lieutenant Commander R. W. Copeland, followed Nelson's traditional injunction and placed herself next to the Japanese cruisers, getting off 608 5-inch shells before being hammered into a burning mass by enemy fire. She sank at 1005, with eighty-nine crew members. The USS *Johnston* began the fray with a torpedo attack that tore the bow from the *Kumano*, and in which she suffered three hits from the *Kongo*'s 14-inch shells; undaunted, the *Johnston* returned to the attack again and again, determined to save the carriers and the transports. She fought on until 1010, sinking with 185 of her crew, including her skipper, Commander Ernest Evans.

The brilliance of the destroyer attacks showed how far the American navy had come, reversing the early days of the war when Japanese destroyers ran rampant. In the course of the war, eighty-two "small boys" would be lost out of a total of 928 destroyers and destroyer-escorts in service. The Japanese lost 126 out of 177 destroyers.

Despite their heroism, however, the destroyers could not prevent Kurita's ships from closing and they began holing the *Gambier Bay* and the *Kalinin Bay*, the heavy armor-piercing shells often passing entirely through the targets without exploding. The *Kalinin Bay* absorbed fourteen hits, most of them 8-inch, and kept on fighting. Like circling wolves, the *Chikuma, Haguro* and *Noshiro* concentrated their fire on the *Gambier Bay* and soon brought her to a halt; she capsized and sank at 0907. (About 100 men went down with the ship; another 750 were estimated to go over the side, only to endure one of the great trials of the war. After forty hours of drifting through shark-infested waters, a total of 183 survivors were eventually rescued. Rescue was delayed because of communication problems and the incessant Japanese kamikaze attacks.)

Aircraft from Taffy 2 arrived just as Taffy 3's planes had to land and rearm, the Avengers launching torpedo attacks while the Wildcats strafed the ships with their machine guns. The *Chokai* was destroyed when four Avengers from the *Kitkun Bay*, led by Commander Richard L. Fowler, put nine 500-pound bombs into her; the destroyer *Fujinami* rescued her crew, then gave the coup de grâce with a torpedo. The *Suzuya* and *Chikuma* were so damaged that they had to be abandoned, the *Suzuya* to be sunk by Japanese destroyers, while the *Chikuma* was sent down later by an Avenger attack. The destroyer *Nowaki* was pummeled by the guns from American cruisers and destroyers that caught up with her after the battle.

The frenzied American destroyer attack was complemented by an unending succession of Avengers and Wildcats coming in at mast-top height dropping bombs, torpedoes and depth charges. Like a swarm of hornets overcoming a bull, it was too much for Kurita, who had only to press on straight through the carrier forces with his mighty *Yamato*, which alone could have sunk the mass of transports like so many ducks on a pond. Unnerved, he ordered a retirement, and his warships, Japan's last hope for saving the Philippines, fled. It was retirement for Kurita too, who was assigned to a dead-end job as head of the Naval Academy, thus ending his career.

The battle off Samar was a magnificent upset victory, a flyweight kayoing a heavyweight champion. The Japanese lost three heavy cruisers, while the Americans lost two escort carriers, two destroyers and a destroyer escort and suffered 2,043 casualties, including 1,130 killed. Both sides had many smaller ships damaged.

Kurita's inept fight was partially compensated for by the fury of the first successful sortie of Admiral Onishi's Special Attack Corps. On October 25, Zeros crashed into the *Kitkun Bay, Santee, Petrof Bay, Sangamon, Suwannee* and the *St. Lo.* The first five ships received varying degrees of damage, but the *St. Lo* was mortally wounded. A single 551-pound bomb dropped by a crashing Zero caused a raging fire and then wracked the ship with eight violent internal explosions as aviation fuel, torpedoes and bombs went off; she sank within thirty minutes. Then two Judy dive-bombers crashed into the battered *Kalinin Bay*, which somehow managed to stay afloat. The *Suwannee* was attacked again the following day, surviving even heavier damage.

The Americans tracked the remnants of Kurita's fleet, planes from the carriers *Wasp* and *Hornet* sinking the light cruiser *Noshiro* and running the destroyer *Hayashimo* aground. The wounded *Kumano*, her captain as bewildered by the scale of the defeat as Kurita, was hounded by planes and submarines through the myriad islands of the Philippines for a month before being towed to Dasol Bay, Luzon, where she was sunk on November 25 by aircraft from the *Ticonderoga*.

The World Wonders at Halsey's Revenge off Cape Engaño

At dawn on October 25 Admiral Halsey began one of the few instances recorded in warfare in which a fantastic victory became an embarrassment. Speeding like an errant fullback toward his own goal line, Halsey had raced after Ozawa's Northern Force of four carriers and the two hybrid battleship-carriers. These had an inadequate defensive screen of three light cruisers and nine destroyers. Ozawa, who had witnessed one accident after another during training in the Inland Sea, had dispatched most of his aircraft to airfields in the Philippines.

Halsey, in the *New Jersey*, threw three of Marc Mitscher's carrier groups against Ozawa, then cruising 205 miles northeast of Luzon's Cape Engaño, in what some have called "the Battle of Bull's Run." Ozawa had only twenty-nine aircraft left, and nine of his screen of fifteen Zeros were knocked quickly into the sea around 0800. The troublesome Curtiss Hell-diver, successor to the beloved Douglas Dauntless, came into its own sink-ing the *Chitose*. The Avengers put a torpedo into the stern of the gallant veteran *Zuikaku*, knocking out her communications and steering. In an amazing anachronism, the *Zuikaku* had used rockets with metal lines at-tached to snag airplanes as a part of her defense. Ozawa transferred his flag to the light cruiser *Oyodo*. The same attack also sank the destroyer *Akizuki*.

The second strike arrived at 0945, damaging the *Chitose*'s sister ship, the *Chiyoda*, so badly that it was left to be sunk later by a force of American cruisers led by Rear Admiral L. T. DuBose, sent out to "clean up the battle-field." The light cruiser *Tama* was torpedoed while rescuing the *Chiyoda*'s crew and was finished off the following day by the submarine *Jallao*, com-manded by Commander J. B. Icenhower, and on her first patrol. The *Tama* was the eighth light cruiser to be sunk by American submarines.

One can only wonder what ran through the mind of Ozawa, Japan's pre-mier carrier commander, as the third wave of American aircraft came in unimpeded by any fighters and with the defensive antiaircraft fire reduced by the fleet being strung out over thirty-five miles. Avengers and Hellcats from the *Lexington* attacked the *Zuikaku*, which finally went down at 1414. The highly maneuverable *Zuiho* was damaged by Helldivers from the *Essex* and left for the next wave to finish. Where once the proud *Hinomaru* in-signia (the red "meatball" in American parlance) had adorned her gleaming yellow flight deck to make sure she wasn't attacked in mistake by her own planes, there was now a "battleship" camouflage, fake turrets and guns painted on the deck, a plaintive request for American planes to seek a more profitable target. How the mighty had fallen!

The fourth wave, from the *Enterprise* and the *Franklin*, sank the *Zuiho* at 1526 and damaged the hybrid *Ise*. The airborne agony was almost over, but the suffering was not. During a night action, the destroyer *Hatsuzuki* was sunk by the cruisers of DuBose's cleanup squad.

Ozawa's decoy had cost him four carriers and many other ships; he re-turned only with the modern cruiser *Oyodo*, the two hybrids *Ise* and *Hyuga* and five destroyers.

Yet long before the battle was over, Halsey had the sweet cup of victory dashed from his lips. Kurita's sortie through the San Bernardino Strait had thrown a degree of panic into the American high command, and at 1000 Ad-miral Nimitz sent the following message to Halsey (normal cryptographic padding underlined): "TURKEY TROTS TO WATER. FROM CINCPAC. WHERE IS, RPT [repeat], WHERE IS TASK FORCE 34. THE WORLD WONDERS."

The message delivered to Halsey had only the first element of cryptographic padding removed, so Halsey read "FROM CINCPAC. WHERE IS, RPT, WHERE IS TASK FORCE 34. THE WORLD WONDERS."

Halsey was furious at the admonitory "RPT" and at the gratuitous "THE WORLD WONDERS," and embarrassed that a copy had been sent to Admiral King as well. Although he was never to admit it, the facts of the situation spoke for themselves: he had erred. This did nothing to diminish his anger at Nimitz for what he deemed to be an insulting message. Later he did say that the June 1944 Battle of the Philippine Sea might have gone better if he and Spruance had switched positions.

Halsey had not been solely to blame; Admiral Kinkaid's reconnaissance had been less than comprehensive. But Halsey's reputation for sloppy planning and inattention to detail had already incurred Admiral King's wrath, and it was only Halsey's immense public popularity that sustained his position. Halsey did not receive his expected promotion to five-star rank until after the war, and suffered further embarrassment when a Court of Inquiry determined that his lack of judgment had resulted in the loss of three destroyers and 800 men during a typhoon in mid-December 1944. But he was too highly revered by the public to replace, and the war situation was not so critical as to demand his removal. Further, in a display of compassion not typical of the military high command, in which incidents like this are often used to settle personal matters of long standing, the navy from Admiral King down seemed to understand that the same qualities that had made Halsey so indispensable in the early days of the war also prompted his problems in the closing months.

Notwithstanding these minor developments, the four engagements that comprised the Battle of Leyte Gulf were, in sum, the largest naval battle in history, employing not only air, surface and submarine elements but introducing kamikaze tactics, which went on in subsequent battles to inflict damage upon other ships, including the *Cabot, Essex, Lexington, Franklin* and *Belleau Wood.* Yet Leyte Gulf was an unmitigated defeat for the Imperial Japanese Navy, which would never again conduct a complex fleet operation; some ships would make valiant but hopeless suicide sorties, while the rest would be hounded by submarines and planes until all but a pitiful few were sunk. The Japanese navy worsened its dying with the pointless sacrifice of its sailors just as the army did with its soldiers, who battled on in Leyte and Luzon with the same futile courage against similarly great odds. Sadly, all their sacrifices were for the unworthy purpose of buying a little time for feckless politicians at home.

34

A blurred photo, but worth study, as it shows the Japanese crewmen of the mighty aircraft carrier *Zuikaku* cheering "Banzai" as their naval ensign is lowered. Many of them yelled "Banzai" aboard the same ship as it launched aircraft at Pearl Harbor. The veteran of many battles, the *Zuikaku*'s sharp list presages its sinking off Cape Engaño on October 25, 1944.

35

As the *Zuikaku* sinks, Vice Admiral Ozawa Jisaburo transfers his headquarters to the light cruiser *Oyodo*. Ozawa was regarded as a "fighting admiral" by his countrymen, even though it was his fate to be defeated in every battle he fought after 1943.

In one of the most daring adventures of the war, American sailors board and
capture the sinking German *U-505*. In service for thirty-four months, and having
sunk seven ships, the *U-505* was an intelligence bonanza and remains today a
remarkable teaching device, on exhibit at the Museum of Science and Industry
in Chicago.

The Japanese carrier *Mogami*, just after it was launched in 1934. The ship
had a long and troubled career, requiring an almost immediate rebuild after
entering service, then being severely damaged at Midway and off Rabaul
before finally being sunk on October 25, 1944, when a night engagement
with U.S. cruisers off Bohol Island was capped by a collision with the heavy
cruiser *Nachi*.

38

Even as U.S. strength grew and Japanese strength diminished, the war continued with unprecedented ferocity. The USS *Princeton*, a 10,883-ton *Independence*-class aircraft carrier, served for a year in combat before its flight deck was penetrated by a single 250-kilogram bomb that set off uncontrollable fires. Munition explosions gutted her, and she had to be sunk by torpedoes from the U.S. cruiser *Reno* on October 24, 1944, during the Battle of the Philippine Sea.

39

The escort carrier *St. Lo* explodes after a Japanese suicide plane attack in the Leyte Gulf on October 25, 1944. She sank within thirty minutes.

40

How the mighty had fallen. Where once the decks of the Japanese aircraft carriers gleamed with yellow varnish and were proudly marked with the bright red *Hinomaru* insignia, the pressures of war now forced a primitive camouflage. A converted submarine depot ship, the *Zuiho*, painted guns simulating a battleship, begins to burn from bomb damage received off Cape Engaño, the Philippines, on October 25, 1944. It was sunk later that day by further hits from U.S. carrier aircraft.

41

The USS *Gambier Bay*, a *Casablanca*-class escort carrier, fights valiantly for her life in an unequal contest with the Japanese cruisers, *Chikuma*, *Chokai*, *Haguro* and *Noshiro*, in a battle off Samar Island on the same day the *Zuiho* went down, October 25, 1944. About 750 men abandoned ship; 700 were ultimately rescued over the next two days.

42

A Japanese Judy kamikaze plane, flames pouring from its wing tank, is shot down by gunners of the USS *Essex* during a November 25, 1944, attack. Considered by many to be the best torpedo-bomber of the war, the Judy, officially known as the Yokosuka D4Y3 *Suisei* (Comet) made the last kamikaze raid of the war on August 15, 1945. Vice Admiral Ugaki Matome, stripped of insignia but carrying his ceremonial sword, squeezed into a Judy with its two regular crewmen, and led an eleven-plane flight that was completely destroyed. Wreckage of a Judy containing a ceremonial sword was reportedly found on a small island north of Okinawa on August 16.

43

Japanese ship handling was excellent; even in the height of battle, when tight turns were necessary to avoid the hail of bombs and onrushing torpedoes, discipline was maintained, as can be seen in this view of three Japanese ships executing the same maneuver. A *Shokaku*-class carrier receives near-misses off her bow and stern as her escort destroyers turn to cover her. The photo was taken on June 19, 1944, west of the Marianas.

44

Crewmen of the new *Lexington* sleep where they fell during a brief lull during the Battle of the Philippine Sea. Originally to be named the *Cabot*, the name was changed to honor the great fighting *Lexington* (CV-2), which was sunk on May 8, 1942.

45

The immensity of the American war effort was impossible for the Axis to comprehend; while the Japanese were being overwhelmed in the Pacific, the Germans could not believe the amount of equipment and matériel being brought to bear against them in Europe. Here vehicles hurry down the causeway of the Mulberry artificial harbor to Omaha Beach in Normandy, while countless others queue up, waiting their turn.

46

The *Franklin*, an *Essex*-class carrier, was commissioned on January 31, 1944; on March 19, 1945, she was hit by two 250-kilogram bombs that pierced the hangar deck and exploded among the aircraft that were waiting, fueled and armed, for the next mission. Through superb damage control, and assisted by ships like the cruiser *Santa Fe*, shown in the foreground, she made it back to Pearl Harbor, and ultimately New York, under her own power.

47

The techniques used at Normandy were learned in the hard classrooms of North Africa, Sicily and Italy. Here the justly famous DUKWs load an LCT (Landing Craft, Tank) on the right, and two LCMs (Landing Craft, Mechanized) on the beach at Scoglitti, Italy.

48

Desperation drove the Germans to improvisations similar to the Japanese human torpedoes. This is a small German submarine of the Biber type, cast up on the Belgian coast. These subs were extraordinarily hazardous; a torpedo was housed on the concave side. Note the shark's eye and teeth painted on the front of the boat; even in the waning moments of the war someone had a sense of humor—or the fighting spirit—to decorate a hopeless weapon.

49

The German battleship *Lützow* in the Stettin Canal, April 1945. It was originally named *Deutschland*; Hitler ordered the name changed because he feared the impact on morale if a ship bearing the country's name should be sunk. But the *Lützow* survived the war until May 4, 1945.

50

The native people were typically friendly to the Americans and unfriendly to the Japanese throughout the Pacific, and nowhere more so than in the Philippine Islands. The Filipinos assembled here to assist the PT boats in picking up survivors from the Battle of Surigao Strait after the second Battle of the Philippine Sea. The PT boats made life an absolute hell for Japanese submarines, which were unable to contend with their speed and firepower.

Life at sea was dangerous at all times; here a Grumman F6F Hellcat strikes the carrier as the LSO (Landing Ship Officer), paddles in hand, runs to get out of the way. 51

The antiaircraft protection of American ships improved steadily throughout the war. Here gunners using Quad 40mm antiaircraft guns defend their carrier from kamikaze attack.

52

Watching a kamikaze attack became an intensely personal experience; the wall of antiaircraft fire put up managed to knock down many of the attackers, but others would somehow find their way through the curtain of shells, many of them proximity-fused. This attack is taking place off the Philippines in October 1944.

53

A therapeutic shot of medicinal whiskey goes well with Lieutenant Donald P. "Rip" Gift, of Marlette, Michigan. The adjuration "Get the Carriers" on the blackboard behind him tells it all, for when the Japanese lost their carriers they had effectively lost the war.

54

Admiral Raymond A. Spruance (left) and Fleet Admiral Chester W. Nimitz aboard the ill-fated cruiser *Indianapolis* in February 1945. The two men were a remarkable combination, not only fighting admirals, but great strategists.

55

56

Air raids on the mainland by the U.S. Navy's Fast Carrier Forces made the Japanese populace realize how desperate their situation was even more than did the B-29 bomber raids. The B-29s could come from long distances—the navy planes had to be operating from carriers from less than two or three hundred miles offshore—something they could not do if the Japanese navy still had any strength.

57

One of the most famous U.S. submarines, the *Wahoo*, which sank twenty ships for a total of 60,038 tons; it was lost while operating west of Honshu, in October 1944, probably the victim of a patrol plane.

58

The *Yamato* angrily responds to an attack by U.S. Navy aircraft at Kure, Japan, on March 18, 1945. The ignominy of this attack in home waters must have galled the crewmen, who had prided themselves on being aboard the most powerful battleship in history. They could not know that the *Yamato* had twenty days to live, for it was to be sacrificed in a futile suicide attack.

Billy Mitchell's dream come true! The most powerful battleship in the world, the *Yamato*, already burning, turns sharply to the starboard as a bomb bursts alongside. Her mighty 18-inch guns were useless against the air attack that sent her to the bottom on April 7, 1945.

59

Within thirty seconds on May 11, 1945, two Japanese Judy kamikaze planes struck the USS *Bunker Hill*, her decks loaded with gasoline-filled and bomb-laden aircraft. The *Bunker Hill*'s crew fought valiantly to save the ship, and it was able to return to a Pacific coast shipyard for repair. But there were 656 casualties, including 392 dead.

60

61

Relaxing as much as possible before what they knew was almost certainly a one-way mission, Japanese aircrew members sit near a Betty bomber laden with a rocket-powered Okha (Cherry Blossom) piloted bomb. It was later discovered that Japan had stockpiled more than 12,000 kamikaze aircraft for use in repelling the expected invasion of the home islands.

62

The sweetest moment of the war for General of the Army Douglas MacArthur, as he signs the instrument of surrender aboard the USS *Missouri* in Tokyo Bay, on September 2, 1945. Immediately behind him on the left is Lieutenant General Jonathan Wainwright, who, referring to his surrender at Corregidor commented, "The last surrender I attended, the shoe was on the other foot." He endured more than three years of harsh Japanese imprisonment. Alongside him is Lieutenant General Arthur Percival, who had surrendered at Singapore and was similarly imprisoned .

63

Among the architects of naval victory were, from the left, Admiral Raymond A. Spruance, Fleet Admiral Ernest J. King, and Fleet Admiral Chester W. Nimitz. Brigadier General Sanderford Jarman, right, escorts them in a photo taken on Saipan before Japan's surrender.

All personality problems temporarily put aside, Admiral William F. "Bull" Halsey (right), Commander of the Third Fleet, greets Fleet Admiral Chester W. Nimitz aboard the battleship *South Dakota* in Tokyo Bay on August 29, 1945. It is a shame that the priceless private conversations between men like these—salty, direct, and no-holds-barred—are lost to history.

The USS *Missouri* in the Brooklyn Navy Yard, all decked out in a spectacular camouflage system.

The Imperial Japanese Navy Submarine *I-58*, whose captain, Commander Hashimoto Mochitsura, sank the *Indianapolis* with three Type 95 Long Lance torpedoes. Hashimoto was later called to Washington to testify in the trial of Captain Charles B. McVay, the captain of the *Indianapolis*. The U-shaped structures held the kaiten human torpedoes in place. The photo was taken at Sasebo, in November 1945. The *I-58*, like most of the surviving Japanese submarines, was taken to sea in 1946 and scuttled with demolition charges.

67

One of the most famous cruisers in the Imperial Japanese Navy, the *Tone*, lies battered on the bottom of Kure harbor, the last survivor of the task force that attacked Pearl Harbor on December 7, 1941. The *Tone* was ubiquitous, appearing in battles all over the Pacific, until she was finally tracked home and sunk in her lair by planes of the Third Fleet.

Only the Japanese had successful torpedoes from the beginning of the war. Here a one-armed Kate takes off for a mission.

68

69

U.S. escort carriers also did invaluable work ferrying U.S. Army Air Force aircraft. In this case the USS *Barnes* carries a deckload of Lockheed P-38 Lightnings and Republic P-47 Thunderbolts, in a photo taken on July 1, 1943.

A sailor on an escort happily adds victory flags to his ship's scoreboard, which shows victories both in the Atlantic and the Pacific.

70

71

President Harry S Truman and Admiral William F. "Bull" Halsey confer on October 19, 1945. They were two men of similar stripe—outspoken and fearless. Halsey's turbulent career delayed his promotion to Fleet Admiral to December 1945.

Vice Admiral Marc "Pete" Mitscher awards the Navy Cross, Distinguished Flying Cross and Silver Star to Lieutenant Cecil E. Harris during a January 17, 1945, ceremony. Harris ended the war as the navy's second highest ranking ace, with twenty-three victories in the Pacific.

72

The Last Bitter Months

The battles of the Philippine Sea and Leyte Gulf finished the Japanese navy as a cohesive fighting force; in a ninety-day period, the U.S. Navy had sunk more enemy tonnage than any other fleet in history. The United States now had to determine the most efficient method of ending the war at a minimum cost in Allied lives. The very nature of the conflict had changed from a war between roughly equal contestants into a massive police endeavor to round up individual surviving warships. From the Philippines forward, not even the most optimistic Japanese still considered the long-sought "decisive victory" possible, especially since it was evident that Germany's defeat was not far off. A small group of fanatics refused to consider surrender; a wider group rationalized that dogged resistance might result in surrender terms that would preserve the Emperor's—and by extension, their own—prerogatives. Underlying both groups was a desire to remain in power as long as possible. Japan's leaders thus adopted a gangster's "come in and get me, copper" attitude, allowing their soldiers to be killed by the thousands while defending a crumbling periphery. Given the demonstrated American preference for spending money on weapons and supplies rather than risking lives, it is difficult to understand how even the most sanguine—in either sense of the word—Japanese could have supported this policy.

Change of Strategy

On October 3, 1944, the Joint Chiefs of Staff ordered General MacArthur to fulfill his dreams by going on to invade Luzon, an order he quite rightly interpreted as a charter to liberate all the islands of the Philippines. After providing air support to MacArthur—"the great blue blanket" that snuffed out Japanese aerial opposition—Admiral Nimitz was tasked to move first to the Bonin Islands, and then to the Ryukyus, to acquire additional bases for bombing Japan. The orders sounded innocuous, but they would eventually involve U.S. ground and air forces in some of the most bitter fighting of the war, while the navy provided air and naval gunfire support, along with the most magnificent logistics effort in the history of warfare.

Curiously, the Bonin Islands had been settled as an American territory in 1830, and Commodore Perry took formal possession of it in 1858. His actions were not sanctioned by the U.S. government, however, and Japan annexed the islands in 1861. In the lower tier of Bonins are three volcanic outcroppings called collectively the Volcano Islands; in the center of this group is an ugly veal-chop-shaped island named Iwo Jima. Small—four and one half miles long and two and one half miles wide—Iwo Jima had no redeeming features except its extraordinary suitability for use as a fighter base for the long-range P-51s coming to the Pacific theater, and as an emergency landing base for B-29s. In the months after its capture 2,400 landings were made by B-29s. Taking Iwo Jima also denied its use to Japan as an advance fighter base and a radar site for early warning of incoming raids.

Previous campaigns had demonstrated the value of fast carrier tasks forces smashing the airfields not only on the invasion sites, but well beyond the immediate theater of operations to prevent timely reinforcements. With the kamikaze threat, this became even more important. TF 58, now under Spruance's command, had grown to unprecedented size: eleven fleet carriers, five light carriers, eight fast battleships, the first battle cruiser built for the U.S. Navy, the *Alaska*, five heavy cruisers, nine light cruisers and seventy-seven destroyers, the latter almost twice the number remaining in the Japanese navy. The *Alaska* was actually a dead-end design, less heavily gunned and armored but no faster than modern U.S. battleships.

TF 58 struck the invasion sites and the Japanese homeland in a fast-moving series of attacks from February 16 to March 10, 1945. Japanese opposition was light and for the most part ineffective. These attacks, useful but not devastating, brought home to the Japanese people their relative military inferiority even more than the B-29 raids, the effects of which had so far been minimal. To have carrier planes raiding the homeland with impunity was a tremendous loss of face.

THE ATTACK ON IWO JIMA, FEBRUARY 19, 1945

The United States conducted its amphibious operations on an ever more sophisticated basis, and the 5th Amphibious Force performed almost flawlessly. The preparatory sea and aerial bombardment of Iwo Jima was followed by two days of carefully plotted naval surface gunfire, with battleships lying within two miles of the beach, pounding targets as they were discovered. This on-the-scene delivery of heavy shells was more effective than all the previous air and sea bombardment combined, for it was directed precisely as the Japanese batteries uncovered to shell the inbound

LCTs, and it protected the almost 900 vessels of specialized types that delivered 9,000 marines to the shore in the first wave.

Even so, the marines were met by a hail of fire from the island's defenders, under the able command of Lieutenant General Kuribayashi Tadamichi, who had 14,000 soldiers and 7,000 sailors at his disposal. Curiously enough, Iwo Jima had benefited from the U.S. submarine campaign and the earlier island defeats, for concrete, reinforcing rods, guns, ammunition and troops originally destined to reinforce the Marshalls and the Marianas remained on hand. The sixty-year old Kuribayashi, a former cavalryman, used his materials to defend the beaches with casemated artillery, concrete blockhouses and antiaircraft guns sited in deep dugouts that gave them a good field of fire upward while affording blast protection. He concentrated his main effort inland. Once again the ground was honeycombed with the trademark Japanese defenses of interconnected and mutually supporting tunnels, bunkers and pillboxes; they differed this time in their number—estimated to be more than 7,000—and in their depth, which rendered them almost impervious to anything but a direct hit in the entrance.

By nightfall, 30,000 marines and their heavy equipment were ashore, but at a cost of 2,000 casualties to Japanese machine-gun, mortar and artillery fire. The black sands of Iwo Jima did not permit foxholes to be dug; the sides caved in, filling in immediately behind the shovel. Once again the marines had to flush the Japanese soldiers from each tunnel and each pillbox with grenades and flamethrowers, not daring to advance a yard beyond until every defender had been killed.

On February 24 the U.S. flag was raised on Mount Suribachi, a moment made immortal by the Joe Rosenthal photographs and Felix de Weldon's sculpture at the Marine Corps Memorial in Arlington, Virginia, but the battle was far from over. Kuribayashi continued the hopeless fight until March 27, when he committed *seppuku;* he was posthumously promoted to full general. Of his 21,000-man garrison, only 2,500 prisoners were taken, most of them injured. The fanatic Japanese resistance had killed 6,766 marines and sailors and wounded another 23,000, the highest casualty rate in marine history, and a sobering forecast of what an invasion of the Japanese homeland might cost. There would be confirmation of that forecast on the next invasion.

The one possibility of avoiding that ultimate invasion of Japan seemed to lie in the new tactics used by Major General Curtis LeMay, who began sending his B-29s over Japan at night at low altitude, dropping a mixture of high-explosive and incendiary bombs that set one city after another aflame. Tokyo was first and the hardest hit; on the night of March 9–10, sixteen square miles were burned out, 267,171 buildings destroyed, 83,793 people killed and more than 160,000 injured. LeMay went on to systematically destroy city after city, but Japan fought on, actually inviting invasion in both its internal and external propaganda, while still hoping to delay it by a stand on Okinawa.

OPERATION ICEBERG: OKINAWA AND THE KAMIKAZE ONSLAUGHT

Okinawa, fifty-seven miles long and twelve miles wide at its broadest point, is some 350 miles southwest of Japan. The Ryukyus, of which it is part, had been annexed by Japan in 1879. Previously an independent kingdom, the Ryukyus' indigenous population was not assimilated but was instead exploited as cheap labor. With its harbors and with room for many airfields, Okinawa made a perfect staging point for the invasion of Japan. Recognizing this, the Japanese Imperial General Headquarters pumped troops, matériel and supplies into the island.

The commander, Lieutenant General Ushijima Mitsuru, had 67,000 regular army troops, along with 33,000 reservists, 9,000 sailors and 20,000 Okinawa home guardsmen. He also had an island population of almost 500,000 to call on for labor and support, although many of these were evacuated to Japan. Despite his lack of air defenses, Ushijima would conduct an incredibly tough defense, making the invasion of Okinawa the most costly endeavor in the Pacific war for the United States. The fanatic fighting on the ground was complemented by Operation Ten-Go, a massive kamikaze campaign headed by Vice Admiral Ugaki, who had been stockpiling aircraft for this operation.

TF 58 made additional forays against the Japanese mainland, and took the first of the long series of kamikaze hits when the carriers *Enterprise*, *Intrepid* and *Yorktown* were struck on March 18, suffering minor damage and relatively light casualties, with two killed on the *Intrepid* and five on the *Yorktown*. The next day, two bombs and a kamikaze aircraft hit the *Wasp*, causing major damage, killing 101 and wounding 269. But the worst was reserved for the *Franklin*, when two bombs caused fires in airplanes on both flight and hangar decks, resulting in a series of six explosions that virtually gutted the ship. Heroic damage-control efforts, made possible by the installation of the new fog-nozzle fire-fighting systems in the *Franklin* and the support from other ships, saved her. The *Franklin* got under way the next day and returned under her own power, though terribly battered and burned, all the way to New York for repair. The attack had killed 724 and wounded 265. She never again operated as a combat unit.

The preassault attacks on Okinawa began on March 23. The U.S. military leaders recognized how difficult taking Okinawa would be, and made a careful approach, securing the Kerama Retto Islands, fourteen miles west of Naha, on March 27 to serve as a base for subsequent operations. The decision to anchor ships so close to so many Japanese air bases was evidence of Allied confidence in their air power, aided now by additions from Great Britain. In the process, 350 fast Shinyo (Ocean-shaking) motor torpedo boats, packed with depth charges for suicide operations, were captured.

With the war in Europe grinding down, Great Britain was eager to assert its presence in the Pacific, and, over the objections of Fleet Admiral King (who saw logistics and command problems), created the British Pacific Fleet for operations against Japan. They fielded TF 57, a balanced force of two battleships, four fast carriers, five cruisers and fifteen destroyers. A small but adequate supply train kept the fleet in action; British carriers, although shorter-ranged, had the advantage of armored flight decks, which would stand them in good stead during subsequent kamikaze attacks.

The Dual Path Joins

Lieutenant General Simon Bolivar Buckner, Jr., commanded the ground forces, including the III Marine Amphibious Corps, three divisions under the redoubtable Major General Roy Geiger, and the XXIV Army Corps, four divisions under Major General John Hodge, a total of 172,000 troops. The landings began on Easter Sunday, April 1, 1945, with the heaviest naval bombardment yet made in the Pacific. The landings were almost unopposed, with 50,000 troops ashore by nightfall.

The Americans had assembled a fleet of 318 combatant ships and 1,390 auxiliaries and transports. Practice makes perfect, and Admiral Turner's amphibious operations went off flawlessly. Control officers in well-marked ships directed traffic, and lanes like a modern highway system were established for entry and exit. Once on the beaches and rolling inland, some confusion was encountered by the DUKWs and LVTs, but for the most part the abundance of supplies overcame any problems.

Ushijima hoped to lure the Americans inland, allowing them to take airfields quickly. He planned to have the kamikazes of Ugaki's Fifth Air Fleet in Kyushu destroy the American fleet with Operation Ten-Go, and then counterattack and wipe the invaders out.

Japanese resistance was concentrated in two areas. The enemy fought in the hills of the northern Motobu Peninsula until April 18. The main center of resistance was in the south, in the hills and valleys northeast of Naha. There Ushijima fought the dogged battle that characterized Japanese defensive efforts, even though by then he personally had little hope for relief by kamikaze operations, whatever their scale.

The Dinosaur's Death Ride

The *Yamato* was sent on Operation Ten-Ichi (Heaven Number One) as a matter of pride for the Imperial Japanese Navy. Spurred by an inquiry from Emperor Hirohito as to the role the giant battleship would play in the defense of Okinawa, the navy elected to sacrifice the *Yamato* rather than be accused of a failure to make sacrifices comparable to the army's. Everyone from Admiral Toyoda down realized that the 350-mile sortie from Kyushu to Okinawa without air cover was suicide, and that it could achieve nothing. *Yamato*'s Surface Special Attack Force consisted of the light cruiser *Yahagi* and eight destroyers, supplied with only enough fuel for a one-way trip. In contrast to the usual complex instructions, orders to the commander of the Second Fleet, Vice Admiral Ito Seiichi, consisted of only five pages of generalities—a sign that the mission was written off before it began. The *Yamato* was ordered to do as much damage as possible to the invasion fleet, then beach herself. Her 18.1-inch guns were to serve as artillery while her crew joined the fighting on land.

At 2000 on April 6 the huge ship sailed through the Bungo Suido entrance to the Inland Sea and was sighted minutes later by the USS *Threadfin* under Lieutenant Commander John Foote and *Hackleback* under Lieutenant Commander Frederick E. Janney. Vice Admiral Mitscher was notified, and he positioned TGs 58.1, 58.3 and 58.4 to pounce on *Yamato*, sending search aircraft off at first light. Almost all Japanese air support had been allocated to the scheduled kamikaze attacks, and the Surface Special Task Force had no air cover. At 0823 on April 7, a vigilant Grumman F6F Hellcat pilot from the *Essex* spotted the Japanese force and, via the air-to-air signal system Mitscher had devised, passed its location back 240 miles to Admiral Spruance, whose flag was on the cruiser *Indianapolis*. Spruance warned Rear Admiral Morton L. Deyo, commanding TF 54, the bombardment group of battleships and cruisers, that Ito's force was en route. Deyo gave orders so that his fleet would interpose between the transports and the *Yamato*—but the latter was never to arrive.

Although not absolutely certain of the location of the Japanese fleet, at 1000 Mitscher ordered the launch. Planes began to lift off from TG 58.1's *Belleau Wood*, *Bennington*, *Hornet* and *San Jacinto*, followed by TG 58.3's *Bataan*, *Bunker Hill* (in which Mitscher flew his flag), *Cabot*, *Essex* and *Hancock*. The first wave of 280 American planes included fifty Helldivers, ninety-eight Avengers and 132 Hellcats, the last armed with 500-pound bombs. Three more waves of aircraft followed; fifty-three planes from the *Hancock* got lost and never entered the battle. TG 58.4, with the *Intrepid*, the *Langley* and the *Yorktown* launched another 106 aircraft at 1045.

The first wave burst out of a low overcast to surround Ito's force. By 1232, the *Yamato* was already reeling from a torpedo that damaged her steering gear and from two bomb hits, even as the *Yahagi* was put out of action and a destroyer was sunk. The Japanese antiaircraft fire, dense but inaccurate, included the San Shiki shells from the *Yamato*'s 18.1-inch guns, fused to detonate at 1,000 yards. Nothing deterred the attackers, and the big battleship was hit by at least seven more torpedoes and many bombs. The Americans had learned from the attack on the *Musashi* to concentrate as many torpedoes as possible on one side to eliminate counterflooding and to make the ship list as much as possible. By 1300 *Yamato* was listing to port with many of her antiaircraft guns out of action; the list steadily increased to 20 degrees. At 1410, a torpedo exploded in the stern, jamming the rudder hard left and sending the battleship in a circle at 8 knots. At 1423 the red bottom of the *Yamato* appeared as she turned turtle, the sailors scrambling for a moment's safety before she exploded in a premonitory mushroom cloud and sank beneath the waves with 2,488 officers and men. The Americans also sank the *Yahagi* and four destroyers, at a cost of ten aircraft and twelve crewmen.

KIKUSUI ATTACKS

Operation Ten-Go called for *Kikusui* tactics, which involved both mass kamikaze attacks and individual suicide sorties. The Americans established fighter-director teams on the radar picket screen of destroyers and small craft placed as far as ninety-five miles and as close as forty miles from Okinawa. Task Force 58 was positioned to the north to defend against attacks from the home islands, while Task Force 57 of the Royal Navy's Pacific Fleet operated to the south warding off attacks from Formosa. The armored decks of the carriers *Indefatigable, Illustrious, Indomitable* and *Victorious* proved invulnerable to the kamikazes.

The kamikaze pilots tended to concentrate on the picket ships, of which more than twenty were sunk. Hundreds of sailors were killed. On April 6, 1945, the Japanese launched the first full-scale *Kikusui* with 355 suicide planes among 700 attackers. More than 250 of these were slaughtered before they passed the radar picket screen; fifty-five were shot down before they reached Okinawa, with another 171 falling in the course of the abortive attack. Within an hour, 476 Japanese planes had been destroyed, 68 percent of the attacking force. But 180 of the suicide planes—51 percent of their total strength—broke through to attack, sinking the destroyer *Emmons*, two ammunition-laden merchant ships and an LST, and scoring hits on the British carrier *Illustrious* and six destroyers. Casualties were high—466 killed and 568 wounded, and morale was sharply shaken by the seeming inability to deter the enemy attack.

The second *Kikusui* consisted of 194 suicide planes accompanied by forty-five Jill torpedo-bombers, thirty Val dive-bombers and 150 fighters. These struck on the afternoon of April 8. Nine of the suicide planes were Yokosuka Okha (Cherry Blossom), the rocket-powered human bomb carried by twin-engine Betty bombers. One of the Okhas sank the destroyer *Mannert L. Abele,* already damaged by a crashing Zero.

Eight more *Kikusui* missions raised the total of 6,300 sorties and 3,000 kamikaze attacks in which twenty-one ships were sunk, forty-three badly damaged and twenty-three forced out of action for more than a month. The U.S. Navy lost 4,907 officers and men killed and 4,824 wounded, more casualties than it had suffered in all its previous wars combined. The losses would have been greater except for simple physics: most of the Japanese aircraft, even when laden with a 500-pound bomb, lacked the mass required to cause fatal damage to a larger warship. Only the tiny seventeen-foot wingspan Okha, carrying a 2,646-pound warhead and reaching a terminal diving speed of 576 miles per hour, had the penetrating power that conventional kamikazes lacked.

Okinawa was finally secured on June 22, 1945, after eleven weeks of the most intense fighting of the Pacific war. More than 135,000 Japanese soldiers had been killed, along with 75,000 civilians. American land battle casualties were 7,374 dead and 31,807 wounded. The American field commander, General Buckner, was killed on June 18 by debris from an artillery shell. On June 22, Lieutenant General Ushijima committed ritual suicide and was given the coup de grâce by his aides.

The surrender on Okinawa was the penultimate step in the Emperor's journey to reality, adding to his dismay at the loss of the *Yamato* and the elimination of the Imperial Japanese Navy. Hirohito had vastly enjoyed the great victories of both Japan and Germany. He supported Tojo to the very end, advocating the concealment of losses from his people. It would take years of unmitigated defeat, the destruction of his merchant marine fleet, a catastrophic bombing campaign and two atomic bombs to move him at last to agree to surrender.

13.

THE DEPTH AND BREADTH OF A LONG WAR

SUBMARINE WARFARE IN THE PACIFIC

During Grand Admiral Karl Doenitz's trial at Nuremburg his defense lawyers solicited and received a deposition from Fleet Admiral Nimitz to the effect that the United States had practiced unrestricted naval and air warfare against Japan from December 7, 1941, to the end of the war. "Unrestricted" was a modest term; the American assault on the Japanese was savagely aggressive and achieved unprecedented success, being far more effective than the German efforts and completely overshadowing the inadequate Japanese submarine campaign.

Before the war the submarine warfare doctrines of both the United States and Japan had been almost identical: the submarine was to operate as an adjunct to the fleet and reduce the enemy's effectiveness by attrition. Both navies developed submarines of generally similar size and appearance, but with capabilities tailored to missions of different type and duration. There were many specialized types, but a typical Japanese scouting submarine like the famed *I-19*, victor over the *Wasp*, had a 3,654-ton submerged displacement and was 356.5 feet long and 30.5 feet in beam. Two diesels of 12,400 total horsepower provided a surface speed of 23.5 knots, while 2,000-

horsepower electric motors gave an 8-knot submerged speed. The densely packed ship was crewed by ninety-four officers and men, and carried seventeen torpedoes. The *I-19* could cruise for 14,000 miles at 16 knots, and submerge safely to a depth of 330 feet.

The *I-19*'s contemporary and rough equivalent, one of the *Gato* class of U.S. fleet submarines, had a submerged displacement of 2,424 tons, and was 311 feet long and twenty-seven feet wide. Diesel engines of 5,400 horsepower provided a top surface speed of 20 knots, and the 2,740 horsepower electric motors gave a submerged speed of 8.75 knots. A crew of eighty to eighty-five, including up to eight officers, lived closely together in a hull that was rated to dive safely to 300 feet, but was capable of greater depths in an emergency. Armament consisted of twenty-four torpedoes, to be fired from either the six forward or four aft tubes. The American submarine was better outfitted for crew comfort than its Japanese counterpart. (After the war, submariners of all nations generally agreed that the German U-boat was the best in the world in terms of equipment—*except for torpedoes*—and performance.)

At the beginning of the war, the principal difference in capability was the vastly superior performance and reliability of Japanese torpedoes. U.S. torpedoes were not substantially improved until the spring of 1943. The initial Japanese advantage was soon eroded, however, as the American submarines had the benefit of much better communications and sonar equipment, and even more importantly, were outfitted with radar relatively early in the war. Japanese submarines began to receive radar equipment in June 1944, but Japanese radar never approached the high American standards of quality and performance.

Japan began the war with sixty-four submarines, and built 126 more, for a total of 190; when the war ended, 130 had been sunk and only thirty-two were operational. (This does not include the many human torpedoes and midget submarines that were built at such great cost and to such little purpose.)

America began the war with 111 submarines, and built another 177 for a total of 288. Fifty-two submarines were lost (forty-five to enemy action)—18 percent of the force, a very high ratio for American combat units, and indicative of the dangers involved. Although built in several classes, the fleet submarine was highly standardized, even as successive improvements were conferred upon the fleet as the technology developed.

Japanese Strategy and Personalities

Japan's had to be the largest and best prewar submarine fleet in the Pacific. Unfortunately for the Japanese, the leadership of the Sixth Submarine Fleet changed rapidly, with no fewer than eight commanders serving between February 1, 1941, and the end of the war. The changes reflected the rapidly changing war situation, which in turn influenced Japanese strategy. Until April 1942, the primary emphasis was on attacking warships. From then until November 1942, the focus was attacks on merchant shipping, an effort firmly countered by American antisubmarine tactics. Japanese attacks on the merchant shipping that streamed in endless lines from the West Coast throughout the Pacific were so lackluster that the American navy shifted the emphasis of its antisubmarine-warfare ships from the defensive to the offensive.

After November 1942, the Japanese leadership lost sight of the whole point of undersea warfare and used their submarines primarily as freighters in *mogura* (mule) supply operations to isolated Japanese island garrisons. Scarce resources were expended upon submersible freight carriers like the Unkato, a 136-foot-long cylinder that could carry 337 tons of cargo, but was difficult to manage under tow, or the Unpoto, a platform carrying artillery, powered by torpedo propulsion units for sub-to-shore transfer. The endemic army-navy feud reached a height of absurdity when the army secretly began building its own submarines, eschewing all help or information from the navy. About twenty-eight relatively small army cargo submarines were built, but little is known of their wartime activities.

The resupply effort continued to the end of the war. From November 1944 on, Japanese offensive efforts were concentrated on the use of suicide weapons, including the Kaiten, one-man human torpedoes, and a variety of small midget submarines. The two-man submarines were not originally intended as suicide craft, even though few crew members survived an operational mission. Carried on submarines and powered only by electric motors, they displaced forty-six tons submerged, were 78.5 feet long and six feet wide. Capable of the high speed of 24 knots submerged, they were equipped with two torpedo tubes that were externally loaded, like an old-fashioned muzzle-loading cannon. The most famous Japanese midget submarine was sunk by the destroyer *Ward* outside Pearl Harbor, the first of five to be lost in that attack. Eighteen more were lost in other attacks.

The Kaiten was developed by two survivors of midget submarine operations, Lieutenant (junior grade) Kuroki Hiroski and Ensign Nishina Sekio. Both men lost their lives with the desperation weapon, Kuroki, like so many others, in training, and Nishina on the first mission. The Kaiten pilots were trained and honored like their airborne kamikaze equivalents, but were to prove far less effective in battle.

The Kaiten was intended as a suicide weapon from the start of its development in late 1942, even though the Japanese Naval General Staff insisted that provision be made for the pilot to escape. It was rushed into high-volume production after the Battle of the Philippine Sea. Essentially a Type 93 torpedo modified with a center section for the pilot, periscope and controls, the Kaiten displaced eighteen tons submerged, was 48.3 feet long and had a slender 3.25-foot diameter. It carried a 3,400-pound warhead, and could attack at 20 knots from a distance of twenty-seven miles. Early Kaitens required the submarine to surface to allow its pilot to enter; later models could be boarded through a lower hatch while the mother ship remained submerged. A total of nine major Kaiten attacks were made, resulting in the sinking of a tanker and a destroyer, but costing almost all the Kaitens and eight of the mother ships that carried them into battle. When the war ended, there were 100 Kaitens and 400 midget submarines available in Japan to attack the Allied invasion fleet. The navy persisted in the program despite its failures, primarily because of the almost childlike claims made for its success; on the basis of the sound of the Kaitens blowing up, without any visual or other reference, the I-boat commanders made grossly inaccurate estimates of the damage they had done. These fantasy games averaged a ship per Kaiten, and not just any ship either, but aircraft carriers and battleships. It is difficult to explain this degree of self-delusion except in the context of an offensive-minded service that had never lost a war and could not believe it was losing this one. The Kaitens were sent: therefore, they must have been successful. Not even the toadies in Hitler's bunker were so blind to the truth.

The officers and men manning the submarines were the elite of the Japanese navy; almost all the officers were graduates of the Naval Academy, while the enlisted were, as the nature of submarines demands, specialists. Discipline was extremely hard, as it was everywhere in the Japanese armed services, but the inevitable propinquity of submarine life resulted in better relations between officers and men than existed elsewhere.

It is thus all the more extraordinary that alone among all the Japanese armed services, the officers commanding Japanese submarines were evaluated after the war by both the Allies and the Japanese as having been nonaggressive and ineffective. The officers were inhibited by too detailed orders and by an absolute adherence to radio silence, even when communications were vital. The degree to which this was carried out was epitomized by the epic of the destroyer escort *England*, which sank six Japanese submarines in twelve days, beginning May 19, 1944. The victory went far beyond just killing the submarines, for it completely wiped out Admiral Toyoda's scouting line, his trip wire for the Battle of the Philippine Sea. When at last aware of the elimination of his six submarines, Toyoda assumed that they must have encountered an enormous force of Americans intent on invading Palau. He sent seventy aircraft from Guam to Palau—just when they were needed on Guam.

The *England* was a *Buckley*-class destroyer escort captained by Lieutenant Commander Walton B. Pendleton, and commissioned on December 10, 1943. She displaced 1,400 tons, and was 306 feet long and had a thirty-seven-foot beam. A turboelectric drive of 12,000-shaft horsepower provided a 26-knot top speed. The *England* was armed with three 3-inch guns, a three-tube 21-inch torpedo mount and two 40mm and six 20mm antiaircraft gun mounts. She carried effective radar, excellent sonar, Hedgehog projectors and depth charges, but more importantly, her crew had been well trained.

The *England* was working in concert with the destroyer escorts *Raby* and *George* on a mission that made naval history. Her first kill was a supply boat, the *I-16*, carrying rice to Buin; five Hedgehog runs resulted in hits at 1433 on May 19. The *England* then began rolling up Toyoda's picket line. At 0444 on the morning of May 22, she put a Hedgehog salvo on the *RO-106*, which exploded and sank. (The RO submarines were of medium size, just under 200 feet long and twenty feet wide and displacing 782 tons submerged. Intended for coast defense operations, they had a cruising range of 3,500 miles and a speed of only 14.5 knots on the surface. Japanese submariners liked them, for they were more maneuverable than the larger I-boats.)

A day later, at 0834, at least a dozen Hedgehogs ripped open the *RO-104*. The *RO-116* went down early in the morning of May 24, a victim of the *England*'s first firing run. Because of the strict radio silence imposed on the Japanese, there was no hint of the carnage being dispensed by the *England*; the fifth submarine in the scouting line, *RO-108*, waited haplessly until 2315 on May 26, when the Hedgehog worked its final magic.

The *England* had help with the last submarine, the *RO-105*; joined by the *George, Raby, Hazelwood* and *Spangler,* the attack began at 0144 on May 30. It was not until 0735 that the *England*'s salvo of Hedgehogs blew the *RO-105* up—the sixth kill, setting a record that will probably never be surpassed. (The sixth submarine in Toyoda's line, the *RO-117,* was sighted south of Truk and sunk by a PBY Catalina.)

The *England* was awarded a Presidential Unit Citation. On May 9, 1944, at Okinawa and under a new skipper, she took a kamikaze hit and had to be towed to port. She later steamed home, to be broken up for scrap; she should have been made into a memorial.

Unlike the destroyers with their slashing night attacks, or the cruisers with their unrivaled torpedo tactics, or the battleships with their accurate gunfire, or the aircraft carriers with their aggressive bombers and torpedo planes, there was no area where the Japanese submarine force excelled at any time of the war. Its strategy was confused, its tactics poor and there was virtually no research and development except for the futile suicide projects. As a result, Japanese submarine successes were very limited, and had virtually no impact on the war, despite victories over the aircraft carriers *Yorktown* and *Wasp* and the escort carrier *Liscome Bay*, and, in the last days of the war, the cruiser *Indianapolis*.

The July 30, 1945, attack on the *Indianapolis* by *I-58* (which was carrying Kaitens at the time) was doubly dramatic, for it caught the ship just after she had delivered the elements of the atomic bomb to Tinian. The *Indianapolis* was unescorted and not zigzagging; Lieutenant Commander Hashimoto Mochitsura put two Long Lance torpedoes into the ship, which went down in fifteen minutes. No radio call for assistance had been made, and no one on shore noticed the ship's failure to arrive at her scheduled destination. Only 316 crewmen survived the four days they were adrift at sea; 880 died. At the postwar court-martial, the cruiser's skipper, Captain Charles B. McVay, was convicted of "Negligence in Suffering a Vessel of the Navy to be Hazarded." Hashimoto was a witness for the prosecution.

Despite the occasional success, the overall performance of the Japanese submarine force was a blot on a proud nation's naval escutcheon; submarines could have made a decisive difference in the battles of the Coral Sea, Midway and the Philippine Sea. They failed dramatically in each instance, and ultimately their failure can be attributed to a rare condition in Japanese military history: a lack of aggressiveness on the part of its fighting men.

American Strategy and Personalities

Pearl Harbor altered American strategy; there could be no fleet battle until the U.S. fleet was reconstituted. The American submarines were unleashed upon the Japanese merchant marine like wolves upon not-too-bright sheep, for the enemy antisubmarine-warfare techniques were bad to begin with and improved only slightly in the course of the disastrous war.

The seeds of the American victory lay in the Two-Ocean Navy so energetically advocated by President Roosevelt in 1940, which provided the ships, equipment, personnel and training that were the essential elements of the later success. Admiral King deserves a full measure of credit for his diligent defense of the Pacific theater at a time when the war effort's primary focus was on Europe, and for his willingness to delegate both authority and responsibility to Admiral Nimitz and his subordinate commanders. Nimitz, a pioneer submariner himself, aided the submarine campaign by providing the necessary resources and placing it in the capable hands of his friend and colleague "Uncle Charlie," Vice Admiral Charles A. Lockwood, who as COMSUBPAC (Commander Submarines Pacific Fleet), was as influential in the American submarine fleet as Doenitz was in the German.

A 1912 Naval Academy graduate, Lockwood's first command was the *A-2*, the fourth submarine to be owned by the U.S. Navy. He spent a lifetime in submarines, and, as part of the "boat culture," he knew firsthand the hazards, the comradeship and the potential. He was respected by his subordinates for being one of them, and admired for the way he took on not only the Japanese, but what at times seemed a tougher opponent, the American naval bureaucracy. It was Lockwood who forced a recalcitrant Bureau of Ordnance to acknowledge that the torpedoes that they had foisted upon the navy with almost no testing had four major deficiencies. His pragmatic "fire-them-into-the-net" tests proved that the torpedoes (which the navy considered so valuable that virtually no practice live firings were allowed) ran not only too deep but also erratically in both horizontal and vertical planes. The top secret magnetic exploder design had been based on Rhode Island's local magnetic fields, and malfunctioned in the magnetic environment near Japan. Finally, the backup contact-exploder mechanism was so delicate that anything but a perfect 90-degree hit caused a failure.

The Bureau of Ordnance insisted that Lockwood's tests were "unscientific," and refused to allow the required changes to be made. Lockwood put his career at risk (a far braver act for most officers than going into combat with the enemy) by going over the heads of the bureau chiefs directly to Nimitz, and convincing him to allow the necessary modifications to be made in the field.

Lockwood was also beloved for the way he took care of his crews, acquiring the best facilities in Hawaii, including the pink Royal Hawaiian Hotel for rest and recreation. In return, his submariners pushed the war ever closer to Japan, until in the final days they sailed openly on the surface, pugnaciously trying to lure Japanese destroyers out for a fight.

After the initial stumbling efforts around the Philippines, where a combination of too cautious skippers and defective torpedoes failed to achieve results, the U.S. submarine effort grew ever more successful, improving with each passing month. The American headquarters setup was not ideal, with the three separate submarine commands (Pacific, Southwest Pacific and Atlantic) functioning virtually autonomously. But the supply of submarines was adequate, the new crop of skippers were fighters and the torpedo problem was eventually solved.

The submarines operated in squadrons composed of two divisions of six subs each, and were assigned either to submarine tenders, virtual floating cities, or to land bases. After a patrol, leave was granted, and then several days were spent in training and loading stores; after five patrols, the sub was sent back to the United States for overhaul.

The results of the American efforts are revealed in the statistics. Japan began the war with about six million tons of "steel" shipping, i.e. ships made of steel and a displacement of over 500 tons. There were in addition many smaller steel vessels and thousands of tiny wooden craft. Japan's civilian economy required about three million tons annually to maintain itself, but with the outbreak of the war, this was arbitrarily reduced to 1.9 million tons.

Japan gained about 800,000 tons through capture and seizure after the start of the war, and during its course, built another 3.2 million tons, reaching a creditable peak of 1.7 million in 1944. It thus had at its disposal in the course of the war more than 10 million tons.

During the war, the Japanese lost 2,259 merchant ships of 8.1 million tons to all causes; a further 275 ships of 755,802 tons were disabled. This almost 90 percent destruction of its merchant fleet caused Japan's imports, which were over 22 million tons in 1940, to decline to a starvation level of 2.7 million in 1945.

American submarines, which accounted for a small proportion of the U.S. Navy's total strength, sank an astounding 59.7 percent of Japanese merchant shipping. Almost 15,000 torpedoes were expended to sink 1,150 ships of a total of nearly 4.9 million tons. Aircraft (army, navy land-based and navy carrier-based) sank 750 ships of 2.5 million tons; mines accounted for 210 ships of 397,412 tons; while the remainder were lost to surface gunfire, marine hazards and unknown causes.

Submarines also sank 214 Japanese naval vessels of all sizes, aggregating 577,626 tons. By the end of 1944, valuable targets became scarce, and the submarines attacked and sank thousands of barges, sampans, small steel ships and fishing vessels, cruising on the surface and picking them off like ducks in a shooting gallery. Although not a gallant way to wage war, it was essential, for the small boats were Japan's pathetic life-support system, barely sustaining her dying gasps. Even these numbers do not reflect the true picture, for the once efficient Japanese repair facilities were ravaged, and many ships still afloat in port were out of commission because of a lack of repairs and the fuel shortage. The Japanese merchant marine suffered 143,000 casualties, including 27,000 killed.

The success of the American submarine force stands in stark contrast to the failure of the Japanese effort; these results were irrevocably influenced by the two nation's respective antisubmarine technologies. As the destroyer escort *England* and her cohorts had demonstrated, and as the Japanese admirals ruefully acknowledged even during the war, the American antisubmarine effort was superb. A profusion of well-equipped ships, manned by eager, aggressive crews, suppressed the enemy submarines. Japan, whose island empire was extremely vulnerable to submarine attack, had made only perfunctory efforts toward developing an antisubmarine-warfare capability. Since such measures were essentially defensive in nature, they were, as such, disparaged by the same warrior mentality that failed to supply armor and self-sealing tanks for their airplanes. But even after the full measure of the American threat became known, little was done. Japanese antisubmarine weapons remained primitive, with inefficient depth charges, inferior sonar and radar and far too few ships devoted to the task.

Individual American Exploits

There are literally hundreds of brilliant examples of American submarine warfare, and, after the war, veterans of the "Silent Service" produced a score of excellent books on their experiences. We can touch on just a few highlights here.

The USS *Tautog*, sailing from 1942 to 1945 under three skippers, sank the most Japanese ships, twenty-six, for 72,606 total tons; these included two submarines and a destroyer. The USS *Flasher* sank the most tonnage, 100,231, sinking twenty-one vessels in just thirteen months, beginning in January 1944. Lieutenant Commander Reuben I. Whitaker earned seventeen of these kills, including the light cruiser *Oi* and two destroyers.

As the Japanese defensive perimeter shrank, the American submarines patrolled ever closer to the home islands, and Japanese convoys began to grow in size and the number of escorts. Each U.S. island conquest severed an oceanic route, and ultimately the Japanese were reduced to hugging the coastline along the mainland of China and Korea. As the supply routes were collapsing in 1944, the United States torqued up its efforts with wolf pack operations.

Operating in groups of two or three, their commanders often bestowed upon themselves a colorful pack name like "Moseley's Maulers," "Blair's Blasters," "Underwood's Urchins" or "Earl's Eliminators." They took the war into the South China Sea and then into the Inland Sea itself, using raw courage and modern detection equipment to thread their way through the extensive minefields, some of which extended from Formosa to Kyushu.

It was in the dangerous waters of the East China Sea that the *Sealion II*, on her third war patrol and commanded by Commander Eli T. Reich, stalked the veteran battleship *Kongo*. Just after midnight on November 21, 1944, the *Sealion* picked up a task force of two battleships (the *Yamato*, carrying Admiral Ugaki, just relieved of his battleship command, and the *Kongo*) and two cruisers, the *Nagato* and *Yahagi*. Escorted by three destroyers, they were returning somewhat hangdog—and, in Ugaki's case, hungover—from their shellacking in the Battle of Leyte Gulf. At 0256, cruising cockily on the surface in the face of dozens of huge guns, including the *Yamato*'s 18.1-inchers, Reich made naval history by pulling a double. He fired his six bow torpedoes at one battleship, then did a hard right turn to fire three torpedoes from his stern tubes at the second. He heard three distinct hits as he raced away to put a five-mile distance between *Sealion* and his quarry. Reich kept the enemy under surveillance while he reloaded and the Japanese ships steamed on, apparently undamaged.

The task force soon separated; the *Kongo* had taken two hits. Although listing 15 degrees to port, she continued to make 16 knots. The destroyers *Isokaze* and *Hamakaze* were detached to escort her. As Reich prepared his second attack, still on the surface, the *Kongo* suddenly exploded and sank, the only Japanese battleship to be sunk by a submarine in the war. After the war, it was learned that Reich's stern-tube attack had blown up the 2,490-ton destroyer *Urakaze*. It was a remarkable achievement: a battleship and a destroyer in one brilliant strike. In her career, the *Sealion II* sank a total of eleven vessels for 68,297 tons.

Even the largest Japanese ships, already vulnerable to air attack, could not elude the submarines. The *Archerfish* ranked twenty-fifth in total tonnage sunk, with 59,800 tons, and achieved this by sinking only two ships, the 800-ton Coast Defense Vessel *#24* and the 59,000-ton aircraft carrier *Shinano*.

Commander Joseph F. Enright, skipper of the *Archerfish*, on its fifth patrol, was cruising about 150 miles south of Tokyo. At 2048 on November 28, 1944, radar contact was made with what seemed to be a large target. Within an hour, it had been identified as a carrier, zigzagging at 20 knots and escorted by four ships. The *Archerfish* was one knot slower on the surface than the carrier's speed, but the zigzagging allowed him to keep up. Enright sent out contact reports, but at 0300 the *Shinano* altered course to the southwest, closing the distance with *Archerfish*. Had she maintained a straight-line course she would have escaped.

The *Shinano* had started life as a *Yamato*-class battleship, and was converted during construction to an aircraft carrier after the losses at Midway. She was the largest carrier in the world when she was commissioned on November 18, 1944. She had an armored flight deck 840 feet long and 131 feet wide, and an interior so cavernous that besides carrying her own complement of fifty aircraft, she was intended to serve as a replenishment and support ship for smaller carriers. When caught by the *Archerfish*, she was en route to Kure for final outfitting; her watertight doors and damage-control pumps had not yet been installed.

At 0317 *Archerfish* sent a lethal spread of six Mark 14 torpedoes at the target; all six hit, smashing the gigantic ship from the propellers to the bow. Incredibly, despite a green crew and the lack of damage-control equipment, the *Shinano*'s captain, Abe Toshio, did not reduce speed, but plowed ahead for seven hours, scooping in water all the time. At 1048, just 160 miles southeast of Cape Muroto, the ten-day-old vessel, the largest and youngest ever to be sunk by a submarine, rolled over and sank, taking 500 men, including Abe, with her. The loss was so mortifying that it was kept secret even from officers as senior as Vice Admiral Ugaki.

In January 1945, the *Barb*, under Commander Eugene B. Fluckey, earned a Presidential Unit Citation for her solo attack on a convoy of thirty Japanese ships; Fluckey was awarded the Medal of Honor. The *Barb* later bombarded the Japanese coast with gunfire and rockets, and on July 17, 1945, nine of her crewmen invaded Japan proper near Otasamu on the east coast of Karafuto. They blew up a rail line and a train, indicating the lengths the American submariners would go to vent their aggressive tendencies. The *Barb* ranked third in the tonnage of ships sunk, with a score of 96,628 tons; she ranked twelfth in total ships, with seventeen.

The veteran aircraft carrier *Junyo*, converted from the 27,500-ton liner *Kashiwara Maru*, had survived the bitter battles of the Santa Cruz Islands and Philippine Sea. On December 9, 1944, she fell prey to torpedoes from the *Redfish*, under Commander Louis "Sandy" McGregor, and the *Sea Devil*, under Commander Ralph Emerson Styles. The *Junyo* didn't sink, but never returned to service, and was broken up for scrap in 1947. Ten days later the *Redfish* was cruising in the East China Sea when a target appeared on the horizon. Ignoring depth charges being dropped by an aircraft (Japanese depth charges had only 200 or 300 pounds of explosives, and usually were not dropped in systematic patterns), McGregor saw the new 18,500-ton carrier *Unryu* obligingly turn toward his submarine. At 1620, he fired four torpedoes, one striking the carrier's bow. The *Unryu* stopped and almost immediately began listing 20 degrees to starboard. A covey of enemy destroyers surrounded the *Redfish* but American submarines were more and more disposed to duel with surface craft, and McGregor fought back with a four-torpedo spread, then circled as his men reloaded. A second torpedo blew up the *Unryu;* it slid under the sea at 1659. The destroyers' depth charges damaged the *Redfish*, but McGregor parked his boat on the sea floor for two hours before surfacing and returning to Pearl Harbor.

The navy's history is replete with similar tales of heroism and achievement; sadly, less is known about the tragic last moments of most of the fifty-two submarines that were lost. In many instances, the boats simply disappeared and were never heard from again; in a few cases, there were survivors. Of the 16,000 men who went on patrol, 3,506 were killed—22 percent! It was the highest casualty rate of all the services.

Other Duties as Assigned for U.S. Submarines

While the U.S. Navy tended to keep focused on the decimation of the Japanese fleet, it also sent its submarines on hundreds of special missions from the very first days of the war, when ammunition and supplies were carried to Corregidor and gold and pilots carried away, down to the very last days, when special agents were landed and minefields probed in anticipation of the invasion of Japan.

Submarines returned to the Philippines frequently, bringing in ammunition and stores to support the guerrilla movement, to take off civilians who were being hunted by the Japanese, and later, to remove liberated prisoners of war. The Japanese occupation was harsh (an estimated three million Filipinos died under their rule, most from starvation) and even the relatively small amounts of supplies that the submarines could bring in were precious.

The *Nautilus* ran special missions to Attu, Dutch Harbor, the Gilberts and practically commuted to the Philippines. Her sister ship, the *Narwhal*, was similarly involved; between them the two ships also sank thirteen Japanese vessels.

As the submarine force built up, and as the occasional rescue occurred, a formal system to station submarines so that they could pick up downed airmen was put into operation during the campaign in the Gilberts in November 1943. The B-29 campaign was accelerating even as Japanese shipping became harder to find, so more and more submarines were allocated to lifeguard duties, at least four submarines per mission. The first B-29 rescue occurred on December 19, 1944, when the *Spearfish*, under Lieutenant Commander Cyrus C. Cole, rescued seven men near the Bonin Islands.

In 1943, submarines had spent sixty-four days on rescue station, and picked up seven aviators; in 1944 the totals were 469 days and 117 rescues, while in 1945 they were 2,739 and 380, respectively. A total of 504 airmen was saved by submariners.

One of the most famous and aggressive submarine skippers Commander Richard H. O'Kane, in the *Tang*, also made many successful rescues. Under O'Kane, the *Tang* sank twenty-four vessels for a total of 93,824 tons, and also rescued twenty-two airmen on a single patrol, going in under the guns of Japanese shore batteries on Truk to do so. Thirty-five airmen had been shot down in carrier strikes on the island, some of them landing in the atoll, and thus impossible to rescue. Whenever possible, the *Tang* remained surfaced, popping at enemy gunners with her small-caliber deck guns. U.S. Navy fighters suppressed the enemy fire with strafing attacks, and from this rescue the Submarine Combat Air Patrol was developed, in which fighters actively cooperated with the submarines in their rescue attempts. (Glad as aviators were to be rescued, most were distressed by the claustrophobic conditions aboard the rescue submarines, and none enjoyed depth-charge attacks and the other routine events in the submariners' lives.)

O'Kane, unquestionably the ace American submariner, was on the *Argonaut* at Pearl Harbor on December 7, 1941. He made five war patrols in the *Wahoo* as executive officer, and then took over the *Tang*. On her fifth patrol, during which she had sunk seven vessels between October 10 and October 25, O'Kane was making another surface attack on a transport when one of his own torpedoes circled around and smashed into the *Tang*'s stern. He and eight others were thrown into the ocean; four survived the night to be picked up by the Japanese. O'Kane was among them, and endured the interminable series of beatings meted out to them. O'Kane survived as a prisoner of war, and when released was awarded the Medal of Honor to go with his five Legion of Merits, three Silver Stars, three Navy Crosses and numerous other decorations.

MINE WARFARE

The submarines of all navies were often called upon to lay mines, and these, differing only in technology from those used in the Civil War, proved to be surprisingly effective in all the oceans of the world.

The mine antedated the rifled cannon, submarine, aircraft and armored ship by centuries. Although they received little publicity during World War II, mines sank more than 200 surface warships and thousands of merchant vessels. The 550,000 mines sown during the course of World War II were inexpensive weapons that gave a good economic return in terms of the damage they caused. Mines did not receive greater use because the United States and Great Britain were offensive-minded naval powers who regarded them as a passive, defensive weapon. The Germans, who led in mine technology, did not use their most advanced mines in the quantities that they might have because they feared the secret of their operation would be discovered and used against them. The Japanese, despite their attack mentality, used mines almost solely for defensive purposes, and then not with good results—four Japanese ships were lost to their own mines in the first months of the war.

World War I mines were largely the contact type; a ship had to physically hit one—or in the case of the mines invented by an American, strike a wire attached to the mine and suspended from a float. By 1918, Germany, England and the United States had all developed concepts for the magnetic mine. It was introduced in combat by the Germans in World War II, but its success was muted because they had so few on hand; they were able to lay less than 500 in the first four months of the war. The British recovered an example from the mudflats off Shoeburyness, and were able to devise countermeasures, including degaussing ships, i.e. passing a current through massive coils of wire placed around a ship's hull to alter or neutralize its natural magnetic field. Nonetheless, German aerial minelaying in the Thames Estuary in November 1939 threatened to close the port of London. In that one month, mines sank twenty-seven merchant ships of 120,958 tons; a destroyer was sunk, and a cruiser and many other ships damaged. The Germans laid only 318 mines off the U.S. seaboard during the war; only ten merchant ships were sunk or damaged, but an inordinate expenditure was made on minesweeping equipment.

Moored mines were relatively easy to sweep; ground mines, which rested on the ocean floor, were far more difficult to remove, although over the years each navy developed painstaking techniques to handle them.

Like electronic countermeasures, a give-and-take evolved in mine and antimine warfare, with some mines being sown in containers that released the active mine only after the container had been swept.

The Germans developed acoustic mines, magnetic-acoustic mines, mines with ship counters (which didn't go off until a specified number of ships passed) and pressure mines, which reacted to the decrease in pressure that occurred when a ship passed. The latter, called "oyster mines," were developed in 1940 but the Germans delayed their use because they feared that the British would retaliate with a similar weapon. Hitler insisted that they be used at Normandy (where the biggest minesweeping operation in history was to be conducted), but only about 4,000 were laid and they had only moderate success, sinking two destroyers and some landing craft. Had Rommel been able to get the quantity of land and sea mines he wanted—more than 40 million—the invasion might have been seriously hampered.

The U.S. Navy had begun mining operations early in the war, despite not having strong doctrinal backing, but it possessed too few mines to be effective. Later in the war, as more mines became available, it didn't pursue as aggressive a mining program as it should have. Captains didn't like to carry mines on aircraft carriers—they took up space and were hazardous, and carrier aircraft could only carry a few per sortie. Submarines were so successful with torpedoes that mines were not highly regarded.

The true potential of mining operations was not realized until late in the war, when the B-29 became available as a long-range minelayer. A classified study by the Naval Ordnance Laboratory of Silver Spring, Maryland, went to great lengths to prove the effectiveness of the B-29 campaign compared to the submarine campaign, a result that was received with mixed emotions by the navy. On the one hand, the navy resented the upstart air force getting the benefit of the study even though the navy needed the study in its own campaign to obtain long-range bombers. The army air force didn't want to drop mines, but did not wish the navy to obtain long-range bombers, and so reluctantly took on the task.

The submarine campaign lasted forty-four and a half months compared to four and a half for the B-29 mining campaign. In those periods, a force of 100 submarines sank 4.8 million tons of merchant shipping (an average of 107,416 tons per month) at a cost of fifty-two submarines sunk. A force of forty B-29s sank 1.3 million tons of shipping (an average of 277,777 tons per month), with the loss of fifteen aircraft. A total of 103 aircrew were lost, versus 3,560 submariners. In cold human terms, 12,135 tons of shipping were sunk for every U.S. casualty in mining operations, while only 1,343 were sunk for every man lost in submarines. In economic terms, the mining campaign cost $6 per ton sunk, while the submarine campaign cost $55 per ton sunk.

The most important conclusion of the study was that air power could now achieve one of Alfred Mahan's doctrinal tenants, a continuous close blockade. This had never been done before, for no matter how many ships the Royal or U.S. Navy possessed, the sheer immensity of the European and Asian land masses meant that only the most important ports could be covered. The result was that the close blockade concept was abandoned, and a distant blockade—essentially removing enemy ships from oceanic waters—was pursued.

Aerial Mining

The offensive aerial mining campaign against Japan began with the Outer Zone Campaign in February 1943, which ranged all around the outer zones of Japan's defensive perimeter, from the Solomons to the China-Burma-India theater, including the rivers and coasts of China, Burma, Thailand, Indochina and the Malay peninsula. During this period, the American Fifth, Seventh, Tenth and Fourteenth Air Forces and XX Bomber Command combined with the Royal Air Force, Royal Australian Air Force and the U.S. Navy to lay 9,254 mines.

The Outer Zone Campaign resulted in 275,000 tons of shipping sunk and 610,000 tons damaged. The minefields and the relentless submarine and air attacks forced Japan to withdraw most of its remaining two million tons of shipping to the Inner Zone, which consisted of the Sea of Japan, the Yellow Sea and the East China Sea.

As the Japanese perimeter shrank, minelaying efforts increased, moving ever closer to the home islands; during the island hopping, every bypassed island was mined to contain its forces and make their resupply difficult. When an offensive in one area was planned, mining was undertaken by U.S. carrier-based aircraft to bottle up the enemy ports that could supply aid. In the Marianas campaign, for example, the stronghold at Palau was heavily mined.

Admiral Nimitz had repeatedly called for a joint aerial mining campaign in which the army would provide the B-29s and crews and the navy would provide the mines and technical personnel. General Henry "Hap" Arnold, the Commanding General of the U.S. Army Air Force, agreed only reluctantly, because the effort would detract from the strategic bombing campaign advocated by air force leaders. He finally directed the commanding general of the XX Bomber Command, Major General Curtis LeMay, to begin a campaign on April 1, 1945. Once the orders were received, LeMay began planning on typical B-29 scale—a huge multi-phase campaign that would include training, reconnaissance, damage assessment and an extension of the effort to more and more areas.

In striking contrast, the Japanese, despite their long experience in mine warfare, were completely unprepared for the mining campaign, lacking minesweepers, equipment and personnel. They were never able to cope with even the initial American effort, and were soon swamped by its rapid expansion in both scope and sophistication.

LeMay selected the 313th Bomb Wing (VH)—very heavy—for the mining campaign, supplementing it occasionally with other forces. The navy was so eager to cooperate that the complex chain of command necessary to integrate the two services' efforts worked smoothly.

The combination of island hopping, submarines and mines had, by March 1945, shut down thirty-five of the forty-seven regular Japanese convoy routes. Traffic could no longer flow from the Dutch East Indies, Singapore and the Philippines. The ports on the Asiatic side of Kyushu and Honshu received the bulk of Japan's vastly reduced imports, while Tokyo, once the heart of Japan's shipping trade, was already of steadily declining importance. A list of twenty-four areas to be mined was compiled, the most important of these being L for Love, the eastern end of the Shimonoseki Strait, and M for Mike, the western end. The Shimonoseki Strait was the only protected waterway that allowed ships to pass through from the western coast to the eastern industrial centers; it was also a traditional route for warships embarking on a mission.

Both tactical and strategic considerations prompted LeMay to mine Shimonoseki first; the attack on Okinawa was scheduled for April, and he wanted to confine the Japanese fleet as much as possible. On the night of March 27, the 313th Bomb Wing, commanded by Brigadier General John J. Davies, sent 105 B-29s in at altitudes from 5,000 to 8,000 feet, flying singly. Each bomber carried a 12,000-pound bomb load—a mixture of 1,000- and 2,000-pound acoustic and magnetic mines to be parachuted into the ocean. Another mission was flown three nights later, supplementing the drop on Shimonoseki and adding mines to the approaches to Sasebo, Kure and Hiroshima. The parachute-retarded mines required the army air force to develop specialized mine-dropping procedures for both visual and radar drops.

The results of the mining campaign can be plotted in two intersecting lines: as the American mine totals rose, Japanese shipping declined. LeMay's plan worked both tactically and strategically; the battleship *Yamato* was forced to sortie through the Bungo Suido (no ship larger than a light cruiser ever passed through Shimonoseki again), to be sighted, tracked and sunk, while Japanese industrial imports fell from 800,000 tons in March 1945 to less than 200,000 tons in August.

The mining entered a new phase on May 3, with the introduction of "unsweepable" pressure mines and the mining of the ports of the Inland Sea as well as Tokyo, Nagoya, Kobe and Osaka. The third phase began on May 13, the mining of all the major harbors of northwest Honshu and Kyushu. (During May, losses due to mines exceeded those due to submarine torpedoes for the first time.) The fourth phase began on June 7, and extended the effort to smaller ports and harbors, forcing the Japanese to begin unloading their ships at sea via lighters. The navy added its weight to the program by using four-engine Consolidated PB4Y-2 Privateers to mine the southern coast of Korea.

The fifth phase intensified all the previous efforts to the extent that every port controlled by the Japanese was immobilized by mines. The situation was so desperate that the Japanese began a system of Russian roulette shipping, ordering its ships to steam ahead regardless of the mine fields, accepting the inevitable heavy losses just to get a few ships through.

By expending less than 7 percent of its Inner Zone bombing effort, the army air force had dropped 12,135 mines in 1,529 sorties. Japanese records indicate that 294 ships were sunk, 137 damaged beyond repair and 239 damaged for repairs that took an average of ninety days. As the Japanese shipping dried up, mines were set to react to smaller and smaller vessels; even wooden ships could not escape the pressure mines. The total mining effort by all parties resulted in almost 25,000 mines being sown, with 515 ships sunk and 560 damaged. A total of 2.3 million tons of shipping was thus removed from the war.

The cumulative total of ship losses is only one measure of the success of the mining campaign; shipping schedules were completely disorganized as delay was piled on delay. Arms production was disrupted because basic materials—primarily coal for power—were sunk or tied up in port. The Japanese ultimately dedicated a mixed group of 349 vessels and 20,000 men to the task of minesweeping, but their approach was as hopelessly outdated as their low estimate of the level of American effort was optimistic. The Japanese thought that only 3,690 mines had been dropped during the Inner Zone Campaign, rather than the 12,135 actually expended.

Along with the mines, the 313th Bomb Wing dropped almost five million propaganda leaflets urging the Japanese people to recognize the seriousness of the situation and to surrender to avoid starvation. Had the war continued for another year—and it would have had an invasion been necessary—probably more than seven million Japanese would have starved to death because the reduction of food imports was compounded by the rice crop failure of 1945.

The 313th Bomb Wing had not been happy about its minelaying assignment, which was regarded as a secondary task, and from which the immediate results could not be observed. Yet Admiral Nimitz pronounced its work "phenomenal." The British, not always the kindest critics of U.S. arms, said that the 313th's mining efforts were "like a dream come true."

(After the war, the United States and Japan worked cooperatively for two years to clear minefields; even so, several ships, totaling almost 80,000 tons, struck mines and sank.)

OTHER WARS, OTHER NAVIES

Italy

Mention has been made earlier of the Italian navy's operations; an unofficial Italian naval history makes the point that the utter failure of the Regia Aeronautica to cooperate with the navy made the navy's defeat at the hands of superior British forces inevitable. The navy fought bravely under difficult circumstances to defend its coasts and continued to ferry troops and supplies even when its convoys were being massacred. One remarkable statistic validates the Italian navy's commitment to battle: in all of the Italian combat vessels sunk during the war, only 30 percent of its crew members were killed. The percentages of fatalities among officers, ship commanders and admirals were 50, 75 and 100 percent, respectively, indicating that in the Italian navy, the officers put their lives on the line with their men.

The Soviet Union

Like the Italian navy, the Soviet Union's Red Fleet has received relatively little attention, in part because of the almost ludicrous way in which Soviet propaganda inflated its successes and minimized its losses. When the war began, most of the Soviet Union's heavy ships were obsolete, but it possessed more submarines, motor torpedo boats and naval aircraft than any other power. Germany's sudden air attacks on all its major western ports from bases in Finland, Poland and Romania did not greatly damage the Soviet navy.

The Russian sea war was split into five separate and essentially isolated fronts. Battles were fought in the frigid wastes of the Barents Sea, in the confined and shallow channels of the Baltic Sea and the Gulf of Finland, back and forth across the Black Sea and its adjacent rivers, and very briefly, late in the war, in the Pacific. The fifth front was the most unusual, the bitterly fought riverine war that resembled in bloodiness if not in equipment the fighting years later in Vietnam.

The nature of sea warfare in these widely separated areas differed not only from the major naval conflicts of the other Allies with Japan and Germany but from each other. There were only two consistent elements. The first was the support rendered by the Soviet naval air arm, which aided at each front and had more than 2,500 aircraft, including 750 fighters. It far surpassed in numbers and aggressiveness the Luftwaffe aircraft so grudgingly allocated the German navy. The second common element was submarine warfare. Soviet submariners were persistent in penetrating minefields and antisubmarine nets to get to battle, but they were not tenacious in their attacks and seemed to lack training. As in all navies but the Japanese, their torpedoes often failed to work, either running too deep, or failing to detonate by magnetic or contact means.

Overall, the Russo-German naval war was defensive; no capital ship engagements occurred, and weather was often an overriding factor. All arms in the Soviet Union were subordinate to the Red Army, and the Red Navy was poorly and meagerly equipped. Imperial Russia had suffered defeats in the 1904–1905 war with Japan and in the subsequent revolution. The navy was further depleted when much of the fleet was sunk as an act of sabotage during the ensuing civil war; the hulks for the most part were sold for salvage. Stalin's purges included the navy, but had an accidental benefit; those who survived were young and capable, so equal to their task that there was very little turnover in command during the entire war.

Admiral Nikolai Gerasimovich Kuznetsov was only thirty-five years old in April 1939 when Stalin appointed him Commissar for the Navy. He had served for only thirteen years, probably a record for promotion for a major fleet. Kuznetsov was valued for his approach to his position; instead of squabbling for assets like other commanders, he pledged himself to economies and to the support of the army.

Affable, but a hard taskmaster, Kuznetsov trained his fleet intensively, both in naval matters and in fighting on land; the latter was to be invaluable during the Nazi invasion. He anticipated the German attack, and, unlike Soviet army commanders, did not suffer significant losses from the initial air attacks. Reportedly a true leader himself, he was able to pick subordinates to carry out his orders and still not evoke jealousy or fear of treachery from

Stalin, an almost impossible task. As a result, any attrition of Soviet admirals came in battle, not in front of a firing squad; it was not so with army generals, for whom a great victory was almost as dangerous as a great defeat.

A leading example of Kuznetsov's ability to select the right man for the job was Rear Admiral S. G. Gorshkov, who repeatedly demonstrated his brilliance in both withdrawals and in landing operations conducted with his river flotillas. (A tradition of lake and river fleets extended back to Czarist times.) With small craft—gunboats, motor torpedo boats, barges and modified fishing boats—Gorshkov plied the Volga, the Sea of Azov and the Danube, always striking when least expected. The battles were often like those of the fabled pirates of the Caribbean. German gunboats were generally larger and more powerful, but the Soviet counterparts would engage in close firefights, boarding the enemy craft and conducting what amounted to bayonet-and-rifle trench warfare in a boat. After 1943, the Americans supplied 202 modern motor torpedo boats (MTBs).

The continental-minded German high command did not use its naval forces effectively to supplement the advance over land toward the disaster at Stalingrad. In contrast, the Soviet Union relied heavily upon sea and river transport both during the period of retreat, and subsequently as the Germans were rolled back. Further, Soviet sailors and marines fought hard and well in the defense of Odessa and Sevastopol. Their stout resistance was a propaganda windfall, and there were dozens of songs and stories about the brave Red Navy men who destroyed Nazi tanks by throwing themselves under the treads while clutching hand grenades, and, almost certainly, singing the "Internationale" as they did. Even allowing for the propaganda, there is no question that the tough sailors' resistance made a difference; it took the Germans 250 days to take Sevastopol during 1941 and 1942, but only four days to lose it in 1944.

Gorshkov's great reward was to succeed Kuznetsov as Commander-in-Chief in 1956, when the latter fell out of favor. (It was the second time for Kuznetsov; the first had come in 1946 when Stalin's jealousy finally caught up with him and he was accused of spying for the British.) Kuznetsov was retired at the age of fifty-one—an infant by the Soviet standards of the time—and was not rehabilitated until the first full-deck Soviet aircraft carrier was named *Admiral of the Fleet of the Soviet Union Kuznetsov*. (It was the third name for the ship; previously she had been the *Leonid Brezhnev* at her launch, then renamed *Tblisi*, and re-renamed *Kuznetsov* after the breakup of the Soviet Union.)

Another of Kuznetsov's selections was Admiral Aresni Grigoryevich Golovko, who was only thirty-four when he was given command of the

Northern Fleet. Golovko used his rather minimal resources to counter the German attack on Murmansk. Prior to 1944, Golovko worked closely with the British to expedite Lend-Lease supplies, and recounts in his memoirs a brush with the redoubtable Sir Philip Vian, who asked him in loud and rather offensive terms if the Russians would provide vegetables, fuel oil, a guard house for British sailors and brothels. Golovko reports that he replied yes to vegetables and fuel, no to the guard house and never to the brothels.

Of all the contests, Golovko's was probably the most important, for it facilitated the steady stream of Lend-Lease materials that kept the Soviet Union alive. The Northern Fleet's battles were fought in impossible conditions of ice, extensive fogs, the endless polar days and nights and, always, the intense cold.

The Red Banner Fleet

The war in the Baltic was curiously constrained until 1944. Both sides used mines extensively, the Germans laying them from self-propelled barges, motor torpedo boats and aircraft. The Nazi mines kept the Soviet fleet bottled up in port until the land campaigns freed them in 1944. Kuznetsov later admitted that his greatest error was his failure to insist on an adequate number of minesweepers. In war's eccentric manner, being in port turned out to be where the obsolete capital ships could be of the most service, fighting as deadly efficient floating heavy artillery in the defense of Leningrad and other coastal cities. The heavy 12-inch guns of the battleships were highly accurate and German ground commanders complained long and hard about the toll they took.

The Soviet Red Banner Fleet, commanded by Vice Admiral Vassily Tribitz, consisted of two battleships, two heavy cruisers, two light cruisers, nineteen destroyers, sixty-five submarines and about 100 smaller vessels—minesweepers, motor torpedo boats and the like. In contrast, the German navy could muster only ten minelayers, five training submarines and 100 smaller units of their own.

The most intensive fighting came in almost daily battles between the smaller boats skirting through the ribbon of coastal islands, just as Peter the Great had brought his oar-powered ships to defeat Sweden. Though the craft were small—often less than 100 feet long—and the weapons light, the fighting was as vicious to the participants as Savo Island or the Battle of Cape Matapan. In the long run, it doesn't really matter if you are killed by an 18-inch shell or a 7.9mm bullet—the result is the same.

In its numerous amphibious operations, the Soviet Union, lacking landing craft, used motor torpedo boats instead; the soldiers, usually inadequately trained and often including women, were forced to lie on the deck of the MTBs, then leap off into the intolerably cold waters of the Baltic to storm some coastal position, always without any heavy equipment.

The situation changed in 1944, when developments in the land battle opened up the Baltic to Soviet forces. Until that time, it had not been necessary for the Germans to operate convoys; afterward, the Soviet submarines scored many successes, the most notable of which have already been related in the account of the evacuations from East Prussia. Admiral Doenitz had pressed hard to keep the Baltic open, for it was only there that he could train the crews for his new fast submarines that he considered to be the sole remaining weapon that might win the war.

The Soviet Union claimed that the Red Banner Fleet had destroyed 624 ships and 1.6 million tons of shipping during the war; postwar German records confirmed only about half that number. Even so, it was a notable effort by a fleet not trained to make quick sorties.

Red War in the Black Sea

The Black Sea Fleet, commanded by Vice Admiral F. S. Oktyabrski, was overwhelmingly powerful for those inland waters, with one battleship, seven cruisers, ten destroyers, forty-seven submarines and eighty-four MTBs, and a Naval Air Arm of 626 airplanes. In addition, it, like the Barents Sea Fleet, had ample time to recover from the surprise of the German invasion. Initially, only the negligible Romanian navy—four destroyers, one submarine and twenty small patrol boats—opposed the Black Sea Fleet. After June 21, the Germans got into the battle by shipping sections of submarines via the Danube River and assembling and arming them in Romania.

The main thrust of the battle in the Black Sea was conducted by the smaller MTBs, many of them stemming from the plans of aircraft designer A. N. Tupelov. The Germans fought back with the ubiquitous Siebel ferries that proved so useful in Sicily, employing them with dash. They were heavily armed and used to transport troops, cover landings and otherwise engage the Soviet forces. The Siebels were disassembled and carted overland on double teams of trailers and assembled at the Black Sea port of Constanza.

A quirk of fate would allow Admiral Kuznetsov to redress almost all of the Russian losses to Japan that occurred as a result of the 1904–1905 war, winning a great triumph on borrowed resources. As a reward for his stewardship of the navy, Kuznetsov wheedled a specialized list of Lend-Lease ships for employment in the war against Japan that Stalin had agreed to at Yalta. The U.S. Navy, flushed with its impending victory over Japan and stocked with more ships than it could use, allocated 250 smaller vessels, including frigates, LCTs, LCIs, LCMs, minesweepers and motor torpedo boats to Kuznetsov's Pacific Fleet. When the Soviet Union declared war on August 8, 1945, he used these to overrun Sakhalin, the Kuriles, and the islands of Kunashiri, Etorofu, Habomai and Shikotan. This quick grab, overlooked by the world in the joy of surrender, was sweet revenge for the indignity of the 1904–1905 war, but is still a bone of contention between Japan and Russia.

OTHER ARMS, LESSER WEAPONS, EQUAL BRAVERY

One of the inexplicable phenomena of war is the almost insane desire that possesses men to risk their lives to come to grips with the enemy and do him harm. It often exceeds rational patriotism. Only the Japanese embraced deliberate suicide as an important tactic; other nations, however, used devices and employed tactics that amounted to almost the same thing. One example already mentioned was the bravery of the Italian sailors who were so successful with their Maiale (pig) boats that operated in the harbor at Alexandria and also at Gibraltar. These were only slightly less dangerous than the dedicated Kaiten human torpedo, corresponding more closely to the British Chariot, a two-man torpedo. Later in the water, Italo-British teams fought together in operations against elements of the Italian fleet captured by the Germans.

The British version of the midget submarines used by Germany and Japan was the X-craft, two-man midget submarines that severely damaged the *Tirpitz* at Kaafjord, Norway, on September 22, 1943.

The United States eschewed suicide weapons, but in many instances tasked its servicemen with almost equally dangerous missions. In the Pacific island-hopping campaign and on the beaches of Normandy, the work of Underwater Demolition Teams was highly dangerous and invaluable. Using equipment just past the testing stage, and operating in strange waters and unknown tides, these frogmen, to use the term of the day, routinely defused mines in the face of hostile fire.

Motor torpedo boats seemed to bring out the most dashing and buccaneering spirit. American PT boats were the bane of Japanese submarines, who were unable either to contain their aggressive tactics or put torpedoes into their low-draft wooden hulls. German E-boats caused tremendous problems to the Allies all during the war, and inflicted the worst seaborne casualties of the Normandy invasion in their famous attacks off the British coast.

The British Special Boat Service found its counterpart in limited numbers in other navies. Never more than 300 men strong, the service acted as commandos in the Aegean and the Mediterranean; using rubber rafts, fishing boats or canoes, they harassed the occupying forces until the Mediterranean was finally secured.

The danger was not confined to those at the sharpest edge of the stick. Sailors doing routine duty on radar picket ships became the special targets of the kamikazes, while there were many merchant mariners who endured more than one sinking from torpedo attack. No one could be braver than the young sailor—probably from some inland town—working thirty feet below the ocean's surface in the heat of a warship's engine room, knowing that the watertight doors leading to safety were closed, and that if the ship were sunk he stood very little chance of making his way to the surface.

A Summing Up

The 1939–1945 war at sea extended to all the oceans of the globe, and to many inland seas; for long after the surrenders, the submarines of the defeated nations were still coming to port and mines were still sinking ships.

The naval war was started by aggressor nations that interpreted the situation erroneously. Germany thought it could use submarines as its primary weapon, deferring a decisive sea battle until after it had won its wars on the continent. Japan thought it could use its fleet to secure a quick victory that would persuade its disheartened opponents to negotiate a satisfactory settlement.

The Allies regarded the naval war as one of long duration, hard work and dogged persistence, pursuing it as systematically as their resources would allow. And that is the key: the Allies' resources, particularly those of the United States, allowed them to create navies of a size and quality never before imagined, and far beyond the capacity of their enemies to emulate.

The quality of the Allied production achievement was matched by the quality of its leadership. Both Britain and the United States enjoyed first-rate naval leadership from the heads of government, who were basically navy men at heart, through the intermediate layers of command down to the commander of the smallest ship. In contrast, the leaders of the Axis nations were less interested in their navies than in their armies. Hitler was totally preoccupied with his army, as was Tojo. Mussolini felt, correctly, that the navy was Royalist and thus anti-Fascist. At intermediate levels of command, the Axis navies were less ably manned, but at the level of ship command, however, the Axis officers, particularly the Japanese, were fully the equal of their Allied counterparts. In a similar way, the sailors of all fleets of all nations executed their tasks in an exemplary way, regardless of the cause, and without respect to the imminence of either defeat or victory.

The Allied production capacity and leadership were greatly enhanced by their extraordinary advantage in intelligence matters, especially code breaking. Neither the Germans nor the Japanese ever understood that the Allies had almost complete and virtually instant access to their most secret transmissions.

The general western political situation, reinforced by the almost mindless quest for disarmament at any cost, had convinced the aggressor nations—Germany, Japan and Italy—that they could enrich themselves at the expense of their neighbors. That same political situation—democracies (with the exception of the Soviet Union) versus totalitarian states—was also the determinant factor. The democratic nations fought with greater unity and they were more disciplined and made great sacrifices. In the end, the absolute Allied triumph in naval warfare was a tribute to the same democratic system that had allowed the conditions for war to occur in the first place.

There was some poetic justice in the way the war ended. In Germany, whose armies had been so badly crushed, the Third Reich formally ceased to exist with Grand Admiral Doenitz as the new Fuehrer, not so much a tribute from Hitler to his navy as a malevolent rebuke to the generals he believed had betrayed him. In Japan, whose navy had been utterly defeated but still possessed an army of millions of men, it was General Umezu Yoshijiro who signed for the armed forces. (Umezu, appropriately, was later to be convicted as a Class A war criminal and sentenced to life imprisonment.)

The moment was sweet for the Allied representatives on the deck of the battleship *Missouri* in Tokyo Bay on September 2, 1945, as they watched hundreds of TF 58's carrier-based planes and hundreds of army B-29s thunder overhead. The new Supreme Commander, General Douglas MacArthur, treated a bewildered and chastened group of Japanese dignitaries correctly but sternly as they did easily what they had so long pronounced impossible, and surrendered.

The long war was over.

Selected Bibliography

Agawa, Hirouki. *The Reluctant Admiral.* Tokyo: Kodansha International, 1979.

Arnold, Henry H. *Global Mission.* New York: Harper & Bros., 1949.

Bagnasco, Erminio: *Submarines of World War II.* London: Arms & Armour Press, 1977.

Barnett, Correlli. *The Desert Generals.* London: Allen and Unwin, 1983.

———. *Engage the Enemy More Closely.* New York: W. W. Norton, 1991.

Behr, Edward. *Hirohito: Behind the Myth.* New York: Villard, 1989.

Bekker, Cajus. *Hitler's Naval War.* London: Macdonald and Jane's, 1974.

Belote, James H. and William M. *Titans of the Seas: The Development and Operation of the Japanese and American Carrier Task Forces During World War II.* New York: Harper & Row, 1975.

Bergamini, David. *Japan's Imperial Conspiracy.* New York: William Morrow, 1971.

Blair, Clay, Jr. *Silent Victory: The U.S. Submarine War Against Japan.* Philadelphia and New York: J. B. Lippincott, 1975.

Boyd, Carl. *Hitler's Japanese Confidant.* Lawrence, KS: University Press of Kansas, 1993.

Bragadin, Marc Antonio. *The Italian Navy in World War II.* New York: Arno Press, 1980.

Breuer, William B. *Devil Boat: The PT War Against Japan.* Novato, CA: Presidio Press, 1987.

Breyer, Siegfried. *Battleships of the World, 1905–1970.* London: Conway Maritime Press, 1980.

Breyer, Siegfried, and Gerhard Koop. *The German Navy at War, 1935–1945.* Vol. 2. *The U-Boat.* West Chester, PA: Schiffer Publishing, 1989.

————. *The German Navy at War, 1939–1945*. Vol. 1. *The Battleships*. West Chester, PA: Schiffer Publishing, 1989.

British Admiralty. *Fuehrer Conferences on Naval Affairs*. London: Greenhill Books, 1990.

British Air Ministry: *The Rise and Fall of the German Air Force (1933 to 1945)*. London: HMSO, 1948.

Buell, Thomas B. *Master of Sea Power: A Biography of Fleet Admiral Ernest J. King*. Boston: Little, Brown, 1980.

————. *The Quiet Warrior*. Boston: Little, Brown, 1967.

Bunker, John Gorley. *Liberty Ships: The Ugly Ducklings of World War II*. Annapolis, MD: Naval Institute Press, 1972.

Busch, Harold. *U-Boats at War*. New York: Ballantine, 1956.

Calvocoressi, Peter, and Guy Wint. *Total War: The Story of World War II*. New York: Pantheon, 1972.

Carpenter, Dorr, and Norman Polmar. *Submarines of the Japanese Imperial Navy*. Annapolis, MD: Naval Institute Press, 1986.

Chesneau, Roger. *Aircraft Carriers of the World, 1914 to the Present: An Illustrated Encyclopedia*. Annapolis, MD: Naval Institute Press, 1984.

————. *Conway's All the World's Fighting Ships, 1922–1946*. London: Conway Maritime Press, 1981.

Churchill, Winston S. *The Second World War* (six volumes). Boston: Houghton Mifflin, 1948–1951.

Clark, J. J., and Clark G. Reynolds. *Carrier Admiral*. New York: David McKay, 1967.

Coffey, Thomas M. *An Imperial Tragedy*. New York: World Publishing, 1970.

Coletta, Paola E. *Patrick N. L. Bellinger and U.S. Naval Aviation*. New York: University Press of America, 1987.

Cook, Haruko Taya, and Theodore F. Cook. *Japan at War: An Oral History*. New York: The New Press, 1992.

Costello, John. *The Pacific War*. New York: Rawson, Wade, 1981.

Craven, Wesley Frank, and James Lea Cate, eds. *The Army Air Forces in World War II* (seven volumes). Washington, DC: Office of Air Force History, 1983.

Cunningham, Admiral of the Fleet, Lord. *A Sailor's Odyssey*. London: Hutchinson, 1957.

D'Este, Carlo. *Bitter Victory: The Battle for Sicily, July–August, 1943*. London: Collins, 1988.

Doenitz, Grand Admiral, Karl. *Memoirs: Ten Years and Twenty Days*. London: Weidenfeld and Nicolson, 1959.

Dulin, Robert O., Jr., William H. Garzke, Jr., and Robert F. Sumrall. *Battle-*

ships: United States Battleships in World War II. Annapolis, MD: Naval Institute Press, 1979.

Dull, Paul S. *A Battle History of the Imperial Japanese Navy, 1941–1945*. Annapolis, MD: Naval Institute Press, 1978.

Eisenhower, Dwight D. *Crusade in Europe*. Garden City, NY: Doubleday, 1948.

Elfrath, Ulrich, and Bodo Herzog. *The Battleship Bismarck*. West Chester, PA: Schiffer Publishing, 1989.

Evans, David C., ed. *The Japanese Navy in World War II*. Annapolis, MD: Naval Institute Press, 1986.

Forrestel, E. P. *Admiral Raymond A. Spruance, USN: A Study in Command*. Washington, DC: U.S. Government Printing Office, 1966.

Francillon, R. J. *Japanese Aircraft of the Pacific War*. Annapolis, MD: Naval Institute Press, 1979.

Friedman, Norman. *Naval Radar*. London: Conway Maritime Press, 1981.

———. *U.S. Cruisers: An Illustrated Design History*. Annapolis, MD: Naval Institute Press, 1984.

Fuchida, Mitsuo, and Masatake Okumiya. *Midway: The Battle That Doomed Japan*. Annapolis, MD: U.S. Naval Institute, 1955.

Fuller, Richard. *Shokan: Hirohito's Samurai: Leaders of the Japanese Armed Forces, 1926–1945*. London: Arms and Armour Press, 1992.

Gannon, Michael. *Operation Drumbeat*. New York: HarperCollins, 1990.

German Ministry of Defence (Navy). *The U-Boat War in the Atlantic, 1939–1945*. London: HMSO, 1989.

Gilbert, Martin. *Churchill: A Life*. New York: Henry Holt, 1991.

———. *The Second World War*. New York: Henry Holt, 1989.

Glines, Carrol V. *Attack on Yamamoto*. New York: Orion, 1990.

———. *The Doolittle Raid*. New York: Orion, 1988.

Golovko, A. *With the Fleet*. Moscow: Progress Publishers, 1988.

Gray, Edwin. *Hitler's Battleships*. London: Leo Cooper, 1992.

Grove, Eric. *Sea Battles in Close-up: World War II*. Vol. 2. Annapolis, MD: Naval Institute Press, 1993.

Halsey, William F., and J. Bryan Halsey III. *Admiral Halsey's Story*. New York: McGraw-Hill, 1947.

Hastings, Max. *Overlord, D-Day and the Battle for Normandy*. London: Michael Joseph, 1984.

Hough, Richard. *The Longest Battle: The War at Sea, 1939–1945*. London: Weidenfeld & Nicolson, 1986.

Howarth, Stephen, ed. *Men of War: Great Naval Leaders of World War II*. New York: St. Martin's, 1992.

Howse, Derek. *Radar at Sea.* Annapolis, MD: Naval Institute Press, 1993.

Ienaga, Saburo. *The Pacific War, 1931–1945.* New York: Pantheon, 1978.

Isakov, Admiral of the Fleet, I. S. *The Red Fleet in the Second World War.* London: Hutchinson, 1947.

Jentschura, Hansgeorg, Dieter Jung, and Peter Mickel. *Warships of the Imperial Japanese Navy, 1869–1945.* Annapolis, MD: Naval Institute Press, 1992.

Kahn, David. *The Codebreakers: The Story of Secret Writing.* London: Weidenfeld and Nicolson, 1967.

Kemp, Peter. *Decision at Sea: The Convoy Escorts.* New York: E. P. Dutton, 1978.

————. *Key to Victory: The Triumph of British Sea Power in World War II.* Boston: Little, Brown, 1957.

Kennedy, Ludovic. *Pursuit.* London: Collins, 1974.

King, Ernest J., and Walter Muir Whitehill. *Fleet Admiral King: A Naval Record.* New York: W. W. Norton, 1952.

Koburger, Charles W., Jr. *Steel Ships, Iron Crosses and Refugees.* New York: Praeger, 1989.

Kriegsmarine. *The U-Boat Commander's Handbook.* Gettysburg, PA: Thomas Publications, 1989.

Larrabee, Eric. *Commander in Chief.* New York: Harper & Row, 1987.

Layton, Rear Admiral, Edwin T. *And I Was There: Pearl Harbor and Midway—Breaking the Secrets.* New York: William Morrow, 1985.

Lundstrom, John B. *The First Team.* Annapolis, MD: Naval Institute Press, 1993.

Macintyre, Donald. *The Battle of the Atlantic.* New York: Macmillan, 1961.

————. *U-Boat Killer.* London: Weidenfeld and Nicolson, 1956.

Martienssen, Anthony. *Hitler and His Admirals.* New York: E. P. Dutton, 1949.

McCue, Brian. *U-Boats in the Bay of Biscay.* Washington, DC: National Defense University Press, 1990.

Meigs, Montgomery C. *Slide Rules and Submarines.* Washington, DC: National Defense University Press, 1989.

Meister, Jurg. *Soviet Warships of the Second World War.* New York: Arco, 1977.

Melia, Tamara Moser. *Damn the Torpedoes: A Short History of U.S. Naval Mine Countermeasures, 1777–1991.* Washington, DC: Naval Historical Center, 1991.

Merrill, James A. *A Sailor's Admiral: A Biography of William F. Halsey.* New York: Thomas Y. Crowell, 1976.

Middlebrook, Martin. *Convoy.* New York: William Morrow, 1976.

Miller, Edward S. *War Plan Orange*. Annapolis, MD: Naval Institute Press, 1991.

Miller, Thomas G., Jr. *The Cactus Air Force*. New York: Harper & Row, 1969.

Mitcham, Samuel W., Jr., and Friedrich von Stauffenberg. *The Battle of Sicily*. New York: Orion, 1991.

Monsarrat, John. *Angel on the Yardarm*. Newport, RI: Naval War College Press, 1985.

Morison, Samuel Eliot. *History of United States Naval Operations in World War II* (15 volumes). Boston: Atlantic-Little, Brown, 1947–1962.

———. *The Two-Ocean War: A Short History of the United States Navy in the Second World War*. Boston: Atlantic-Little, Brown, 1963. (A selection rather than a condensation of the previous work.)

Muellenheim-Rechberg, Baron Burkhard von. *Battleship Bismarck: A Survivor's Story*. Annapolis, MD: Naval Institute Press, 1980.

Naito, Hatsuho. *Thunder Gods: The Kamikaze Pilots Tell Their Own Story*. New York: Farrar Straus & Giroux, 1989.

Naval Ordnance Laboratory. *Mines Against Japan*. Washington, DC: U.S. Government Printing Office, 1973.

O'Kane, Rear Admiral, Richard H. *Wahoo: The Patrols of America's Most Famous World War II Submarine*. Novato, CA: Presidio Press, 1987.

O'Neil, Richard. *Suicide Squads*. New York: Ballantine, 1984.

Orita, Zenji, with Joseph Harrington. *I-Boat Captain*. Canoga, CA: Major Books, 1976.

Padfield, Peter. *Doenitz: The Last Fuehrer*. London: Victor Gollancz, 1984.

Parillo, Mark P. *The Japanese Merchant Marine in World War II*. Annapolis, MD: Naval Institute Press, 1993.

Pelz, Stephen E. *Race to Pearl Harbor: The Failure of the Second London Naval Conference and the Onset of World War 2*. Cambridge: Harvard University Press, 1974.

Pogue, Forrest. *George C. Marshall: Ordeal and Hope, 1939–1942*. New York: The Viking Press, 1966.

———. *George C. Marshall: Organizer of Victory, 1943–1945*. New York: The Viking Press, 1973.

Polmar, Norman. *Aircraft Carriers*. New York: Doubleday, 1969.

Potter, E. B. *Nimitz*. Annapolis, MD: Naval Institute Press, 1976.

———. *Sea Power: A Naval History*. Annapolis, MD: Naval Institute Press, 1981.

Potter, John Deane. *Fiasco*. London: Heinemann, 1970.

Prange, Gordon W. *At Dawn We Slept: The Untold Story of Pearl Harbor*. New York: McGraw-Hill, 1981.

———. *Pearl Harbor: The Verdict of History*. New York: McGraw-Hill, 1985.

Preston, Anthony. *Aircraft Carriers*. New York: Gallery Books, 1979.

Raven, Alan, and John Roberts. *British Cruisers of World War II*. Annapolis, MD: Naval Institute Press, 1980.

Reynolds, Clark G. *The Fast Carriers: The Forging of an Air Navy*. Annapolis, MD: Naval Institute Press, 1992.

Robertson, Terrance. *Channel Dash*. London: Evans, 1958.

Roessler, Eberhard. *The U-Boat*. Annapolis, MD: Naval Institute Press, 1981.

Rohwer, J., and G. Hummelchen. *Chronology of the Great War at Sea, 1939–1945*. Annapolis, MD: Naval Institute Press, 1992.

Roscoe, Theodore. *On the Seas and in the Skies*. New York: Hawthorne Books, 1970.

———. *United States Destroyer Operations in World War II*. Annapolis, MD: Naval Institute Press, 1953.

———. *United States Submarine Operations in World War II*. Annapolis, MD: Naval Institute Press, 1949.

Roskill, S. W. *The Navy at War, 1939–1945*. London: Collins, 1964.

Ruge, Vice Admiral Friedrich. *Sea Warfare, 1939–1945*. London: Cassell, 1957.

———. *The Soviets as Naval Opponents, 1941–1945*. Annapolis, MD: Naval Institute Press, 1979.

Scheina, Robert L. *Latin America: A Naval History, 1810–1987*. Annapolis, MD: Naval Institute Press, 1987.

Sherrod, Robert. *History of Marine Corps Aviation in World War II*. Washington, DC: Combat Force Press, 1952.

Shores, Christopher, and Brian Cull, with Yasuho Izawa. *Bloody Shambles*, Vol. 1. London: Grub Street, 1992.

Showell, J. P. Mallmann. *U-Boats Under the Swastika*. Runnymede, England: Ian Allan, 1987.

Slessor, Marshal of the Royal Air Force, Sir John. *The Central Blue*. London: Cassell, 1956.

Spector, Ronald H. *Eagle Against the Sun: The American War with Japan*. New York: The Free Press, 1985.

Spurr, Russell. *A Glorious Way to Die*. New York: New Market Press, 1981.

Stafford, Edward P. *The Big E: The Story of the USS* Enterprise. New York: Random House, 1962.

Stephen, Martin. *Sea Battles in Close-up: World War 2*. Annapolis, MD: Naval Institute Press, 1988.

Swanborough, Gordon, and Peter M. Bowers. *United States Naval Aircraft*

Since 1911. Annapolis, MD: Naval Institute Press, 1976.

Tarrant, V. E. *The U-Boat Offensive, 1914–1945*. Annapolis, MD: Naval Institute Press, 1989.

Taylor, Theodore. *The Magnificent Mitscher*. New York: W. W. Norton, 1954.

Tedder, Marshal of the Royal Air Force Arthur, Lord. *With Prejudice*. London: Cassell, 1966.

Terraine, John. *A Time for Courage*. New York: Macmillan, 1989.

————. *The U-Boat Wars, 1916–1945*. New York: Putnam, 1989.

Toland, John. *Rising Sun: The Decline and Fall of the Japanese Empire, 1936–1945*. New York: Random House, 1970.

Turner, John Frayn. *Service Most Silent: The Navy's Fight Against Enemy Mines*. London: George G. Harrap, 1955.

Ugaki, Admiral, Matome. *Fading Victory: The Diary of Admiral Matome Ugaki, 1941–1945*. Pittsburgh: University of Pittsburgh Press, 1991.

United States Strategic Bombing Survey (Pacific). *The Campaigns of the Pacific War*. New York: Greenwood Press, 1969.

U.S. Division of Naval Intelligence. *Allied Landing Craft of World War II*. London: Arms and Armour Press, 1985.

van der Vat, Dan. *The Atlantic Campaign: World War 2's Great Struggle at Sea*. London: Hodder and Stoughton, 1988.

————. *The Pacific Campaign: The U.S.–Japanese Naval War, 1941–1945*. New York: Simon & Schuster, 1991.

Von der Porten, Edward P. *The German Navy in World War II*. New York: Ballantine, 1969.

Werner, Herbert A. *Iron Coffins*. London: Arthur Barker, 1969.

Whitley, M. J. *German Coastal Forces of World War II*. London: Arms and Armour Press, 1992.

Willmott, H. P. *The Barrier and the Javelin: Japanese and Allied Pacific Strategies, February to June, 1945*. Annapolis, MD: Naval Institute Press, 1980.

————. *The Great Crusade*. New York: The Free Press, 1990.

Winterbotham, F. W. *The Ultra Secret*. New York: Harper, 1975.

Y'blood, William T. *The Little Giants: U.S. Escort Carriers Against Japan*. Annapolis, MD: Naval Institute Press, 1987.

————. *Red Sun Setting: The Battle of the Philippine Sea*. Annapolis, MD: Naval Institute Press, 1981.

INDEX